Fiscal Policy
for Industrialization and Development
in Latin America

Latin American Conference, 21st, University of
" Florida, 1971.

Fiscal Policy
for Industrialization and Development
in Latin America

Edited by
David T. Geithman

A University of Florida Book

The University Presses of Florida
Gainesville

Proceedings of the

21st Annual Latin American Conference

Center for Latin American Studies

University of Florida

Printed by Storter Printing Company, Incorporated
Gainesville, Florida

Library of Congress Cataloging in Publication Data

Latin American Conference, 21st, University of
    Florida, 1971.
    Fiscal policy for industrialization and development
in Latin America.

    "A University of Florida book."
    Proceedings of the conference held in February, 1971
and sponsored by the Center for Latin American Studies,
University of Florida.
    1. Fiscal policy—Latin America—Congresses.
2. Latin America—Industries—Congresses. 3. Finance,
Public—Latin America—Congresses. I. Geithman, David
T., ed. II. Florida. University, Gainesville. Center
for Latin American Studies. III. Title.
HJ799.52.L38 1971   330.9′8′003   74-2231
ISBN 0-8130-0397-0

Preface

THIS volume grew out of the Twenty-First Annual Latin American Conference, held at the University of Florida in February 1971. It consisted of nine working sessions, each of which contained formally prepared papers and comments followed by a general round-table discussion. This format was designed to encourage scholars who have been working independently on related research to come together, share insights, and develop conclusions which hopefully will benefit all concerned with the economic and social development of Latin America.

The central theme of the conference was to analyze and evaluate the interaction among fiscal problems, fiscal tools, and fiscal systems in the industrializing economies of Latin America. Obviously, many other issues of economic development are related to this theme. A conscious attempt was made not to exclude these from the conference—perhaps somewhat diluting the fiscal policy theme but, I believe, adding considerably to the intellectual substance of the papers and discussions. Moreover, as the papers and discussions indicate, issues in both theory and policy arose in each session. The participants found ample opportunity to join the more theoretical to the more applied aspects of fiscal and developmental problems.

The conference could not have taken place without the generous financial and logistical support of the Center for Latin American Studies at the University of Florida. Its success depended in large measure on the complete and enthusiastic cooperation of William E. Carter, Director of the Center, and on the unfailing assistance of Raymond J. Toner, Assistant Director, Mrs. Vivian G. Nolan, and the entire Center staff. I wish also to place on record my appreciation to Dean Robert F. Lanzillotti of the University of Florida College of Business Administration and Irving J. Goffman, Chairman of the Department of Economics, for their support and encouragement, to Manuel Carvajal for his personal contribution, and to Mark Waldman for his assistance in preparing the manuscript.

D. T. G.

v

Conference Participants

FUAT ANDIC, University of Puerto Rico, Rio Piedras, Puerto Rico.

SUPHAN ANDIC, University of Puerto Rico, Rio Piedras, Puerto Rico.

WERNER BAER, University of Illinois, Urbana, Illinois.

RICHARD M. BIRD, University of Toronto, Toronto, Canada, and Tax Policy Division, International Monetary Fund, Washington, D.C.

ANTHONY CHURCHILL, International Bank for Reconstruction and Development, Washington, D.C.

DAVID FELIX, Washington University, Saint Louis, Missouri.

EDMUNDO FLORES, Universidad Nacional Autónoma de México, Mexico City, Mexico.

DAVID T. GEITHMAN, Russell Sage College, Troy, New York.

JOSEPH GRUNWALD, Brookings Institution, Washington, D.C.

HARLEY H. HINRICHS, United States Naval Academy, Annapolis, Maryland, University of Maryland, College Park, Maryland, and George Washington University, Washington, D.C.

DONALD L. HUDDLE, Rice University, Houston, Texas.

NICHOLAS KALDOR, King's College, University of Cambridge, Cambridge, England.

GEORGE E. LENT, International Monetary Fund, Washington, D.C.

JONATHAN LEVIN, International Monetary Fund, Washington, D.C.

DENNIS J. MAHAR, Ford Foundation and Instituto de Planejamento Econômico e Social, Rio de Janeiro, Brazil.

JAVIER MÁRQUEZ, Centro de Estudios Monetarios Latinoamericanos, Mexico City, Mexico.

JOHN F. MORRALL, University of Florida, Gainesville, Florida.

ELLIOTT MORSS, Consultant, Washington, D.C.

RICHARD A. MUSGRAVE, Harvard University, Cambridge, Massachusetts.

IFIGENIA M. DE NAVARRETE, Universidad Nacional Autónoma de México, Mexico City, Mexico.

OLIVER OLDMAN, International Tax Program, Harvard University, Cambridge, Massachusetts.

JUAN PABLO PÉREZ-CASTILLO, formerly Centro de Estudios del Desarrollo, Universidad Central de Venezuela, Caracas, Venezuela.

FREDERIC L. PRYOR, Swarthmore College, Swarthmore, Pennsylvania.

DANIEL M. SCHYDLOWSKY, Boston University, Boston, Massachusetts.

LARRY A. SJAASTAD, University of Chicago, Chicago, Illinois.

VITO TANZI, American University, Washington, D.C.

RICHARD S. THORN, University of Pittsburgh, Pittsburgh, Pennsylvania.

DALE TRUETT, University of Texas at San Antonio, San Antonio, Texas.

WILLIAM G. TYLER, University of Florida, Gainesville, Florida.

JAMES W. WILKIE, University of California at Los Angeles, Los Angeles, California.

Contents

1

Fiscal Policy in Latin America

An Overview

DAVID T. GEITHMAN

IN the less-developed countries of the world today, fiscal policy and the development process are inextricably intertwined. During the course of the past quarter century, the overlapping objectives of industrialization and socioeconomic development have become such constant policies of government as to be virtually taken for granted, and in the future, governments themselves will increasingly be judged by the strength of their commitment to development and their effectiveness in achieving it. It is, therefore, crucial for governments to determine the different priorities for each possible role of the public sector at each stage of planning a development strategy. The range of these public sector functions characteristically includes mobilizing human and material resources and ensuring productive employment for them, avoiding disruptive domestic price-level and external balance-of-payments instabilities in income, wealth, and consumption standards.

Within the broad purview of public policy, fiscal policy embraces all government budgetary transactions and operations on both the revenue and expenditure sides of account that have as their objective the support of general economic and social policy. The true engine of economic development, as Musgrave has noted, is increased productivity, which in turn is a matter of real capital formation and more efficient real resource use rather than finance. Thus fiscal policy exercises its economic development role largely by assisting the processes of capital formation and the movement of resources into their most productive employments. At the same time, it must somehow reconcile these requirements with the nation's near- and long-term social development goals. Taxes and subsidies, then, cannot be treated merely as means of transferring resources to public use in an equitable manner, although equity is important. Together with the pattern of public expenditures, they are more generally the most economically rational and effective method of systematically diverting resources to preferred uses and away from low-priority uses. In other words, like

1

all development policy, fiscal policy is inherently resource reallocative by modifying the use to which resources would be put if guided solely by the private sector. It is a consequence that some degree of tension inevitably occurs between the private and public sectors, even when both presumably endorse the ultimate goal of economic and social development.

The task of harmonizing public policy and private enterprise confronts every developing society, although the specific problems which this implies assume different forms and degrees from country to country. Presently, the government of each Latin American nation is deeply engaged in the process of working out a reconciliation of public control and private decision making which is relevant to the character of its economy, consistent with its societal values, and effective in achieving its national development goals.

In the first paper in this volume, Nicholas Kaldor presents a formal exposition of the structuralist interpretation of industrialization in Latin America that relates industrialization to Latin American inflationary experiences and explains why industrialization in Latin American countries has led to structural bottlenecks when in other countries it has not. He argues that Latin American inflations are fundamentally caused by a disproportion between incomes generated in the urban sector and available food supplies derived from the agricultural surpluses of the rural sector. This disproportionate development is, in turn, a direct consequence of the policy of industrialization through import substitution, which has been pursued without sufficient regard either for the import requirements of industrialization or the export capabilities after import-substitution industrialization.

Indiscriminate import-substitution industrialization has yielded three major consequences for Latin American development. It has increased import requirements relative to export capacities; it has increased demand for food by the urban sector, driving up agricultural prices; and finally, it has caused a change in the terms of trade against the agricultural sector, with negative consequences for agricultural productivity. The rise in food prices (in money terms) would improve the terms of trade for agricultural products *if* the rise in food prices did not call forth an equivalent rise in money wages in industry. But money wages *do* tend to be adjusted to keep pace with the rise in the cost of living, so real wages do not decline and the agricultural terms of trade fail to improve as a result of the inflation. Inflation is a process of rising prices, not just high prices, and money wages must continue rising to compensate for the rising prices of consumer goods in order to keep the inflationary process in motion. While demand for food by the urban sector is increasing, agricultural supply tends to be inelastic due to backward land-tenure systems, marketing problems, and stagnant technology—in addition to the lack of a strong incentive to produce, because of inappropriate agricultural terms of trade.

Nor can the growing food demand be satisfied (at stable prices) through foreign trade, due to the occurrence of severe import constraint. It is precisely the existence of the import constraint that distinguishes the inflationary from the noninflationary countries in Latin America and elsewhere. The seriousness of the balance-of-payments problem in Latin America derives from the original bases of the Latin American industrialization programs. These focused primarily upon substituting domestic production for goods imported from the more-developed countries. Domestic markets were generally narrow and highly protected. Industrial enterprises organized on this basis have not proved to be well adapted to competing in the world market with the more-developed industrial producers. Latin American inflations are therefore structural in the sense that money supply expansion, although necessary to the inflation process, is basically passive and responsive to other, underlying economic pressures. While it cannot be denied that monetary and fiscal restraint is necessary to end inflation, an *enduring remedy* to structural inflations must involve industrial and agricultural rationalization, increased export earnings, and expanded food production for domestic consumption.

Vito Tanzi's paper, in treating taxation as the most efficient and rational method of transferring resources from the private sector to the public sector and to higher-priority uses, explores some difficult issues raised in analyzing the proper role of taxation in promoting capital formation and industrialization. He focuses on the two major, related questions of whether or not there is an optimal tax burden (or average tax ratio) and whether or not a relationship exists between the structure of taxation and the level of economic development. On the first question, he underscores the basic need to increase the real resources available to governments in order to allow them to carry out those functions required by a development policy. However, the solution to the problem is more complicated than merely always to specify an increase in the average tax ratio. One reason is that taxation can exert a negative impact on the distribution of income via the structure of public expenditures financed by taxes. Analyses of tax burden and tax structure should explicitly consider uses to which tax revenues are put. A second reason is that government's concern over investment is not confined to creating infrastructure but also extends to the level and quality of private investment. Assuming a flow of public funding for private investment that equalizes the marginal productivities of investment in the public and private sectors, the case for higher taxation is strengthened if the marginal propensity to save in the public sector exceeds that in the private sector. Even this proposition must be qualified if a severe balance-of-payments constraint exists, since there is a direct connection between an increased rate of saving-investment and an expanding level of capital goods importation. The *structure* of taxation, however, can affect the availability of foreign exchange in several ways, and therefore the tax structure can help determine the optimal *level* of taxation by influencing the attainable rate of investment. Finally, there are various tax level and tax structure considerations in the context of countercyclical fiscal policy.

On the second question of whether or not a relationship exists between the structure of taxation and the level of economic development, Tanzi arrives at a predominantly negative conclusion. There are two general theories of tax structure change during economic development, those of Hinrichs and Musgrave; but both theories suffer from overgenerality. Numerous series of statistical results also exist, many of which are contradictory, that statistically "explain" how a particular tax, or more often a group of taxes, changes when per capita income or openness or some other economic variable changes in a cross-section sample. The value of nearly all these results is seriously compromised by certain purely statistical problems as well as by the occurrence of technological innovations in the tax field, changing social and political trends which affect taxation, and the omission of change on the expenditure side of the budget. While recent work on tax structure change in relation to economic development is an exciting area of research, much still remains to be accomplished before it can be directly applied in helping to design a tax structure for development and in answering normative questions about the kind of tax structure a country should possess at a given stage of development.

More immediately useful research for policy-making purposes should concern itself with a comparison of the structure of *particular* taxes and the development of the structural characteristics of a *specific* tax. In this regard, Tanzi argues on behalf of two tax proposals. The first advocates for Latin America a system of income taxation characterized by highly progressive rates on individual incomes coupled with very low rates on corporate incomes and unrealized capital gains. The second proposal involves a tax on the *potential* value-added of business enterprises, especially for those firms operating in the manufacturing subsector.

Harley Hinrichs's innovative case study of Guatemala is designed to sort out and assess the influence and implications of several interwoven strands of taxation theory and tax reform theory in a world of practical policy making. The analysis embraces some of the special fiscal problems of membership in a common market, together with the constraints that such membership imposes upon tax reform. More importantly, it stresses the importance of timing and political and administrative constraints in the formulation of a successful strategy for fiscal reform. Hinrichs argues strongly and persuasively that a government's position regarding taxation reform in effect cannot be stronger than its position on general development priorities. Sound tax reform proposals imply a sound conception of the role of taxation reform in some larger developmental scheme. The latter requires a realistic understanding about which goals tax reform can properly and reasonably undertake to accomplish and which problems can be better dealt with by other means.

The fiscal capacity of a country can be evaluated on both macro and micro bases. The former looks at the determinants of taxation capacity by means of indicators such as national income or product, foreign trade, value-added in manufacturing, etc. This approach shows Guatemala to be a serious fiscal underachiever. Among the salient reasons that the country has not measured up to its revenue potential are special internal and external political pressures, which have curtailed the growth of its foreign trade-related revenues, and the failure to shift to heavier internal progressive taxation, direct and indirect, as its revenues from foreign trade have stagnated. However, such macro measures of tax *capacity* are in reality only measures of past tax *effort*, and as Tanzi's paper on tax structure argues, a description of past tax effort offers no necessary conclusions about *potential* sources of future taxation.

Consequently, Hinrichs offers a second and somewhat innovative micro approach to tax-capacity estimation that examines various potential tax bases. He considers here the bases for personal income, business income, property, general sales, excise, and foreign trade taxes. Both the size and growth of these tax bases are treated, and tax rates are applied to them to determine the potential yields that might be obtained with tax rates achieved on similar bases in comparable countries. The procedure results in an estimate of the extent of unused tax potential, which can be exploited to finance a shift toward prodevelopmental public expenditures. Certain Guatemalan tax bases have been seriously eroded—notably its foreign trade and business income tax bases—largely due to generous programs of investment incentives. The costs (in terms of lost revenues) of these incentive policies probably exceed their benefits to the nation, especially since there is no need for international rivalry over fiscal incentives among the Central American Common Market countries. Beyond this, Guatemala should begin concentrating its scarce administrative capacity and limited political support for tax reform in those areas where the greatest potential tax revenue is located and where fiscal objectives are most vital. At the same time, it must be recognized that tax reform is subject to several political constraints whose effects are approximately quantifiable. Finally, Hinrichs attempts something quite unusual in contemporary tax reform analyses: he summarizes, in a large policy matrix, numerous alternatives for tax reform (including twelve different taxes and other revenue-raising measures, plus fifteen different policy moves) as each relates to the achievement of various tax policy objectives and the occurrence of political and administrative constraints on tax reform. In this way, the government has at its disposal a menu of tax reform alternatives and can select for itself a reform package designed, for example, to maximize total revenue or achieve a better balance in the balance of payments or minimize political opposition.

The problems associated with the wide range of instruments and often conflicting objectives involved in agricultural taxation policy, in both theory and Latin American practice, are discussed by Richard Bird in the fourth paper presented here. The sheer size of the agricultural sector in Latin America makes it appear inevitable that agriculture must serve as the main source of the real resources required for the industrialization of these economies. Effective agricultural taxation is often seen as the principal instrument with which to effect the net transfer of resources out of agriculture into industry. This overall perspective of the development process derives largely from the fascination that the dualistic and labor-surplus models of development have held for developmental economists. Unfortunately, these models minimize the numerous difficulties that surround the problem of extracting the surplus from agriculture. Even more seriously, they beg the entire question of whether or not a surplus of unutilized potential in the agricultural sector in fact exists. On the latter issue, Bird argues that whether or not the net flow of resources should be *from* or *to* the agricultural sector must depend ultimately upon the particular circumstances of a given country, and that appropriate policy treatment of agriculture at this level of abstraction is not a subject about which useful recommendations can be formed apart from specific real-world situations. The policy conclusions that emerge from any *general* model of the interaction between agricultural and industrial development will be either so empty as to be useless or else applicable at most to a highly limited group of countries. Even when an agricultural surplus does exist and a net outflow of resources from agriculture is therefore feasible, a large proportion of such a surplus may have to be reinvested in the agricultural sector itself to finance certain vital projects necessary to maintain or accelerate the growth of agricultural productivity and agricultural surplus.

Whether a net outflow of capital from agriculture to industry occurs, or merely a gross inflow of capital for certain key agricultural projects, the role of tax policy in mobilizing saving in the agricultural sector is crucial. Heavier reliance upon taxes levied on agricultural land appears to be the most desirable way to extract an increase in public revenues from the agricultural sector, primarily for reasons of incentives. Latin American experience suggests that the most viable form of land taxation reform is to concentrate on establishing a solidly based, simple property tax with meaningful rates, rather than designing complicated special taxes on idle lands and similar devices which attempt to achieve primarily nonfiscal purposes. At present, nowhere in Latin America does direct taxation of agricultural land significantly contribute either to public resource mobilization for developmental purposes or to resource reallocation within the agricultural sector. In those countries where the agricultural sector does appear to be moderately to heavily taxed, the task is generally accomplished through taxes on agricultural exports. Although several explanations are commonly offered for the widespread failure to tax agricultural land adequately, political and especially administrative constraints provide the best answer to this anomaly. Some evident reasons why the use of agricultural taxation to provide incentives has not succeeded in Latin America are that the legislation almost always has been poorly written, inadequately based on facts, and lacking in political support. Considerations of this sort argue on behalf of a piecemeal, incrementalist adjustment of an agricultural tax system, involving the employment of relatively simple taxes, both in valuation technique and in structure, coupled with as many benefit taxes and user charges as possible, plus careful research on the appropriate level of the net intersectoral resource flows in the particular country.

In developing and developed countries alike, the active factor in government budgeting is the decision to spend. While taxes may be more or less equitably imposed and with more or less desirable incentive effects, their raison d'être is to make possible the social provision of public services. Basic questions concerning the appropriate level of expenditures at various stages of economic development, the optimal structure of public expenditures at each stage, and the appropriate instruments for public expenditure planning are all dealt with by Richard Musgrave in the fifth paper in the volume. He initially presents empirical data on the size of the public sector, as measured by the expenditure ratio or, with substantially unchanged results, the tax to national product ratio. His evidence supports Wagner's Law of a growing public sector with rising per capita income when comparing the average low per capita income country with the average high-income country, but no such significant relationship is found to exist within the subgroup of low-income countries. Nevertheless, a positive relationship between public sector size and per capita income does exist for the Latin American countries as a group, although their average expenditure (or tax) to national product ratio is below the average ratio for the rest-of-the-world sample. The degree of industrialization in the Latin American countries also enters the regression with a positive sign to help explain variation in public sector size, while the degree of openness enters with a negative sign but is not statistically significant.

From the viewpoint of assessing an expenditure policy for development, the intractable question, of course, is: should the statistical average performance of a group of countries, controlled for level of per capita income, degree of industrialization, extent of openness, etc., determine the "correct" fiscal performance for a single country; or should it indicate a minimum (or perhaps a maximum) performance level to be attained; or does it say nothing whatsoever about an appropriate performance level for an individual country? This is substantially the same question that Tanzi addresses with respect to optimal tax effort during development. General rules about expenditure levels are elusive, but economic theory can point out certain considerations relevant to the issue of the social goods share of total product as income rises. First, the importance of externality-intensive consumption goods relative to private-type consumption goods is probably less at lower per capita income levels than at higher income levels. This suggests that the income elasticity of demand for public consumer goods is probably unity or less over the low-income range, although this conclusion may be crucially modified by a greatly unequal distribution of the gains from overall income growth and by the association of rapid urbanization with economic development. Second, the importance of externality-intensive types of investment relative to private-type capital goods is greater at lower per capita income levels than at higher income levels, as is the overall share of output (public and private) to be allocated to capital goods formation. This suggests a greater-than-unity income elasticity of demand for public investment goods, at least in the earlier stages of economic development. Such an elasticity is all the more plausible if human capital investment is considered as part of public capital formation, as it surely should be. Third, although transfer payments have historically risen more than proportionately to the rise in per capita income in Latin America, and greater equality of income distribution will probably be essential to orderly economic, social, and political progress in the future, the transfer payment approach is not the most effective mechanism for income redistribution. Rather, expenditure policy should rechannel into capital formation (via progressive consumption taxes) high incomes which now flow into excess consumption. Through careful direction of such investment, government must assure that the resulting income gains are widely shared by the population. Several instruments for expenditure planning can help achieve this as well as other objectives, including the creation of coordinating councils between finance ministries and planning agencies, and the proper use of cost-benefit analysis. The latter, although difficult to apply in developing economies due to sizable price and discount rate distortions and significant secondary effects, should include income distribution weights in its objective function.

Of course, Musgrave is aware that neither the optimal size of the public sector nor the proper extent of fiscal centralization or decentralization can be properly analyzed purely on the basis of economic efficiency considerations, but rather that both depend in large degree on historical, political, and social factors. In this respect, his paper is a companion piece to James Wilkie's. Wilkie, an expert on the political and economic history of Mexico, Bolivia, and Costa Rica, presents a comparative analysis of budgetary policy in these three countries in an attempt to get beneath the conventional wisdom about the impact of widespread decentralization of national government expenditures in Latin America.

In modern government, the budgetary process normally serves as a coordinating and decision-making mechanism for the diverse organizational forms of the public sector. The budget itself usually incorporates a plan for management of the public sector, prepared by the central executive authority and presented to the legislature for modification and adoption. It includes decisions about the size and composition of government outlays as well as the intricate relations between public and private sectors. But in Latin America, or at least in the three countries for which Wilkie carefully compiles budgetary data, the normal budgetary process has been subverted. Analyses of public expenditures both by function and by centralized-versus-decentralized governmental authority in Mexico, Bolivia, and Costa Rica are presented. These attempt to show the total impact of the public sector on national development by drawing a distinction between the part of the public sector that can be manipulated by the central government to support state policy and the part that is essentially beyond central government control. Because of real or imagined abuses of presidential authority over the central government, which is after all the single most powerful element in most Latin American societies and one whose influence is multiplied indirectly by licensing, credit and foreign exchange policies, etc., the power of the central government has been increasingly restricted to social and administrative affairs, Wilkie argues. Real or imagined efficiency considerations have also reinforced this historical pattern.

Public enterprises, mixed public and private corporations, governmental commissions, institutes, independent agencies, etc., have all been designed to execute economic policy free from the vagaries of "politics." With their proliferation, vast and important economic activities of the state have been effectively removed from central government review and authority. Thus, an institutional structure has grown up in Latin America which is not necessarily responsive to changing political pressures and interests and which, by its decentralized nature, can prevent planning and frustrate new policy directions. Some very real and perplexing problems of political economy are involved. What are the political powers of presidents who have given up important economic decision-making powers relating to development? What are the prospects and avenues for incorporating the decentralized sector into state economic planning, and how to prevent new kinds of challenges to central government authority? How can the autonomous agencies be made subordinate to the central government but retain certain prerogatives of autonomous action for efficiency reasons? Since the mid-1960s, the central governments of all three countries have begun to bring their decentralized sectors under greater presidential authority and control in order to develop and enforce national development plans responsive to new demands for social and economic improvements. The task has been difficult, and only modest success has so far been achieved. This drive for budgetary "recentralization" marks an important turning point in twentieth-century history which will help determine the course of future Latin American economic development.

Another dimension of the public budget is explored by Werner Baer in his study of the role of government enterprises in Latin America. In a pure typology of government activities, three more-or-less distinct organizational forms are evident: general government, which provides goods and services to the community on a nonexclusionary basis free or for a nominal charge; trust funds, which are characterized by a specific group of contributors and beneficiaries in which linkages exist between contributions and benefits received; and public enterprises, whose functions most closely approximate the types of activities carried on in the private market. Public enterprises provide goods and services to the community but also charge prices for discrete units of output. They usually maintain accounts approximately along commercial lines, and thus they possess at least the potential for meeting most or all operating costs with proceeds from sales rather than by calling upon general government revenues for their financing. In the real world, however, organizational forms often become blurred. In Latin America, on one hand, general departments and agencies are conducting public enterprise activities. On the other hand, public enterprises are engaged in a wide variety of functions that range from the provision of purely public goods and services to the production of purely private-type goods and services. Indeed, traditions in Latin America more nearly resemble those of continental Europe than those of the Anglo-Saxon countries. These traditions have always admitted a highly complex interrelationship between the state and the private sector.

As Baer shows in a brief survey of government enterprise activities in several Latin American countries, a combination of circumstances explains the greatly increased importance of direct state participation in the economy over the last three to four decades. Probably most central are the industrialization ambitions of the governments, which often necessitated public sector activities in key areas where no private domestic or foreign enterprises would venture. In some cases, nationalist considerations prevented foreign private enterprises from being allowed to enter certain fields. In still other cases, especially involving public utilities, welfare considerations prompted government controls to prevent private groups from entering or enlarging their facilities.

Clearly, public enterprises in Latin America are almost invariably subject to a large degree of political policy determination, and their divergent goals frustrate attempts at comparative analysis of their performance. When judged by criteria customarily applied to private firms, Latin

American government enterprises are poor performers. But there are several sound reasons why a government may desire its firms to intentionally charge prices that result in losses for the enterprises, with a part or all of their activities subsidized out of general revenue. This consideration implies that, in the final analysis, a reasonable evaluation of public enterprise performance can be made only according to broad distributional criteria that specify who (or, what socioeconomic classes) should bear the costs of public enterprise activities and who should receive the benefits.

The final two papers of the book assess the relationship of fiscal and economic policy to industrial structure and industrial exporting. They focus on the capacity of the export market to (a) absorb additional output arising from fuller utilization of existing industrial capacity, and (b) alleviate the foreign exchange bottleneck stemming from the need to continue importing inputs for production. Each of the studies begins with recognition that a necessary condition for sustained industrial export expansion in Latin America is the achievement of long-run competitiveness in world markets. Both papers attempt to evaluate the probable effectiveness of an industrial export-promoting fiscal policy from this perspective.

In his case study of recent Argentine experience, David Felix concludes that successful long-run export expansion hinges on a rationalization of the country's overprotected and high-cost industries. This task involves as much the flexibility of political power relationships in Argentina as it does the technical efficacy of fiscal promotional stimuli. Essentially, Felix backs into this conclusion after detailed empirical analysis of the relative contributions to Argentina's recent industrial export growth of export tax subsidies, Latin American Free Trade Area tariff concessions, and excess capacity in export industries. The findings are that industrial exports did not respond well to favorable relative prices, including export tax subsidies, but instead reacted primarily to the introduction of intra–Latin America trade concessions and the existence of excess capacity in the industrial sector.

The plausibility of these results is supported by empirical examination of the factor intensity biases in Argentina's industrial export mix, which apparently violate the Heckscher-Ohlin dictum that countries possess a comparative advantage in goods produced with factors of production in which they are relatively abundant. To the extent that Argentina is exporting industrial products for which the basis of its comparative advantage is dubious, doubts arise concerning its ability to sustain a high industrial export growth rate and the possibility that the present growth rate might have been higher if the factor composition of exports had been different. Argentina's perverse factor intensity biases of industrial exports are linked to characteristics of its industrial market structure and domestic price behavior. Any "real-world" analysis of the

Argentine economy must inevitably turn to sociopolitical phenomena, and Felix suggests that stalemated sectoral conflicts over basic economic policy exist and that these continue to block rationalization of the industrial sector. More than thirty years of import-substituting industrialization have raised Argentina's industrial value-added–GNP ratio to the highest level in Latin America, but they have also left the industrial sector woefully unprepared to serve as a dynamic leading sector for future economic growth.

Daniel Schydlowsky is considerably more optimistic than is Felix about the prospects for future Latin American industrial export expansion, an interpretation which derives in part from his earlier research on the structures of Latin American exchange rates. Schydlowsky views the Latin American economies as generally characterized by simultaneous underutilization of installed industrial capacity and by large-scale industrial labor force unemployment and underemployment. A number of factors are cited as barriers to full-capacity utilization, including small market size, shortage of working capital, insufficient skilled personnel, the labor cost structure, and the tax structure. The immediate cause, however, for the presence of concurrent labor and capital unemployment and underemployment is lack of demand. Domestic demand could easily be stimulated through expansionary domestic monetary and/or fiscal policies. But, due to the import-intensive content of industrial production, imports would rise significantly along with the expansion of domestic industrial output and bring the balance of payments into disequilibrium. For this reason, a better alternative from the point of view of the balance-of-payments constraint is the expansion of industrial exports. Industrial export promotion would, at the same time, create the additional demand necessary for industrial growth and provide the foreign exchange required to purchase the imports to sustain full-capacity utilization. As industrial exporting expands, adoption of an expansionary domestic aggregate demand policy also becomes feasible, and thus additional industrial output could be absorbed by the domestic market. The point of equilibrium in this expansionary process exists where the new industrial exports exactly offset the new import requirements, which are generated by the industrial output expansion itself and the growth of domestic income.

Of course, industrial exports would have to be competitive in the world market, but Schydlowsky sees this as less improbable than does Felix. Schydlowsky argues that existing Latin American financial exchange rates are in fact poor measures of Latin America's true competitiveness. They do, however, create an "inefficiency illusion." Actual industrial costs are based on exchange rates substantially above the financial rate, and a comparison of these industrial costs with world prices by means of the financial rate considerably overstates dollar costs. The antiexport bias in the Latin American exchange rate systems means that, at private prices, industrial exports are frequently unprofitable. At social (shadow) prices, however, export of a share of the increased industrial production resulting from full-capacity utilization would leave a positive net benefit for a wide spectrum of industrial activities. "Socially corrected prices" should be developed through the use of industrial export subsidies. These would provide the necessary profitability to make industrial exportation economically feasible for private enterprise. Thus, the problem posed by the simultaneous existence of both idle labor and capital is not fundamentally a "structural" one. It is more Keynesian in nature and is largely solvable by providing the correct incentives through appropriate fiscal policy.

2

The Role of Industrialization
in Latin American Inflation

Nicholas Kaldor

MOST Latin American economies have been characterized by a proliferation of policies designed to promote industrialization, and by persistent rapid inflation. The extent to which there is a causal connection between these two phenomena is, however, a controversial subject. The views held by many of the professors of economics in the United States and in Europe are not shared by many distinguished economists in Latin America, and neither are they shared by what was once called the "underworld" of economics—people of heterodox views who are not well represented among those holding academic appointments. In order to examine the basis of the controversy, it is necessary to examine the fundamental issues concerning not only industrialization, but also the broader issues concerning economic development and trade.

It is best to start with the peculiarities of Latin American inflations. It is generally agreed that Latin America is "peculiar" in its inflations in that they are not like other countries' inflations, or have not been considered to be such until recently. In recent years the difference has undoubtedly become less pronounced. The rate of inflation in the United States and in the countries of Western Europe has accelerated, although it has not yet reached Latin American dimensions. In Latin America the countries which have suffered from these inflations have maintained very high rates of price increases, of the order of 25 to 50 percent per year on the average, over periods as long as thirteen or fifteen years. And their further peculiarity has been that such fast rates of price increases have been maintained over long periods without exploding into what we call "hyperinflations." Hyperinflations occur once the annual rate of price increases exceeds a kind of "sound barrier" of 400 percent a year. Past experience has tended to show that once a rate of price increase of 400 percent per year is attained, inflation becomes a "galloping" phenomenon, with a strong built-in acceleration, leading to a situation where prices are doubled weekly or even daily. This is what happened in Germany

14

after the First World War and in a number of other countries (such as Hungary and Greece) after the Second World War; and it invariably ends with a complete collapse of the currency and its replacement by an entirely new monetary system.

But nothing like this ever happened in Latin America. One reason is that the rates of inflation, although they were high, were never very steady, and this is their second important characteristic. If one looks at the graphs, the rates of inflation fluctuated; they reached and sometimes exceeded 100 percent for one or two years, but then they slowed down again to under 50 percent or even to 20 percent, and afterwards they tended to start up again. So, the course of these inflations has never been *certain* for the near future—the movement of prices is unpredictable in the short term even though, on past showing, one may be confident of the continuance of rising prices in the long term. All the inflationary countries exhibited these queer fluctuations—periods of high inflations followed by years of relative quiescence; in some cases, violent inflations flaring up after quite a long period of price stability, and in other cases inflations apparently dying out altogether, although no one can ever be certain that they will not start up again without any major visible cause (such as a major war or a revolution).

The third characteristic is that although all Latin American countries show important similarities in political and social framework, in the matter of inflationary experience they are by no means all alike. The high inflations were confined to a particular group of countries, notably Chile, Brazil, Bolivia, Argentina, Paraguay, and, more recently, Uruguay. Other Latin American countries may have had inflations in the past, but in the postwar period they have escaped it altogether or almost entirely; in the latter category I would put Mexico, Peru, Venezuela, and many, but not all, of the Central American republics.

On the face of it, there is nothing very much to distinguish one of the two groups of countries from the other: we have some more-developed and some less-developed countries, some un-developing countries (as someone called it), and some rapidly growing countries both in the inflationary group and in the noninflationary group.

The questions which need to be answered are why these inflations occurred, and why they had the peculiar characteristics described.

ALTERNATIVE EXPLANATIONS

The possible explanations are of three different types, which I should like to call the "monetary," the "terms-of-trade," and the "structural," respectively. Not all of these are mutually exclusive; and, except for the naive version of the monetary explanation, none can be dismissed as wrong.

The "naive version" of the monetary explanation attributes inflations to an increase in the "money supply" per se. The most distinguished proponent of this view is Professor Milton Friedman of Chicago, whose views could be paraphrased in a sentence or two: "Show me a country which had a major inflation *without* an increase in the money supply. Until such an example is found, and until somebody shows that the money supply *cannot* be controlled by the monetary authority, the change in the money supply must be the 'main and only necessary cause' (to use a famous classical expression) of the rise in prices. In other words, provided a good correlation is found between the GNP and the money supply in *all* cases, and especially when the change in the money supply *leads* the GNP, there is no need to go beyond that relationship and to look for a 'mechanism' or a 'model.'" This is the message of the so-called "positive economics" à la Chicago.

The more sophisticated adherents of the monetary explanation do find the intellectual need for something more, and look for the causes of inflation either in excessive private investment financed out of bank credit or in excessive government borrowing, i.e., a lax fiscal policy by the government. In other words, the ultimate cause of inflation according to this view must be looked for either in the government's ability to cover its needs by printing money, combined with its inability, or disinclination, to raise enough in taxation to avoid having recourse to the printing press; or else in the greed of the banks and other financial intermediaries to expand their business and increase their profits through excess lending, which is insufficiently kept in check by the central bank.

There are possible hypotheses—the question is, do they receive enough empirical support to be preferred to other explanations? Excessive lending to private business should manifest itself in an "excessive" proportion of the GNP being devoted to private investment, either in the form of fixed investment or of addition to stocks. Lax fiscal policy leading to excessive borrowing (or "resort to the printing press," which comes to the same thing) should show itself in relatively large fiscal deficits as a percentage of the GNP.

I do not think that either of these hypotheses can be adequately supported by the available evidence. The countries which experienced large inflations do not show that private investment (as a proportion of GNP) was large relative to that in the noninflationary countries. If anything, the statistics point the other way. If one looks at the budgetary deficits, it is true that, taking the inflationary group as a whole, deficits as a percentage of the GNP tended to be somewhat larger; but there is not very much in it. The important exception is the Argentine, where the fiscal deficit reached 4 to 5 percent of GNP for a number of years. (On the other hand, Venezuela, a noninflationary country, had even larger budgetary deficits.)

My feeling is that insofar as the budget deficits of inflationary countries have been larger percentage-wise than those of the noninflationary countries, this was a symptom (or consequence)—not the cause—of the inflationary process. It is well known from European studies that inflation causes budgetary deficits simply on account of the lag in tax collections; so even when a country's level of taxation is adequate, the process of inflation can cause the rise in tax receipts to lag behind the rise in expenditure. But this would not in itself add to the inflationary fuel; the larger fiscal deficit may have its offset in enlarged "tax reserves" of the private sector. Hence, the existence of a budget deficit does not necessarily indicate the presence of a demand inflation emanating in the public sector.

Of course, the true Friedmanite would say that it does not matter what *causes* inflations; if the central bank resolutely refused to countenance any increase in the money supply, there would be no inflation—in that sense, inflation is always the fault of the central bank! According to this view, if Venezuela and Mexico avoided inflations, it was because their central bankers were clever and/or virtuous; if Chile and Brazil did not, it was because they were wicked and/or stupid. There is nothing to explain why some countries should be so much luckier in their choice of central bankers than others.

A more reasonable view (in my opinion) is that central bankers are much the same kind of people everywhere; what differs is the pressure to which they are subject. They always, I presume, wish to do the right thing; but they cannot resist certain pressures, they are not the "powerful people" they are made out to be. This is only another way of saying that the "money supply" is not *really* under their control; the supply of money (in each country) responds to the demand, and this, in my view, is the basic explanation of the correlations found between the money supply and the changes in the money-GNP, both in Latin America and elsewhere.

One important feature that distinguishes the inflationary group of countries from the noninflationary group in Latin America is the existence of import restrictions. Every country which experienced inflation for any length of time restricted the import of consumer goods—i.e., imposed quantitative import controls of some kind—either through direct import licensing or the licensing of foreign exchange. If this is accepted as an empirically valid generalization (and I have no doubt that it must be), then the question is whether the "balance-of-payments constraint" which caused the adoption of quantitative import restrictions is itself an effect, or symptom, of the inflationary process or whether it may have a causal role in creating inflation. The answer to this clearly depends on an analysis of the causes of the "shortage" of foreign exchange. If it is a consequence of inflationary excess spending in the domestic economy due to budgetary deficits, this would show itself in an "abnormal" rise in the volume of imports resulting from the fact that home demand exceeded the capacity to produce.

But the need for import restrictions *could* arise from other causes, which are not associated with excessive demand and are not "monetary" or "fiscal" in origin. One such cause is a sharp deterioration in the terms of trade—a fall in the prices of a country's exports relative to the prices of imports—an extreme example of which was the collapse of export earnings during the Great Depression of the 1930s. It could also occur as a result of crop failure or of a fall in world demand for the particular product which provides the major source of exports to a particular country. In all these cases a country may be compelled to restrict imports; if as a result, the domestic price of some basic consumer goods rises, there will be pressures to find compensation for the fall in urban living standards (manifesting itself in a rise in the cost of living) through compensating increases in money wages and salaries. In these cases the consequential inflation is really a reflection of the inability of the country to distribute an inevitable reduction in its real income in a manner that is acceptable to its inhabitants.

Finally, one can conceive of situations in which there is a disproportion between the structure of production and the structure of final demand which, for special reasons that need to be explained, cannot be eliminated through international trade—and which leads to a disproportion between the import requirements and the export capacity associated with the production structure of a particular country.

Of course, it is true of any region or country which is not wholly self-contained that the proportion in which it produces different things is not the same as the proportions in which they are required for consumption or investment. This difference between the "product mix" and the "consumption mix" or "final-demand mix" should, in normal cases, be eliminated through international trade—any particular region or country exports the things which it produces in excess of domestic needs and obtains in return, through imports, the goods in which it is deficient. Under ideal conditions the world market is an enormous mart in which any particular "mix" of goods can be changed into any other "mix" at given conversion ratios, i.e., at the given system of world prices.

"Structural bottlenecks" arise when this harmonization of the "product mix" with the "final-demand mix" cannot take place in the normal manner through international trade; and the explanation for this lies at the heart of the problem of "structural inflations."

INDUSTRIALIZATION AND STRUCTURAL INFLATIONS

That the basic cause of Latin American inflations is "structural" and not "monetary" has been repeatedly asserted in the past, mainly by Latin American economists, and if their views have failed to carry conviction among the more sophisticated academic economists of the United States or Western Europe, this was perhaps because they failed to show the "necessary and sufficient" conditions for the occurrence of such "structural bottlenecks." Why should these bottlenecks have occurred in Latin American countries (or rather in *some* Latin American countries) and not elsewhere?

My contention is that the changes in the production structure of Latin American countries which caused the prevalence of "strong" inflations as a long-continuing process had their origin in the circumstances and manner in which industrialization and the associated urbanization proceeded in these countries, following upon the collapse of export earnings during the Great Depression of the 1930s and the further stimulus to industrialization afforded by the Second World War.

To understand this it is necessary to begin by drawing attention to the basic connection between industrialization and economic development, and to the preconditions of industrial development.

It is perhaps not sufficiently understood that the kind of economic growth that involves the use of modern technology and eventuates in high real income per head is inconceivable without the development of modern manufacturing industry. The reason for this is not only (or even mainly) because, as real income rises, only a diminishing proportion of income is spent on food and a rising proportion on industrial products and services. The main reason is that when primary production is efficiently conducted, high-productivity agriculture (or mining) cannot absorb more than a fraction of the labor force on the exploitation of the available land and mineral resources. Hence, a country that specialized entirely in primary products and obtained all its industrial goods from abroad could never be a country with a high real income per head. The best proof of this is that even those "advanced" high-income countries which "specialized" in the exportation of agricultural goods, forest products, or minerals (such as Australia, New Zealand, Denmark until recently, and Sweden in the earlier part of the century) have nevertheless had only a low proportion of their labor force in agriculture and mining, not only absolutely but relative to the labor force in industry. Wherever the proportion of the labor force in agriculture is large (as it still is in the countries of Latin America), this is a symptom of poverty, underdevelopment, and the existence of "disguised unemployment" on a large scale.

In a self-contained economic region—and the world was divided into such nontrading regions, particularly in landlocked areas, before the great transport revolution of the nineteenth and twentieth centuries—the rate of growth of manufacturing or "processing" activities was conditioned by the rate of growth of land productivity (in yields per acre, rather than per man) that made it possible for a surplus to emerge over the consumption needs of the agricultural producers. This "agricultural surplus" generated a market demand for industrial goods; it also provided the supply of "wage goods" for nonagricultural employment. Under favorable conditions, the expansion of these two sectors had a stimulating effect on one another. While the growth of marketable food supplies increased the demand for industrial goods, the increased availability of industrial goods led to further technological improvements in agriculture. Before the advent of the industrial revolution, however, the pace of this "chain reaction" was normally too slow to be perceived as a continuing process by contemporary observers.

With the transport revolution of the last two centuries, vast areas of the world became accessible to trade, and regions previously self-contained were increasingly drawn into the network of the world economy. Historically, this had two consequences. First, the cheap products of the manufacturing industries of the developed capitalist countries increasingly displaced the local manufactures of primitive small-scale industry. Second, with the growth of industries in the "advanced" countries of Europe, markets were created for temperate foodstuffs, tropical products, and minerals. Frequently this meant the establishment of foreign-owned mines and plantations, the products of which were mainly destined for export. As a result of both these factors, industrial development became increasingly polarized in certain "industrialized" countries, whilst the others (such as the countries of Latin America) became "specialized" in the production of raw materials and foodstuffs for the use of the industrial countries. The countries of Latin America, up to the 1930s, enjoyed rising export earnings from the sale of foodstuffs, minerals, and plantation products, which they spent on industrial goods produced in Western Europe or the United States. While their export earnings were growing, and there was a prosperous land-owning class in all these countries, the standard of living of the population remained low. This was true partly because wages were low, but mainly because only a fraction of the population was in regular employment.

In order to raise real income per head, the Latin American countries should have pursued from an early stage the same policies of fostering domestic industries by judiciously chosen methods of "import substitution"—the replacement of imports of manufactures by domestic production—which were so successfully pursued by the countries of Western Europe, North America, Japan, and other "developed" countries in the late nineteenth century and the present century. Apart from the case of Britain, which initiated the industrial revolution and for a time had a near-monopoly of the world market in factory-made goods, all the other present "developed" or "industrialized" countries established their industries through import substitution by means of protective tariffs and/or differential subsidies. As the German economist Friedrich List first emphasized in the middle of the nineteenth century, productivity in manufacturing industry is very low to start with; hence, without special measures of protection such industries cannot be established because they cannot compete with the products of the industrial centers at higher stages of development. However, owing to the existence of increasing returns to scale and learning-by-doing, productivity rises rapidly as these industries develop under the umbrella of protection; and assuming that wages remain low in comparison to those in the more advanced industrial centers, the industrializing country will pass from the stage of import substitution to become an exporter of manufactures on an increasing scale. For such a policy to be successful, the protective measures must be both moderate and discriminating. They must not encourage the mushroom growth of high-cost enterprises, and the protection itself should be reduced with the growth of domestic output as the industries pass beyond their "infancy," so as to put them in a position to develop an export potential. Moreover, the policy needs to be selectively applied; the "light industries" (such as textiles), which require less industrial know-how and smaller scale for efficient production, should be established first and the "heavy industries" (such as chemicals, steel, and engineering) at a later stage, when the "light industries" have already passed into the stage in which they export an important share of their output.

The Latin American countries did not follow this pattern. The initial impetus to industrialization did not come from suitably designed policies for industrial promotion. It came as a by-product of widespread and severe import restrictions imposed on account of sudden collapse of export earnings. The prime motive was the necessity to save foreign exchange. The stimulus to the establishment of local industries came from the rise of internal prices brought about by the shortages of goods previously imported. These import restrictions were thus the equivalent of an indiscriminate protection of a rather violent kind—raising the prices of industrial goods sometimes by several hundred percent in terms of agricultural products. Thus it was made profitable to produce goods for the home market even when the cost, in terms of primary products, was many times as high as the external price (or the world price) of such products.

This led to considerable investment in industrial capacity, increased urbanization, and an increase in total employment. In the earlier phases of this process, the gross domestic product grew quite rapidly (even in terms of world prices, not only domestic prices) because the newly established industries meant a net addition to resources, both capital and labor. The newly created capacity was the fruit of additional savings generated by the rise in profits, and the increase in industrial employment meant a net addition to employment—it did not cause any offsetting reductions in the effective utilization of labor in the rest of the economy.

However, while the additional output went largely to replace goods previously imported, the additional incomes which the new productive activity generated led to an increase in demand for consumption goods, primarily food, which was greater than could be satisfied by the available supplies. At the same time, the industrial activity did nothing to alleviate the balance-of-payments constraint. Though many goods previously imported were replaced by domestic production, the process itself generated an additional demand for imports—partly because the investment needed to establish productive capacity had a very high import content; partly because some of the current inputs of raw materials and components had to be imported; and partly because industrialization meant additional incomes—additional profits, salaries, and wages—which generated additional consumption, and some part of that consumption, however severe the restrictions, was inevitably spent on imported goods or services. At the same time, owing to the circumstances of their creation, very few of the new industries were efficient enough to develop a capacity to export. Thus, the pressure for imports in excess of current earnings became greater, not less; the balance-of-payments constraint was not alleviated by industrialization, but aggravated by it.

Even this constellation of circumstances would not have necessarily caused prolonged inflations if it had not been combined with a third factor: the failure of agriculture to respond to increased urban demand by increasing marketable food supplies in an adequate manner. This lack of response on the side of agriculture had partly institutional and partly economic causes. It may have been due to vestiges of feudalism, ancient forms of land tenure, and absentee ownership, or it may have been due to an adverse change in the terms of trade (despite the shortage of agricultural products). The relative importance of these two factors varied in different countries. In the Argentine, where agriculture was more "commercialized," the unfavorable change in the terms of trade (particularly in the years of the Perón regime) was the important factor. In Chile, on the other hand, it was more a matter of absentee ownership and lack of incentives in the absence of land reform.

It was the combination of an increase in both the volume of employment and output per head in nonagricultural employment and the absence of a corresponding increase in food supplies that made continued inflation inevitable. It caused a persistent upward pressure in the prices of food paid by the urban consumer, and it was the rise in food prices which caused the persistent rise in urban wages and salaries (in order to maintain real wages), which in turn raised the general level of industrial costs and prices. The inflation, therefore, was "demand-induced" as far as food prices were concerned, and "cost-induced" as far as the rise in the prices of nonagricultural goods and services was concerned. Or, putting it in different words, the basic cause of the inflation was the disproportionality in the growth of production in different sectors of the economy, particularly between "wage goods" and "nonwage goods." Given this fact, inflation could only have been prevented if (a) production and employment in the nonagricultural sectors had been cut so as to eliminate excess purchasing power for foodstuffs, and (b) nonagricultural employees had been ready to put up with a cut in real earnings without demanding (and obtaining) compensating increases in money wages. As it was (in some of the countries at any rate), real wages tended to remain constant and the share of wages in the national income fell. It must also be borne in mind that when real wages are low enough for the cost of food to take up a high proportion of the wage earner's budget (as is the case in most Latin American countries), it is not in the interest of a capitalist employer to allow the purchasing power of his employees to fall, since any reduction might cause a rise in costs through reduced work performance (owing to lower food intake) that is greater than the increase in cost involved in paying higher wages. In other words, there is a certain real wage that minimizes the cost of labor per unit of output, and it is in the interests of the employer to ensure that wages do not fall below that level. The periodic upward adjustment in money wages to compensate for the rise in living costs (which alone made the inflation a *continuing* process) was, therefore, not just a matter of "trade union pressure"; it might have occurred in much the same way even if such pressure had not existed.

In a paper on Chile written in 1956,[1] I predicted that "no lasting cure of the inflationary tendencies of Chile can be found either in stricter monetary and credit policies or even in administrative reform which secured more effective taxation"; it can "only be found through a more rapid increase in food availabilities—either through a more rapid increase in the productivity of agriculture (which in turn hinges upon the reform of land tenure) or a more liberal policy of importing food-stuffs from abroad."[2] Events in the subsequent fifteen years have certainly not contradicted this prediction. Despite repeated attempts to secure "stabilization" by far-reaching monetary and fiscal reform (some under the aegis of the International Monetary Fund), inflation could not be slowed down, let alone halted, for more than brief periods.

The orthodox instruments of credit control cannot prevent the in-

1. Nicholas Kaldor, "Economic Problems of Chile," a study prepared for the Economic Commission for Latin America, reprinted in *Essays on Economic Policy*, vol. 2 (London: Duckworth, 1964), pp. 233-77.

2. Ibid., p. 277. As was noted in that paper, the deficiency in domestic food production was increasingly supplemented by food imports; but owing to the ever-present shortage of foreign exchange, these imports were not on the scale required to satisfy the growth in demand resulting from the rise in employment and incomes. In another (unpublished) paper on the Argentine, it was also argued that the acceleration of its inflationary trends in the post-Perón period in the 1950s could be traced to the restriction of food availabilities for domestic use owing to the need to restore (or prevent a further erosion of) the volume of agricultural exports.

crease in bank credit required in consequence of the rise of the money value of the "normal" working capital, which is a consequence of the rise in money wages. The banking system could only withstand this pressure at the cost of serious interference with the normal processes of production and circulation of goods, or by causing a general breakdown on contracts. It would be idle, for example, to charge the banks with the responsibility of *preventing* increases of money wages through a refusal of credit if the employers themselves regard the adjustment of money wages as fair and reasonable in the light of the rise in the cost of living. It would be equally idle to expect the banks to force businesses to reduce their scale of operations by enforcing a reduction in working capital tied up in "goods in process" in order to compensate for a rise in demand that originates from another quarter—e.g., from increased government spending. The responsibility of the banking system cannot be extended beyond ensuring that an inflationary process is not aggravated by abnormal speculative demands arising out of the process of inflation itself; and there is no evidence, in the case of Latin American inflations, that such "speculative demands" (fed by easy credit) played an important role in the process. Moreover, if monetary measures *could* be made effective, they would remedy the disproportionality by cutting output and employment in the nonagricultural sectors; this is clearly not a solution that would recommend itself on welfare criteria.

It is equally idle to expect that the basic disproportionalities can be eliminated by devaluation. For countries whose main exports are primary products (like coffee or copper), the prices of which are determined by world markets, devaluation is unavailing in increasing the export proceeds in terms of such products. To develop industrial exports, on the other hand, the necessary devaluation would have to be pretty severe— partly because industrial costs and prices in these countries, when measured in terms of primary products, are so much higher than world prices, and partly also because there are high initial marketing and selling costs connected with such exports. And devaluations of this order, by raising the domestic prices of traditional exports as well as imports, cause a further bout of inflation that cancels the effects of devaluation in a fairly short period.

Devaluation may be an appropriate remedy for balance-of-payments disequilibria of industrialized countries which export manufactured goods and which become uncompetitive (or insufficiently competitive) in relation to other industrial exporters because their "efficiency wages" (money wages divided by productivity) are excessive at the prevailing exchange rates. But in the case of "developing" countries whose major exports are primary products, the trouble is not with the general level of costs or prices. The trouble is with the price *structure* rather than the price *level* —the cost of industrial products is too high not just in terms of international currency, but in terms of food and primary products—and this defect cannot be remedied by an overall change in the exchange rate, for much the same reasons that a rise in the cost of living is unavailing in securing a lasting reduction in real wages.

The countries of Latin America that succeeded in avoiding inflations, or in gradually eliminating the inflationary process, were those that succeeded in avoiding or getting out of the impasse of a chronic balance-of-payments constraint, one way or another. One country, Venezuela, escaped inflation largely because her foreign exchange earnings, on account of oil, were large enough to permit liberal importation of foodstuffs, as well as investment goods and goods serving luxury consumption. The lag in agricultural production in relation to the growth of urban food requirements was no different, as far as I can see, than in Chile; but unlike Chile, Venezuela was able to import all basic foods that were needed to prevent shortages and rising prices in the domestic markets. Then there were countries which from the start paid more attention to the development of an export potential. That is true of Peru, which developed a large export in fish meal and various other products and, thanks to rising export earnings, could allow a far more liberal import policy. A third type of country is one that, thanks to land reform or to a revolution which gave the land to a new lot of owners, managed to make agriculture more "dynamic" or "responsive" and thus to keep the growth of marketable food supplies in line with the growth of urban demand. This is the explanation for the comparative absence of inflation in Mexico. And finally, there is a group of countries which did not attempt to industrialize (or not on any scale), were therefore not subject to the pressures arising from an industrialization policy, and were able to take the reduction of their export earnings in the 1930s in stride without the need to impose severe import restrictions. This includes many Central American republics, many of which escaped the need for such severe import controls partly because, in the critical period, they were still the colonies of European powers.

REMEDIES

If the above analysis is correct, the remedies to Latin American inflations will not be found in monetary or fiscal reforms—though this is not to say that these, particularly fiscal reform, may not be necessary and important as accompanying measures. The remedies must be "structural," and this means changing the framework of institutions and of basic policies, which takes some time to become effective. The two basic remedies are, first, stimulating domestic food production, which requires far-reaching land reform in most countries, as well as public investment and promotional policies, e.g., in irrigation schemes; and second, appropriate policies for industrial rationalization and the promotion of exports of manufactures.

Industrial rationalization is necessary because as a result of excessive protection, production is scattered over too wide a field and in too many separate plants, each of which is operating on an uneconomic scale. There is also (in relation to developed countries) too much surplus operating capacity. This, as noted, was the unintended consequence of quantitative import restrictions (the original purpose of which was to cut "luxury" consumption—like motor cars—not to stimulate the domestic production of such "luxuries"). The remedy lies, in the first place, in replacing import quotas by protective duties, which has already taken place to a considerable extent; and in the second place, in cutting the "peaks" and leveling up the "troughs" in the ad valorem equivalent of import duties so as to withdraw protection from those activities or enterprises which are exceptionally inefficient. One needs to make a sharp distinction between the *average level* of import duties—which may have to remain pretty high if industrial activity and employment in the aggregate is not to contract—and the degree of unevenness in the incidence of the duties between different goods. Of course, it is desirable that the average level of protection should also be reduced as rapidly as possible, provided this is consistent with the continued growth in the scale of industrial activities. But whatever the average level of protective duty that is found necessary for that purpose, the policy of leveling out the height of the tariff between one industrial product and another allows the law of comparative costs to operate within the industrial sector; less efficient firms and industries will be eliminated, and the more efficient will expand and thereby achieve further gains due to increasing returns. It is in this way that a situation could be created in which the Latin American countries might secure an increasing share of world trade in manufactures.

The other aspect—deliberate export promotion—is best undertaken by a system of "dual exchange rates," a suggestion which I developed in a paper in the ECLA *Bulletin* several years ago.[3] Because protection involves a change in the internal price structure (between industrial goods and primary products) in relation to the structure of world prices, no *single* exchange is appropriate for promoting industrial exports without an undue domestic rise in the prices and incomes of primary producers. The ideal way of promoting industrialization, as several economists have pointed out, is not by tariffs at all but by straightforward subsidies paid to industry by the government, the money being raised by taxes collected on incomes of primary producers. In that way the *internal* cost relationship is adjusted to the *external* price structure and not the internal price structure to the internal cost structure. But this involves large budgetary transfers—the raising of large sums in taxation from the agricultural sector,

3. Nicholas Kaldor, "Dual Exchange and Economic Development," *Economic Bulletin for Latin America* (September 1964), reprinted in *Essays on Economic Policy*, vol. 2, pp. 178-99.

which most countries (not only those of Latin America) find very diffi-cult.[4] However, much the same result could be attained without the need for large budgetary transfers if the protective import duty on industrial goods were "matched," so to speak, by equivalent export subsidies. This means that if the level of import duties is 50 percent, there should be 33 1/3 percent subsidy on industrial exports, and so on. Assuming the duties on industrial goods are uniform and the export subsidies are uni-form, this means that the industries which remain profitable at the chosen rate of tariffs and subsidies can compete with the goods produced by other countries on the same terms, in their own internal market as in the world market. The industries that will prosper under this system will be those in which the comparative efficiency of any particular country is greatest. Each country will go on developing its industrial activities, but these developments will be consistent with the maximum benefit of in-ternational specialization. Such a policy, if universally pursued, would combine the advantages of free trade with the elimination of the handi-cap to economic development of the less-developed areas arising from the very existence of more highly developed countries. No amount of re-search and planning could predict beforehand which particular industry any particular country is best fitted to develop. (Who could have pre-dicted, for example, that Hong Kong in a matter of a few years would develop an export trade of $150 million in wigs?)

The simplest and most effective way of giving effect to such a policy is through a system of dual exchange rates—with one particular rate ap-plicable to "traditional" exports (of primary products) and basic imports (of foodstuffs and industrial materials) and another exchange rate appli-cable to both the exports and imports of manufactured goods—the greater the difference between the two rates, the less developed the country's industry. The present international rules regarding money and trade (Bretton Woods and General Agreement on Tariffs and Trade) rule out both dual exchange rates and export subsidies. These rules were invented for the benefit of the developed countries (who are, however, as recent events have shown, also ready to break them whenever it suits their in-terests); and clearly, in a sensible world they would not be applied to developing countries. There would be different rules for the one group and for the other. Indeed, the developed countries have already acknowl-edged the case for giving preferential treatment to imports from the developing countries and have taken effective steps to this end, albeit on a rather meager scale. Much the best way to give effect to the principle of helping the developing countries through the adaptation of the "ground rules" in their favor would be to abolish quantitative restrictions on im-

4. The countries which have succeeded in doing this—such as Japan through the land tax after the Meiji restoration—and were thereby able to establish industries through subsidies without the need for high protective tariffs, reaped their reward in an early development of industrial exports.

ports from the developing countries (which many of the developed countries now maintain, under the escape clauses of GATT, to protect themselves from "trade disruption") and to permit them to operate dual exchange rates (or a linked system of import duties and export subsidies), provided they agree to eliminate in stages their own quantitative import controls and also their protective duties other than those involved in the operation of the dual exchange rate or its equivalent. This would be a far better way of developing the world economy than the creation of discriminating blocks (common markets or free trade areas), among either the developed or the developing countries, and in the particular matter of inflation, would be the best way to get Latin America out of the wood.

Comment—Javier Márquez

ALTHOUGH I am not a Kaldorian scholar, I am not unfamiliar with his writings. There is not a great deal I can say concerning his model, but I will venture some misgivings concerning several theoretical and policy points which he makes.

The first refers to Kaldor's contention that the rate of migration from rural to urban areas depends on the demand for labor in the towns, on the growth of job opportunities. Labor transference, he notes, is entirely dependent on the growth of the demand for industrial labor, as defined by him (manufacturing, construction, and public utilities). This may be the case (that is, a net transference) in a very few Latin American countries (perhaps Argentina is one) where rural manpower has decreased in absolute terms and where total population grows slowly; but it is difficult to accept that the rate of migration from rural to urban areas in a country like Mexico, for example, with a population growth of 3.5 percent per year, has had much to do with the urban demand for labor. The continuous growth of open unemployment, which is a typical urban phenomenon, seems to contradict Kaldor's point, which I believe assumes a fairly constant rate of unemployment. Between 1950 and 1965 open unemployment in Latin America grew from 3 to almost 9 million people, that is, from 5.6 to 11.1 percent of the labor force. If this trend continues, by 1980 open unemployment will be the equivalent of 18.6 percent of the labor force. People are "expelled" from the land, they do not move because they are "demanded" elsewhere even in the medium run (twelve months?). Perhaps equally significant, in this respect, is the fact that between 1950 and 1965 Latin America's agricultural labor force grew from 27.5 million people to 33.6 million (in relative terms it diminished from 55.3 percent to 47.5 percent of the total), while the growth of the urban population was far larger. If, as Kaldor contends, the (indispensable) increase of the yield per acre is dependent on the transfer of people engaged in agriculture, I shiver at the manifold consequences of such an increase of the yield per acre in Latin America.

This brings me to a second point—namely, the argument for land reform, which seems to conflict with other points that he makes, in particular with his emphasis on the increase in food production and the requirements for it. Agriculture, I agree, must be made responsive to the stimulus of increased demand coming from the urban sector. He attributes the present lack of response partly to a feudal system of land tenure. I understand this to mean that the wealthy landlord is satisfied with what he is already getting from his land, and consequently the increased demand and prospective larger profits (surplus) do not induce him to produce more. Although it is not explicit in his paper (but he has emphasized it on other occasions), the gimmick to force an increase in food production is a tax system that penalizes unutilized or poorly utilized land; but the wealthy landlord is politically so powerful that he is able to evade taxes or to prevent the establishment of such a tax system. With land reform we would have the land in the hands of smaller farmers without the same political power, and taxes could force them to produce more (as occurred in Japan in the last third of the nineteenth century). Land reform then becomes a roundabout way of imposing taxes on agriculture and thus forcing an increase in production. Whatever its merits in solving a social problem that might otherwise bring about a collapse of the whole economic system, land reform per se does not increase agricultural production, as the small farmer is no more *homo œconomicus* than the wealthy landlord.

What worries me here is, to the extent that land reform is implemented, the size of agricultural holdings is reduced (or at least that is the Latin American idea of such a reform), while—as Kaldor himself points out—the larger units are more productive than the smaller ones. Also, if the reduction of the rural population is a prerequisite for increasing yields per acre, is land reform not contrary to such a reduction? Kaldor's preferred example of increases in food production in Latin America, the case of Mexico, does not seem to me to lend much support to the argument for the benefits of taxes on land, since the increases that have occurred are, I believe, entirely independent from such taxes and mainly the result of a complex of causes such as response to demand (domestic and foreign), protectionism, improved infrastructure, improvements in seeds, fertilizers, plague control, the building of an official agricultural credit system, selective credit controls on private banks, etc.

The promotion of industrialization and of industrial exports is basic to his model. Industrialization always requires protection for newcomers, for those that started late in the industrial field, but protection should be temporary infant-industry protection, and uniform for all industries, in order to stimulate the play of comparative costs both at domestic and at international levels. Exports should not be stimulated through devaluations, for the problem is not one of the general price level but of the structure of prices; the right stimulation is through internal subsidies, and the easiest way to implement such subsidies is through a dual exchange system that gives industrial exports a rate which should be the equivalent of a certain proportion of a uniform import duty.

Here occurs a problem of definition. In the context of his paper, infant-industry protection seems to mean protection of all industries, whether existing or potential, at the early stages of industrialization with a diminishing scale as industrialization advances. (It would mean infant "industrialization" protection.) It is not, I understand, a uniform protection to selected industries as and when they appear. One starts with a uniform tariff on industrial goods of 100 percent today and reduces it gradually to zero at the end of, say, fifty years. It is not that each industry when established gets 100 percent protection which is reduced gradually to zero in fifty years. If my interpretation of Kaldor's definition of infant-industry protection is correct, I am somewhat doubtful about the operational virtues of the concept. It would imply an unnecessarily high price level, since industries that do not exist are protected, and the level of protection depends on the date at which an industry is established. At the same time, if an industry is not given more protection than it needs to get started, protection which is then reduced gradually, would one not have the same advantages as in Kaldor's proposal? The trouble is not with the diversity of degrees of protection, but with permanent protection. Perhaps his proposal is based on the idea that as you become a more mature, industrialized country, even new industries need less protection.

This latter possibility would be consistent with the proposal for export subsidies as it appeared in his 1964 article for ECLA.[1] In 1964 he advocated a dual exchange system in the sense of an official, or basic, rate which would apply to traditional exports and essential imports, while industrial exporters would sell the exchange proceeds of their exports in a "free" market where importers of luxury goods and other buyers of foreign exchange for nonessential purposes would also have to go. The premium in the free market would be the subsidy—the more industrial exports and consequently the larger the supply of foreign exchange in the free market, the smaller would be the premium, or subsidy; that is, there would be a diminishing subsidy as the country became more industrialized, or more competitive in world markets. In this new version, there is no self-regulating mechanism for a diminishing subsidy: the subsidy is estimated as a percentage of the protective tariff (33 percent if the tariff were to be 50 percent; 50 percent if the tariff were to be 100 percent).

1. Nicholas Kaldor, "Los tipos de cambio duales y el desarrollo económico," *Boletín Económico de América Latina* 9, no. 2 (noviembre de 1964): 214-23.

The need to export nontraditional goods is today understood in all Latin American countries; the demand for traditional exports is inelastic, while the demand for industrial exports is not. Kaldor emphasizes this need as a way to overcome the balance-of-payments constraints of development. There is more to it than that. Given the size of the domestic markets of the great majority of Latin American countries, most efficient, low-cost industries require foreign markets if they are to be operated at or near full capacity without undue effects on the domestic price level. I would not be satisfied with artificially promoted exports of industrial goods while the domestic price of these goods remains very high, for such a situation is bound to affect the whole price and cost structures of the country and thus require recurrent devaluations which, we agree, are not to the long-run benefit of anybody.

I am not clear whether Kaldor advocates the same policies of protection and export subsidies in all cases—that is, even for those countries (he mentions Venezuela, Peru, and Mexico) that have escaped inflation; or only for those that, for one reason or another, have not been able to increase food production and/or have not been able to increase their export earnings. Assuming that some of the presently inflationary countries were able to increase agricultural production and/or develop their exports, would he still advocate the same protectionist and export subsidizing policies? I suppose that he would, for inefficiency would still be there in the short run, but then we would have the cost effects which I have just mentioned. In any case, some of the remedies proposed to deal with development problems through the promotion of industrialization seem to be rather inflationary to the extent that they imply the acceptance, indeed the promotion, of high costs—and consequently high prices —in industry which would permeate the whole cost structure.

His main explanation of inflation in Latin America is that it is due to structural factors arising out of a disproportionate development between the output of various economic sectors, which reflects itself in a disproportion between import requirements and export capacity. He also says that there were demand-induced increases in food prices which led to cost-induced increases in industrial wages. The countries of Latin America were unable to increase their exports, Kaldor notes, while their import requirements grew up because their national income and industrial investments grew. And the agricultural surplus was not rising because of the very policy of deteriorating the terms of trade against agriculture. He maintains that too many people are engaged in producing things other than food and too little food is available to meet their requirements. He accepts that fiscal deficits and credit expansions are inflationary, but contends that the main or most frequent cause of inflation is structural.

In general, I find this theory a successful attempt to prove that some inflations are being triggered by disproportions in the structure of production and prices and that not all pressures come from an expansion of money, or that the expansion of money is not always autonomous. Moreover, Kaldor does not contend that industrialization (which is a necessary condition for development) per se brings inflation, but just industrialization of the wrong kind and under the wrong policies (indiscriminate and permanent protection, insufficient emphasis on industry or manufacturing,[2] too many people on the land, not enough emphasis on agriculture, etc.). Some Latin American countries have been able to escape inflation because they have been "lucky," because they developed exports or because they developed agriculture.

An interesting aspect of Kaldor's exposé is his acceptance of the monetarist contention that, if central banks resist the pressures for increasing the money supply, inflation could not go on for any length of time. If I am not mistaken, on previous occasions Kaldor did not make such a concession, but argued that if the central bank were to refrain from increasing the money supply, inflation would go unabated because the velocity of money would increase sufficiently to finance the increases in costs and prices. Velocity was elastic; now he says that the money supply is elastic because central bankers are unable to resist the pressures to which they are subject. This is a very fortunate situation, for, in the absence of elasticity in the velocity of money, and given the downward inelasticity of wages, stability would be achieved through increases in industrial unemployment. If deflation were the alternative, we could get close to the situation of the famous medical report which, after describing the positive reactions of a patient to successive treatments, ended with something to the effect that "the patient died in much better health."

My final remarks concern Kaldor's policy remedies for inflation. I find that, with the possible exception of land reform (to the extent that it is more than a means of being able to impose taxes on land), his remedies are implicitly or explicitly monetary and/or fiscal. In fact, if the purpose is not just stability but stability *with* development of the right sort (a socially oriented development), then it seems obvious that all sorts of policies have to be applied simultaneously. No single policy—monetary, fiscal, incomes, etc.—would do, and monetary policy should play an important role.

2. Here I am frequently at a loss as to whether he means industry including construction and other components, or only manufacturing.

Comment—Dale Truett

KALDOR has supplied an eloquent and reasonably complete exposition of the structuralist interpretation of inflation in Latin America. I am particularly pleased by the attention he has called to the *reasons* for monetary expansion and the role of price *structure* in countries characterized by relatively high rates of inflation. The criticism which I offer stems from the rather loose and general terms in which he has couched his argument and his propensity to utilize examples which do not quite conform to my view of fact.

Let me begin by saying that Kaldor's analysis certainly does not destroy the monetarist argument that expansion of the money supply is essential to any explanation of persistent Latin American inflations. Indeed, where real output is increasing, it would be difficult for anyone to put together an explanation of prolonged inflation based on a stable money supply. Thus, as Kaldor himself has said, the inflation *is* tied to actions of central bankers. I would agree with him that central bankers are much the same kind of people everywhere and what differs is the pressure to which they are subject. However, Kaldor's subsequent discussion does not link structural problems to the discretionary actions of central bankers and their ultimate decision to feed the inflationary process. This issue is dismissed by the assertion that the money supply is not *really* under their control and that the supply of money responds to money demand. It seems to me that the response which Kaldor envisions is not automatic and cannot occur without some discretionary action by the central bank. It follows that central bankers must desire to have a certain rate of inflation, either for developmental purposes or for fear that failure to inflate, whatever the consequences for economic development, will lead to their demise. In either case, they are responding to the *pressure* to which Kaldor made reference, and their actions have both social and private costs and benefits.

The upshot of the foregoing is that structural bottlenecks, imperfections, or maladjustments may well be at the root of initial inflationary pressure, but they are in the continuing process combined with the central bank's willingness to feed the inflation. As Kaldor suggests, the pressures may well emanate both from unplanned imbalances in the growth process and from deliberate policies (such as protectionism) which may kick off an initial round of price increases.

I am surprised that in his brief discussion of the behavior of the monetary authority Kaldor did not admit a deliberate policy of forced saving as a possible explanation for expansion of the money supply. This is strange, especially in light of the evidence on this score brought out during the Rio Conference of 1963. For example, Baer and Kerstenetzky, in reference to Brazil, stated that "we are convinced that the forced-saving mechanism played a definite part during the inflationary period. . . ."[1] Kaldor's discussion of "lax fiscal policy" simply dismisses the forced-saving premise too lightly. Further, his treatment of bank lending to the private sector whets our appetites for an explanation but concludes with none, and he writes off this issue with allusion to the rather stable investment rates found in inflationary countries. It seems to me that he should have noted that "excessive lending" is a blind alley in the explanation of private banks' role in an inflationary economy. After all, once inflation has gotten under way, pecuniary lending will have to increase in order to have even marginal increases in the real value of lending for purchases of goods and services (or inventories) at higher prices. Obviously, private banks will be called upon to increase lending in this setting. Here is the demand for money affecting its supply, à la Kaldor, but the supply response ultimately comes up against a policy variable. Private banks seeking real growth in the volume of their operations and returns will, in this setting, place considerable pressure on central bankers to undertake expansionary monetary policy. Perhaps it is the private bankers who are the "powerful people" affecting the money supply.

Let us turn now to the structural bottlenecks setting off inflationary pressure, to which the money supply eventually responds. It is widely accepted that in a developing economy such structural impediments are continuously present, and they are generally identified as supply bottlenecks of one kind or another. In Kaldor's analysis, the existence of these supply bottlenecks is reflected in a distorted internal price structure, caused primarily by discriminatory protective policies implemented through *quantitative* controls on imports. The cyclical variation of export earnings may be the culprit in the establishment of the controls. Kaldor emphasizes the ad hoc quantitative structure of import controls in inflationary countries, since this fits nicely with his later prescription of a system of dual exchange rates. However, the examples used in Kaldor's description of import controls do not quite fit his proposition that discriminatory quotas and licenses produce the maladjustments in the price structure which underlie inflation. Kaldor states: "Every country which experienced inflation for any length of time restricted the import of consumer goods—i.e., imposed quantitative import controls of some kind—either through direct import licensing or the licensing of foreign exchange." Brazil, which had long periods of spiraling inflation, relied primarily on the tariff and did not use import licensing to any great extent. Its exchange control system (terminated in 1962) relied on auction of certificates, and after 1962 more-or-less free exchange was permitted.[2] Fur-

1. Werner Baer and Isaac Kerstenetzsky, "Some Observations on the Brazilian Inflation," in Baer and Kerstenetzky, eds., *Inflation and Growth in Latin America* (Homewood, Ill.: Richard D. Irwin, Inc., 1964), p. 367.
2. See International Monetary Fund, *Annual Report on Exchange Restrictions* (1960, 1962, 1964, 1967).

ther, to turn the table on Kaldor's argument, Mexico has utilized an intricate system of quotas and licenses but has not had spiraling inflation. I would suspect that although the structure of import controls plays a role in price distortions, the set of forces underlying demand pressure on the money supply is much more complex. This is why generalizations for all of Latin America never seem to hold up.

Of course, Kaldor himself is not satisfied to look only for price distortions caused by import control systems. In fact, he turns to the entire structure of dualistic development, with which we are all familiar, to find further support for the price distortion argument. I fully agree with him that high real income per head cannot be achieved in the absence of an urban-industrial complex, since I find his labor-absorption argument quite convincing: high-productivity agriculture or mining cannot absorb more than a fraction of the labor force on the exploitation of the available land and mineral resources. Import substitution, therefore, *is* necessary and has been practiced by every industrializing country since Britain. Again as we all know, the infant-industry argument for protectionism is valid, not only because of increasing returns to scale (the only reason given by Kaldor) but also because externalities and interindustry linkages abound in the industrial growth process. The protectionist systems in Latin America have indeed fostered the development of urban-industrial complexes, but, as Kaldor notes, agricultural production for internal markets in general has lagged. Both land tenure systems and fluctuating terms of trade have aggravated this situation, but they have not been the sole reasons for bottlenecks in agriculture. In Chile, for example, indiscriminate protectionism has led to high tariffs on fertilizers and agricultural machinery—an absurd situation for a country with chronic food shortages. Thus, there is ample evidence, Kaldor argues, that the basic cause of inflation was the disproportionality in the growth of production in different sectors of the economy, particularly as between "wage goods" and "nonwage goods." In this setting, inflation proves the easiest means to reduce the effective demand of the nonagricultural sector. It is certainly simpler than fighting the clamor for wage increases or taking positive steps to increase the productivity of agriculture (especially when such steps alienate the landed aristocracy). Further, in an expanding economy it is quite possible that an inflationary solution to the supply dilemma might keep real wages about constant while increasing the share of capital in national income and stimulating overall growth.[3] We are back to the rationale of the central bankers and development authorities, and at this point expansionary monetary policy appears to be an easily accepted alternative.

Kaldor devotes the final section of his paper to remedies for Latin American inflations, but he is really dealing with strategies for overall

3. As Kaldor notes, this may be in the capitalists' interest.

economic growth. He rightfully calls for increasing domestic food production and rationalizing domestic industry through a sensible system of export promotion. In the latter context, he certainly has not left the dictates of comparative advantage behind. Again, most of us are faced with an overall position with which we cannot disagree. However, there are a number of policies that could be employed to achieve these ends, and those prescribed by Kaldor seem not entirely consistent with his explanations of the inflationary and industrial growth processes.

In an attempt to instill automaticity in the growth process, Kaldor comes out for a policy of leveling out the height of the tariff as between one industrial product and another in order to allow the law of comparative costs to operate within the industrial sector. This seems an odd prescription in light of his earlier argument that protection needs to be selectively applied. Can the law of comparative cost be depended upon to make automatically the best choices when rates of change in returns to scale and externalities vary from industry to industry? I seriously doubt it. Excessive protection *is* to be avoided and comparative advantage specialization *is* desirable. But a proactive policy of determining which infants to protect is probably better than one of "more or less" letting the market do it. I would suspect that the comparative successes of Mexico and Brazil in recent years have had much to do with such direct application of incentives and disincentives. This is not to say that eventual reliance on a more-or-less automatic internal market is not desirable, but such reliance may only be the best policy at relatively high levels of industrialization. Kaldor's system of dual exchange is subject to the same criticism as his uniform tariff system—it may rely too heavily on market forces when differential rates of scale economies, external economies, and interindustry linkage are present. Thus, although I would agree with the overall strategies of agricultural development, industrial rationalization, and export promotion, I would hope that the incentive system for industry would be less dependent upon current market forces which do not accurately reflect future prospects for many industries.

Comment—Larry A. Sjaastad

IT is at once a privilege and a responsibility to comment on the many varied, and sometimes contradictory, things contained in Kaldor's paper. As a long-term admirer of Kaldor, I approach this task with rather mixed feelings. Kaldor's contributions to economics are impressive; to my thinking, his *Expenditure Tax* stands out as an all-time classic. As a student of public finance I grew up with the *Expenditure Tax,* and I have been permanently influenced by it, just to mention one of his many distinguished contributions.

Our task, however, is not to review the history of Kaldor's economic thought, but rather to attempt to assess his most recent contribution. Turning to that, I had thought that by now structural inflation had become somewhat of a relic of the history of Latin American economic thought. That is, I had thought this until Kaldor's presentation. With considerable skill of clarity, however, Kaldor has reintroduced and rejuvenated and lent, some would say, intellectual respect to a theory best described as lacking rigor and frequently described as lacking content. I, for one, am not favorably impressed with this resurrection.

To begin with, Kaldor's treatment of the monetarist position is as misleading as it is cavalier. Most simply put, the monetarist position is that monetary policy is the immediate cause of inflation; this is obviously true when the increase in the price level, or the rate of change of the price level over time, is purely a monetary phenomenon. It is also true that inflation is caused by monetary policy even though the increases in prices do not originate in the monetary sector. This is the case of a passive monetary policy, one in which the change in the nominal money supply is merely to validate changes in prices which originate in the real sector. Changes in the price level that originate in the real sector cannot be sustained without being validated by monetary policy. The monetarist position does not claim to explain *why* the changes in the money supply occur; rather, it simply points to the theoretical and empirical evidence that inflations do not last long without concomitant rises in the money.

In refuting the monetarist position, Kaldor clearly errs in his appeal to the empirical evidence in pointing out that if the monetarist position were correct, then inflation should be accompanied by increases in private investment made possible by increases in the money supply being fed out in the form of additional credit to the private sector. In a closed economy, increases in investment would have to be matched by increases in saving; there is nothing about an inflation which necessarily causes saving to increase. Similarly, in an open economy there is nothing about an inflation which should in itself cause either saving or the savings gap to increase. Indeed, quite the contrary may well happen; it is usually the case that, as inflation begins, the stock of real bank credit dwindles, and it is frequently also the case that the private sector's share of that stock diminishes, both effects tending to cause private investment to shrink as well. Kaldor goes on to point out that he views budget deficits as more a symptom than a cause of inflation; he fails to recognize that it is not so much the size of budget deficit that is relevant, but rather the manner in which it is financed. It is true but trivial that, as Kaldor observes, the existence of a budget deficit does not necessarily indicate the presence of a demand inflation emanating in the public policy sector.

At this point I submit that much of the controversy between the monetarists and structuralists is somewhat redundant. I find it useful to look at inflation as a way in which a government systematically collects taxes. If we define H as the quantity of high-powered money in the economy and P as price level, then H/P is the amount of government non-interest-bearing debt measured in real terms. A policy of inflation is essentially a policy of systematically attempting to reduce the real value of H/P. The manner in which you do this is through inflation, and the rate at which you are reducing the real value of this non-interest-bearing debt is, of course, the rate of inflation times the amount of outstanding debt: $(\dot{P}/P)(H/P)$. This is a measure of the accrual of capital gains brought about by systematically inducing inflation. On the other hand, $\dot{H}/P$ is the rate of realization of capital gains. Now abstracting from growth and matters of that sort, it is going to be true (and clearly is true over fairly long periods of time) that the integral of tax collections tends to be about the same as the integral of tax accrual:

$$\int \dot{H}/P \, dt \cong \int (H/P) \, (\dot{P}/P) \, dt$$

Over short periods of time, of course, this is not true. If one looks at quarterly or semiannual data, or even annual data, he finds little support for the monetarist position. All I am saying, at this point, is that there is no reason why one *should* expect, over short periods of time, that tax collections equal tax accruals—or, put another way, that accruals of capital gains and realization of capital gains over short periods of time be equal. Over long periods of time, however, there just is no way of avoiding the conclusion that inflation is a monetary phenomenon.

Kaldor makes much of differences among the Latin American inflationary experiences, and I think quite correctly. These differences do exist. I would submit, however, that these differences, rather than reflecting the real factors which Kaldor has emphasized, reflect primarily institutional factors. They reflect the degree to which central banks are autonomous in some countries and captive in others. It is no accident that Central America has not experienced an inflation problem. The central banks of Central America are about the most autonomous institutions that exist. It is no accident that Panama has not had inflation; it has not had the ability to have inflation because it does not have a central bank. The Panamanian case is relevant because there is nothing in the structural inflation "theory" that requires the existence of a central bank.

In his discussion of the "terms-of-trade" explanation for inflation, Kaldor makes much of his observation that "no country experiences inflation for any length of time which did not restrict the importation of consumer goods." In this part of his paper, Kaldor seems to leave the impression that trade restrictions themselves may be responsible for inflation. But this can hardly be the case, since for every country that has had inflation and import restrictions, one can find a country that has had import restrictions but no significant inflation. I would cite the cases of Colombia, Mexico, and Panama as evidence in this connection.

Kaldor then goes on to develop his own particular version of structural inflation (which differs very little from existing versions) in which industrialization, or lack thereof, plays a key role. The story is essentially one in which import substitution was induced by a variety of forces—primarily collapsing export earnings—and, as a consequence of the movement of resources out of agriculture and into industry, the demand for food increased. This demand could not be met by importation and, more importantly, was not met by increased agricultural output. This, Kaldor claims, caused a persistent upward pressure in the prices of food paid by the urban consumer, and it was the rise in food prices that caused the persistent rise in urban wages and salaries, which in turn raised the general level of industrial costs and prices. In this connection, I have two comments. First, it would appear that at best this could explain a rising relative price of food and the products in which urban industrial labor represented a large part of total cost. It cannot, however, explain a rising absolute price of food. (I am reminded of David Meiselman's famous comment that structural inflation is a situation in which all relative prices are rising.) Kaldor's argument and that of other structural inflationists can explain only a structure of relative prices and not a rate of change-of-price level, which is one of the key defects of the structuralist position. This brings me to my second comment in this connection, which is the question of empirical evidence. I know of no evidence that countries with so-called structural inflations are also countries in which food prices are either high in relative terms or leading the inflation process. If such evidence exists, I am very surprised that no structural inflationist has brought it forward.

Kaldor concludes that inflation could have been escaped only if the output of the nonagricultural sectors had fallen sufficiently to eliminate the excess demand for food or if the workers in these industries had been willing to accept a cut in real income. He rejects devaluation as a way of increasing exports and hence possibilities for importation of food, and does so for a rather curious reason: for those countries whose main exports are items whose prices are determined by world markets, he argues that devaluation would be ineffective in increasing export proceeds. What he seems to be saying is that if a country is a price taker in the world market, then the fact that the demand for its exports is perfectly elastic implies that its supply of those exports is perfectly inelastic. This interpretation does not make a great deal of sense, but I can find no other that is consistent with the terms Kaldor employs.

Kaldor's conclusions that structural inflation can be avoided or remedied only by far-reaching land reform and industrial rationalization follow directly from his analysis. Consequently, the errors in that analysis, particularly with respect to the role of the price of food, cast doubt upon the validity of the conclusions. I think that no further comment on the food hypothesis is necessary at this point; but I do have some comments on his proposals for industrial rationalization. Kaldor's conception of industrial rationalization in the context of developing countries characterized by inflation seems to be that nontraditional export activity should be given approximately the same treatment as import substitution. That is, if import substitutes were to enjoy 50 percent protection, then sufficient subsidies should be given to nontraditional exports to permit marginal cost of that production to also exceed the world price by 50 percent. He does not say what sort of treatment he would give to importation of capital goods, raw materials, and intermediate goods. Neglecting those three items for the moment, it is easy to show that Kaldor's proposal is equivalent to taxation of traditional exports. Let us define the units of all traded goods such that their world price is unity; and let us assume that, in a situation where all imports are subject to a 50 percent duty and all exports to a 33 1/3 percent subsidy, the equilibrium rate would be 100. Elimination of the import duties and export subsidies together with a 50 percent devaluation would, as is well known, leave the situation unchanged if trade were initially balanced. Hence, the imposition of import duties and export subsidies at the suggested rates would have no effects, assuming that the exchange rate would find its appropriate level to maintain balanced trade. Kaldor's proposal differs, however, in that he would give export subsidies only to *nontraditional* exports. Consequently, the Kaldor proposal is equivalent to a situation in which imports are not taxed, nontraditional exports are not subsidized, but in which traditional exports are taxed. When viewed in this fashion, there is considerable similarity between the industrial rationalization proposal of Kaldor and the commercial policies of Perón. It is not clear, however, how Kaldor would treat imports of capital goods and inputs for the domestic industrial sector; nevertheless, it remains true that the key feature of Kaldor's proposal for industrial rationalization is the taxation of traditional exports, and I find it rather amusing to point out that this is the policy that has long since been followed by both Argentina and Chile—two of the countries for which the structural inflation theory was designed.

Julio Olivera once provided a fig leaf of respectability for the theory of structural inflation in the form of a set of internally consistent propositions.[1] I have no doubt that Kaldor has failed to improve upon the Olivera model. Also, I would like to refer to some insights by Mario

1. See *Oxford Economic Papers* 16 (November 1964): 321-32.

Simonsen at the 1963 Rio Conference on Inflation and Growth. His best comment in this connection was that the architects of structural inflation should be somewhat more modest in their ambitions; that is, with the set of propositions underpinning the structuralist position, it is very hard to explain inflations of more than 5 to 10 percent per year. But what we are talking about, and what Kaldor is talking about, is the Argentine experience, the Brazilian experience, the Chilean experience, in which inflations frequently have been 40 percent per year and occasionally as high as 100 percent per year. I find it inconceivable that the inflations of the ABC countries of Latin America can be explained satisfactorily without heavy reliance on monetary factors. Indeed, this proposition is currently so widely accepted that we now have had a great deal of empirical study of the Latin American inflationary process, and understand it much better than if we had begun with the position outlined by Kaldor in his contribution to this conference.

Discussion

D. HUDDLE: Kaldor's conclusions seem overly pessimistic to me. Numerous studies of import substitution [hereafter IS] in Latin America have shown the IS strategy is to have been "successful."[1] In Brazil and Mexico the payoff was high; IS industrialization was rapid and balanced, especially during the decade of the 1950s in Brazil. That rapid IS cannot continue ad infinitum is, of course, true; however, new strategies for development have been successful by the test of real GNP growth over the past few years in Brazil and Mexico.

Aside from successful IS, there are other encouraging alternatives. Carnoy's study of the comparative efficiency of a wide variety of industry plants at large scales of operation indicated that a Latin American common market with product specialization *could be* quite competitive with the United States in many lines of production.[2] Though I suspect that much of the competitiveness stems from U.S. technology and management inputs into many of these firms, the results nevertheless show that all inputs have to be provided from external sources to get efficient infants going. Complementary to Latin American specialization, export-led growth *has* occurred (contrary to much opinion) and much more can

1. Cf. D. Huddle, "Postwar Brazilian Industrialization: Growth Pattern, Inflation, and Sources of Stagnation," in E. Baklanoff, ed., *The Shaping of Modern Brazil* (Baton Rouge: Louisiana State University Press, 1969), pp. 86-109. A recent study demonstrates higher IS in Brazil by including indirect impacts via the 1959 input-output table for Brazil. See S. Morley and G. Smith, "On the Measurement of Import Substitution," *American Economic Review* (September 1970), pp. 728-36.

2. M. A. Carnoy, "Welfare Analysis of Latin American Economic Union: Six Industry Studies," *Journal of Political Economy* 78, no. 4, part 1 (July-August 1970).

occur in the future with "appropriate" policies.[3] That much of the rapid IS observed in Brazil was attributable to foreign firms should not, at the same time, rule out the wisdom of efforts toward IS industrialization.

Employment creation has been a major problem, but choice of technique is not necessarily fixed and biased toward capital-intensity. Factor-intensity is amenable to skillful manipulation without efficiency losses under a variety of realistic conditions.

For these and other reasons, continued progress in Latin America has not been as uncommon as models incorporating structuralism imply. Stagnation is there, but it is unusual, not usual. While Kaldor's model is both interesting and stimulating in its policy implications, as we have learned to expect from him, it does not incorporate the major factors which have been operating in recent years. Its explanatory and predictive power is, therefore, less than its power of stimulation.

A. CHURCHILL: Kaldor has proposed a theory, or hypothesis. One must ask: does it work and what is the evidence? I am not sure if it is Kaldor's lack of knowledge of Latin American experience that led him to pick a case which perhaps can most appropriately be fitted to Argentina and perhaps Chile, but the rest of Latin America has had a quite different experience. The only example of a structural inflation with some evidence for it turned out to be a case *not* of the kind of steady Latin American, or Argentinian-Chilean-Brazilian, type of inflation, but one which exploded. The example occurred in Indonesia, where in fact there was a very inelastic supply of food; the government paid its army and civil service in kind, and the only way it could get the food was to bid the price up and buy it from the countryside. The result was a 1600 percent per month rate of inflation. However, with appropriate monetary measures it came to an end in something less than a year.

The whole idea of structural inflation hinges on what one estimates is the elasticity of supply in the agricultural sector, and I would hold that the evidence is quite contrary to what Kaldor suggests. The evidence in Argentina, which is the prime Kaldor example, says that Argentine agriculture was extremely price-elastic. If the price response is *more* elastic in agriculture than in industry, then a policy, actively followed by the Argentine government and others, of deliberately holding down agriculture—by holding down agriculture I mean not just price controls, which usually did not work, but also via credit policy and import restrictions on inputs into agriculture—is extremely detrimental to the economy.

N. KALDOR: In order to raise agricultural prices one must lower

---

3. Although there have been no export booms in Latin American countries comparable to the pre–World War I era, export growth in value terms has not been absent. In addition, future prospects may be very good, as Y. M. Ho and D. Huddle demonstrate in a forthcoming discussion paper, "Income Elasticities and Future L.D.C. Exports," Program of Development Studies, Rice University.

industrial prices. That is the point. One cannot talk of prices in money terms. The exchange rate would remedy the situation *only* if it meant an improvement in relative prices for agriculture. It is the domestic terms of trade that are relevant.

A. CHURCHILL: Yes, but in an open economy that is not relevant.

N. KALDOR: In an open economy there is no inflation.

A. CHURCHILL: But the inflation results in a deliberate attempt *not* to make the economy open. So perhaps the best policy recommendation you come out with is to have an open economy.

N. KALDOR: If a country's earnings come from coffee and coffee prices collapse, it inevitably follows that it has to restrict imports. To say (or to imply) that the restriction of imports is a deliberate attempt not to make the economy open is a tautological use of words.

A. CHURCHILL: The growth rate experience in Latin America suggests that those economies which have grown fastest have been those that have deliberately remained reasonably open, with a few exceptions. In fact, I suspect for most of Latin America that if one correlated the rate of growth to the rate of industrial growth, the relationship would be negative.

H. HINRICHS: Kaldor actually advocates devaluation. Promoting exports and providing import protection is de facto devaluation, because devaluation is technically simply negative excises or subsidies on exports and taxes on imports. In the context of Latin America, one cannot say that devaluation does not change relative prices, since both the import and export content of consumption and production are affected by the fact that there are really segregated groups in Latin America which have different demand functions, preferences, incomes, all affected by devaluation.

I. NAVARRETE: I want to make two points, the first on Sjaastad's remarks: is he not overemphasizing the effect of the rate of interest? What role does the rate of interest play when the capital market is virtually nonexistent? Or when inflation turns the real rate of interest negative? These situations, common in Latin America, explain why the monetarist school has so little attraction for development policy.

The second comment is addressed to Kaldor's point about land reform. Land reform effects are more significant from a political than from an economic point of view. Its political importance arises because it tends to break the structure of power that hampers the adoption of policies conducive to development. In Mexico public investment created an irrigated, commercialized sector in agriculture that is very responsive to price changes. This fact allowed a substantial increase in food supply and exports, while a traditional type of agriculture—unresponsive to price increases and still employing the majority of the rural population —persisted, so that nowadays Mexico has a dual system of agriculture.

Closely related to this process was Mexico's experience with different stages of price stability. At the beginning of the development process, Mexico fitted very well into the scheme of what is called structural inflation; in a second stage, after a commercialized sector was developed, the elasticity of supply of food became more elastic and the price level relatively stabilized.

J. GRUNWALD: I thought we had put structural inflation to bed once and for all at the Rio de Janeiro Conference on Inflation and Growth in 1963, and I am surprised that today we should still discuss a rationale for it. We all know that if the only objective were to eliminate inflation, it can be done. There are monetary and fiscal tools and foreign trade policies which can be used to stabilize prices effectively. But, in the real world, inflation control is not the only objective. Other important objectives in Latin America are industrialization, full employment, and a better distribution of income.[4] Given such a preference pattern, there is very little one can do with monetary tools and traditional stabilization measures, because they would lead to unemployment, a dismantling of industrial protection apparatus, restraint of industrial expansion, lower real wages, etc. This kind of result Latin American governments cannot accept. And this has little to do, I would say to Sjaastad, with whether central banks are autonomous or not. Unless these basic development strategies can be modified, the structural nature of inflation is built into the economy automatically.

L. SJAASTAD: With respect to the point about the rate of interest, one of the great tragedies, it seems to me, of the Latin American inflations has been the fact that they have generally been suppressed. A number of years ago Martin Bailey studied the cost of inflation in terms of substitutions of real resources for money in effecting transactions. I believe, and this is an empirical judgment, that this cost is rather trivial. The more important costs of the Latin American inflations have arisen because the inflations have been suppressed. As a consequence, capital markets have been all but destroyed; they have not been permitted to work. In the foreign exchange market the same thing has frequently occurred. The costs of inflation in Latin America, or in those countries where inflation has been a problem, have been greatly magnified by these efforts to pretend that there is no inflation. I think that open inflation of maybe even 100 percent per year probably is not a terribly costly thing. But when a government insists that the rate of interest for time deposits cannot exceed 7 percent per year while the rate of inflation is 100 percent per year, it greatly raises the costs of inflation.

4. See Joseph Grunwald, "Invisible Hands in Inflation and Growth," in *Inflation and Growth* (Yale University Growth Center: Richard D. Irwin, 1964), and "The 'Structuralist' School on Price Stability and Development: The Chilean Case," *Latin American Issues, Essays and Comments,* Albert O. Hirschman, ed. (New York: The Twentieth Century Fund, 1961), pp. 95-124.

N. KALDOR: Sjaastad has made a lot of far-reaching assertions, but he produced no mechanism, no explanation. Inflation always occurs (according to him) because H/P, the money supply divided by the price level (which is the real value of cash balances), is somehow "expropriated" by the government. There is very poor evidence for the contention that inflation proceeds via a *reduction* of H/P. In Brazil, one of the most inflationary countries, it was high, remained high, and remained constant, despite their fantastic inflation.

With regard to the question of inflationary pressure caused by an insufficient urban food supply, there is nothing in this view that is in any way inconsistent with the proposition that there is a high (price) elasticity of supply for farm products *in real terms*. In other words, the fact that, under the existing terms of trade between agricultural and industrial goods, not enough food is produced and marketed to meet the urban demand does not rule out the possibility that food production *would have been* substantially higher (or increased faster) if the terms of trade had been more favorable. In agriculture, however, a rise in food prices in money terms would only serve to improve the terms of trade if the rise in food prices did not call forth an equivalent rise in money wages in industry. But if money wages are always adjusted so as to keep in step with the cost of living, real wages are not reduced and the agricultural terms of trade are not improved (as a result of the inflationary process, at any rate) beyond a certain range. Inflation is a *process* of rising prices, not just *high* prices. And to keep the process going, money incomes have to rise the whole time in order to keep up with, or to compensate for, the rising prices of consumer goods.

As a result, the "equilibrium" relationship between industrial wages and food prices can never be established, or if it is momentarily established, it cannot be maintained without both wages and prices rising. This is the essence of "structural inflation." I suppose monetarists like Sjaastad would argue that if the central banks were really autonomous they would prevent, by monetary measures, the rise in wages that occurs in response to rising food prices. This is what he appears to have been saying. In my view, this is precisely what cannot be done. Monetary measures cannot prevent the rise in wages: the most they could do is to reduce the volume of employment. Such "deflationary" policies can alleviate the inflation through a shrinkage of employment and output, but there are obviously severe limits to the extent to which any community would tolerate a reduction in employment as a means of dealing with inflation. Hence, there will be a combination of a demand-induced rise in food prices with a wage-induced (not demand-induced) rise in industrial prices. It is because the terms of trade do *not* change as a result of the demand-induced price changes that the process of inflation goes on; it would not go on if real wages could be cut or imports be allowed in more freely. The monetary economist's standpoint is again a very crude one: there is no need for import controls; why not let in imports freely and allow the rate of exchange to find its own level? The point is that if there is a huge gap between import requirements arising out of the existing structure of production and employment and the country's export capacity, this kind of policy is not feasible since in balancing imports and exports through free market forces the real wage bill would be reduced too much, which means that either employment or real wages per worker would be reduced (or both). This is not politically feasible, or rather, the attempt to do so would lead to more inflation and thereby would recreate or perpetuate the old price structure. We saw this happen on several occasions in various Latin American countries, in Chile and in Argentina, for example, where every act of devaluation led to new bouts of wage-induced cost inflation.

A lasting remedy requires structural measures, which imply that either industry is made more efficient (and this is a gradual process) or that there is an increase in food production for domestic use at the existing price relationships on account of distributional changes or a land reform of some kind. I entirely agree with Navarrete that in Mexico the remarkable increase in the food supply for urban areas was mainly the consequence of the increased commercialization of agriculture. But the commercialization of agriculture was a form of agricultural revolution; it was "land reform" of the kind which historically occurred in Britain two centuries earlier through the "enclosure" movement. This eighteenth-century type of land reform meant that the landlords expropriated the peasants, instead of the other way around. In Britain, the efficient landowners or farmers—people who were able to farm efficiently and on much larger farms than the peasant cultivators—replaced the previous small holders, at a high cost in social misery for the appropriated peasantry (who then formed the source of cheap manpower for the industrial revolution); but it also brought about a large increase in the marketable output of the land. In Mexico, the reform was largely the result of the expropriation of the estates of feudal landlords rather than those of small tenant-holders and was not (as far as I know) attended by an impoverishment of the peasantry.

The point about the growth of industry, and its association with the accumulation of capital and the growth of employment, is that the growth of both capital and labor is a consequence of industrial growth, rather than the cause of it. They are the consequence of a structure of demand —an increase in the effective demand for industrial products, which is brought about either through a rising agricultural surplus or a growing foreign demand (through exports) or both. It is only when production increases *in response to* a rise in demand that an economy gets, through an "accelerator effect," an increase in capital accumulation and the transfer of labor to industry, which results in a faster rate of growth.

Would a more suitable choice of techniques involving *less* capital-intensive methods of production in industry be a *cure* for structural inflation? I would say it would worsen it. The structural inflation arises because too much urban labor is employed in relation to the supply of wage goods (meaning food). With higher productivity of labor in industry, fewer people would be employed per unit of output; hence, it would be possible to improve the terms of trade in favor of agriculture and this would tend to restore the balance. A redistribution of income within the industrial sector cannot do this because the higher that wages are as a share of industrial output, the greater is the excess demand for wage goods; and it is the lack of wage goods which is the cause of the difficulty.

H. HINRICHS: You pointed out before that a growing demand for industrial products is needed; therefore, income distribution would be critical to industrialization.

N. KALDOR: This is a misunderstanding of the meaning of "growing demand" in this context. A bigger *demand* for industrial products, in the sense in which I use this notion, is the same thing as a bigger *supply* of nonindustrial goods (foodstuffs, raw materials, or convertible foreign exchange, which is an entitlement to both) offered in exchange. One cannot have a bigger "demand" for industrial products if the complementary element, a growing supply of primary products, is lacking. That is what leads to disproportionalities. Giving the wage earners employed in making, say, television sets, more money to spend does not increase the demand for television sets; it increases the demand for food. The workers of Latin America prefer to eat more before they spend money on television sets; unless they are paid in special money (which can only be spent on, say, bicycles or television sets), one cannot stop them from spending the wages earned in industry on food which is not produced by industry. If one could direct that wages paid for industrial labor should also be expended on the products of that labor, the situation would be very different.

3

The Theory of Tax Structure Development and the Design of Tax Structure Policy for Industrialization

Vito Tanzi

TRADITIONAL tax analysis, more than perhaps any other branch of economics, reflects its neoclassical heritage and idiosyncrasy. Its major preoccupation is generally with neutrality and equity, which were very valid objectives in a world in which equilibrium was the norm and growth was an almost natural consequence of economic activity. Since growth was not the overwhelming policy objective, there was little point in speculating about the relationships among, for example, average tax ratios, tax structures, and per capita income. Furthermore, lack of data would have prevented any such analysis.

The Keynesian attitude toward taxation is, of course, quite different from the neoclassical one, but it too has no particular interest in the structure of taxation except for the impact that it may have on consumption. Its major preoccupation is with full employment and stability, and for these, what counts most is the net contribution of the public sector to aggregate demand.

With the intense preoccupation with economic growth that has characterized the last two decades, with the much greater availability of statistical information than ever before, and with the generally different attitude toward the role that the governments are supposed to play in the economic development of their countries, a new and growing interest has developed toward comparative tax analysis. This is a new area with very little relationship to the traditional tax analysis, which for so long has dominated the field of public finance and which at one time prompted Paul Samuelson to take Pigou to task for devoting to it no less than 200 of the 285 pages of his *A Study in Public Finance*.[1]

It is easy to imagine the chain of causation that has led to this departure from tradition. First, as already stressed, there has been this obsession with growth which has called for the addition of a Growth, or

1. Paul A. Samuelson, "Aspects of Public Expenditure Theories," *Review of Economics and Statistics* 40, no. 4 (November 1958): 332.

Development, branch to Musgrave's trilogy of Allocation, Distribution, and Stabilization.[2] The main function of this new branch is obviously the reallocation of resources away from low-priority toward high-priority uses. This, of course, includes also a reallocation of resources away from consumption toward saving and investment. One needs to add a Growth branch because the type of allocation which concerns the Allocation branch is the traditional one of provision of public goods.

Second, the formal recognition that the government must play the leading role in the development of the economy has led to the taking of inventory of the various instruments available to the governments of mixed economies. This action has shown that, in the ranking of those instruments in order of efficiency, taxation may very well be "the most efficient and rational method of systematically diverting resources to preferred uses . . . including the promotion of industrialization."[3]

Finally, and perhaps most importantly, the tax instruments themselves have been analyzed to find the various ways in which they can be used for this programmed departure from neutrality. This analysis inevitably heightens the interest in the tax structure of other countries—how that structure relates to the level of economic development, how it relates to the structure of the economy, to the total tax ratio, etc. Also, new tax schemes have been proposed with increasing frequency and with varying degrees of originality and feasibility. The objective of this intellectual activity has been the same; to discover the kind of desirable nonneutrality in the tax structure which will accelerate economic development.

Perhaps it is not completely accurate to say that the ultimate goal of modern tax structure analysis is the acceleration of economic development. It is possible that, even if growth had not been such an important objective, the increasing availability of statistical information would have led, in any case, to the development of this branch of public finance. After all, some researchers might have been concerned with these relationships for historical curiosity. I believe, however, that without the utilitarian motive mentioned above, much less work would have gone into this area. Proof of this is that much of that work was either carried out within, or at least financed by, international organizations concerned mostly with economic development.

This paper will consist of three distinct parts: the first will discuss in more or less general terms some aspects of taxation in relation to economic development and industrialization; the second will survey and discuss as briefly as possible some of the major conclusions reached by vari-

2. Richard A. Musgrave, *The Theory of Public Finance* (New York: McGraw-Hill, 1959), chap. 1.

3. Jan Little, Tibor Scitovsky, and Maurice Scott, *Industry and Trade in Some Developing Countries* (London: Oxford University Press, 1970), p. 333.

ous studies of tax structure comparison; the third will present two proposals aimed at making the tax system nonneutral in a desirable sense.

Before moving to the next section, I want to make explicit some of the underlying assumptions on which especially the proposals made in the third section are based. First, the analysis will accept the concept that the developing countries in general and Latin America in particular will have to industrialize as they go along the road of development. Of course, this does not mean that, as has happened in Latin America and elsewhere with the import-substitution industrialization policy, the other sectors should be ignored.

A second assumption, which may be less acceptable, is based on my reading of economic history; it states that the corporate form of business organization is by far the most efficient, especially for what concerns industrial development. It may also be very efficient for agriculture if we attribute to it the success of many commercial enterprises in the Latin American agricultural sector.

Thirdly, I will assume that, in the long run, the level of investment is less important than its quality. Finally, I will assume that in the absence of a perfect capital market, *where* savings occur determines, to a large extent, the types of investment that will be carried out. For example, in most countries, on the average, investment in housing is very close in magnitude to household saving; thus measures that try to increase household saving, to the extent that they are successful, will generally lead to additional investment in housing.

INDUSTRIALIZATION, TAXATION, AND THE ROLE OF GOVERNMENT

It is difficult to talk about tax structure without dealing first with some aspects of the role of government in capital formation and growth and their relationship to tax levels. The main objective of this section is to raise questions concerning the level and the structure of taxation, which I think should be analyzed within the context of the present literature on tax structures and tax burdens.

Public Investment and Income Distribution

Almost everyone seems to agree that the overwhelming objective of tax and expenditure policy in the Latin American countries must be the acceleration of economic development. The tax system must transfer resources from the private to the public sector so that the public sector will have the capability to carry out those functions which are basic to the role of the government—defense, police, administration, justice, etc.—as well as those functions which are related to the development of the countries. The tax system must also induce a transfer of resources within the private sector away from low-priority toward high-priority uses.

Among the growth-related expenditures, the creation of infrastructures—both economic and social—has received most of the attention. Taxes put resources in the hands of the governments and these resources can be used for carrying out certain investment programs which are supposed to be productive to the economy, especially in the long run. These programs normally involve the building of roads, railroads, dams, power plants, etc. Lately, it has also become fashionable to include some expenditures for education and health among the types which directly contribute to the growth of the economy.

An increase in tax burden is often defended along the lines indicated in the previous paragraph. In other words, the higher the average tax ratios are, the more resources the governments will have for the building of infrastructures; this assumes, of course, that, contrary to what Stanley Please has argued, political pressures do not bring about a "waste" of the extra resources on unproductive current expenditures.[4]

In economies where human capital is at a relatively low level and where the returns to real property are consequently very high, the distribution of income will normally be very skewed. Wealth will often be concentrated in a few hands which will receive a very high share of total income. Also, the proportion of total wealth accounted for by land will be very high.[5] The Latin American countries, of course, fit this description to varying degrees.

In such a setting, a good share of the expenditure for public investment (for roads, power, irrigation, harbors, etc.) may very well lead to an increase in the returns to private property by making the existing tangible wealth more productive. This will be particularly true if substantial unemployment or underemployment keeps wages (especially agricultural wages) at low levels. If, furthermore, public investment is financed largely through regressive taxation or through inflation, the negative impact on income distribution caused by public investment might be even greater. In other words, in the short run the higher the level of public investment is, the worse the distribution of income will be, especially in the agricultural sector.[6]

Thus, here we have one example of a general shortcoming in the recent discussion of tax structure. By and large the relationship between the structure of taxation and the structure of public expenditure has been ignored although, as I will argue later, some evidence exists that such a relationship may exist at least in the developed countries. Furthermore, if, as it is often argued, industrialization is aided by a better distribution of income which enlarges the size of the market for mass-produced, man-

4. Stanley Please, "Saving Through Taxation—Reality or Mirage?" *Finance and Development* 4 (November 1967).

5. In the United States, land accounts for only about 5 percent of total wealth.

6. It would be easy enough to make the above point using A. Lewis's model of economic development with unlimited supply of labor.

ufactured products, the change in income distribution will not help in this direction.

In passing, I would like to call attention to a proposal made in the report of the Musgrave mission to Colombia which is related to the above point and which I find very intriguing. The proposal was to increase the use of property taxes and to link the revenues obtained from this source to additional expenditures for elementary education. If my analysis is correct, this proposal can be justified along the lines of benefit-received taxation for what concerns the tax, while the earmarking can be considered as a corrective measure for the worsening of the income distribution caused by public investment.

It would be interesting to find out to what extent the distribution of income in Latin America has, in fact, been worsened by the increase in public investment which has generally accompanied the increase in the average tax ratios for most of the countries of the continent. Much work and many unavailable data would be needed to ascertain the significance of this factor.

In conclusion, the above discussion indicates that it is really not very useful to discuss what constitutes an optimal tax structure unless the use of tax revenues is also considered. As an example, an increase in taxation which was to be used to finance the building of infrastructure should probably involve increasing taxes on land and on other property.

Budget Surplus and Entrepreneurial Ability

In the previous paragraphs, the emphasis has been on the contribution that the government makes to capital formation through the building of infrastructures. Obviously, however, the productivity of these public investments is closely related to the *level* and the *quality* of the investment in the private sector. In fact, one can really think of public investment of the type outlined above as a kind of input for private investment. The *direct* contribution of public investment to potential output is generally very low; its effect on the productivity of private investment is what makes public investment desirable. It follows that the government has the responsibility not only of creating the infrastructure but also to see that the level and the quality of the forthcoming *private* investment are as good as possible.

Entrepreneurial ability is the capacity to foresee investment opportunities, to put together the team that will produce the product at a low cost, and to organize all those other functions connected with the production, distribution, and marketing processes. This is an extremely important and scarce quality, especially in developing countries, and it should therefore be fully utilized and not wasted. The degree to which the available entrepreneurial ability is utilized determines to a large extent the quality of the investment and, in some cases, may even determine the quantity. It follows that the government has the responsibility to see that it be utilized to the fullest degree.

An interesting aspect of this ability is that it is not very strongly concentrated in any particular income or social group of the population, although it may be concentrated in certain ethnic groups. There is, in fact, no particularly strong reason to assume that those with high incomes also possess a monopoly of those qualities that Schumpeter associated with the successful investor, especially when those incomes are generated by inherited wealth. Thus it is likely that those who have financial resources often do not know what to do with them except perhaps spend them or invest in land and residential construction or take them out of the country. On the other hand, many people who because of their mental qualities and general aptitudes could be successful entrepreneurs have often neither personal wealth nor access to resources through the capital market.

If a well-working capital market does not exist to take care of this problem, it should be the responsibility of the government to try to develop one. This, however, is only a long-range enterprise. In the short run the government will have the option of providing a kind of proxy for the capital market.

If the previous discussion is correct, it would argue for a planned budgetary surplus in excess of what the government needs to spend itself. In other words, the government should aim its tax burden at a level that would leave a surplus which could be made available to the private sector. Of course, the greater the potential entrepreneurial ability, the greater the surplus (and therefore the higher the average tax ratio) that the government should aim at. There is, therefore, a relationship between tax levels and absorptive capacity of the economy.

Several surveys carried out in some Latin American countries have shown that the inability on the part of many enterprises and many individuals to obtain credit is a very considerable obstacle to development. Probably a good case could be made that credit incentives are more important than tax incentives, especially for the creation of new enterprises. Tax incentives by increasing the liquidity of the already established enterprises may facilitate their development, but normally will not help very much the potential enterprises or the individuals who do not have funds for the fixed, initial investment. Credit incentives on the other hand will be able to do this.

Approach to the Determination of Optimal Tax Burdens

In the previous two sections several references have been made to the need for increasing the resources available to the governments in order to allow them to carry out those functions needed by a growth-oriented policy. Does this mean that one of the requirements of such a policy is always the increase in the average tax ratios? And if we emphasize, as I have done above, the efficient use of resources as a determinant of the optimum tax burden, is there any direct relationship between that level and the tax structure of a country?

When the emphasis is on the efficient resource use and not on the "ability to collect," then one could follow a kind of capacity approach to the question.[7] In other words, can the capacity of the economy to produce be increased by an increase in the tax level? Assuming that investment is defined comprehensively to include those public expenditures for education, health, etc., which also add to the productive capacity of the economy, and assuming that part of the public saving is used to finance private investment so as to bring about the equality of the marginal productivity of investment in the public and private sectors, then total tax revenues should be increased if the marginal propensity to save is higher in the public sector than in the private sector.

One problem with this conclusion which is of particular relevance to Latin America is the balance-of-payments bottleneck. In fact, if taxes are increased and capital formation increases accordingly, under present circumstances much of the additional capital will be imported. Since in the short run the export variable is assumed to be exogenous, the balance of payments of the country will worsen. Therefore, given the present tax structure, and thus the structure of private consumption, investment, and relative prices, the balance of payment of the country may impose a limit to the desirable tax burden, especially in those cases in which the government is supposed to be doing the right thing with the extra money, i.e., investing it.

Under these circumstances a change in the tax structure that reduced the need for foreign exchange, or at least increased the availability of foreign exchange, would make possible a higher tax burden, which in turn would make possible a higher level of investment. Conversely, a higher level of investment would require a different tax structure. Thus, here we find once more a relationship among the structure of taxation, the tax level, and the structure of expenditure.

Requirements for a Flexible Fiscal Policy

As the Latin American countries develop and their economies become more dependent on the manufacturing sector, they will start experiencing fluctuations in national income originating not in the foreign sector but in investment. When this happens—and countries like Brazil, Argentina,

7. Richard A. Musgrave, *Fiscal Systems* (New Haven: Yale University Press, 1969), pp. 159-62.

and Mexico may very well be reaching that stage—some of the traditional objections to the use of Keynesian fiscal policy in developing countries will no longer be valid.[8] The question then arises as to whether their tax systems will be ready for the new fiscal policy role. What characteristics should the tax systems exhibit to make fiscal policy for stabilization a possibility?

First, it is evident that the impact of the tax system on the economy will be greater, the higher the average tax ratio. If this ratio is low, a given percentage increase or decrease in total taxes will not affect the economy in the same way as when that ratio is high.

Second, even a high tax ratio may not be sufficient if the public sector is highly decentralized. In other words, from the point of view of stabilization policy a highly centralized public sector would be desirable.

Third, there must also be a substantial concentration of tax revenues in a few taxes. Fiscal policy has normally been most effective in those countries where a few taxes provide most of the tax revenues. In most of the industrialized countries, one finds that a couple of taxes provide more than half of the total government revenues. In many of the Latin American countries, on the other hand, there is a tremendous number of taxes in existence. This proliferation of taxes not only complicates their administration, confuses the taxpayers, and facilitates or even invites tax evasion; it also renders very difficult the use of an active fiscal policy. The reason for this is that if the government wants to raise more revenues for stabilization purposes, it needs to change the nominal structure of many taxes. In other words, it needs to study each of the many taxes, decide on the changes desired, and then go to the congress, where ideally each tax would be discussed and voted upon. If the time available is very limited, this introduces rather obvious complications and difficulties.

Thus, in our analysis of tax structure change we should start paying attention to this aspect. Perhaps we could develop some coefficient of concentration—say, the ratio of total tax revenues (or of national income) accounted for by the three or four most important taxes. It would then be interesting to analyze the factors which determine this ratio, how it changes with the change in the total tax level, how it is related to per capita income, etc.

Fourth, the tax structure should also be analyzed with respect to the degree of synchronization between legal imposition and actual collection. Again, is there an average lag which can be determined? What factors influence that lag? How is it related to the tax structure? How is it related to the tax level? Of course, from the point of view of fiscal policy, the longer the lag, the more difficult is the application of fiscal policy for stabilization. A long lag may even make fiscal policy disstabilizing.

8. V.K.R.V. Rao, "Investment, Income and the Multiplier in an Underdeveloped Economy," *Indian Economic Review* (February 1952).

Fifth, there is the problem of tax evasion, which may also contribute to the ineffectiveness of fiscal policy for stabilization. An effective fiscal policy requires that the authorities be able to, first, estimate what change in revenue would be required to correct the disequilibrium, and, then, be able to estimate what changes in the legal or nominal structure of the tax system will bring about the desired increase or decrease in revenues. To do this, the tax authorities need much statistical information that they often may not have, but they also need to assume that evasion either is nonexistent or will continue at a constant rate. Unless this can be assumed, there will not be any possibility of relating a given change in nominal rates to a given increase or decrease in revenues. Since the government can only directly manipulate the legal structure of the taxes, if it cannot assume a direct relationship between that structure and the size of tax revenues, it will not be able to pursue a successful fiscal policy. It has often happened in some Latin American countries that the government would push through some tax reform in the hope of raising a given amount of additional revenue and would find that its projections were in substantial error.

Even when there is little evasion, or the degree of evasion can be assumed to be constant, fiscal policy can be made ineffective if, for a variety of reasons, people declare their tax liabilities but abstain from paying them. This problem, which is common to many Latin American countries, became most serious in Argentina in the first half of the 1960s, when more than 50 percent of the total taxes declared were not paid due to great scarcity of credit availability and the low fines for postponing payments.

Finally, the degree of built-in flexibility of the tax systems will be important in the context of countercyclical fiscal policy. To the extent that the Latin American tax systems do not exhibit this characteristic, the burden placed on discretionary policy will of course be all the greater.

THEORY OF TAX STRUCTURE DEVELOPMENT

Is there a relationship between the structure of taxation and the level of economic development of the countries? Can the nature of this relationship be specified? These are the questions to which a growing number of scholars have addressed themselves in recent years. The questions are somewhat similar to those raised by Chenery in his well-known article on industrial structure.[9] Through the application of statistical techniques to cross-section data on the industrial composition of the GNPs of many countries, Chenery derived the kind of average, or "normal," structure

9. Hollis B. Chenery, "Patterns of Industrial Growth," *American Economic Review* 50 (September 1960).

that he thought one would expect in a given country at a given stage of economic development. Thus, an industrial composition too far out of line from the average would require some particular explanation.

It would be nice if we could derive a normal structure for tax revenue in a way similar to Chenery's. The truth of the matter is that we are still far from it. What we have so far is a theory which, though interesting, is just a bit too general to be useful and a whole series of statistical results, many contradictory, which in most cases "explain" statistically how a particular tax (or more often a group of taxes) changes in a cross-section sample when one changes per capita income or openness or some other economic variable.

Hinrichs's General Theory

Hinrichs[10] claims that his empirical analysis reveals an "ideal type" of tax structure change during the process of development. In fairness to him, he does emphasize that by "ideal" he does not necessarily mean "desirable," and that "no country may necessarily follow the exact pattern depicted. . . ."[11] I shall attempt to summarize some of the main conclusions of Hinrichs's interesting work.

He points out that traditional societies derive their tax revenue from what he calls "traditional direct" taxes which would include taxes on land and agricultural output, on livestock, heads, water rights, etc. These sources lose ground when societies begin to modernize and are in part replaced by indirect taxes in general and foreign trade taxes in particular. In this context he stresses the importance of openness both in the level of the average tax ratio and in its composition. His empirical analysis leads him to conclude that the more open the economy, the higher the average tax ratio and the larger the share of revenue from the foreign trade sector.

As development advances and—either naturally or with an assist from a conscious policy of import substitution—a sizable local manufacturing sector comes into existence, the foreign trade taxes begin to decline in importance while internal indirect taxes become more significant. Eventually, modern direct taxes, which all along the way have been replacing the traditional ones, will become important enough to make the ratio of direct to indirect taxes rise. Therefore, over the whole period of development, the ratio of direct to indirect taxes will follow a U-shaped curve, being high at first, then falling to a low level, and rising again with the traditional direct taxes being replaced by the modern ones.

10. Harley H. Hinrichs, *A General Theory of Tax Structure Change During Economic Development* (Cambridge: Harvard Law School, 1966).
11. Ibid., pp. 97-98.

Musgrave's Theory

Musgrave[12] emphasizes that economic in addition to social and political factors will affect the development of tax structure. The economic factors will influence tax structure through the creation of what he calls "tax handles" as well as through the changes in the economic objectives of tax policy. The tax structure which is best when the most important economic objective is growth will no longer be good when the objective has changed to, say, income redistribution or stability.

Musgrave pays little attention to traditional societies in Hinrichs's sense. Instead, he distinguishes an early period from a later one. His general discussion seems to be more normative than Hinrichs's: he seems to be as much concerned with which taxes can or, perhaps, should be used as with those that have been used. For the early period he stresses: that land taxes are very important; that consumption taxes have to be mostly excises and should be limited to certain major products produced in large establishments; that public enterprises should follow pricing policies aimed at generating revenue; that personal income taxes have to be limited to highly schedular ones and will probably be limited to civil servants and employees of large firms; and finally, that the foreign trade sector is one of the important handles.

For the later period he foresees a broadening of the scope of indirect taxation in view of the increase in the average size of the production and sales establishments. This development will also make possible the effective taxation of business income as well as the taxation of personal income. In general more tax bases become available, so that finally the tax structure comes to depend more on social or political decisions than on economic factors. In Musgrave's words, it becomes a "free policy choice."

Criticism of Cross-Section Studies

Both Hinrichs and Musgrave make extensive use of data; however, in spite of occasional forays into history—mostly, Japan for Hinrichs and the United States, United Kingdom, and Germany for Musgrave—their conclusions, as well as those of practically all the investigators in this area, are firmly based on cross-section evidence. Then the obvious question, which, incidentally, is the same one raised by Kuznets[13] with respect to Chenery's work on industrial structure, is whether we can use these results, obtained for a specific point in time, to project future trends or even to

12. Musgrave, *Fiscal Systems,* chaps. 5, 6.
13. See Simon Kuznets, *Modern Economic Growth* (New Haven: Yale University Press, 1966), p. 433.

infer past trends in tax structure associated with development. We have several problems.

First, there are the purely statistical problems.[14] For example, is the sample large and representative enough? Are the data accurate enough not to generate the common econometric problems associated with errors in the variables? Have purely short-run factors been eliminated? Has the nature of the relationship been accurately specified so that linear functions are not applied when the true relationship is nonlinear?

With respect to the first of these questions, I want to mention that, often enough, the choice of the sample, which is largely determined by the availability of data to the particular researcher, leads different scholars to different conclusions. With respect to the second question we have, first, the basic problem of making different income levels comparable and, second, the problem created by the existence of different levels of government which always makes one dubious about the comprehensiveness of the tax data. As to the third question, it is doubtful that it has been possible for the various scholars to correct their data for cyclical factors which may distort the tax structure in particular years; at best the data have been averaged for two or three years in the hope that this would smooth out cyclically generated distortions. The last question requires no comment except to point out that, generally, either linear relationships or those implying constant elasticities have been assumed.

Second, there is the problem of technological innovation in the tax field. Just as it is true for production functions, the usefulness of the results obtained from cross-section analysis is limited by the implicit assumption of a given technological knowledge. But economic development is associated not only with the discovery of new tax bases, or handles, but also with the theoretical discovery of new tax forms. To take the most obvious example, how many people had heard of a value-added tax twenty years ago? If, as seems likely at this time, the use of this tax spreads to the developing countries,[15] should we attribute its adoption to the emergence of new tax bases or simply to the discovery of a new tax? Suppose that Kaldor's expenditure tax[16] had been seriously imposed and administered in India and Ceylon; would we have attributed the change in these countries' tax structures to the technical innovation or to the change in the bases?

14. Some of the points raised here with respect to tax structure are very similar to those raised by Kuznets with respect to industrial structure. Ibid., pp. 431-37.

15. In Latin America the tax has already been introduced in Brazil (1965) and Uruguay (1968) and has been proposed for Mexico, Chile, and Argentina. Venezuela and Ecuador are also considering it.

16. Nicholas Kaldor, *An Expenditure Tax* (London: Unwin University Books, 1955). See also the two selections by Kaldor in Richard M. Bird and Oliver Oldman, eds., *Readings on Taxation in Developing Countries* (Baltimore: Johns Hopkins University Press, 1967).

There is no reason to assume that we have already thought of all the possible taxes which could exist; new taxes will probably be "discovered," introduced into the literature, and adopted. The results obtained from cross-section analysis ignore this aspect. Japan in 1870 not only did not have available the tax handles, or tax bases, of Japan in 1970, but also did not have recourse to the various theoretical tax forms available to that country today or to a present-day developing country at the same stage of economic development as Japan in 1870. We must recognize that as time passes, the tax menu will acquire new entries so that the governments' degrees of freedom will increase.

Third, there is the problem of change in what could be called "consumer tastes" and the related one of demonstration effect. Both Musgrave and Hinrichs recognize that "tastes" may change. In his discussion of historical development in tax structure, Musgrave, for example, attributes the increasing importance of the taxes on income not only to the change in the structure of the economy which makes more feasible the imposition of these taxes, but also to the spreading of "social and political trends toward redistribution that have characterized the last half century or more."[17] As to the demonstration effect, suppose that France had never adopted the value-added tax and that the European Common Market had never come into existence; would the developing countries be seriously considering this tax? Of course, results based on cross-section data ignore these historical developments.

Tax Structure and Structure of Public Expenditure

The remarks made in the previous several paragraphs concern specifically the use of cross-section data in deriving a general theory of tax structure change. There is, however, another aspect of all the studies on tax structure which I consider unsatisfactory and which, I think, deserves much more attention. This is the relationship, if any, between the structure of taxation and the structure of public expenditure. Is it reasonable to assume that there is no relationship between these two? And if such a relationship does in fact exist, what characteristics will it show?

These questions have not been raised in the literature on tax structure. As far as I know, almost no research has gone into this aspect of tax structure determination. Yet if, for example, instead of basing the conclusions of his historical view on the statistical evidence provided by the United States, the United Kingdom, and Germany, Musgrave had included Italy and France, he probably would have been surprised at the different development of their tax structures. He might then have been led to the possibility that their tax structures changed in a different way

17. Musgrave, *Fiscal Systems*, p. 141; see also p. 143.

because the composition of their expenditures changed differently; or perhaps it was the other way around.

The only piece of evidence I know on this aspect is perhaps too simple to tell us much.[18] For what it is worth, that study pointed in the direction of a relationship, among twelve developed countries, between tax structures and share of total expenditures accounted for by transfers to households. More specifically it was found that the countries for which the share of transfers to families in total expenditures was low, were the ones which most likely relied more on direct taxes. In other words, the direct/indirect breakdown in the tax structures could, to a large extent, be explained statistically by the composition of public expenditure.

When income redistribution becomes an important policy objective, it is obvious that it can be pursued either on the expenditure side or on the revenue side. It seems, then, reasonable to assume that what happens on the revenue side will be related to what happens on the expenditure side. Under these circumstances a theory which tries to explain the change in the tax structure without considering the changes in the expenditure side will not be very satisfactory.

Statistical Evidence on Specific Taxes

My discussion of the theory of tax structure development has been based exclusively on Musgrave's and Hinrichs's work. This is because they are the only two authors who, in my judgment, have provided us with what could be called a genuine theory of tax structure change. Many other authors have, however, supplied statistical support on specific hypotheses.[19] I could not possibly survey all of these studies; I shall, therefore, refer briefly to some of their results.

A common hypothesis states that, during the process of economic development, the ratio of direct to indirect taxes will increase. This hypothesis is supported by the work of Musgrave, S. Lewis, Williamson,

18. Vito Tanzi, "Governments' Approaches to Income Redistribution: An International Comparison," *National Tax Journal* 21, no. 4 (December 1968).

19. Among these, one should see the following: A. Martin and W. A. Lewis, "Patterns of Public Revenue and Expenditure," *Manchester School of Economic and Social Studies* 24 (September 1956); Jeffrey G. Williamson, "Public Expenditure and Revenue: An International Comparison," *Manchester School of Economic and Social Studies* 29 (January 1961); Stephen R. Lewis, Jr., "Government Revenue from Foreign Trade: An International Comparison," *Manchester School of Economic and Social Studies* 31 (January 1963); Jorgen R. Lotz and Elliott R. Morss, "The Tax Structure of Developing Countries, An Empirical Study," IMF Departmental Memorandum (January 21, 1969); John F. Due, *Indirect Taxation in Developing Economies* (Baltimore: The Johns Hopkins University Press, 1970); Douglas Dosser, "Indirect Taxation and Economic Development," and K. S. Krishnaswamy, "The Evolution of Tax Structure in a Development Policy," both in Alan T. Peacock and Gerard Hauser, eds., *Government Finance and Economic Development* (Paris: Organization for Economic Cooperation and Development, 1965).

Krishnaswamy, and Due.[20] This support, however, seems to be dependent on the pooling together of the data for developing and developed countries. Those authors who separate the two groups find very little evidence for the hypothesis within each group. Musgrave finds that, replacing per capita income with the share of agriculture in GNP, the relation is improved and becomes negative; Lotz and Morss, on the other hand, show that monetization, rather than per capita income, is the most important variable.

A second hypothesis, which is probably the best-supported one, states that, as countries develop, the importance of the taxes on foreign trade will decline while that of the internal indirect taxes will rise.

Levin[21] and Lewis[22] have provided strong historical backing to this hypothesis with their interesting work on Colombia and Pakistan. For cross-section studies, the fall in foreign trade taxes is demonstrated by Hinrichs, Musgrave, S. Lewis, and Due. Musgrave and Due indicate that if the countries are separated into two groups—one including the developing countries and the other the developed ones—the relationship between these two variables becomes very weak. The analysis by Lotz and Morss shows little relationship between foreign trade taxes and per capita income. Their work, as well as that of S. Lewis and Hinrichs, emphasizes openness as the major determinant of the ratio of foreign trade taxes to total taxes.

Musgrave and Williamson both find that direct taxes on households, including social security contributions, are positively related to per capita income, as would be expected from the theory of tax structure change. The disaggregation of these taxes, however, brings conflicting results. Personal income taxes are barely related to per capita income (Musgrave, Lotz, and Morss). For the corporation income taxes, Williamson finds a positive, but weak, relationship to per capita income, while Musgrave finds none for the whole sample but a significant, positive one if only the high-income countries are considered. Interestingly enough, Lotz and Morss find openness to be the most significant determinant of the share of corporate income taxes. They also find that per capita income and monetization are the most significant, positive determinants of social security taxes.

Theory of Tax Structure Development: Concluding Remarks

My brief overview of the recent work on tax structure development indicates clearly that up to now the marriage between the two general theo-

20. The hypothesis is rejected by Dosser.
21. Jonathan Levin, "The Effects of Economic Development on the Base of a Sales Tax: A Case Study of Colombia," *IMF Staff Papers* 15 (March 1968).
22. Stephen R. Lewis, Jr., "Revenue Implications of Changing Industrial Structure," *National Tax Journal* 20 (December 1967).

ries outlined above and the statistical analysis carried on thus far to verify those theories has not taken place yet. The truth of the matter is that we still do not have an answer to the question of what kind of tax structure a country should have at a given stage of economic development. So far the most ambitious and successful of the statistical studies in this area—and the one which comes closest to answering that question —is Lotz and Morss'.

But even that study really gives us no theory—only some equations which in most cases "explain" statistically only a small fraction of the total variation. It is inevitable that one should ask why those relationships —calculated for many countries with different backgrounds—should be relevant to the policies of any particular country. If we believe, as we all seem to do, that the tax structures of most developing countries are far from what they should be and that they should be changed, why should we use as our reference point the average of all those distortions? A statistical average of thirty or fifty distorted tax structures cannot give us the norm against which a country should evaluate its own tax structure. And if those statistical relations do not do that, then what do they do?

Finally, quite apart from the points raised in the last two paragraphs, the literature on tax structure will not be very important for policy use as long as the dependent variables are such broad categories as direct taxes, personal taxes, foreign trade taxes, and so on. The really important questions are more concerned with the structure of particular taxes than the structure of the tax system. What is really important is to find out how, for example, the structure of the personal income taxes changes as the countries develop. What happens to the relative size of the exemptions, the deductions, etc.? What happens to the ratio of taxpayers to labor force? To the treatment of specific incomes? What happens to the structure of the taxable income, to the ratio of taxable income to adjusted gross income, and to the ratio of each of these to national income?

These and similar questions ought to be raised not only for the personal income taxes but for all the other taxes. So far there is almost no literature on the comparison of the structure of specific taxes or on the development of the structural characteristics of a particular tax.[23] Perhaps this is explainable by the tremendous amount of data necessary to carry out such studies, and by the difficulties in getting them. But as data become more available, this is a territory that we have to explore if we want to give relevance to the work on tax structure change.

23. For two examples see: Vito Tanzi, *Individual Income Tax and Economic Growth: An International Comparison* (Baltimore: The Johns Hopkins University Press, 1969), and Levin, "Case Study of Colombia." See also Due, *Indirect Taxation.*

TAX STRUCTURE POLICY FOR INDUSTRIALIZATION

I am somewhat reluctant to turn to tax proposals for Latin America—mainly because there are enough proposals around and a good argument could be made that, in the particular case of Latin America, the problem is not one of a limited menu but one of unwillingness to pay the price for some of the items on that menu.

In making these proposals I am aware that no tax structure is universally valid; if I ignored that truth, I would be ignoring the lessons which we should have been taught by the literature on tax structure development. Consequently, no tax structure or for that matter no tax proposal can find equal applicability or equal relevance in the whole Latin American continent, which includes countries with per capita income as low as $80 and as high as $800. However, if we exclude the few really backward countries, most of the others have now achieved a level of economic development which makes possible the introduction of rather sophisticated tax schemes. Of course, this is true as long as the governments are willing to introduce them and make them work.

For most of the Latin American countries I think that, quoting Musgrave a bit out of context, ". . . the incantation of 'administrative difficulties' . . . is more often a pretext to avoiding comprehensive taxation than a justified cause for rejecting tax reform."[24] If anyone doubts that this is true, let him analyze the Brazilian experience of the last five years. Brazil has demonstrated that, given the political will, almost any increase in the tax burden and any change in the tax structure can be brought about even in a country with a per capita income of $350 and a remarkably unopen economy. The Brazilian success with income taxation and especially with *personal* income taxation, for example, proves that the popular arguments concerning the preconditions for the successful application of an income tax are not really as relevant as they sound. That success is, incidentally, also a serious challenge to the conclusions reached by the literature on tax structure change.

Because of lack of space and time, it is not possible to give full and detailed justification of the two proposals. For the first and, I believe, less controversial of the two proposals it is not necessary to do so, because it has already been done elsewhere by the author.[25] As to the second, the objective is, frankly, to stimulate interest in a direction that has been ignored in the literature. Thus, I do not find it necessary to work out here all the implications and details of that proposal, since it is not made to be adopted at its face value.

---

24. Musgrave, *Fiscal Systems*, p. 131.
25. Vito Tanzi and Joseph Aschheim, "Saving, Investment, and Taxation in Underdeveloped Countries," *Kyklos* 18, facs. 2 (1965).

The First Proposal

I reiterate here that I believe: (a) that industrialization is necessary for development of Latin America and must therefore be stimulated; (b) that it will require and be aided by the development of the corporate form of business organization and that form must therefore receive a preferential treatment; (c) that where the investment takes place is, perhaps, more important than how much investment is undertaken; and (d) that the allocation of investment depends substantially on the allocation of saving.

These assumptions, together with some empirical evidence on the marginal propensity to consume of individuals in Latin America,[26] provide the background for the first proposal: what is needed for Latin America is a system of taxation with high progressive rates on the incomes of individuals; these would be coupled with very low rates, or no taxes at all, on the incomes of corporations and on unrealized capital gains.[27]

The special treatment of corporations suggested by the above proposal has been supported by many scholars.[28] The combination of high personal income taxes—with rates of, say, up to 50 percent—and a low, or zero, tax on corporations (and no tax on unrealized capital gains) should increase total private saving for the country[29] and put it where it is more likely to be invested productively. In other words, personal saving and consumption are likely to fall while corporate saving is likely to rise.

The tax on personal income could be complemented by a special tax on income from capital withheld at the source. Ideally, this tax on capital income should be levied with a rate equal to or close to the maximum rate for the regular income tax. In other words, we could conceive of a personal income tax with two schedules: one progressive and starting with relatively low rates to apply to most incomes; the other proportional and with a rate very close to the maximum rate in the other schedule, to apply to the dividends paid by the corporations. Retained earnings would thus escape taxation.

26. See, for example, the evidence for Colombia in Richard M. Bird, "Income Distribution and Tax Policy in Colombia," *Economic Development and Cultural Change* 18, no. 4, part 1 (July 1970).

27. See, for details and implications, Tanzi and Aschheim, "Saving, Investment, and Taxation," especially pp. 217-21.

28. See, inter alios, Carl S. Shoup, "Taxes and Economic Development," *Finanzarchiv* N.F. 25, Heft 3; Nicholas Kaldor, *An Expenditure Tax* (London: Unwin, 1955), p. 141; Stephen R. Lewis, Jr., "Aspects of Fiscal Policy and Resource Mobilization in Pakistan," *The Pakistan Development Review* 4, no. 2 (Summer 1964); Little, Scitovsky, and Scott, *Industry and Trade in Some Developing Countries*, p. 202.

29. For a defense of this point, in addition to the *Kyklos* article, see Vito Tanzi, "The Effect on Private Saving of a Change from an Income to an Expenditure Tax," *Rivista di Scienze delle Finanze* (June 1969).

The Second Proposal

For many Latin American countries the flagrant underutilization of land, due in part to the overconcentration of land holdings, has led to many proposals aimed at forcing the land into more productive uses. Many tax experts believe that a tax on potential production (which for the agricultural sector is very close to potential value-added) would go a long way toward making land more productive. There has been the general feeling that developing countries cannot afford to keep scarce resources underutilized, and land is definitely a scarce resource.

In view of this interest in the tax on potential production for the agricultural sector, and in view of the declared concern on the part of tax experts for the underutilization of scarce resources, it is strange that the same idea and the same concern have not been transferred to the manufacturing sector. This sector is often as guilty as the agricultural sector in wasting resources and it should be subjected to the same opprobrium and the same treatment. Let us consider some aspects of the Latin American reality.

It is generally agreed that perhaps the scarcest resource in many Latin American countries is foreign currency. Because of this scarcity and because of the industrialization policy followed by the governments of the countries, the scarce foreign exchange is often made available to many concerns at prices which are far below its shadow price. The pursuit of this policy of import-substitution industrialization has led to the creation of productive processes which not only are probably more capital-intensive than they could and should be but which are substantially underutilized for most of the time. To students of the Latin American economic scene, there must be few statistics more depressing than those on capacity utilization in the manufacturing sector. This is especially so when one realizes that, while the unutilized land was a gift from the sky, that unused capacity has been bought with the hard-earned foreign exchange.

The suggestion made here is simply to borrow the basic idea about the tax on potential output of the agricultural sector and apply it to the manufacturing sector, especially to the modern manufacturing sector. The proposal is simply to impose a tax on something fairly close to the potential value-added of the enterprises.

Thus, the proposal involves the following steps:

(a) The government would have to survey the various enterprises once a year and determine how much they could produce if they were fully utilized.

(b) On the basis of the estimated full-capacity output, the value of that output would be calculated. Of course, some assumption concerning the elasticity of demand would have to be made. The simplest would be to assume that prices would remain the same as output increased.

(c) From that estimate of the value of potential output, actual inputs from other firms would be subtracted. That is, only what the firm actually buys from other firms, and not what it would buy at full capacity, would be deducted.

(d) The difference, which is actually higher than the potential value-added, would be taxed at a certain rate.

Thus, assume that the government has estimated that enterprise A, if it were working at full capacity, could produce an output which at current prices could be sold at 100 pesos. Suppose that the rate of the tax is $T = 10$ percent. Suppose also that the purchases from other firms are valued at 20 pesos. Then the tax would be 10 percent of 80, or 8 pesos. But the enterprise could be producing only, say, an output of 50. This means that the actual value-added for that enterprise would be 30 and that the tax paid would be almost 27 percent or 8/30. If the value of the output increased to, say, 60 pesos, both the tax rate and the tax payment would fall. In other words, the enterprise could increase its output up to 100 pesos without any increase in tax liability and, in fact, with decreases in the rate and amount of the tax. This should provide a stimulus toward higher utilization of the existing capacity.

In conclusion, while the land tax would force a better use of land, the tax on the potential value-added would have the purpose of forcing a better use of capital. I have been purposefully vague about the details of the proposal because, as I stated above, the basic objective is to stimulate some thinking along these somewhat nonorthodox lines. I would actually combine the two proposals to get my ideal tax system for the more advanced of the Latin American countries. In rough outline, that system would include, but not be limited to, a tax on potential agricultural production, a tax on the potential value-added in the manufacturing sector, a progressive income tax on most incomes (excluding those from capital received from enterprises), and a proportional tax on the latter with a rate equivalent to the maximum rate for the other incomes.

CONCLUSIONS

While the recent work on tax structure change in relation to economic development is certainly one of the most exciting areas of research, much remains to be done before it can be of immediate use for the design of tax structure for industrialization. We have learned a lot from it, but there are still too many aspects to be analyzed and too many questions to be answered before that work becomes much more than an intellectually satisfying exercise. In the meantime, those responsible for designing tax structures for development in specific countries are well advised to read it; but they would be unwise to rely too much on its conclusions in making their proposals.

Comment—Jonathan Levin

TANZI'S paper is so rich and diverse in its content that one could go on for a long time touching on almost every aspect of public finance. I think that it would be wisest, therefore, to limit myself to three topics. The first will be the general area of tax structure analysis; second, the proposals advanced in Tanzi's paper; and third, the other nontax means of transferring resources to the public sector and the importance that they have assumed.

A great deal has now been written on the analysis of tax structure development in relation to general economic development, and we have a tendency to forget the basic purpose for which this field was first developed. Though one may find valid criticism for some of the analytical techniques utilized, the underlying rationale behind the field was to prevent what had occurred in many areas previously, that is, the simple transplanting of taxes and tax devices from industrial countries to less-developed countries. In order to counteract the idea that the tax of the expert's own country is automatically applicable in the country he visits, a great deal of work was done to show that there are sound reasons why different tax systems are applicable in different circumstances. I think the analysis of tax structure has been successful in this basic objective. It has also been successful in giving a direction to research which is outside the analysis of general tax structure, such as research on specific tax instruments. It has given many students an economic and developmental framework to which they can relate the individual tax. Despite these achievements, however, the entire field of tax structure analysis is still relatively undeveloped; a great deal of work remains to be done and little more than direction now exists.

One aspect of tax structure development studies which merits comment here is the question of normativeness. A great deal of controversy has arisen as to whether the analyses of tax systems in relation to development should be normative: should they be taken as descriptive of what exists in different countries, or should they be taken to indicate a desirable pattern of tax levels toward whose attainment tax structure should be changed? As a means of counteracting the normativeness of the previous tendency for transplantation of taxes, I suppose there could be little argument against the prescriptions of some tax structure development analyses. Like Tanzi, however, I do not find great persuasiveness in an argument for changing taxes that is based on the tax structure in other countries at the same level of development. A comparison of one country with other countries at its level of development provides very little incentive for change; if other countries have a better tax system, why are they at this level of development? Much more persuasive are the lessons that we can learn from an examination of taxation in several countries which may help us to identify sectors in a particular country that are not being adequately taxed. Rather than argue that taxation is inadequate in comparison with other countries, one can then argue that the level of effective taxation of a particular sector or activity—which may have prospered or developed in recent years—is out of line with taxation elsewhere in the economy and could justifiably be increased.

Certainly, tax structure studies are not without shortcomings. Probably the greatest shortcoming is a tendency to lose touch with reality— a tendency to identify countries as industrial or developing and to locate them along any of several indices, such as per capita income or openness. There are also differences in structure and in time, however, which are important to an understanding of tax structure. An oil country, for example, may have available to it distinctive sources of revenue in the foreign companies at work in the country and may be characterized by a reluctance to tax the rest of the country, the domestic sector. Another country at the same level of per capita income and openness may have very few foreign companies to tax, an export sector characterized by small holders producing a stable or stagnant export crop, and a much higher level of domestic taxation. Therefore, openness and per capita income do not tell us enough. Fresh in our minds are the recent news stories of the hard bargaining between the oil-exporting countries and the oil companies. The result was a higher level of base prices for exports and, in effect, higher taxation. On the basis of some models of tax structure change, however, all that may be discernible will be a strengthened relationship between openness and taxes on foreign trade. When in fact one is dealing with protracted negotiations between an organization of exporting countries and foreign companies which work their oil fields, one is several steps removed from reality if one speaks only of a statistical relationship between openness and the importance of foreign trade revenues.

In a recent experience in one developing country in Latin America, I found that the desired interchange of experience with other countries was very far from such general issues as overall tax structure or tax level. There was no interest in learning from other countries to what height taxes should be increased. While there was an awareness that taxes should be higher, this grew not out of a comparison with other countries but out of the ambition to fulfill a development plan. It was from this direction that much of the impetus came. However, there was an interest in more specific questions, such as how to tax agriculture through a presumptive income system; how to tax retailers through such a system; how to institute physical reports of development expenditures; how to develop a budget system which would not produce fictitious annual surpluses that might dissuade parliament from passing necessary taxes. There is a gap between these very specific questions of technique, drawing upon the applicable experience of other countries, and the very simple lessons which we have thus far been able to derive from the study of tax structure development. Eventually, as we push forward with tax structure study, this gap should close.

Moving to the second major theme, I should like to examine the proposals advanced by Tanzi in his paper. I am not sure whether there is one proposal in the paper or two, for while one proposal would call for the effective elimination of taxation on corporations, the other would impose taxation on corporations based on potential value-added or potential capacity. I will assume, therefore, that there is one proposal and that it calls for the taxation of corporations on the basis of full capacity. There are some advantages, of course, which would derive from such a tax. As we all know, there are certain distinctive effects which arise from taxes. Perhaps the worst would arise from a tax on gross receipts which at some level of production, in the case of increasing cost, would make the marginal product unprofitable. One can avoid this by moving to a system of net taxation, in which case the less profitable marginal item would still be profitable. One could go a step further by having a fixed tax, which makes the marginal product completely profitable without any subtraction of taxation so long as the taxation has not imposed so large a burden as to make production unprofitable to begin with. In some ways the proposal to tax on the basis of potential full capacity bears a resemblance to taxation of specified fixed value, which would occur in a land tax. It resembles also what would occur in the case of taxation based on certain indices of profitability, such as the number of square feet of floor space, of horsepower, and of many other rough indices. In the sense that it is based on a national tax-paying capacity which does not vary, it leaves the taxpayer free to argue about the appropriateness of the particular level while increasing production at no tax cost.

A major difficulty would arise, however, just from the measurement of full capacity. Obviously, this would be rather difficult, and even a rough measure might face some insurmountable obstacles. For one, there is the question of limited market. Felix's paper in this volume refers to excess capacity in a number of export industries. When one taxes land, one does not have this limitation; one feels that there are alternate crops which, in one case or another, would be profitable. However, when one is dealing with an industrial plant with a limited domestic market and a cost structure which may make it incapable of competing in foreign markets at the prevailing exchange rate, potential full capacity may very well be unattainable and a tax based upon it unrealistic.

Another aspect of this proposal runs into a separate set of problems which can only be briefly referred to here. The proposed tax would return fiscal incentives from industry to a relatively free, open, and uncomplicated situation. What exists now in most of Latin America is an immensely complex combination of fiscal instruments which are already being used to render incentives for industrial production. These range from reduced taxes to outright subsidies and to combinations of the two. Tanzi has clearly pointed out in his paper that the alternatives between expenditure and taxation must be studied together and that income redistribution, for example, can be promoted either through expenditure or through taxation. This is true as well in other areas, such as the rendering of incentives to various branches of production. Indeed, the interaction of fiscal instruments and the exchange system is so great in many Latin American countries that the two are difficult to untangle. Thus, even with the shift to a single tax on the full-capacity income of corporations, there would have to be a decision either to eliminate or maintain the other incentives which now exist, including export bonus schemes, exemption of income from exports, awarding of import entitlement certificates, duty exemption of raw material imports, drawbacks, and a large range of other instruments. One could either eliminate all of these and face the problems of readjustment, or maintain them and add to the existing complexity with a relatively simple and direct instrument. The choice would, at least, require considerably more analysis.

Another relevant point is made in the paper in this volume by Baer. He finds, in the cases studied, that public enterprises do not themselves generate adequate investment funds, even though presumably most or all of them do not pay taxes. Thus, even without the payment of any taxes there could still be the question of the provision of adequate funds for investment. This does not mean that each proposal must solve all problems, but it does suggest that the provision of funds is a problem which may go beyond taxation.

As with all taxes, the possible revenue effects must be dealt with, and in this case the question of taxation of eventual capital gains from the corporation. One would also wish to consider carefully the problem of evasion through nondividend payments which is likely to occur.

To move to my third topic, the point is made early in Tanzi's paper that taxes are considered to be the most rational and effective way of transferring resources from the private to the public sector. There is also an assumption made that saving in each sector in a developing country gives rise to investment in that same sector and that there is very little transfer of savings from one sector to another. This, of course, is one of the measurements of development itself, since the mobility of financial resources from one sector to another identifies development of the financial market. However, it may not be entirely correct to assume that what we are dealing with is simply the transfer of resources from the private sector to the public sector. One cannot overlook the great importance in many of these countries of government lending programs, which are carried out through agrarian banks, development banks, housing banks, and other channels. This implies a relaxation of the assumption of strict application of all savings in the same sector. I think it is entirely proper to depart from this assumption. Indeed, one of the government's objectives should be to increase the mobility of financial resources between sectors. Some care must be taken, however, as to how this is done. Thus, the proposal for running a budget surplus, which can then be offset by increased credit to the private sector and particularly to new entrepreneurs, runs into a major difficulty. It is the same difficulty that gives rise to government lending programs in many countries: the extreme rigidity which characterizes the domestic credit market. Credit will normally go to established customers, to those with political or special influence in the banks; it will go to financing imports or traditional exports. Credit will not go, generally, to the new growth industries and to the small entrepreneurs who may need it the most. It is because of these rigidities in credit that government lending is in fact a very important part of many countries' programs in Latin America today.

Quite apart from taxation as a means of mobilizing resources from the private sector to the public sector, many governments in Latin America today are utilizing the capital markets. These are not perfect capital markets, to be sure. In fact, governments are mobilizing resources for public use through the sale or placement of government securities by means that are not available to the private sector. This type of debt placement works through reserve requirements for banks, insurance companies, and mutual firms; it works through index clauses on government securities where that is found necessary; and it works in some cases through the maintenance of redeemability for public securities, which is something private firms cannot afford. As a result, though the government deficit may disappear as an inflationary device and the government tax ratio may not be very high, the government may still be taking resources from the private sector through mobilization of savings in imperfect capital markets. While the merits of this allocation of resources must be judged in each individual case, it cannot be argued in such circumstances that the government is making resources available to the private sector by leaving the tax ratio low.

I would like to compliment Tanzi for covering such a wide area in his paper. I am sure that, were we to meet some years from today, we would find a much narrower gap between tax structure studies and the questions which arise in international discussions among those concerned with tax policies.

Comment—Eliott Morss

THE cross-sectional analysis that Tanzi reviews attempts to characterize what happens to the tax levels and tax structures of countries as they develop economically. Something of a pattern does emerge. But there are a sufficient number of important exceptions to the pattern to suggest that any particular country will not *have* to comply with the general pattern. There is clearly no evidence to suggest that economic, political, or other factors will force a country to follow the pattern.

Since developing countries have considerable latitude to deviate from the general pattern, the next logical question is: should they deviate? I see no compelling reason to believe that past behavior should serve as a guide for today's fiscal policy decisions. Certainly it would be difficult to argue that fiscal policies made in the past were the correct ones for the past; and even if they were, conditions today are different enough to cast further doubt on the appropriateness of past policies for today's decisions.

Views on industrialization and on how it should be accomplished have in recent years changed quite dramatically in both developed and developing nations. In the past, industrialization was considered desirable to all nations, whereas today considerable disillusionment exists. The sources of this disillusionment are not always the same. In the developed nations (and particularly in the United States), the role of private industry is being questioned (rightly or wrongly) for its materialistic emphasis, for its role in the military-industrial complex, and for its contribution to the destruction of the environment. In the developing nations, the disillusionment stems from the feeling that too large a portion of the benefits from industrialization are being siphoned off by large foreign investors.

Given that this characterization of the setting in the developing world is correct, one can seriously question the relevance of past fiscal policy relationships between government and business for the future. Indeed, it would seem far more appropriate for developing countries to ask how much *should* be given up to attract foreign capital rather than to ask what is customarily given up. Putting it more colloquially, the developing country's attitude might be to stop asking what it can do to attract foreign investment and instead to start asking what foreign business can do for it.

At the risk of being presumptuous, let me carry this line of thinking a bit further. It seems to me that the developing countries want three things from foreigners: capital, technological knowledge (both production and marketing), and access to foreign markets. It is clear that the needs for these three "goods" will differ substantially among developing nations, and this suggests that the amounts they should be "willing to pay" (in the form of tax relief, various types of government subsidies, currency convertibility guarantees, etc.) will differ. Contrast this approach to the one that is implicit in the tax studies discussed by Tanzi, which is to ask, "How does our tax rate compare with the tax rate in fifty other developing countries?" Rather than follow this approach, I would urge the developing countries to view what they are willing to pay foreigners as fees for services rendered, and to set these "fees" no higher than is needed to get the services performed.

This, I would argue, is the realistic way to deal with foreign investors. By approaching them in this manner from the outset, most of the unpleasant confrontations and threats of exploitation, which stem from a feeling that foreigners were given too much in the past, could be avoided in the future.[1]

If developing countries were to follow the approach I suggest, would there be any use for the sort of research discussed by Tanzi? I think so. For even the most Machiavellian finance minister would probably be interested in knowing how the tax burden of his country compares with other countries in similar circumstances. After all, in deciding what "fee" to pay for foreign and domestic investment benefits, some idea of what other countries are paying would be useful. And there is a second way in which comparative tax structure studies might be useful to the finance minister. Once he has decided what fee to pay he will probably, for public relations purposes, want to offer some justification for it. It is a bit brash to be perfectly frank and say, "That is all we will have to pay to attract foreign and domestic investors," just as in the past it would have been brash for colonialists to talk about how far they could go in exploiting their colonies without causing a revolution. Hence, to the extent that comparative studies can be drawn upon to show that relative to other countries the fee being offered is generous, finance ministers might as well use them.

Discussion

N. KALDOR: Taxation is one field where simple comparative study of what happens in different countries is *not* in itself of any use in deciding how one can improve the system in any particular country. Each country has its own problems. I think comparative studies are terribly important to learn about economic development and how economic systems behave.

---

1. Perhaps this statement does not have general applicability. To the extent that Latin American countries are following a successful policy of "draw foreigners in, let them get their capital in place, and then take it away from them," my suggestion is not appropriate.

But, as to how governments behave in their tax systems, we do not know whether any of them behave well or badly. Therefore, we cannot just "buy" the technique of regression equations and thereby establish that because a majority of countries with an income per head of $800 have some particular set of taxes, these are good things to have at that income level. Different countries have different needs.

I have strongly urged some countries to adopt particular taxes, and I have strongly urged other countries not to adopt the very same taxes. For example, take the value-added tax. When I was in Latin America I was a strong advocate of the value-added tax for one very important reason: Latin American countries suffer from an enormous amount of tax evasion. The difficulty of collecting what is legally due under any tax is much greater there than in almost any other part of the world. There are huge taxes on paper, but very little of the full liability gets collected. The value-added tax is a very good revenue-raiser from a collection point of view. It has self-checking features (even if it is not really self-checking, people think that it is, which is what matters) in comparison to an ordinary turnover tax or a sales tax. This is why it was introduced in France and from there it spread to other countries. On the other hand, the economic merits claimed for it are very largely spurious. From an administrative point of view, it is an extremely clumsy and difficult tax to introduce, and when it was a question of its being introduced in the United Kingdom I was strongly against it. Instead, the U.K. invented an entirely new tax called a selective employment tax, which I think is a most excellent tax *for the U.K.* I think the selective employment tax is the last tax I would recommend at the moment for the countries of Latin America. But, I can predict there will be some countries, e.g., Japan, that will adopt a selective employment tax in the next ten years or so. I merely mention these examples to show that the kinds of taxes required in different countries are very different.

In this regard, I think Tanzi's paper understates the case for an agricultural land tax on the value of potential output. The case is much stronger than he makes it appear. It is not just a matter of incentives and of land being a scarce resource. There is also the fact that the distribution of the burden of taxation among the different sectors of the economy is highly inequitable. This is a very important reason in itself. Another point is that, at the stage of economic development in which many Latin American countries are today, increasing the marketable surplus of agriculture—that is, the part of agricultural production that has to be monetized—plays a very important role. Any Japanese economic historian would tell you that the land tax in Japan had an enormous impact in stimulating industrialization. There is no equivalent to such a tax in the industrial sector. The corporation tax, I would still say, is the best tax for many countries. There are all sorts of considerations involved; it is all very well to say that one ought to heavily tax personal incomes, but sometimes one simply cannot do so. Given the machinery of administration, the corruptibility of officials, and other limitations on what one can do, the idea that one can collect a lot of money on the personal income of capitalists or property owners may be just illusory. Corporations, on the other hand, particularly large corporations and multi-national corporations, have a high degree of taxability and provide a reliable source of revenue.

I agree that corporation taxes are bad from an incentive point of view. I would, however, reform the tax in a somewhat different (though perhaps not very different) direction from what Tanzi suggests, along lines sometimes proposed in Italy, namely that taxes on corporations should not be on profits (or at least not entirely on profits) but should be expressed as a percentage of capital employed. In other words, this could be a tax on the net worth of companies, provided the administrative problems could be solved. Instead of a tax on profits earned, this tax would give a differential incentive to those companies that earn a high rate of profit in relation to the capital employed and tax more heavily those companies that employ too much capital in relation to the profits they earn. It is exactly the opposite of an excess profits tax. It is an excess profits subsidy.

Under the present system of the corporation tax, the tax as a percentage of capital employed is all the lower, the lower the profits are; if the corporate tax rate is 50 percent, a company that earned an amount equal to 50 percent on its capital employed would pay in taxes an amount equal to 25 percent of its capital employed. A company that earned less profits would pay in taxes an amount equivalent to a smaller percentage of its capital employed. On the other hand, if one levied a tax on net worth, then the company which earned 50 percent on its capital employed is bound to be "undertaxed" in relation to another company which earned only 5 percent on its capital employed. I think a combination of a dual tax, partly on profits and partly on capital employed, is preferable to the type we now know, provided the administrative problems of getting a tolerably good measure of net worth or capital employed (on the basis of historical costs and depreciation) can be solved.

O. OLDMAN: If it is difficult to tax income or if it is difficult to estimate a person's actual income by any of the administrative means available, think how inconceivably greater the difficulty would be of trying to tax somebody's potential income, something that might have been if he had used his resources in some better way or used his brains in some better way. It is for this reason that I object to the Tanzi proposal. I am afraid I also have to object to Kaldor's proposal about taxing potential agricultural income. I agree with him wholeheartedly that we have to tax agriculture; as Hinrichs's paper shows, we indeed do that. But, to think about going after agricultural potential, some mythical amount, is very much like going after the economist's concept of pure economic rent. It would be nice to do it, but until we can identify it with numbers that the tax collectors can deal with, it seems that we really ought not spend a great deal of time refining concepts of this sort. They are interesting to discuss philosophically, but we ought not to be too serious about trying to convert others.

Tanzi also thinks that we could eliminate taxes on corporations. If we literally exempted corporations from taxation, it would be very easy for any of us to figure out ways in which we would incorporate all of our economic activities and thereafter forever defer tax on any of our incomes. Therefore, I argue that we ought to face up to the fact that corporate income must be taxed as it is earned. The important current questions are those relating to integrating this tax with the personal income tax in more-or-less practical ways. We have already gone beyond the point that, in the real world, we can think seriously about eliminating taxes from corporations.

N. KALDOR: I take a tax on potential agricultural output to be the same as the old British land tax in India, or what you call a property tax; that is to say, you assess the man on the annual value of his property. You have this in the United States. The valuations are always out of date and so on, but you cannot say that it cannot be done. This has been done for centuries.

O. OLDMAN: Insofar as you are talking about any of the typical range of annual taxes measured by the capital value of property, I could not agree more. But, insofar as one uses the phrase that the Argentines and others have used, which happens to employ the language "taxing agricultural potential income" and which seeks to measure a potential income on a current basis, then it seems we are going beyond the realm of practicality.

Ecuador has in fact installed the value-added tax, but I do not think I could believe anybody who tells me that they are not having any trouble with it, just as I discount similar statements by the Brazilians, because others who work with that tax there tell me otherwise. Everybody ought to note that the Latin Americans actually were using the value-added tax technique before the Europeans. Argentina had it for many years; they did not call it by that name, unfortunately, so they never got full credit for it. If one remembers that it is essentially just a conversion of the withholding device we use on personal income taxes to the sales tax area, and an administrative device for collecting taxes a bit more efficiently, we see in it a modern scheme for sales tax collections. It too has problems of evasion similar to those of the other sales taxes. But while people are afraid of new taxes, it takes them a while to learn the "tricks of the trade." The Latins have not yet learned about the French entrepreneur who created a corporation which manufactures value-added tax deduction slips. A beautiful system of evasion was developed; invoices were sold for only a one percent commission. When word gets around about how these different schemes work, the value-added tax is as evadable as any other tax. Nevertheless, it does build effectively on the tax systems of countries which have been accustomed to gross turnover taxes in the past. The basic administrative mechanism is there, a new wrinkle of modernization is added on as a gloss, and for a period you may get some injections of additional revenue. But one ought not assume there is anything magic here.

R. THORN: Concerning the tax on potential agricultural productivity, I agree that the agricultural sector has to be incorporated into the tax base. But, I would criticize this particular tax. There must be an assumption missing here when one talks about this tax as stimulating productivity. If we own a capital asset which has the capability of giving forth a potential income stream and then a fixed annual charge is levied on it, the only thing that happens is that the capital value of the asset decreases. Perhaps there are other assumptions that would force an increase in productivity.

N. KALDOR: The effect of a heavy tax on land is to force inefficient farmers out of business. Since the amount of land is limited, their elimination enables the more efficient farmers to acquire more land, and to consolidate farms into larger units cultivated by more efficient "entrepreneurs." The peculiarity of land is that the available amount is fixed. Hence, competition does *not* eliminate bad farmers, because to do so the good farmers would have to increase their output sufficiently to drive agricultural prices below their costs. But, they cannot increase output sufficiently precisely because they do not have control of the land.

R. THORN: I would like to make a few brief comments on the corporate income tax. First, the statistical phenomenon of the decline of the corporate income tax with a growth in per capita income should not discourage us from the usefulness of the tax; the tax has a good income elasticity. Part of the reason for its secular decline with the growth of GNP is another statistical phenomenon, the tendency for the share of capital to fall and the share of labor to increase as a country's income grows.

Another point I would bring out in connection with the corporate income tax is that, in large measure, our opinion of the corporate tax depends on how efficient one is in the taxation of personal income. If one is efficient with the personal income tax, I would tend to downplay the importance of the corporate income tax. However, one of the ways to catch high-income receivers is via the corporate income tax. Of course, they try to convert their current income into capital gains when capital gains receive special treatment, as in the United States and United

Kingdom. I do not think we can make an a priori judgment whether the corporate income tax is good or bad. This has to be determined, in part, on grounds of administrative convenience as to where one is going to tax personal income, especially the higher incomes which are so elusive.

D. FELIX: Concerning a tax on potential industrial output, there is a problem of incidence shifting in the industrial sector which requires spelling out a price model. The prevalence of wage-price spiraling in a number of Latin American countries suggests that the industry pricing pattern is some version of full-cost pricing. Assuming this to be the case, there is a question of the impact of a tax levied on potential output on the price of industrial goods. In other words, what sort of tax shifting is likely to occur?

A second question deals with the issue of resource misallocation, or a badly structured industrial sector. The chronic excess capacity which has arisen in the past decade or so seems to reflect not only micro-inefficiencies but also industrial structures, which in many of these countries cannot be sustained at full capacity for long without running into balance-of-payments problems. The industrial structures are too import-intensive without at the same time offsetting these import requirements by substantial exporting. If this is in fact the case, then a scheme that pushes these firms toward a full-capacity utilization cannot succeed unless it also incorporates techniques for overcoming the balance-of-payments constraint. Schydlowsky's paper in this volume rigorously deals with this problem.

Third, if one of the functions of the tax is to squeeze out firms that somehow cannot reduce costs, then one must also confront the nature of the investment function. Often these are mercantilistic economics, where the purposes of protection and the various kinds of subsidies for import substitution are not merely to raise the expected profit rate but to reduce the risk variance. Tanzi's tax scheme would increase the risk to private firms contemplating new production, and thus could have a depressing effect on the rate of investment in the private sector because of a reduced willingness on the part of new firms to step in and draw resources away from firms that are squeezed out. All this suggests that the potential output tax could be ineffective or even disruptive, unless embedded in a larger package of measures designed to modify the industrial structure, push more industrial output into export markets, and provide against transitional aggregate demand difficulties.

W. TYLER: Regarding the idea of Tanzi's capacity utilization tax, or tax on potential value-added, there is some question, in a conceptual sense, of the definition of capacity utilization. Given an orthodox U-shaped short-run average cost curve, the question arises as to where the point of 100 percent capacity utilization lies. Is it the point of economic capacity, the minimum point on the SAC curve? Or does it lie closer to the point—or even at the point—of physical capacity, where the SAC curve becomes vertical? If the former is chosen as the point of full-capacity utilization, any firm producing a level of output below that resulting in the minimum SAC would presumably benefit under a tax scheme designed to eliminate the economy's idle capacity. On the other hand, if the physical capacity concept is selected, certain allocational inefficiencies become evident. In either case, the burden on the tax administrator in deciding which standard to apply and identifying its conditions will be great.

4

Tax Reform Constrained by Fiscal Harmonization within Common Markets

Growth without Development in Guatemala

HARLEY H. HINRICHS

THIS paper is concerned first with the theory of tax reform—the methodology and approach whereby individual cases "should" be studied;[1] second, with the case of Guatemalan tax reform; and third, with the constraints upon tax reform set by membership in a common market—in particular, the effects of structural revenue falloffs from foreign trade revenues, the merging of fiscal incentives within such markets, and the pressures for achieving allocative fiscal neutrality within such markets (such as by uniform indirect tax systems). Such pressures for allocative uniformity may please fiscal purists, but should not obscure more important structural reforms related to income distribution, tax administration, and expenditures for human development. Thus, the reader should be warned that fiscal harmonization is treated more as a constraint on the achievement of some optimum of an interrelated set of objectives rather than as the prime objective itself.

1. See Harley H. Hinrichs, *Reforming Tax Reforms, The Reform of Tax Theory, The Theory of Reform* (Agency for International Development, 1969).

In addition to primary research conducted in Guatemala in April-May 1970, this paper is based on (and indebted to) Michael H. Best, "Determinants of Tax Performance and Developing Countries: The Case of Guatemala" (Ph.D. diss., University of Oregon, August 1969); Alan Cohen and AID Economic Staff, "Economic Development of Guatemala," unpublished (Guatemala, 1970); Virginia G. Watkin, *Taxes and Tax Harmonization in Central America* (Cambridge, Mass.: Harvard Law School International Tax Program, 1967); Joint Tax Program OAS/IDB, *Tax Systems of Latin America: Guatemala* (Washington, D.C.: Pan American Union, 1966); Marion H. Gillim, *The Fiscal Aspects of the Central American Common Market in Fiscal Harmonization in Common Markets*, vol. 2 (New York: Columbia University Press, 1967); John H. Adler, Eugene R. Schlesinger, and Ernest C. Olson, *Public Finance and Economic Development in Guatemala* (Stanford, Calif.: Stanford University Press, 1951); Richard N. Adams, *Crucifixion by Power: Essays on Guatemalan National Social Structure, 1944-66* (Austin, Tex.: University of Texas Press, 1970); *Una Política para el Desarrollo de Guatemala*, Administración de la Revista Economía y Instituto de Investigaciones Económicas y Sociales (Guatemala, 1969); and numerous government documents, reports, and studies, especially by the Ministerio de Hacienda y Credito Público and Banco de Guatemala.

The major theoretical innovations, or emphases, herein include a greater than typical concern with income distribution; the division of expenditures into "developmental" and "nondevelopmental" as contrasted to current and capital; and the timing and tactics of tax reform as constrained by political and administrative capabilities. Probably the most interesting innovation is the analysis of fiscal capacity from both a "macro" and a "micro" side. This "micro" approach of individual tax bases had been suggested in my early work,[2] was fathered in the impressive empirical work of Jonathan Levin, and was first applied to Guatemala by Michael Best. I am in debt to both these pioneers.

SUMMARY OF THE FISCAL DILEMMA, ISSUES, AND APPROACH

The Guatemalan fiscal system faces the classic dilemma of many developing countries: revenues grow less rapidly than incomes, current expenditures more rapidly. Public sector savings, already at a low level, will vanish in the next few years. This dilemma has occurred in the past and has resulted in halted public investment programs, a lack of government expenditures for long-term human development needs in education and health, and spasmodic increases in tax rates, fraught with political uncertainties, to cope with such recurring dilemmas. A new government has the opportunity to foresee and prevent such dilemmas in the future by constructive fiscal planning and action now. This is the challenge for the Guatemalan fiscal system.

Although this classic fiscal dilemma is similar to that of many developing countries, Guatemala is different. Its differences suggest issues and approaches not typical for many countries. Throughout this paper certain themes and issues will be explored: (a) the special fiscal problems of membership in the Central American Common Market (CACM); (b) the lesser importance of public sector savings as a planning benchmark relative to the greater relevance of total "developmental expenditures," both current and capital, to meet both economic and human needs; (c) the importance of income distribution in fiscal analysis, especially for measuring fiscal capacity and in achieving other than "equity" goals such as balance of payments and economic development objectives; and (d) the importance of both political and administrative constraints in planning tax strategies based on a systems analysis of tax instruments and objectives within the entire public sector.

OBJECTIVES

A fiscal strategy for Guatemala is a function of the nation's objectives. The role for the public sector may include resource mobilization, resource

2. See Harley H. Hinrichs, *A General Theory of Tax Structure Change During Economic Development* (Cambridge, Mass.: Harvard Law School International Tax Program, 1966), pp. 33, 63.

reallocation, stabilization of prices, employment and the external balance, redistribution of income, and other goals. It is critical for any government at an early stage of planning to determine for itself the different priorities to be put on each possible role.

The past performance of the public sector in Guatemala may suggest where past priorities have been placed (either consciously or by default) and where they might be reordered for the future:

The quality and quantity of government current expenditures for social development, especially education and health, have provided one of the lowest performance records in the hemisphere (see Table 1).

Public sector savings, averaging only 1-2 percent of GNP, have been of little help in raising an overall poor savings performance of the economy (see Table 2).

One of the most unequal distributions of income within the hemisphere has been little affected by the performance of the public sector (see Tables 3a-d.)

Even current and short-run prospects for economic growth at promising rates of 5-6 percent may coincide with little if any corresponding social development and the widespread dispersion of such economic gains to improve the quality of life.

Long-run development, both economic and human, may well rest on the public sector's future priorities to readjust its performance. Objectives in the future may need to be broader than simply maintaining a stable currency and meeting government payrolls. As any government can be seen as a "system" wherein certain inputs or instruments can be used to optimize some set of objectives, it is critically important to analyze sufficiently such possible objectives. Unless the objectives are clear, any possible strategy is merely set in limbo, and only when the consequents of policy actions are made clear can the initial problems or objectives be formulated.

THE FISCAL GAP AND FISCAL CAPACITY

Fiscal Gap

If the government undertakes no significant fiscal program, a fiscal crisis is inevitable during 1971-76. Public sector savings will vanish by 1976 at the same time investment expenditures are to double (see Table 4). In 1969, central government current account savings (Q20.4 million), along with savings from the rest of the public sector (Q7.1 million) and various capital receipts (Q3.7 million), supported nearly 70 percent of public sector investment expenditures, although at a modest level. By 1974 central government savings will go to zero, and by 1976 the entire public sector will show negative savings. But, the level of investment expenditures will have grown from Q45 million to Q95 million. Obviously,

TABLE 1

RELATIVE PERFORMANCE OF GUATEMALAN ECONOMIC GROWTH AND SOCIAL DEVELOPMENT COMPARED WITH 10 OTHER MIDDLE-INCOME LATIN AMERICAN COUNTRIES IN 1960s (RANKED IN ASCENDING ORDER OF OPTIMAL PERFORMANCE)[a]

ECONOMIC GROWTH		HEALTH			EDUCATION		
Per Capita Income Level	Growth Rate 1961–69 (GDP)	Death Rate	Infant Mortality Rate	Life Expectancy	Literacy Rate	Primary School Enrollment Percentage	Secondary School Enrollment Percentage
Mexico	Nicaragua	Dom. Rep.	Honduras	Costa Rica	Chile	Chile	Peru
Costa Rica	Mexico	Costa Rica	Nicaragua	Mexico	Costa Rica	Peru	Costa Rica
Chile	El Salvador	Chile	El Salvador	Chile	Mexico	Costa Rica	Brazil
Nicaragua	Costa Rica	El Salvador	Mexico	Colombia	Colombia	Mexico	Colombia
GUATEMALA	Peru	Honduras	Costa Rica	Brazil	Brazil	Dom. Rep.	Mexico
Peru	Honduras	Colombia	Dom. Rep.	El Salvador	Dom. Rep.	El Salvador	Chile
Brazil	Brazil	Mexico	Colombia	Peru	Peru	Honduras	El Salvador
Colombia	GUATEMALA	Brazil	Chile	Dom. Rep.	Nicaragua	Colombia	Nicaragua
El Salvador	Colombia	GUATEMALA	GUATEMALA	GUATEMALA	El Salvador	Brazil	Dom. Rep.
Dom. Rep.	Chile	Peru	Brazil	Nicaragua	Honduras	Nicaragua	Honduras
Honduras	Dom. Rep.	Nicaragua	Peru	Honduras	GUATEMALA	GUATEMALA	GUATEMALA

NOTE: These rankings for particular countries may appear to be highly suspect (e.g., Dominican Republic and Honduras rank highest in mortality rate statistics). However, they do serve to demonstrate an overall poor performance for Guatemala.

SOURCE: Tables, *Progreso Socio-Economico en America Latina, Noveno Informe Anual, 1969* (Washington, D.C.: Banco Interamericano de Desarrollo, 1970)), pp. 1–161.

[a] "Middle-income" countries are here defined as those with 1968 per capita incomes between $250 and $500.

a greater domestic effort must be forthcoming if such an investment level is to be attained and foreign institutional finance obtained. Even if net external finance were to reach a significantly higher level in 1974-76 compared to 1969, a financing gap of Q40-60 million will remain, after allowing for a reasonable amount of net domestic borrowing.

The timing of the fiscal gap has significant implications and political constraints that can be foreseen. The central government fiscal crisis is

TABLE 2

RELATIVE PERFORMANCE OF GUATEMALAN SAVINGS AND TAX EFFORT (COMPARED WITH 10 OTHER MIDDLE-INCOME LATIN AMERICAN COUNTRIES IN 1960s)

1961–68		1963–65		
Rank	Private and Public Savings as Percent of GDP	Rank	Tax Ratio (%)	Rank of Tax Effort[a] (Among 52 Countries)
Mexico	18.2	Brazil	21.4	1
Peru	17.8	Chile	20.9	9
Brazil	16.4	Dominican Republic	17.9	12
Colombia	15.7	Peru	16.0	24
Costa Rica	13.5	Costa Rica	13.8	38
Nicaragua	13.2	Nicaragua	13.5	37
Honduras	12.7	Colombia	10.9	43
El Salvador	12.6	El Salvador	10.9	48
Chile	12.0	Mexico	9.9	49
Dominican Republic	9.5	Honduras	9.9	50
GUATEMALA	9.3	GUATEMALA	9.3	51

[a]Rank based on per capita income and "openness" (foreign trade ratio); see Harley H. Hinrichs, *A General Theory of Tax Structure Change During Economic Development* (Cambridge, Mass.: Harvard Law School International Tax Program, 1966) and Jorgen R. Lotz and Elliott R. Morss, "Measuring Tax Effort in Developing Countries," *IMF Staff Papers* 14, no. 3 (November 1967).
SOURCE: *Progreso Socio-Económico en America Latina, Noveno Informe Anual, 1969* (Washington, D.C.: Banco Interamericano de Desarrollo, 1970), pp. 69, 78.

expected to occur in 1974, an election year. If the 1969-70 election period has been any guide, it will then be difficult to initiate a tax program to cope with the crisis. Indeed, in 1969 some tax collections, such as property taxes, even fell by 10 percent from the previous year despite expanded property tax assessments. Furthermore, the government may be able to function financially during its first few years in office while the investment program is still being geared up and vigorous tax enforcement generates additional revenue flows, but by the end of its tenure in office it will face both the election and a potentially severe fiscal crisis. By then it may have lost the opportunity to mount a serious fiscal program: the experience in many countries is that tax reforms are most successfully installed during the first year or two of a new government coming

TABLE 3

(a) DISTRIBUTION OF INCOME

| | 1950 (%) | | 1962 (%) | |
	Population	GNP	Population	GNP
Subsistence economy	71.3	24.0	72.7	21.9
Commercial economy: low income	21.1	24.2	20.0	20.9
Total subsistence and low income	92.4	48.2	92.7	42.8
Commercial economy: middle and high income	7.6	51.8	7.3	57.2

SOURCE: Richard Newbold Adams, *Crucifixion by Power: Essays on Guatemalan National Social Structure, 1944-66* (Austin, Tex.: University of Texas Press, 1970), p. 383; table drawn from work of the General Secretariat of the National Economic Planning Council.

(b) DISTRIBUTION OF AGRICULTURAL HOLDINGS, 1960

| | Number of Fincas | | Area of Fincas | | |
Type of Holding	Number	Percent	Total Area (Hectares)	Percent	Aver. Size (Hectares)
Microfincas	74,270	21.3	28,600	0.8	0.4
Subfamilial	233,800	67.1	504,600	13.5	2.2
Familial	33,040	9.5	500,800	13.5	13.2
Medium multifamilial	7,060	2.0	1,167,500	31.4	165.4
Large multifamilial	520	0.1	1,519,300	40.8	2,921.9
Total	348,690	100.0	3,720,800	100.0	

SOURCE: Comite Interamericano de Desarrollo Agricola, *Tenencia de la Tierra y Socio-economico del Sector Agricola, Guatemala* (Washington, D.C.: Pan American Union, 1964), p. 58.

(c) DISTRIBUTION OF GROSS INCOME REPORTED ON INCOME TAX RETURNS, 1966-67

	Number	Percentage of Returns	Percentage of Gross Income
Returns with gross incomes below Q50,000	31,383	93.6	18.5
Returns with gross incomes above Q50,000	2,523	7.4	81.5
Total	33,806	100.0	100.0

SOURCE: Statistical tables, Dirección General del Impuesto sobre la Renta, Guatemala.

to power. Thus, timing suggests that serious consideration and implementation of structural reforms in the tax system not be delayed.

The reasons for the imminent demise of public sector savings in Guatemala are evident: the major generator of public savings, the central government, faces a future growth rate of current expenditures of 8.5 percent while current revenues, at best, are not likely to grow faster

TABLE 3—*Continued*

(d) DISTRIBUTION OF PROPERTY TAX ASSESSMENTS, 31 DECEMBER 1969

Property Listings		Property Assessment Values: Categories	Total Assessed Value		Total Tax Payable		Applicable Tax Rate(%)
Number	%		Q(000)	%	Q(000)	%	
9,767	4.0	Q20,000 and above	Q698,140	58.0	Q4,189	72.2	0.6
100,667	40.9	Q1,000 to Q20,000	Q437,604	36.4	Q1,413	24.4	0.3
135,710	55.1	Q100 to Q1,000	Q37,131	5.6	201	3.4	0.3 (Theoret. aver.)
246,144	100.0		Q1,232,875	100.0	Q5,803	100.0	0.5 (Actual aver.)
			Q4,000,000[a]		Q4,700 (Actual collected)		0.1

NOTE: One owner may have more than one property listing; thus, table understates concentration.

[a]Hinrichs's estimated market value.

SOURCE: Statistical tables, Sección de Matrícula y Cadastro Fisca, Dirección General de Rentas, Guatemala.

than 4.6 percent a year (see Table 5). This revenue growth will be about one percentage point higher than the 3.6 percent annual growth rate that would have been experienced in 1961-68 without tax rate increases and structural changes. This ex ante, or automatic, growth rate will be higher because of the shift in the composition of the tax structure toward more income-elastic tax sources. This revenue growth rate is also premised on a Gross Domestic Product growth rate about one percentage point higher than experienced in the last decade. However, the revenue growth rate of 4.6 percent will still fall short of both the 6 percent GDP growth rate of the National Development Plan and the 8.5 percent cur-

TABLE 4

THE LONG-RUN FISCAL CRISIS, 1970-76 (MILLIONS OF QUETZALES)

	1969	1970	1971	1972	1973	1974	1975	1976
Central government current revenue	150	160	168	175	184	191	200	210
Current expenditures	129	137	152	163	177	191	206	223
Current A/C surplus	21	23	16	12	7	0	− 6	−13
Savings from rest of public sector	7	7	11	12	13	12	13	12
Total public sector savings	28	30	27	24	20	12	7	− 1
Capital receipts	4	4	3	3	4	4	4	4
Investment expenditures	45	57	74	80	89	93	93	95
Overall deficit (−)	−14	−22	−45	−53	−66	−77	−82	−92

NOTE: Totals may not add due to rounding.
SOURCE: *Current Economic Position and Prospects of Guatemala,* International Bank for Reconstruction and Development Report No. CA-3a, Central America and Caribbean Department, 17 December 1970; hereafter referred to as IBRD Report.

rent expenditure growth rate (which is also one percentage point higher than its 1965-69 rate). Thus, new measures will have to be forthcoming if the current and capital expenditure programs are to attain adequate domestic and foreign financing. In the past, such fiscal crises were resolved only at the cost of significant shortfalls in expenditure programs below budgeted levels, frequent and often traumatic increases in tax rates, and in the longer-term stagnation of the investment program (1965-69). The new government now has the opportunity to prevent future fiscal crises by restructuring its tax system to make it more income-elastic and to improve its contribution toward other national objectives, such as more efficient resource allocation, economic and social development, wider sharing of the gains from economic growth, and an improved balance of payments. Alternatives for this restructuring will be discussed in a later section of this paper. It is necessary first to consider the possibilities or capacity for increased government revenues.

Fiscal Capacity

An estimate of Guatemala's fiscal capacity can be made on both a macro and micro basis. The former looks at determinants of tax capacity as related to such factors as GDP, "openness" (the ratio of imports and/or exports to GDP), value-added in manufacturing, income distribution, or any other determinant found significant in international comparisons.[3] The second approach examines various potential tax bases, both their size and growth, and present tax rates applied to them as a means of determining what potential yields might be obtained with tax rate levels achieved on such bases in comparable countries.[4] This second approach

TABLE 5

CHANGE IN ELASTICITY OF REVENUE SYSTEM OF 1970s COMPARED TO 1960s

| | 1961-68 | | % of Revenue System | | 1970-76 |
Income-elastic taxes	Aver. Annual Growth Rate[a] (%)	Elasticity (re GDP)[a]	1961	1970	Est. Growth Rate (%)
Income taxes	5.8	1.04	8.2	11.2	6.4
Property taxes	10.9	2.00	2.3	4.4	9.4
Stamp taxes	8.53	1.55	6.6	21.2	7.0
Averages, or total elasticity of taxes	9.0	1.5	17.1	36.8	7.1
Inelastic revenue sources	2.3	.42	82.9	63.2	3.2
Overall revenue system	3.6	0.33	100.0	100.0	4.6

[a]Excluding effect of tax rate changes.
SOURCE: First two columns, Consejo Nacional de Planificación Económica, Government of Guatemala, *National Development Plan, 1971-75* (Guatemala City, 1970), as corrected by IBRD Report.

has the further advantage of suggesting alternative tax strategies to follow, or at least where the most untapped revenue sources might be located.

On a *macro* basis, Guatemala's bottom ranking among eleven middle-income countries in Latin America as to its tax ratio (taxes as percent of GDP) at least suggests that a greater tax effort is possible despite all the difficulties and limitations of international comparison (see Table 2). Indeed, among seventy-two countries studied by the International Monetary Fund, Guatemala's tax ratio (9.3 percent as the 1963-65 average) was in sixty-ninth place.[5] If the comparison of tax effort is made on the

3. See Hinrichs, *General Theory*; Jorgen R. Lotz and Elliott R. Morss, "Measuring Tax Effort in Developing Countries," *IMF Staff Papers* 14, no. 3 (November 1967); and Best, "Determinants of Tax Performance."

4. See Hinrichs, *General Theory*; Jonathan Levin, "The Effects of Economic Development on the Base of a Sales Tax," *IMF Staff Papers* (March 1968); and Best, "Determinants of Tax Performance."

5. See Lotz and Morss, "Measuring Tax Effort," p. 479.

sole basis of per capita income, Guatemala would finish even worse, seventy-first out of seventy-two; the same result would hold true if openness were added to the determining variables.[6] These ordinal rankings suggest that Guatemala's tax effort is exceptionally low.[7] The methodology used in these studies may also provide a range of "normal" tax effort performances by countries with similar tax-determining characteristics: the Hinrichs "rule of thumb" for low-income countries would suggest an approximate 13 percent ratio of current revenues of the public sector to GDP for 1969 (within a range of 10-16 percent), compared to Guatemala's 11.6 percent performance for 1969. (Thus, Guatemala would be in the predictable range but on the low side.)[8] The Lotz-Morss formulation would estimate an expected 16.1 percent performance on the basis of per capita income alone and a 15.4 percent performance using both per capita income and "openness," compared to a "tax effort" (excluding nontax current revenue sources) of about 10 percent for the public sector.[9] Finally, the formulation by Michael Best would yield 13.2 percent for "tax effort" using openness and the manufacturing share of GDP, or 14.3 percent using per capita income only.[10] Thus, from all these broad macro tests Guatemala would have the fiscal capacity to in-

6. Ibid., p. 487.

7. These rankings should not be taken to mean that simply increasing taxation is necessarily associated with the rate of economic development (note Mexico), but they are suggestive of what fiscal capacity may exist that could be applied to development purposes.

8. See Hinrichs, *General Theory*; the 11.6 percent current revenue ratio may be overstated for Guatemala to the extent that cash flows of public enterprises are included rather than net earnings; but this is offset by the noninclusion of public revenues involved in the indigenous Indian sector. However, even an optimistic estimate here would not increase total public sector revenues by more than one percentage point; see Manning Nash, "Capital, Saving and Credit in a Guatemalan and a Mexican Indian Peasant Society," in Raymond Firth and B. S. Yamey, eds., *Capital, Saving and Credit in Peasant Societies* (Chicago: Aldine Publishing Co., 1964); and Melville J. Herskovits, *Economic Anthropology* (New York: Norton, 1940). Thus, even if local indigenous public revenues accounted for 10 percent of income for 2 million Indians earning Q100 per year, the result would only be Q20 million, or just a little more than 1 percent of GDP.

9. See Lotz and Morss, "Measuring Tax Effort"; applying their 1963-65 computed equations to 1969 data: $T/Y = 13.48 + 0.0081$ (per capita income) and $T/Y = 10.47 + 0.0081$ (per capita income) $+ 0.0790$ (imports plus exports/GDP).

10. See Best, "Determinants of Tax Performance"; applying his 1967 regressions to 1969 data: $T/Y = 5.51125 + 0.1165$ (imports plus exports/GDP) $+ 0.30346$ (manufacturing share of GDP) for countries with per capita incomes below $300 and $T/Y = 8.53295 + 0.01732$ (per capita income) for countries between $300 and $750 per capita income. Both tests were used, as there is some question (see Cohen, "Economic Development of Guatemala") as to the possible overstatement of the Guatemalan per capita income (1969 official estimate used here is $336) by as much as 20 percent. However, even using a lower per capita income figure for the Lotz-Morss and Best tests would not lower the predicted fiscal capacity by more than one percentage point; for the Hinrichs test, per capita income is not used, but instead the "rule of thumb" (5 percent plus half the "openness" ratio [defined as imports/GDP] for low income countries [$300 and below]).

crease its tax effort by at least the 2-3 percentage points envisaged in the coming fiscal gap of Q40-60 million.

On a macro basis, analysis of past revenue trends suggests the salient reasons for Guatemala's "underachievement" of its fiscal potential: (a) even though foreign trade has been a large and rapidly growing sector during the past decade, internal political pressures (reduction in coffee export tax rates, increase in import tax exemptions under fiscal incentives) have combined with the special external political alignment within the CACM (elimination of tariffs on most intraregional trade) to reduce government revenues by about the two-percentage-point shortfall from what might be expected under the Hinrichs "rule of thumb";[11] (b) the failure to shift more rapidly to a higher level of internal indirect taxation (excises, sales tax), as a substitute for the stagnating revenues from foreign trade, probably cost another percentage point of GDP for the public sector;[12] and (c) if the highly uneven income distribution is added as a tax ratio determinant increasing fiscal capacity without sacrificing consumption needs of the broad majority, the failure to generate significant revenues from progressive income, property, and/or net wealth taxes probably cost another two percentage points from public sector revenues.[13] If all of these failures had been avoided, the tax ratio in 1969 would have been closer to 15 percent rather than its actual 10 percent.

In more operational terms, filling a fiscal gap of Q40-60 million during the 1971-76 period means, for public sector current revenues, finding the capacity to increase the revenue ratio by only about 2-3 percentage points (to a level of 13.7 percent of GDP) over the automatic revenue growth level, which would lower the tax ratio from 11.6 percent in 1969 to 11.1 percent in 1976 owing to revenue inelasticity with respect to income growth. For the central government, this means a tax increase of only a little more than one percentage point over the current ratio. (The National Development Plan would increase the tax ratio of the central government from the 8.16 percent level of 1969 to 9.06 percent by 1975.) This implies a growth rate for central government revenues of only about

11. Reduced coffee export tax rates cost one-half percentage point; import tax exemptions cost one percentage point; and the impact of the CACM on customs duty revenues costs one-half percentage point if adjustment is made for the higher CACM tariffs on nonregional trade and the trade diversion to CACM import sources because of tariff reductions and eliminations.

12. The failure here includes the relative stagnation in tax revenues from the manufacturing-commercial-urban sector via either company income taxes or excises which could not always be shifted forward; had company income taxes grown at the same rate as this sector during the past decade, the tax ratio would have gained one percentage point. Here the explanation is also tied to generous income tax exemptions not compensated for by a shift to more effective internal indirect taxes.

13. Direct taxes for similar countries fall at least in the 3-4 percent of GDP range rather than in the 1-2 percent of GDP range experienced in Guatemala. See Hinrichs, *General Theory.*

10 percent, a growth rate achieved by many developing countries and a rate approximated by Guatemala during 1967-69. In terms of the required "marginal propensity to tax," the task for the public sector can be seen in a less optimistic light: the required marginal tax rate on increments to GDP during the 1971-76 period will be 17.6 percent. (Using 1970 as the base, GDP will increase by Q755.7 million; current revenue increments projected plus the fiscal gap by 1976 are Q132.9 million.) This marginal tax rate (or, more precisely, public sector marginal current revenue rate) compares to a 14.7 percent marginal rate in 1965-69. For the central government the marginal tax rate was 9.8 percent during 1961-69, but this must increase to 13.3 percent during 1971-76 if the central government intends to fill the fiscal gap by central government revenue measures. Without such measures, the projected central government marginal tax rate is only 6.6 percent (less than the *average* tax burden at present owing to the inelasticity of the tax system). Thus, in macro terms the true performance required by the central government is virtually to double the projected marginal tax rate during 1971-76. A look at the micro fiscal capacity side may indicate where such an increase is possible.

On a *micro* level of analysis one can examine the potential tax bases available, their growth, and potential yields of tax revenues both in relation to politically feasible tax rates and to the experience of other countries. This approach toward tax capacity analysis is somewhat new and innovative, but it can suggest more precisely what revenue instruments have been thus far "underutilized" as well as which sectors of the economy have been relatively "undertaxed."[14] The tax bases considered here are those for the personal income tax, business income tax, land tax, general sales tax, sumptuary sales (excises), and foreign trade taxes (imports and exports).[15]

This micro analysis of tax potential in Guatemala can be seen summarized in the following table comparing existing revenue yields, revenue potentials (estimated both by Hinrichs and Michael Best), and the absolute monetary difference between the existing and potential revenue yields.

Such a micro analysis can provide insights into tax strategy for the seventies: it should be clear that the range of "unused tax potential" of Q95-225 million provides an ample revenue source from which to fill the fiscal gap of Q40-60 million during the seventies. It also suggests that the area of most "unused potential" lies in the direct tax area: the potential for personal income taxation is at least five times greater than present

---

14. See Hinrichs, *General Theory*; Levin, "Effects of Economic Development"; and Best, "Determinants of Tax Performance."

15. This is much indebted to the Best analysis, "Determinants of Tax Performance."

TABLE 6

MICRO-ANALYSIS OF GUATEMALAN TAX POTENTIALS

Revenue Sources	Revenue as % of GDP (1969)	Potential Revenue as % of GDP (Hinrichs Est., 1970-76)	Difference between Potential and Present (Q Millions)	Potential Revenue as % of GDP (M. Best Estimate)
Central government				
Personal income tax	0.2	1.0+ +	Q15–20	7.0–9.0
Business income tax	0.8	2.0+	20–25	1.0–3.0
Property taxation	0.3	2.5–5.0	40–80	4.0–8.0
General sales (incl. stamp tax)	2.0	2.0+	0 to +	0.5–1.5
Excises	2.4	3.0+	10 to 10+	2.2–3.0
Foreign trade: imports	1.8	2.0+	0–5 ⎱	2.0–2.5
exports	0.4	1.0–2.0	10–30 ⎰	
Nontax Revenues	0.9	1.0+	0–5	No estimate
Total	8.6	14.5–18.0	Q95–165	16.7–27.0
Rest of public sector (approximate)				
Social security system	1.0	1.0–2.0+ +	0–20	No estimate
Municipalities	1.0	1.0–2.0	0–20	No estimate
Public enterprises and decentralized organizations	1.0	1.0–2.0	0–20	
Total	11.6	17.5–24.0+	Q95–225	

NOTE: Totals may not add due to rounding.
SOURCES: IBRD Report, and Michael H. Best, "Determinants of Tax Performance and Developing Countries: The Case of Guatemala" (Ph.D. diss., University of Oregon, August 1969).

yields;[16] the potential for business income taxation is at least double; the potential for property taxation is at least ten times greater; and the potential for export taxation may be double or triple existing yields.[17] Contrariwise, the potential for greater internal indirect and import taxation has been virtually exhausted. Thus, adoption of a general sales tax as a sub-

16. Although the Michael Best analysis conceives of a much greater potential for personal income taxation (7-9 percent of GDP), such a potential is highly theoretical, as no country at Guatemala's level of development (and income distribution) has even approached such a level from purely personal individual income taxation. Total income taxation levels greater than 1-2 percent of GDP have virtually always depended on the business income component. In addition, both political and administrative constraints would make a level above 1-2 percent of GDP, from personal income taxation, highly unrealistic.
17. Export taxation is here considered direct taxation, as the incidence of this tax in all probability cannot be shifted forward, given Guatemala's role as a price taker rather than a price maker in the international coffee market, nor can it very likely be shifted backwards, given virtually subsistence labor costs.

stitute for the stamp tax—however laudatory for other reasons—*cannot* be seen as a revenue panacea in terms of resource mobilization.

The future limits on extending indirect taxation are due to a number of reasons: the concentration of income and wealth into the hands of 5,000 or fewer upper-income recipients (0.1 percent of the population), the relatively small middle class (50,000 or fewer even qualify for income tax), and the generally small urban, industrialized, monetized sector above subsistence level which makes expenditures for other than food and housing (usually not touched by general taxation) or sumptuary items (either locally produced and difficult to tax or already subject to fairly high excise taxes).

This conclusion would seem to be contrary to general theoretic grounds that internal indirect taxation might be the most pragmatically accessible revenue source.[18] But this would be a misleading inference from the data: internal indirect taxation already has been the most successful revenue growth source for Guatemala, i.e., the potential already has been exploited (as expected).[19] During the sixties the falloff in foreign trade tax revenues (1961-69) from 3.7 percent of GDP to 2.2 percent, a loss of 1.5 percent, was primarily countered by increasing internal indirect taxation (which rose by two percentage points from 2.4 percent to 4.4 percent of GDP). On the other hand, direct taxes (income and property taxes) contributed less than one-half of one percentage point increase in GDP flowing to the public sector (rising from 0.85 percent in 1961 to 1.32 percent in 1969). Thus, Guatemala has now moved to the next stage of tax structure change in the course of economic development wherein direct taxes (including new social security taxes) may be expected to play a much more important role. This is especially true for Guatemala, given both the severe income distribution limits to mass spending power to purchase consumption goods and the limits to revising import taxation because of membership in the CACM.

THE EXPENDITURE STRUCTURE: "DEVELOPMENTAL EXPENDITURE" GROWTH

Since 1965 current expenditures have been growing at an annual rate of 7.5 percent (see Table 7), about one-fourth more rapidly than GDP growth (which was almost 6 percent per year during 1965-69). This has increased current expenditures of the central government from a level of 7.3 percent of GDP in 1965 to about 7.7 percent of GDP in 1969, still a comparatively modest level for a middle-income country. This income-

18. Hinrichs, *General Theory.*
19. Ibid.; internal indirect taxation is considered to be the historical substitute for the decline in importance of foreign trade taxation; only later in the development process do modern direct taxes become revenue sources of substantial magnitude.

TABLE 7

Central Expenditures: Central Government (Q Millions)

	1965	1966	1967	1968	1969	1965–69 Annual Growth Rates(%)	1970	1971	1972	1973	1974	1975	1976	1970–76 Annual Growth Rates(%)
Total current expenditures	97	109	118	119	129	7.5	137	152	163	177	191	206	223	8.5
Economic services	11	17	7	15	17	12.9	19	23	25	27	29	31	33	10.0
Agriculture	3	3	3	3	3	0.0	4	7	7	8	8	8	8	10.4
Transport	3	8	8	7	8	25.1	8	9	10	10	11	12	13	8.6
Communications	4	4	4	4	4	0.0	5	5	6	6	7	8	8	10.1
Other	2	2	2	2	2	—	2	3	3	3	3	4	4	11.6
Social services	42	45	50	51	58	8.2	62	69	76	85	96	106	120	11.6
Education	22	23	26	27	29	7.5	31	34	38	43	50	57	64	12.6
Health	11	12	13	14	17	11.9	19	23	26	29	33	36	42	14.3
Social welfare	8	7	8	8	7	—	8	8	8	8	8	8	9	—
Housing	1	—	—	—	—	—	—	—	—	—	—	—	—	—
Other	1	3	3	2	4	—	4	4	4	4	4	5	5	—
General services	44	47	50	52	54	5.1	55	60	62	64	67	69	70	4.0
General administration	17	18	17	18	19	3.0	20	21	22	23	24	25	26	5.0
Defense and police	21	21	25	24	24	4.5	25	25	25	25	25	25	25	0.0
Justice	2	3	3	3	3	7.2	3	4	4	4	4	4	4	—
Interest on public debt	5	6	7	8	8	12.5	8	10	11	12	13	14	15	—
Unclassified	—	—	1	1	1	—	1	1	1	1	1	1	1	—
Total current expenditures	97	109	118	119	129	7.5	137	152	163	177	191	206	223	8.5
"Developmental"	44	52	56	56	63	10.0	69	80	89	99	112	124	139	12.4
Economic services	11	17	17	15	17	12.9	19	23	25	27	29	31	33	10.0
Education	22	23	26	27	29	7.5	31	34	38	43	50	57	64	12.6
Health	11	12	13	14	17	11.9	19	23	26	29	33	36	42	14.3
Welfare, general, other	54	57	62	63	66	5.5	68	73	75	78	81	83	85	3.8
Investment expenditure	35	27	30	26	30	-3.3	33	58	63	69	71	72	71	13.7
Total current developmental and investment expenditure	79	79	86	82	93	4.2	102	138	152	168	183	196	210	12.8

Note: Growth rates based on unrounded numbers; dash indicates negative or zero or irrelevant growth rate.
Source: IBRD Report.

elastic growth rate for current expenditures was achieved during this period despite a virtual halt during the fiscal retrenchment of 1968 when salaries of government employees earning Q300-500 a month were cut by 5 percent and those earning above Q500 a month by 10 percent. However, after the 1968 halt current expenditures have returned to a 7-8 percent growth path (1969 actual, 1970 budget).

A system of limited program budgeting was introduced in 1965, allowing for a greater focus on functional budget classifications. Under this system, the ministry of finance has greater control over public expenditures than before. Disbursements are centralized in the treasury with quarterly reviews of expenditure authorizations and central control over the switching of funds among agencies or between programs within any agency. However, no long-term series are available for analysis of salary and wage payments within the central government for the roughly 48,000 regular employees, an equal number of part-time, or contract, workers (mostly in public works), and an approximate 12,000 members of the military. Legislation has been under consideration for the past few years to provide semiautomatic salary increments to civil servants, partly related to productivity and partly in response to growing labor unrest in the public sector.

Although the overall 7.5 percent growth rate of current expenditures for 1965-69 was greater than the growth rate of GDP, the composition of this expenditure growth has been erratic. During this period, there was virtually no growth in expenditures for agriculture, communications, and social welfare (see Table 7). Even in transport, the 25 percent annual growth rate for the period is misleading, as it reflects a doubling of expenditures between 1965 and 1966 but no growth thereafter. Thus, omitting the one-year jump in transport expenditures, the growth rate of current expenditures for economic services (agriculture, transport, communications, and others) would not have been the 12.9 percent shown in Table 7 but only 6 percent. In the social service area, the overall growth rate of 8.2 percent better reflects the growing activity in both its major components, education (7.5 percent) and health (11.9 percent). General services have been growing at a much more modest level of 5.1 percent, with general administration expenditures just matching the population growth rate (3 percent) but with defense expenditures growing rapidly in 1967 to produce a 4.5 percent growth rate for the period. However, as defense expenditures have been on a plateau since 1967 and with the general elimination of violence in rural areas, more of these outlays might be directed toward developmental civic actions, which were successful in the mid-sixties, as well as more education and training programs.

The forecast of current expenditures (and the growing fiscal gap) for 1970-76 is based significantly on the combined growth of investment expenditures (13.7 percent) and developmental current expenditures (12.4 percent) at rates roughly double the projected 6.1 percent growth rate of GDP. Indeed, the forecast for the developmental current expenditures is tied to both the current expenditure component (economic services) of investment programs in agriculture, transport, and communications and to the social development effort to increase the quality of education and health services. In addition, the 1970-76 forecast assumes a slower-than-GDP growth rate for general services of 4 percent. It is assumed that the level of defense expenditures will remain on its relatively high-level plateau, but that general administration costs will rise at a 5 percent rate (compared to a 3 percent rate for 1965-69) as salary levels may be increased in respect to pending legislation for automatic increases and as the overall task of administration grows along with a growing public sector. A larger public debt with higher levels of interest rates in the seventies is another growth factor. However, the overall growth rate of 8.5 percent forecast for current expenditures during 1970-76 is still not much above the 7.5 percent growth rate achieved in 1965-69. Given both a higher projected GDP growth rate for the 1970-76 period and a greater tax effort as previously outlined, such an overall growth rate would appear to be feasible. The distinctive feature will be the shift in composition of current expenditures toward the development effort (economic services, education, and health) that is needed to match the investment program and to provide long-run social development with economic growth.

By 1976 such a program will expand the share of total GDP devoted to government current expenditures to 8.8 percent compared to 7.7 percent in 1969, a shift of only about one percentage point of GDP over a six-year period. The combined growth of both current and investment expenditures will require a two-percentage-point shift of GDP into public sector activities (9.5 percent of GDP in 1969 compared to a projected 11.6 percent share in 1976). The importance of this shift for development is highlighted by the nearly three-percentage-point shift of GDP into "developmental expenditures" (both current and investment): 5.5 percent of GDP in 1969 contrasted to 8.3 percent projected for 1976. This is the crux of the projected development effort.

Tax Strategies for Development: Issues and Alternatives within a Policy Matrix

Fiscal incentives within the Central American Common Market.—Since 1947 Guatemala has maintained a program of generous investment incentives for both new desirable industries and expansion of existing ones. In addition to Guatemala's more well-known 1959 industrial development incentive statute, adopted in anticipation of the Central American Agreement on Fiscal Incentives for Industrial Development (discussed in 1957, adopted in 1962, ratified in 1969, and finally effective in 1970), Guatemala provides many nonindustrial incentives for agrarian development, tourism, and construction, plus exemptions and incentives under the income tax. The long-awaited Central American Agreement on Fiscal Incentives for Industrial Development has harmonized incentives among the member states but is limited to the industrial area. Individual countries may still provide different incentives elsewhere in the economy. For Group A new industries, the industrial incentives provide 100 percent exemption (a) on import duties for machinery (ten years), raw materials and semifinished products (five years, 80 percent for next three years, 50 percent for next two years), and fuels other than gasoline (five years); (b) on income taxes (eight years); and (c) on taxes on assets and net worth (ten years, but Guatemala has no net worth taxes). (Group A includes producers of raw materials and capital goods, and consumer and semi-finished-goods producers using half of their material inputs from CACM sources.) For existing industries, the import tax exemption is for only six years and limited to machinery; the income tax exemption is for only two years, and the net worth and asset tax exemption is for four years.[20] The CACM incentives agreement is slightly less generous than Guatemala's 1959 statute for raw materials, semifinished products, and fuels (except gasoline), which allowed full ten-year exemptions; but the CACM agreement is somewhat more generous on exemption of income taxes (providing six, eight, or ten years depending on category) than the Guatemalan 1959 statute, which provided 100 percent exemption for the first five years, 50 percent for the second five years, for new industries. However, for existing industries the income tax exemption is only zero, two, or four years depending on category, compared to Guatemala's 50 percent exemption for five years.

Overall, there should be no significant difference between the two incentive systems, especially since the Guatemalan 1959 statute was designed to parallel the eventual CACM agreement; if anything, the tightening of the liberality of the import tax incentives (for raw materials, semifinished products, and fuels) would probably outweigh the loss in revenue from income taxes because the income tax system is less important for revenue purposes and has alternative incentives and exemptions that would reduce company income taxes without the windfall from the CACM agreement. Guatemala had already in 1964 expanded its 1959 statute to allow further exemptions on the import of raw materials and semifinished goods if the local producer could show that similar exemptions within the CACM were placing the local producer at a competitive disadvantage.

The cost of the fiscal incentives has been considerable: the revenue losses (tax exonerations) from import duties on industrial enterprises

20. See Watkin, *Tax Harmonization*, and Gillim, *Fiscal Aspects of the CACM*.

have grown from Q3.75 million in 1962 to Q14.7 million in 1968, or from about 15 percent of import tax revenues to more than half of such revenues (which were Q26.1 million in 1968). (Other exonerations for public, especially military, and nonprofit groups raise the exemption level by about another Q9 million, or totaling about four-fifths of all import duties in 1968.) The revenue loss from the income tax exemption is more difficult to measure, but since the value-added in the industrial sector doubled between 1965 and 1969 while company tax revenues remained constant (except for the 10 percent surcharge levied in 1967) at about Q13 million during this period, one might estimate at least about Q10 million in loss revenues because of income tax exemptions. This also roughly parallels the approximate Q1 million payment each year by exempt firms as the 10 percent (of tax exonerations) contributions they are obliged to make to the Industrial Development Bank capitalization fund (adopted in 1964 to coincide with a further expansion of tax incentives to small handicraft producers and other industrial enterprises not enjoying benefits under the law but obtaining at least half their raw materials from Central America). Thus, the total cost of fiscal incentives in 1970 may well have exceeded Q20-25 million.

The issues here are: the degree to which the costs, enumerated above, are justified by the benefits; and, as a tax strategy instrument, the degree to which these incentives, which might be justifiable for one country in competition with neighboring ones, may now be less important in attracting new investment when there is no comparative advantage (under tax laws) for a group of countries within a common market. In the first instance, increases in investment (both foreign and domestic) in favored sectors (primarily industrial), which are the prime objective of Guatemalan tax incentives, have been much more closely related to the pattern of Guatemalan growth analyzed by several economic models of the Guatemalan growth process: increases in exports lead to GNP, investment, and import booms.[21] Thus, given this pattern of growth for an export-led economy, the strategic place to key incentives into the growth pattern would be export-oriented firms.[22] During the total period of fiscal incentives (1947-70, but chiefly 1959-70), the variations in private investment appear to be a function of other factors (export booms, the development of CACM, and the Guatemalan political climate) rather than from the long-time existence of fiscal incentives. The recent surge in private investment (1967-70) cannot be directly related to the fiscal incentives as such, which have been in existence in their present form for more than a decade.

21. See Cohen, "Economic Development of Guatemala," and Erik Thorbecke, *Guatemala's Economic Development* (Ames, Iowa: Iowa State University Press, 1970).
22. See Richard M. Bird, *Taxation and Development: Lessons from Colombian Experience* (Cambridge, Mass.: Harvard University Press, 1970).

The real test of the fiscal incentive program is the degree to which the Q20-25 million in revenues now foregone annually in the incentive program would have a higher marginal use in other areas: government current expenditures (especially education) or capital expenditures (such as industrial infrastructure) or, if directed to the private sector, in selective loans to new enterprises or in reduced taxes on other activities. If the goal is GNP growth, the Q20-25 million annual "tax expenditure" in the incentive program might be more productive elsewhere, such as in tourism or activities directly related to export growth. Another test would be to measure the incentive program funds (which flow to all qualifying enterprises regardless if the incentive itself were the only marginal factor in the determination of investment decisions) against the marginal increase in investment (although value-added, gross output, or exports might be a better index). The increase in new private fixed investment in all sectors has been ranging between or below Q15-30 million (about equal to the selective Q20-25 million cost of the incentive program). It is highly unlikely that the incentive program was the critical factor for all of this new investment. The extensive literature in this area[23] suggests that such incentives account for only a minor part of new investment. Therefore, on this basis the "cost" of the program clearly overshadows its benefits.

The second critical issue is the degree to which *conditions* have changed by 1970 with a fairly successful functioning CACM, as contrasted to the earlier competitive conditions of the 1950s. With a now-unified set of fiscal incentives, there is no need for intercountry rivalry as to fiscal incentives. With a uniform higher tariff wall and with current and prospective healthy economic growth rates, the CACM might well benefit from more investment and growth by using its "losses" through the fiscal incentive program elsewhere: export and/or tourism promotion, regional infrastructure, regional or national development banks, etc. With no need to compete with its neighbors in offering competitive tax incentive packages, Guatemala could well use these "lost" funds elsewhere, such as to ameliorate the growing fiscal gap and *to insure a sufficient flow of public* as well as private investment funds. Of course, to revise the CACM fiscal incentives programs requires regional action, but as the first country to deposit ratification of the 1962 CACM fiscal incentives agreements, Guatemala might well take a leadership role in reducing the level of fiscal incentives now available in the CACM or in devising substitute measures (such as expanding the 10 percent con-

23. See Joel Clark, "Tax Incentives in Central American Development," in *Economic Development and Cultural Change*, 1971; Bird, *Taxation and Development*; and especially Jack Heller and Kenneth Kauffman, *Tax Incentives for Industry in Less Developed Countries* (Cambridge, Mass.: Harvard Law School International Tax Program, 1963).

tributions to an industrial development bank) to recoup the sizable revenue losses. One possible course of action—to sidestep the legalities of concessions already given—might be to require firms within the CACM to contribute a share (10-50 percent) of their tax exonerations to either national or *regional* industrial development banks. (A regional industrial development bank might be a "private sector" counterpart to the regional development bank concerned with public investment and might attract additional funds from the DFC of the World Bank Group.) As with the European Common Market (EEC), it was the common tariff wall and prospects for regional growth which prompted sizable new investment, not an overgenerous set of fiscal incentives which curtailed the public sector's role in providing needed infrastructure (both human and capital) for such expanded investment.

Moving toward an optimal internal indirect tax system.—The Guatemalan Development Plan, as well as other sources such as SIECA, the permanent Secretariat for the Economic Integration of Central America, suggests the prime source of tax reform (at least in terms of revenue) should be a shift from the stamp tax to a general sales tax. This presumably would be a single-stage levy focused for administrative reasons on a few thousand wholesalers or large retailers, with small retailers exempt or "covered" by their purchases from the large wholesalers or importers, as in Honduras. Public finance specialists generally favor such a "single-levy" (really a pseudo single-levy because of the wholesale-retail split) tax to the multiple-stage turnover-type tax such as the stamp tax in Guatemala. The basis of this preference is generally twofold: the single-stage tax (or a value-added tax at all stages) would be "neutral" in effect among products and industries irrespective of the number of stages of production through which the product must pass; thus it is argued that resource allocation would be more efficient. Secondly, such a tax is more certain and visible, whereas the "cascading," or pyramiding, effects of turnover taxes (which result in taxes on earlier tax rounds) will obscure the actual tax rate on a commodity by the time it reaches the retail stage. However, given the existing imperfections in the market structure and prices in Guatemala and the divergence between social and private costs and benefits, the adoption of a "neutral" tax might not have all the advantages claimed for it. But, above all, given much higher-ranking priorities (resource mobilization, economic growth, balance of payments, and improved income distribution), any minor improvements in relative pricing achieved by a shift to a general sales tax should not be high on the agenda for tax reform.

Guatemala already has the highest percentage (54 percent)[24] of its tax revenues coming from internal indirect taxes compared with all other

24. But 46 percent if adjustment is made for the shift to local oil refining and excise taxation in 1963-64.

countries in Central America, which generate only about one-fifth to one-third of their tax revenues from this source. As discussed earlier, Guatemala has primarily passed through its stage of rapid revenue growth from internal indirect taxation as a replacement for foreign trade tax revenues. Thus, any further changes in the internal indirect tax system should be seen not in terms of another burst of revenue growth based on untaxed potential, but rather in using scarce political and administrative resources (which would be required in shifting to a general sales tax) for the purpose of marginal improvements in resource allocation without any great hope for achieving other (higher-ranked) goals of revenue growth, income distribution, economic growth, balance of payments, and so on. Even though such a move to a general single-stage or value-added levy may be desirable in the abstract, it should not now be used as a substitute for real action needed elsewhere, chiefly in the areas of personal and especially corporate income taxation, property taxation, and export taxation.

Indeed, there are even a few "hidden" virtues for the existing stamp tax: (a) even though the private sector complains of their "nuisance," this may also suggest that the tax works effectively in mobilizing revenue, as supported by both the size and growth of their revenues; (b) the combination of a low rate (1 1/2 percent) and a broad base (Q2,000 million) is superior for both reducing disincentive effects and tax evasion than a higher rate (3-10 percent) single-stage levy on a smaller base (Q300-500 million); (c) the stamp tax covers exports and capital transactions which might be excluded under a retail sales tax and thus provides a "tax break" to sectors already "undertaxed"; (d) since the stamp tax falls on virtually all stages of production, some of it may be absorbed out of the profits of businesses, as some studies have indicated[25]—thereby applying some tax to "undertaxed" businesses, especially those with fiscal exemptions—whereas the general retail sales tax would be almost totally shifted forward to higher consumer prices; and (e) in a politically uncertain climate there may be some virtue to sticking with an "old" tax where the incidence has already "settled" and adjustments have already taken place rather than risk the political and administrative uncertainties of moving to a new system when so little extra revenue potential is involved.

In short, the move toward improving the internal indirect tax system should be seen as a low-ranking priority for tax reform. Simply because Colombia, Honduras, and Nicaragua have moved toward such reform does not make a compelling rationale for Guatemala—with differing cir-

---

25. In both Pakistan and Nigeria, studies have indicated that, given imperfect market structures, indirect taxes on earlier stages of production are partly absorbed out of company oligopolistic profits; see Hinrichs, *General Theory*.

cumstances—to follow the same bandwagon and thus divert energies away from much more needed reforms.

Trade-offs and complementarities among objectives for tax policy.— Guatemala is fortunate in that much of a strategy for tax reform in the 1970s involves few difficult "trade-offs" (that is, giving up some of a desirable objective in order to achieve more of another desirable objective) and involves a number of propitious "complementarities" (here defined as the achievement of more than one objective by use of one policy instrument and/or the achievement of one objective by the simultaneous use of more than one policy instrument). Thus, in the direct tax area, substantially higher property taxation, as a tax on capital, might normally involve the "trade-off" of reducing new investment and thereby output. In the Guatemalan case, *higher property taxation* might well achieve greater output by putting more of the unused land into productive uses, by forcing some land redistribution into the hands of those with greater incentive to produce, and/or improving the productivity of existing holdings by increasing the cost of holding idle land for speculative purposes or in submarginal uses (awaiting more favorable opportunities since the "cost of waiting" is so low).[26] Thus, higher property taxation would not only achieve goals of resource mobilization and equity (income redistribution), but could also increase economic growth.

Higher export taxation on coffee not only would have sizable equity benefits (in taxing a "windfall surplus" accruing to a small group of high-income individuals) but also would have no short-run (or likely serious long-run) effects on output and exports. Indeed, if the "income effect" is stronger than the "substitution effect" (that is, if the attempt to preserve before-tax income levels is stronger than any disincentive from a lower per unit after-tax profit), there might even be an attempt to increase gross output and exports. For the longer run, if diversification of agricultural output away from the coffee sector is desired, such a tax could fulfill that purpose (if indeed the long-run response is significant in reducing new investment in the coffee sector).

Income redistribution, as an ultimate objective, may be debated as a goal in and of itself, at least the degree of redistribution. However, even though both Guatemala[27] and the IBRD[28] have shown official sympathy for this goal, there are important complementary objectives that can be

26. See Best, "Determinants of Tax Performance"; Adams, *Crucifixion of Power*; and OAS, *Tax Systems.*

27. As a signatory of the *Declaration to the Peoples of America* (Punta del Este, Alliance for Progress), Guatemala accepted as one of its goals: "To reform tax laws, demanding more from those who have the most, to punish tax evasion severely, and to redistribute the national income in order to benefit those who are most in need. . . ."

28. Robert S. McNamara, address to the Columbia University Conference on International Economic Development (New York, February 20, 1970).

achieved by income redistribution through both the tax and expenditure sides of fiscal operations.[29] Income redistribution might favor the objectives of (a) economic growth and fuller resource use (in higher property taxation); and (b) a better balance of payments (by reducing foreign spending, foreign traveling, and foreign investing by upper-income groups—above all, given a much higher marginal propensity to import on the part of the upper-income groups, this might reduce consumption imports); and (c) shifting more total resources from consumption to saving and investment—assuming tax revenues went into public saving and investment, the reduction in private saving and consumption would very likely lead to an overall saving increase, especially in Guatemala's case, where the upper-income groups have a record of low (5 percent)[30] propensities to save *domestically* with higher propensities to consume or save abroad. In addition, income redistribution might well provide a larger mass or middle-class consumer base, which would not only encourage greater industrialization and employment but also increase the revenue potential from the (indirect) consumption tax base.

Timing and tactics of tax strategy within political and administrative constraints.—Timing is important both for the imposition of tax reforms and the sequence in which they are carried out. As discussed earlier, any major tax reforms would have to be completed fairly early in the four-year tenure of the present government; in most successful instances of tax reform, it is the early years in which reforms have been initiated rather than in periods preceding new elections. This is especially important in the Guatemalan case, for the next elections coincide with the period when public sector savings vanish and when either current expenditures and investment plans might be forced to a halt or ad hoc short-term revenue measures will be needed (reminiscent of the 1967-68 period). But the sequence of reforms is also important: it is far more efficient (from both a political and administrative point of view) to push administrative improvements first, before tax rates are increased. Likewise, for the property tax and income tax, it is much more effective to expand the tax base (especially to increase assessment values, either by some "automatic" escalator or by rapid reassessment of high-value properties) before increasing tax rates. This course of action usually meets much less resistance from taxpayers, who may accept a higher tax base (assessment) at abnormally low rates, but then are "frozen into" recorded tax bases when tax rates go up and they find themselves stuck with higher tax bases as well (bases which would be rigid downward in most cases). Thus, the dilemma here is that delay in pushing administrative

29. See Bird, *Taxation and Development,* for his strong emphasis on the balance-of-payments objectives aided by income redistribution (via progressive income taxation).

30. Cohen, "Economic Development of Guatemala."

improvements will preclude most legal reforms later. If vigorous tax collection procedures are not successful during 1970-71, then immediate legal reforms (rate increases) should be ready to be put into effect to generate additional revenues in 1972. By 1973 it would probably be too late.

Administrative constraints suggest further strategic elements for Guatemalan tax reform. Thus, usual suggestions for Guatemalan tax reform[31] advocate expanding the tax base for agricultural, income, and property taxation. It is asserted that the personal income tax exemption level is too high (Q3,200 for a family of four) and the agricultural tax exemption level (Q15,000) excludes most farmers. The major reassessment effort for the property tax has focused on the number of assessable plots (most small) with the major reform proposal being to double the 0.3 percent property tax rate on properties under Q20,000 to achieve a proportional rate structure. However, given administrative constraints (few effective tax assessors, auditors, and collectors), existing massive tax evasion, and the severely unequal income distribution, such a course of widening the property tax base would be unwise: it focuses on the wrong objectives, it would be politically uncertain, and it would be administratively difficult, if not impossible.

An opposite strategy would make more sense: concentrate limited administrative capacity where the potential revenue is located and where the fiscal objectives are most important. Instead of broadening the nearly 50,000 tax filers under the income tax, given less than two dozen active income tax auditors[32] it would be far more efficient to concentrate audits and collection on the few thousand who have the bulk of the taxable income and pay most of the tax. Likewise, it would be far better to exempt or ignore the 55 percent of property parcels (135,710 parcels) valued at under Q1,000, which represent less than 6 percent of total assessed value, and concentrate (both by reassessments and tax increases) on the 4 percent of the parcels (9,767 parcels) which represent 58 percent of all value. Agriculture, especially coffee, is more effectively taxed under export and property taxation than by attempting to broaden the base and collect taxes under income taxes. With a benefit-cost ratio of at least 15-1, in terms of dollars collected from each dollar put into tax administration (auditing), far more revenue is generated by focusing on higher-income returns rather than by attempting to diffuse an already limited administrative capacity in an effort to cover a broader base. The lower-income farmers, workers, entrepreneurs, and property holders can be much more efficiently taxed, and in a politically safer fashion, through

31. National Development Plan, AID, U.S. Internal Revenue Service, Foreign Tax Assistance Program.
32. Income tax filing requirements for employees might be raised to about 23,000 from the present 21,800 level in order to reduce paperwork.

increased social security taxation (where visible benefits are earmarked to the taxpayer), export and import taxation, and consumption taxation.

An important *political constraint* is the government's desire not to increase tax *rates* but to achieve fiscal gains through administrative improvements only. This carries the danger that the first few years of the new administration may be limited to administrative improvements which, if unsuccessful in mobilizing sufficient revenues, would lead up to the dilemma, as in 1963-64, of being faced with an ominous fiscal gap and new elections. Furthermore, even if administrative improvements are enacted to reduce tax evasion by half in both the income and stamp tax areas, from 50 to 25 percent of the tax yield if there were no evasion— *a highly important effort, but also a highly uncertain one*—this would still cover only about half of the revenue increases required by the National Development Plan, 1971-75. The only way such a strategy might conceivably work would be to combine it with other reforms—even though these would not be officially "rate increases."

Such a package would require (a) rapid increases in property tax assessments; if these were automatically or expeditiously doubled or trebled to reach market value, the revenue gain might be Q5-10 million coupled with exempting properties below Q1,000 in value; (b) an increase in "effective" company income taxation requiring, say, 20 percent of tax exonerations granted under the fiscal incentives program (compared with the current 10 percent) to be used as additional capital inputs into the Industrial Development Bank; this would yield about Q1 million or more; (c) a special contribution by coffee exporters into a stabilization fund, development bank, or diversification fund based on some percent of the export proceeds over domestic cost plus "normal profit," perhaps yielding Q5-10 million; (d) an expansion of the social security system into the pension area, which might generate savings in the early years of Q5-15 million based on a 1-2 percent payroll tax on employees (who might be compensated by *higher* exemption limits under the income tax, which would lose insignificant revenue) and a 2-4 percent payroll tax paid by employers (who might not be able to shift the tax, thus letting it serve as another substitute for effective company income taxation, especially under the fiscal incentive program); (e) encouraging an expansion of municipal revenues (increasing national limits on their use of the property tax or tying their property taxes to the more efficient national assessment base); and (f) increasing fees and prices of public enterprises (including auto license, passport, and exit fees), which would be consistent with the commitment not to increase "taxes," perhaps generating another Q5-10 million. This package might thus total as much as Q21-46 million as a supplement to—and fallback position for—the administrative improvements, which the Government

Plan estimates at best will yield about Q25 million by 1975—only half the fiscal resources needed by then to prevent a gap.

Another *political constraint* is the importance of the coffee growers in Guatemalan political life. Political realities indicate that the coffee growers may easily block any increased taxes on their present and future "boom," given high coffee prices in the early seventies; they might even succeed in reducing existing levies on coffee exports (coffee export taxes will grow from Q6 million in 1969 to about Q9 million during the early seventies). The argument is made by the coffee growers that they should not be "discriminated against" by suffering a special export tax. They would be correct if there were an effective way to tax their true wealth and income in a nondiscriminatory fashion via effective property, income, and net wealth taxation. However, in a "second-best" world, no other way now exists. Economic, political, and administrative realities are such that the income tax would not be an effective substitute. All of agriculture pays less than Q1 million in income tax revenues, or 7 percent of total income tax collections; likewise, the present export tax credit against income taxes payable is only used to offset about Q1.5 million in income taxes otherwise payable, allowing other millions of potential credits to remain unused because no tax would be due anyway. Thus, eliminating the export tax on coffee might only increase taxes on the coffee export sector from less than Q1 million to Q2-3 million at most, a far cry from the export tax levies of Q6-9 million (which themselves are among the lowest in the world, less than 10 percent of total export proceeds, and even low by Guatemalan standards in the fifties). Likewise, even increasing property taxes to an effective 1 percent tax rate (nearly ten times the present effective rate) would raise at best only Q2-3 million in tax revenue.[33]

Thus, it would be totally unrealistic to expect the existing income and property taxes to be a substitute for the present coffee export tax. Other countries have found it both necessary and legitimate to tax the windfall gains (due to unusually high international prices over which the local producers have no control) by the most efficient device available: coffee export taxes. Such taxes would be especially appropriate for Guatemala, given the severely unequal income distribution in the coffee sector: although there are 60,000 coffee farms, 2,500 farms (over 45 hectares) produce nearly 90 percent of all coffee; only 200 to 300 farms account for virtually all the income tax from coffee production; and only 8 farms account for as much as 25 percent of coffee production. Given the windfall of Q25 million in increased export earnings due to high coffee prices, it would seem ill-advised for the Guatemalan government to forego some

33. There are 240,000 hectares in coffee production, yielding a net return of about Q130 per hectare; market value per hectare, even at higher coffee prices, would be only Q1,000-2,000.

share of these gains. This is especially true when these gains might enable a relatively few Guatemalans to increase capital flight, travel, imports, or consumption with a lower marginal product (for Guatemala's development), rather than if they were used in government programs or in lending to the private sector for development purposes.

The strategic element is now introduced: how can the government "control" the use of some of these windfall gains? Given the political constraint blocking higher export taxes as such, the government might well suggest a combination package of abolishing all coffee export taxes below some minimal international price (say, Q30 per quintal), which would provide future security by guaranteeing no taxes on "normal profit" and cost elements in coffee production, but applying a sizable marginal "recovery" rate on windfall gains above such a minimum guaranteed tax-free return. Such marginal recoveries (say, 50 percent of windfall gains above an international price of Q30) would not be "taxes" but deposits for either a "coffee price stabilization fund" or a "coffee diversification development bank" or any other purpose as long as they fulfill the essential function of taxation, i.e., the removal of discretionary purchasing power from the private sector. Of course, the coffee growers will not rush to approve such devices, but it is the government that has the power to select alternatives. The choice may well be expanding a general sales tax to hundreds of thousands, with all the political ramifications this implies, or helping a few hundred major coffee producers contribute to the economic development of Guatemala.

A final *political constraint* lies in being frozen into the set of past fiscal incentives already granted and the regional set of rules under the CACM fiscal incentives agreement. In 1964 Guatemala had already partly bypassed this impasse by requiring a 10 percent remission of these exonerations to the Industrial Development Bank capitalization fund. Such ingenuity will have to continue. Other countries have found other means to tax such exempt or partially exempt firms once they have made their investments and are thus frozen into an investment position. These include selective manufacturers' excises, other indirect taxes that cannot be totally shifted, social security levies partly paid by employers, dividend taxation (not exempt in Guatemala for domestic recipients), net wealth and transfer taxes, or compulsory contributions to development banks (already tried in Guatemala). Such devices should be further explored and expanded as indicated elsewhere in this paper.

Not only should the administration of future exemptions be made more selective, but new avenues might be attempted. One such device (in practice in northern Nigeria and recently debated in the United States) is the concept of a "minimum income tax."[34] Companies as well

34. Hinrichs, *General Theory.*

as individuals might be subject to either the existing progressive net income tax system *or* a minimum gross income tax levy, *whichever is greater.* Given the Q1,300 million gross income tax base for the income tax system, even a 1 percent minimum gross income tax levy would yield about as much as the total net income tax system currently does; a 2 percent minimum levy would insure that otherwise exempt firms and individuals would make some contribution toward government developmental expenditures (or deposits in some development bank, thus complying with any legal constraints).

On the basis of the previous analysis, an outline or agenda of tax reform in Guatemala is now possible. The following potential reforms are first outlined and then their quantitative significance and timing are measured. In line with any systematic analysis, one must keep in mind that the focus is on the achievement of objectives; those intended for Guatemala on the basis of the Government Plan, or at least the possible objectives within which the Guatemalan government can set its own priorities, include: resource mobilization (both the absolute amounts of revenue generated and the automatic growth, or structural elasticity, of such revenues, thus necessitating fewer future structural changes); resource allocation (or the most efficient use of all inputs to maximize outputs); economic development (both social and capital); equity (sharing development benefits and costs in a fair distribution); balance-of-payments goals; and finally, both political and administrative constraints.

Income taxation is highly ineffective at present: extensive exemptions and deductions vitiate the revenue potential of the system. In Columbia, for example, taxable income is 43 percent of gross income and in the United States it is 58 percent; in Guatemala it is less than 10 percent. Deductions (such as insurance premiums) should be reduced, although the exemption level might be raised (say, to about Q3,000 for employees) to concentrate the limited administrative resources on the source of major tax revenues. Given the roughly 50 percent evasion rate, administrative improvements can be highly productive (such as cross-checking auto ownership, import licenses, passport issuance, exit visa clearances, property ownership, etc.). The *major legal reform* would be to split the income tax between an individual income tax and a corporate income tax (as done in El Salvador). This would allow both a progressive income tax schedule for individual taxpayers and a *proportional tax schedule for businesses,* thus eliminating the present implicit bias toward small-scale producers. (Such a bias would be less than optimal given the expanded market within the CACM.) Along with this should be a separate tax on dividends (now exempt) to encourage reinvestment by companies. These taxes should be withheld at the source. In addition, there should be a shift in the concept of income determination for individual income taxpayers to include foreign-source income, in order to encourage investing in Guatemala instead of capital flight. At least for individual taxpayers (and possibly also for companies, to compensate for the revenue losses under the fiscal incentive program), there might be introduced a "minimum gross income" tax to simplify administration and to guarantee some revenue from middle and upper income taxpayers who might be able to otherwise minimize tax burdens.

Property taxation is the greatest potential source for new future revenues in Guatemala, and at the least cost to economic development incentives. In fact, greater taxation here might even promote growth by pushing land into more productive uses. In terms of equity and tax capacity, it is understandable for low-income countries to have lower tax burdens than richer countries, but there is no justification for wealthy individuals in low-income countries to bear low tax burdens. At present the property owner in Guatemala with a Q40,000 property may pay only Q40 property taxes per year compared to the Q400-800 that the same property owner might pay in a richer country. A greater reassessment effort is necessary, concentrating on upper-value properties. The problem here is less administrative than political: the number of property reassessments in the past has exceeded 10,000 per year (equal to the number of high-value parcels), but these have occurred in a nondiscriminate fashion, in some years resulting in rising reassessments (or low or nontaxable properties) but also in falling property tax collections. Other changes are necessary as well. To simplify administration (and to achieve popular political support) properties below Q1,000 (equal to more than half the parcels) might well be exempted or ignored. Properties above this value should be shifted to a straight proportional rate structure (say, 1 percent at the beginning) to prevent proliferation of property titles. In addition, it would greatly aid collection efforts to shift from an ad personam basis to an ad rem basis of enforcement so that absentee owners cannot escape the tax. Initially, the government may wish to automatically double or treble existing assessments (based on a sliding scale dependent on the length of time since the property was officially assessed) with the taxpayer given the option (after paying the tax) to appeal the assessment. Given the revenue needs of the government, it is far better to run an equitable property tax system (with varying assessment/market value ratios) at a high level of revenue mobilization than at a miniscule level. Higher tax payments would tend to generate taxpayer support for more equitable assessments.

Property transfer taxation is another method with administrative feasibility that can generate revenues with few detrimental effects on economic development. In one sense, the property transfer tax (now levied at 1 percent) can be an effective substitute for the present ineffective capital gains tax. By raising the property transfer tax to, say, 10 percent, the government can regard it both as a substitute for effective capital gains taxation (primarily on socially derived increments to value during the development process) and as a means to recoup some of the property tax revenues lost in the past because of inadequate assessments and tax rates. Such a tax would also fit into the recommended tax mix by retarding any proliferation in property ownership, which might occur in an attempt to avoid the higher taxation proposed for higher-value properties and the exemption (or administrative amnesia) in regard to taxing lower-income properties.

Foreign trade taxation is constrained both by the CACM (except for the expected revenue increase from the San José protocol in applying a 30 percent import duty on capital and raw material imports from non-CACM sources) and by the political realities of taxing coffee exports. But, as discussed earlier, the government must find some way to siphon off part of the Q25 million windfall gain accruing to the coffee export sector. Such a "painless extraction" in terms of economic development incentives would reinforce almost all the earlier stated objectives of the fiscal program. In addition, the present loopholes in taxing foreign air passenger travel can be eliminated according to the Government Plan program. Further measures to be contemplated would be income tax exit clearances (which would tend to reduce foreign visits and foreign spending by Guatemalan citizens) and a sizable exit fee or passport fee to discourage foreign travel and shopping expeditions by the upper-income groups.

Internal indirect taxation has been discussed in terms of the low priority placed on shifting to a general sales tax, at least until other items on this tax reform agenda are accomplished. In addition, the auto license fee (an increase is also recommended in the Government Plan) is a suitable place for "presumptive" income taxation since half of the passenger auto owners do not file income tax returns. Here, equity can be served by a sizable increase in the passenger auto fee (from Q31 to, say, Q100 per year) with part of this (say, half) allowed as a tax credit on one's income tax return. Thus, the "honest" income taxpayer would experience only a small increase in his license fee, but the tax evader would be caught with little means to escape. Other areas of concern might well be reducing the widespread exemptions and commercial selling (through military and diplomatic channels) in alcohol taxation; indeed, more tax revenue might be realized by *reducing* the tax rate on certain liquors and wines, thus diminishing the advantage of evasion and shifting consumption from illicit to legal consumption channels. As in other indirect taxes, it is not always clear that tax revenues are maximized by increasing tax rates; at some point on the demand schedule, tax revenues increase when the effective price is lowered.

Tax efforts outside the central government should not be minimized; they might account for half of the program to fill the impending fiscal gap. Such efforts include revitalization of municipal revenues (especially coordination with the national property tax assessment and collection system), expansion of the social security system, and reevaluation of fees and prices charged throughout the public sector, especially by public enterprises.

The timing and rough quantitative effects of these suggested reforms are presented in Table 8. Although these reforms are not necessarily additive (i.e., they may overlap or substitute for one another), it is obvious that there is a sufficient menu of fiscal alternatives from which the government may pick and choose to achieve its fiscal goals for the seventies.

A Policy Matrix

A policy matrix to summarize and to interrelate these alternatives for tax reform may be useful. In Table 9 all the alternatives are considered— how they relate to numerous objectives of tax policy and how they might complement or offset each other. Objectives, or the outputs of the system, include resource mobilization (revenue effects);[35] economic development (here to include not only effects on the current growth rate, but also roughly relating the three key ingredients in the growth process: capital investment, employment of human capital, and entrepreneurship); equity (both horizontal—equals treated equally, and vertical—redistribution of income); and balance-of-payments effects. In addition, two constraints— political and administrative—are put into the matrix. On the "input" side of the matrix are the various tax instruments (direct, indirect, and other) together with the "policy moves," or alternatives, previously discussed in the "alternatives" and "issues" sections of this paper. The symbols within the matrix (+, −, 0) indicate the probable effect of the policy moves: the positive or negative effect of the input on the desired output, the "zero" symbol indicating "no significant effect," and a " + / − " indicating opposite effects.

In summary, this policy matrix highlights some of the differences between my findings and the National Development Plan tax reform. Of the Q100 million potential from this tax menu (which is additive as the earlier list of alternatives was not), about Q20 million come from administrative improvements (reduced evasion) whereas nearly Q80 million come from other reforms. In 1974 the expected gap to be financed is close to Q40 million. The National Development Plan tax program has no contingency plan to put into effect if its half of the gap from administrative improvements is not realized on time. Another difference is that the plan relies on indirect tax measures by the central government—which could

35. The year 1974 was selected to typify revenue effects during the 1970-76 period studied; this is the last year of the present term of the new administration and also the year when central government current savings will go to zero unless something is done to offset this result. This timing dilemma was discussed earlier.

be a politically unpopular course—for about two-thirds of its revenue increase (counting both administrative and legal reforms). The menu of alternatives in Table 9 has within it about one-third (Q30 million) from sources outside the central government (social security, municipalities, public enterprises) and, of the remaining two-thirds, has half from direct tax sources and half from indirect.

The government is also left the option of a *"nontax increase"* route to filling the fiscal gap: Q20 million from administrative improvements;

TABLE 8

TIMING OF REVENUE INCREMENTS—SUMMARY OF REVENUE EFFECTS OF
AVAILABLE FISCAL ALTERNATIVES (IN MILLIONS OF QUETZALES)

	1971	1972	1973	1974	1975	1976
Revision of coffee tax	10	10	8	7	6	5
Automatic property reassessments	6	6	6	6	6	6
Revise auto license fees	2	2	2	2	2	2
Vigorous tax collection/admin.						
Income tax (reduce evasion to 1/4)	2	4	6	8	9	11
Stamp tax (reduce evasion to 1/4)	1	3	6	9	12	15
Property reassessments	2	2	2+	2+	2+	2+
Property transfer tax	1	1	1	2	2	2
Property tax rate increase (1%)	5	5	6	6	6	7
Property tax (1%); full assessment	33	34	35	36	38	40
Substitute sales for stamp tax	5	6	7	8	9	10
Broaden social security system	10	12	14	16	18	20
Exit fee for Guatemalans	1	1	1	1	1	1
Minimum income tax	8	9	10	12	14	17
Separate corporate income tax, tax dividends at source, reduce fiscal incentives	6	7	8	10	12	15

Q12 million from the income tax package of a separate corporate income tax, fewer fiscal exonerations, taxing dividends and foreign-source income, and reduced individual deductions coupled with a higher personal exemption (or filing) level; Q6 million (at least) from property tax reassessments (either "automatic" or concentrated on high-value property); and at least Q10 million from social security savings. This totals Q48 million, which allows some slippage in revenues from administrative improvements. (This also leaves about Q20 million in additional revenue possibilities from municipalities and public enterprise current savings.)

Another route would be a tax package focused on *maximizing economic development*. Taking from the matrix the major tax policy moves that have "plusses" under Economic Development, such a package would pick up the Q20 million in administrative improvements (which would improve relative prices and rewards between taxpayers and tax evaders), Q12 million from property taxes (which might encourage better use of

TABLE 9

POLICY MATRIX FOR GUATEMALAN TAX REFORM

Instruments	Policy Moves	Objectives					Constraints	
		Resource Mobilization (Q Millions) Revenue Increase by 1974	Economic Development	Equity		Balance of Payments	Political	Administrative
				Horizontal (Administrative)	Vertical (Income Distribution)			
Direct taxes								
Income: individual	Reduce evasion	+8	+	+	+	+	+	−
	Increase exemptions, reduce deductions	+2	+	+	+	+	+/−	+
Income: company	Separate tax, reduce fiscal incentives	+10	0	+		0	−	+
Property tax	Reassessments	+6	++	+	++	++	0	−
	Increase rate	+6	++	0	++	++	−	+
	Property transfer tax	+2	−	0	+	+	−	+
Foreign trade								
Import taxes	San José Protocol	+5	+/−	+	++	+	+	++
Export taxes	Revise coffee tax	+7	+	−	++	0	−	++

TABLE 9—Continued

Instruments	Policy Moves	Objectives					Constraints	
		Resource Mobilization (Q Millions) Revenue Increase by 1974	Economic Development	Equity Horizontal (Administrative)	Equity Vertical (Income Distribution)	Balance of Payments	Political	Administrative
Internal indirect								
General	Substitute retail sales tax for stamp tax	+8	0	+	−	0	−	−
Auto fees	Increase fee	+2	−	−	++	++	−	+
Administration	Reduce evasion	+12	+	++	++	++	+	−
Exit fee for Guatemalans	Increase fee	+1	−	−	+	+	−	+
Other								
Social security	Expand program, increase rates	+10	−		−	0	+	+
Municipalities	Increase revenues	+10	++	++	+	+	−	−
Public enterprises	Increase charges	+10	++	++	0	0	−	+
Total		+99						

idle land), and Q7 million from export taxes (on a windfall surplus, and thus not acting as a disincentive to output, at least in the short run). This package equals Q39 million, just equal to the fiscal gap in 1974. Note that the San José protocol has a "+ / −" designation under Economic Development, indicating the opposite effects achieved: the 30 percent surcharge on non-CACM capital goods and raw material imports would tend to reduce investment and output on the one hand, but it might also encourage local production and use of such goods as well as shifting relative prices in favor of less capital-intensive production functions, thus fostering greater employment, which is included under the Economic Development objective.

The optimal "tax mix" for *balance-of-payments purposes* would focus on the direct tax increments based on the use of progressive income and property taxes to remove purchasing power from upper-income groups, which have a much higher marginal propensity to consume imports, plus selective excise measures on automobiles and "exit fees" (passports, airport and other exit taxes for Guatemalans), thus cutting foreign spending.

From an *administrative viewpoint*, the easiest bases to tax would be property (rate increases or automatic reassessments, not individual reassessments), imports, exports, autos, exits, and social security. Also included is the simplification of income and company taxation (higher exemption or filing levels coupled with reduced deductions or with a "minimum income tax" on gross income, which was not included in this matrix but is nevertheless an important option which should not be underrated).

From a *political strategy viewpoint*, the focus would be on the simplification of the income tax including higher exemption (filing) levels, administrative improvements, import tax revisions (San José protocol), and the expansion of the social security system. In addition, to reach the required Q39 million gap, rapid but fair *individual* reassessments of high-value property (coupled with the exemption of properties under Q1,000) would fit together to make a politically palatable package of tax reforms.

Acknowledgment.—Initial research for this paper was partly financed by the Naval Academy Research Council (July-August 1970). The views within do not necessarily reflect its policies. Helpful comments were received (or rejected) from Klaus Huber, Euric Bobb, Enrique Lardau, Michael Best, John Adler, Stanley Please, and Elliott Morss, to whom I am very grateful but whom I exonerate from all errors contained within. This abbreviated version excludes much of the data and substantiating analysis and tables in the larger paper originally prepared and distributed at the conference.

Comment—Oliver Oldman

A point Hinrichs makes which is worth mentioning at the outset concerns tax administration. He, as well as many others, agrees that tax administration is a cornerstone of tax reform. Yet practically everyone working on tax reform in developing countries does little more than make that kind of assertion. There is too little thinking in terms of trying to improve tax administration or to intellectualize a good bit of what is in fact going on in the whole world of administration.

In dividing up my limited time I shall devote almost half to tax harmonization and the rest to issues of tax reform, primarily in Guatemala. I do this even though Hinrichs's paper has, I believe, a better allocation of space to the two subjects. In the paper only a few pages are devoted to harmonization, which I think is quite correct and presents a sound judgment as to the relative importance of the two subjects.

If one asks himself why tax harmonization for Central America or why tax harmonization for Latin America generally, it is hard to come up with a great deal that is of current importance (leaving aside customs tariffs). There are such matters as simplifying aspects of taxes that impinge on interregional trade and investment. One would want to clarify the laws and perhaps make considerably more uniform a good bit of the terminology, both in the concepts and in the procedures for dealing with the application of taxes to international trade and investment. One might want to use tax harmonization arrangements to reduce or eliminate unusual tax obstructions which interfere with international trade and investment among the countries concerned. At present in Central America, the only important device of this sort that has been developed is the tax treaty on uniform tax incentives, which assures that no one of the member countries will grant more tax incentives—to industry at least—than is agreed to in the treaty. Unfortunately, this type of treaty has the unintended effect that it almost compels all the countries to grant all of these incentives as a minimum. That is, the treaty not only legally sets a maximum, but it also for practical purposes represents a minimum. One can question whether or not the extensive number of incentives agreed to in that tax treaty can be justified as a minimum tax incentive program for all member countries of the Central American Common Market.

Another point that might be made—and I take it that Hinrichs agrees with this—is that whatever comes up in the way of tax harmonization, each country should be allowed maximum freedom to use its tax system as an instrument of economic policy objectives in general without hurting the other member countries of the group. There is a question, however, as to what that really means when you try to translate it into practical measures. Perhaps as an overall guideline it tells us that there is not very much that can or needs to be done by way of tax harmonization in

Latin America today, at least compared to the extensive tax harmonization measures taken in Europe. In my view, the sum total of this is that it is not really a very important, immediate issue nor one on which much in the way of resources ought to be expended at the present time, other than a limited amount of continued academic research and thinking to identify and organize the problems.

In the practical sphere, what is most needed in Latin America today, and which could be described as harmonization, is the careful preparation of accurate and reasonably current descriptions of existing tax systems. This seemingly simple thing does not exist today. The Harvard International Tax Program published a single volume on the Central American tax systems a few years ago.[1] While it is now getting a bit dated, those systems have not changed very rapidly. That volume represented the first comprehensive, detailed description of the Central American tax systems. A similar effort has not yet been forthcoming for the rest of Latin America, although this should be an early goal of any tax harmonization group in the Latin American Free Trade Association.[2] Beyond this, currently such a group can usefully think in terms of unifying tax concepts and procedures and matters of that sort. But the time is a long way off before LAFTA has to worry about looking at the kinds of things that the Europeans in their common market are looking at now. It will be enough if a few academicians and institute researchers keep Latin American tax harmonization under study. I doubt that now is the time for the subject to be carried into the world of serious, practical policy making.

The remainder of the Hinrichs paper is essentially an analysis of tax reform. His presentation inevitably gives us his thinking on tax reform, on reforming tax reform, and on tax theory. He uses Guatemala as his illustration, essentially to show how his general theory can be converted to an application at a particular time in a particular country where you have enough information to go about it and are willing to make some judgments and then give some advice.

Some observers may be surprised that Hinrichs puts Guatemala at the particular stage of tax structure development that he does, especially with respect to sales taxes. Nevertheless, when he comes to the sales tax issue he is cool on much reform for Guatemala, the idea being that Guatemala has gone as far as it need go at the present time. This fits neatly into one of the Hinrichs stages of tax structure development in that Guatemala is now ripe for the modern stage of emphasizing direct taxes once again, both property and income taxes. The paper goes on to de-

1. Virginia G. Watkin, *Taxes and Tax Harmonization in Central America* (Cambridge, Mass.: Harvard Law School International Tax Program, 1967).

2. The Harvard Tax Program has published World Tax Series volumes on Brazil (1957), Colombia (1964), and Mexico (1957).

velop in some detail the kinds of changes in these taxes that are needed in Guatemala to bring its tax system into the modern era.

His proposals in the property, or real estate, tax area include taxing real estate in practically every way one can imagine. There is a present transfer tax which he suggests should be raised from 1 percent to 10 percent on all transfers of real estate. I find a problem with this recommendation on administrative and technical grounds: when one starts raising the rate very high on this kind of tax, one finds that people cease transferring real property; instead, they transfer pieces of paper called shares in corporations or interests in trusts or something else that is not a transfer of real property, and then somehow or other the tax does not apply. By the time the tax law catches up with this, the lawyers are one step ahead figuring another way of transferring the *use* of real property, which is after all what people want in the typical case. In short, there are some operational problems here that would have to be examined. His proposals for reassessing property, for raising the rates, and so on, I have no basic quarrel with. They are essentially conventional recommendations but ones not often carried out in practice, which reflects not only the political difficulties but also the administrative and technical difficulties that are involved.

In the income tax area, Hinrichs would raise rates and eliminate exemptions under the personal income tax and numerous exemptions and incentives under business taxes. He would forget base-broadening in terms of the numbers of taxpayers. He would focus his attention on where the money is, believing that this is really the key. He suggests that corporations ought to be taxed in Guatemala much as they are now taxed in El Salvador. I could not agree more with him on that, since I had something to do with designing that system. But the Salvadorians, since the years I last worked in that country, have gradually been chipping away at that corporation tax reform, and I am not sure how much is really left of it. I am not sure that Hinrichs means to say "copy what is there now." He may mean "copy what they started off with about five years ago." But that is the problem of dealing in this area; obtaining current information on which to pattern a current recommendation is always a difficult matter.

In the sales tax area I suggested earlier that he recommends essentially no reforms, not because the system is good—it is basically a 1 percent or 1.5 percent gross turnover tax—but because the benefits which would result from modernizing that tax would be relatively small compared with the benefits from his other recommendations. He recognizes, as a strategic matter, that there are only a limited amount of tax reform resources available. The political, administrative, and legal energies that go into tax reform ought to be focused where the need is greatest. Since the indirect, or sales tax, area is now producing sufficient revenues, it is time to move on to other things. He does not say so, but I suspect he would not object to recognizing that it may not be far in the future, and that after his reforms get adopted, indirect taxes would come back into their own in the next important increase in the revenue ratio for Guatemala. Once one starts trying to raise these gross turnover taxes beyond 1.5 percent, then one might be very much concerned about their effects and want to switch to another form of single-stage sales tax. Since that is in the future, he does not particularly deal with it.

The paper is full of nuggets from one end to the other on one point or another. Some of them are gold; others are not pure gold but nevertheless still valuable. One of them is a recommendation for a big increase in auto license fees. The idea behind this recommendation is to allow something like half of the auto license fee to serve as a credit against income taxes. The purpose of this is not what you might think, to increase the burden on auto users. The purpose is to get people who are liable for income tax to file income tax returns. If auto taxes were high enough, it might begin to pay. At the very least, if people do not file returns they do not get the credit and have paid an extra tax (and so too have those who are not liable for income tax). He has perhaps half a dozen ideas of this sort, some of which are new to me and may have been thought up after all by some ingenious Guatemalans. I have found that Latin Americans are as ingenious as anybody when it comes to thinking of ways in which you can extract something from the taxpayer to increase the level of collections. Sometimes their ingeniousness turns out to be a form of ingenuousness, unfortunately, and some of their gimmicks have backfired. Therefore, one has to be careful in relying on these devices as a solution to a major tax problem. Nevertheless, they have their place and their uses, and Hinrichs is intelligent enough to see that this is the case.

If this paper is to be of maximum use in Guatemala—and it seems to me important for it to be used there—it needs further condensation. But this is a common defect many of our papers have. It also has a great many valuable points and some approaches toward handling material that are not often used. At the end of the paper Hinrichs has what he calls a tax policy matrix in which all the tax policies, together with their pros and cons, appear on a single page. If one can read and understand that single page and if that page can be presented in a way in which Guatemalan policy makers can read and understand it, then one may be quite confident that they will make their decisions a good bit more rationally than they now make them. The tax policy matrix is a useful device that requires some refining and further explanation. We should admire this work and hope that it gets more fully developed.

Comment—Richard S. Thorn

LIKE most tax reformers in Latin America, Hinrichs is arguing for a political revolution. He hopes to achieve radical social and political change through the back door of the ministry of finance that could not be obtained through the ballot box or in the streets. The tax systems extant in Latin American countries are not primarily the result of inadequate technical skill, but rather are expressions of political systems that have not placed high priority on economic development and fiscal stability. If Hinrichs were submitting his proposals subject to some future period when a number of necessary political conditions would be met, I could be more sanguine about the prognosis for success. Unfortunately, this is not the case. Many of his proposals are included in an official report to be presented to the Guatemalan government as a program for immediate action which, I fear, may suffer the fate of other similar volumes that line the shelves of the offices of the ministers of finance of Latin America.

The general formula Hinrichs recommends is essentially the old one of "tax the rich." The rich have successfully resisted campaigns of this type in developed countries. There is little evidence that an undeveloped country such as Guatemala under its present political system will be more successful in this endeavor. Guatemala has one of the highest illiteracy rates and one of the lowest voter participation rates in Latin America. It is no accident that it has achieved such a low level of fiscal effort. However, since neither Hinrichs nor I are experts in the art of political reform, I shall confine the remainder of my remarks to the technical approach underlying Hinrichs's analysis. These relate to four areas: the objectives of tax policy, the general strategy of Guatemalan tax planning, the timing of tax reform, and the presentation of alternatives.

THE OBJECTIVES OF TAX POLICY

Hinrichs sets forth three objectives for tax policy in Guatemala. The first and foremost is the need to increase government revenues over the near term so that they will rise consistently with the rate of growth of government expenditures. The second objective is to improve the distribution of income, and the third is to improve the allocation of resources within the country. I would like to take issue with Hinrichs's second objective, worthy as it may be. Experience in many countries has shown that the tax system is a poor instrument for redistributing income. The major force that redistributes income in developing countries is the absorption of people from the subsistence sector into the modern sector of the economy—that is, the process of economic growth. In view of this, I would argue for placing overwhelming emphasis on the tax strategy to be followed for economic growth and then following the consequences of this decision. I would be willing to trade off, for example, some adverse effects on the distribution of income in the short run for higher growth, if this were the only alternative (and I do not believe it is). This is not, however, necessarily an argument for granting tax incentives for investment. Guatemala is an excellent example of a country in which many so-called tax incentives for promoting growth have not proved effective, and consideration should be given to their removal, as is proposed by both the Guatemalan authorities and Hinrichs. Giving predominance to economic growth in tax policy in developing countries will result in fewer conflicts with the ideal of vertical equity than might intuitively seem to be the case. Indeed, many attempts to introduce tax measures designed to improve vertical income equity have, in fact, had the opposite effect as a result of poor compliance with the new measures.

GENERAL STRATEGY

The strategy advocated in the Guatemalan draft investment plan for 1971-75, prepared by the Consejo Nacional de Planificación Económica, laid heavy emphasis on administrative reform; half of the increment in tax revenues to finance the plan is to be obtained through administrative reform. Hinrichs, on the other hand, projects only about one-quarter of the total increment in tax revenues from this source. A detailed comparison of the Guatemalan and Hinrichs programs is shown in Table 1. If we exclude the Q30 million in the Hinrichs program to be obtained from social security, municipalities, and public enterprises, which are not considered by the Guatemalan tax program, the principal difference lies in the Guatemalan emphasis on import taxes and Hinrichs's emphasis on the property tax and coffee export tax. In effect, Hinrichs is attempting to deliver a triple whammy to the upper-income classes by increasing the income tax, property tax, and coffee export tax largely on the basis that these taxpayers evade so much that all three forms of taxation are necessary to get them to assume a reasonable burden. The Guatemalan draft plan follows a more conventional route in combining greater compliance with the existing law together with a moderate increase in the legal burden on the upper-income groups via the property tax, import tax, and other forms of indirect taxation. This is most clearly shown in the income tax. Both Hinrichs and the Guatemalan draft plan project similar increases, but the Guatemalan draft plan hopes to obtain these largely through administrative reform and Hinrichs through new legislation.

TIMING OF TAX REFORM

Hinrichs advocates greater emphasis on direct taxation in the immediate future in order to achieve a greater income elasticity of government revenues. He argues that economic development, especially that occurring within a common market, is likely to diminish the importance of the external sector relative to the domestic sector and, therefore, the external tax base relative to the domestic tax base. This reasoning has been widely supported by the Joint Tax Program of the Organization of American States and the Inter-American Development Bank, as well as by many foreign fiscal experts including myself. There is no question that in the long run, Latin America will depend more heavily on direct taxation and that the external tax base will diminish in relative importance. But, the

TABLE 1

PROJECTED REVENUE INCREMENTS FROM GUATEMALAN AND HINRICHS TAX PROGRAMS, 1971-74 (IN MILLIONS OF QUETZALES)

	Guatemalan Tax Reform Program			Hinrichs Tax Program		
	Administrative	Legal	Total	Administrative	Legal	Total
Income tax	17.4	6.2	23.6	8.0	12.0	20.0
Property tax	2.0	5.5	7.5	6.0	8.0	14.0
Import tax	8.2	17.5ᵃ	25.7	—	5.0ᵃ	5.0
Indirect (alcohol, petroleum, tobacco)	8.6	—	8.6	—	—	—
Stamp tax	7.3	—	7.3	9.0	—	9.0
Sales tax	—	7.5ᵇ	7.5	—	8.0ᵇ	8.0
Vehicle tax	—	3.5	3.5	—	2.0	2.0
Nontax revenue	3.8	—	3.8	—	1.0	1.0
Coffee export tax	—	—	—	—	7.0	7.0
Social security	—	—	—	—	10.0	10.0
Municipalities	—	—	—	—	10.0	10.0
Public enterprises	—	—	—	—	10.0	10.0
General administration	—	—	—	3.0	—	3.0
Total	47.3	40.2	87.5	26.0	73.0	99.0

ᵃSan José Protocol.
ᵇSubstitute for stamp tax.

time dimension here is important. The issue is: at what rate can we reasonably expect this to occur? It is interesting to note that in an earlier book Hinrichs has a graph showing the change in relative importance of the various forms of taxation over the course of economic development.[1] The horizontal axis of the graph representing time has been left without a scale. I think this was a wise thing to do. A large part of the problem with the present paper is the very short scale that Hinrichs substitutes for the unknown scale of his earlier graph.

I think we must be aware of what I like to call the clock of social revolution ticking away in Latin America. Latin America is deeply involved in a social revolution. It has been going on for a long time and

1. Harley H. Hinrichs, *A General Theory of Tax Structure Change During Economic Development* (Cambridge, Mass.: Harvard Law School International Tax Program, 1966), p. 100.

will probably continue for a long time. I would argue that Hinrichs is advocating an increase in direct taxation at a rate too fast for it to be tolerated without some concomitant political changes. Hinrichs suggests that most changes in tax systems (and we could expand this to include major reforms of any kind) should occur in the first hundred or two hundred days of a new administration for the best chance of success. Few would disagree with this view. In fact, the ideal time for tax reform would be in the closing days of an outgoing administration, but such political cooperation rarely presents itself. In these terms, the time for tax reform in Guatemala is running out, if it has not already run out.

There is another rule of a similar type to which Hinrichs does not pay sufficient attention: the historical principle that major reforms most frequently grow out of major crises. It is, I believe, unwise for any tax expert to suggest major tax reforms without a major crisis if his intention is to have an immediate impact on the current fiscal situation. We all know the wisdom of planning ahead, but in politics this principle seldom operates. I would estimate that the average planning horizon of the U.S. government is eighteen months; for Latin American governments it is probably a year or less. It is difficult for governments to accept advice to prepare for the next generation or the next administration when the benefits will also accrue in the long run. In the absence of an immediate crisis, realistic fiscal experts should present radical reform programs for what they are, namely as long-run plans to be implemented when the opportunity presents itself and not as immediate action programs. One cannot outrun the pace of social progress that is occurring in Latin America. Tax reform programs should be adjusted accordingly. Furthermore, there is little that external influences can do to alter the rate at which the social clock is running.

ADMINISTRATIVE REFORM

Applying this reasoning to the case at hand, I am somewhat more sympathetic to the tax strategy presented in the Guatemalan draft plan than is Hinrichs. I would go so far as to say that were there structural reform without administrative improvement, the new tax laws Hinrichs proposes would turn out to be empty boxes. Tax paying is essentially a voluntary activity, in spite of how we may sometimes personally feel about it. If major inequities are allowed to develop in the tax system, people will not tolerate them. If we are considering a major increase in tax effort, as both the Guatemalan draft plan and Hinrichs advocate, we had better ensure that we are increasing both horizontal and vertical equity. From the viewpoint of both timing and equity, there is much to be said for a tax program heavily weighted on the side of administrative improvement combined with a less potent dose of Hinrichs's structural reforms.

Administrative reform is difficult to implement in any country. In Guatemala, however, perhaps one may be more sanguine than in some other countries about the possibilities of achieving short-run gains in this area. It would involve, in large part, removing the excessive number of exemptions that have eroded the tax base, rather than attempting to obtain higher compliance with existing law. Furthermore, Hinrichs omits from his discussion the differences in compliance between the capital city and the other provincial urban centers. My own observations in Latin America indicate a wide variation in compliance between the capital and provincial cities. Most of the tax compliance effort is frequently concentrated on the first two or three major cities with the result that compliance in the other provincial cities falls off sharply. It would appear that modest efforts in dispersing the administrative effort geographically might produce substantial collection results.

It is interesting to note the rather high ratio between taxable income and taxes paid by foreign affiliates and domestic stock companies in Guatemala. The effective tax rate on taxable income of foreign corporations and branches of foreign enterprises is 30 percent and on that of domestic stock companies 20 percent, compared to a rate of 14 percent for general partnerships and limited responsibility companies. The reasons for this are not discussed, but these facts suggest that legal changes to make the corporate form of organization more attractive might contribute to better tax compliance in the future and should not be overlooked in long-term reforms.

A criticism that Hinrichs makes of the draft plan's emphasis on administrative reform—namely, that given the political, administrative, and forecasting problems involved, it may be necessary to fall back on other strategies— seems to me to apply equally well to his alternative program. It seems wise and preferable to pursue the avenues of administrative improvement and structural reform simultaneously. Indeed, the short-run potential of administration reform, particularly removing exemptions, may be superior to that of structural reform. On the other hand, over the long haul there is no question that structural reform is desirable and should be continued.

TAX REFORM AND TAX ALTERNATIVES

One of the shortcomings of many past tax missions to Latin America was the lack of alternatives they presented to the governments they were serving. Faced with the simple choice of accepting or rejecting the tax packages presented, many finance ministers found it necessary to reject them on the grounds of political expediency. It is highly undesirable for a tax expert or a mission to be too dogmatic in its advice, especially when it has critical political implications. In this respect, I like very much the final part of Hinrichs's paper, in which he presents different tax menus emphasizing different objectives. Presenting proposals for tax reform in the form of alternative menus and letting the politician choose which menu he wants to eat, or choke on, as the case may be, may attract a few more to the table of tax reform. While this may leave the tax expert open to the charge made by George Bernard Shaw that if you laid all the economists end to end you would still not arrive at a decision, it still might be a more attractive alternative than to invite some of the other accusations that governments have leveled at foreign tax missions.

In summary, I am arguing that a balanced program of administrative and structural tax reform is most desirable in less-developed countries. If any special emphasis should be given in Guatemala in particular, I support the case that it should be on administrative reform. Above all, I would ask that tax reformers pay heed to the time on the social clock. Let them present their programs neither too early nor too late, but on time. I do not visualize revolutions being launched in the back room of the ministry of finance reserved for visiting foreigners.

Discussion

N. KALDOR: Hinrichs recognizes, as I do, that in the underdeveloped countries the tax burdens of the poor are high and those of the property owners are low. This in itself creates a revolutionary situation. In an article I wrote for *Foreign Affairs* some years ago, I tried to explain that a revolutionary situation exists in any case. That is to say, it would require a revolution to change the existing state of affairs, but on the other hand there is an acute danger of revolution if you *do not* change this state of affairs. I conceive of my job as a tax expert to suggest what should be done, but I always warn the governments of the ill consequences to themselves of adopting my advice. It is not my job to assess the political risks involved.

Every Latin American economist and Latin American politician says that changing the distribution of income is absolutely essential, and if they ask you to come as an adviser you go and make suggestions. But you always retain a high degree of skepticism about the extent to which reforms will be adopted *in fact*. My feelings in many cases, particularly in Mexico, were that these reforms were never intended very seriously, that the business of wanting reform is itself part of a political game, of giving people the appearance that something is going to be done when the government does not really want to do it. In that way, I think many of us advisers were being "had."

I do not agree that tax reforms can be accomplished only in times of crisis. In the U.K. we introduced one of the biggest tax reforms of the century in the 1965 Finance Act at a time when there was no crisis.

L. SJAASTAD: I am in complete agreement with the pressing need to change the distribution of income in Latin America, but I do not think there exists any evidence that the fiscal mechanism has been successful in bringing about a significant redistribution of income in any country except for short periods. A better way to change the distribution of income is through investment, particularly investment in human capital.

I want to underscore the point that tax rates should be low, particularly personal income tax rates—say 20, 30, or 40 percent, but not higher. The idea that tax proceeds can be increased by raising rates is frequently wrong. We have to be careful in setting up income tax rates in developing countries because a good bit of the labor force in these countries is in the international market; that is, their wages are determined by the international market rather than by the domestic market. Perhaps a Ph.D. economist in the United States earns, on the average, eight to ten per capita incomes in salary. In Colombia, a Ph.D. teaching economics earns fifty per capita incomes, in Chile he is earning forty, and in Argentina he is earning thirty-five, and so on. Now if you take what would appear to be a "reasonable" income tax schedule and apply it to these people, you will drive them out of the country. That is why it is terribly important not to make these rates excessively progressive, since by those high tax rates you may drive out the very people that you need and want to keep in the country.

My second point is that there exists a great deal of misplaced emphasis on simply bringing money into the public sector by taxation. This frequently seems to be treated as an end in itself. I submit what is probably a rather unpopular hypothesis, but one which I could defend —namely, that there is not one Latin American country that has the capacity today to spend *well* the amount of money that it is *currently* collecting.

J. PÉREZ-CASTILLO: I am in complete agreement with Sjaastad that, for Latin American countries to develop and for income redistribution to occur, human capital investment must increase considerably.

I am also in agreement with Sjaastad that most if not all countries (and especially my own country, Venezuela) are not spending their limited resources productively in the full sense of the term. At Centro de Estudios del Desarrollo at Universidad Central de Venezuela, we began to study this phenomenon. Although only preliminary results are on hand, these indicate rather conclusively that over the past eighteen years the efficiency of government expenditures (measured in terms of the productive capacity generated in the overall economy) has been decreasing steadily and continues to do so.

5

Agricultural Taxation in Developing Countries
Theory and Latin American Practice

RICHARD M. BIRD

AGRICULTURAL taxation is important to economic development because agriculture is important. As the largest economic sector in many developing countries, agriculture is bound to play a key role in their economic and social development, whether as an obstacle to be overcome or as a foundation upon which to build. The crucial significance of adequate agricultural development for general economic development has recently received new emphasis as a result of experience in many parts of the world. The sheer size of the agricultural sector makes it appear inevitable that agriculture serve as a potentially important source of tax revenues in most developing countries, where revenues seem always to lag behind expenditure needs. Even more important, the tax system is often the principal instrument available by which to effect that transfer of resources out of agriculture, which has generally been considered to be a cardinal ingredient of effective development policy. Furthermore, the array of tax instruments available for this purpose is, at least in theory, also capable of affecting the volume, composition, and disposition of production within the agricultural sector itself.

In stark contrast to these apparently strong reasons for heavy taxation of agriculture, the agricultural sector is in fact taxed relatively lightly in most countries. Indeed, the inadequacy of the prevailing level of agricultural taxation is a recurrent theme in the literature on economic development and on development finance. Similarly, recommendations to increase taxes on agriculture, and in particular taxes on agricultural land, appear almost ritualistically in reports on the appropriate role of the fiscal system in this or that developing country. It is indeed hard to find a tax expert who has not at some time in his career made such a recommendation—though it is perhaps even harder to find one whose recommendation for heavier agricultural taxation has been accepted.

Earlier discussion of this subject in the Latin American context has been very much along these lines. At the 1962 Santiago Conference on

Fiscal Policy for Economic Growth in Latin America, for example, the principal paper on agricultural taxation, by Haskell P. Wald, argued strongly that heavier agricultural taxes were a necessary ingredient of a developmentally oriented tax policy in Latin America. "Experience shows," said Wald, "that the penalties of too light taxation of agriculture are a stagnating farm sector, a financially starved public sector, and a retarded rate of economic growth in the country as a whole."[1] Nicholas Kaldor in his paper to the same conference went even further when he stated that "it is *only* the imposition of compulsory levies on the agricultural sector itself which enlarges the supply of 'savings,' in the required sense for economic development"—that is, by increasing the marketed surplus.[2] These propositions were favorably received by many conference participants, as was the argument made by both Wald and Kaldor (with some variation) that taxation of the *potential* output of agricultural land was the best way to remedy the ills of the present system and hence to facilitate economic growth. Subsequent discussions in Latin America have generally repeated and reinforced these arguments.[3]

The aim of the present paper is to reexamine the evidence and reasoning behind these general policy conclusions. Is heavier agricultural taxation a necessary condition for economic development?[4] Is taxation of potential agricultural income the best way to tax agriculture? The next two sections discuss some aspects of these and related questions.

AGRICULTURE, DEVELOPMENT, AND TAXES

Agriculture is now the largest economic sector in most developing economies. History suggests, however, that it will shrink in importance as development proceeds.[5] The corresponding expansion of the nonagricul-

1. Haskell P. Wald, "Reform of Agricultural Taxation to Promote Economic Development in Latin America," Joint Tax Program, *Fiscal Policy for Economic Growth in Latin America* (Baltimore: Johns Hopkins University Press, 1965), p. 329.

2. Nicholas Kaldor, "The Role of Taxation in Economic Development," Joint Tax Program, *Fiscal Policy for Economic Growth in Latin America* (Baltimore: Johns Hopkins University Press, 1965), p. 75; emphasis different in original.

3. See, for example, Dino Jarach, *El impuesto a la renta normal potencial de la tierra* (Cuaderno de Finanzas Publicas, 5, Programa Conjunto de Tributación, Union Panamericana, Washington, n.d.), and the various authorities cited there.

4. Public policies other than taxation may also affect, intentionally or otherwise, the allocation of resources and the distribution of income between sectors and within the agricultural sector, but they are not discussed here: an excellent survey and comparison of alternative techniques of taxing agriculture (including some outside the formal tax system) is Stephen R. Lewis, Jr., "Agricultural Taxation in a Developing Economy," in Herman M. Southworth and Bruce F. Johnston, eds., *Agricultural Development and Economic Growth* (Ithaca, N.Y.: Cornell University Press, 1967), chap. 12.

5. This point is stressed, for example, in Simon Kuznets, *Modern Economic Growth* (New Haven: Yale University Press, 1966), pp. 113-27. Considerable supporting evidence for the proposition that the agricultural sector will secularly decline in

tural sector requires an increase in the marketed supply of food, an increase in the nonagricultural labor force, and an increase in nonagricultural capital formation. Inevitably, these three needs must be supplied largely from the agricultural sector.

Agricultural taxation thus becomes the instrument charged with the vital task of transferring surplus food, labor, and capital to the nonagricultural sector, as well as with reallocating resources within agriculture to increase the transferable surplus. Taxes on agriculture are also potentially important means of restraining the rise in consumption of the rural masses who account for the bulk of the population in most developing countries. Unless it is restrained by taxation, the principal effect of increased rural consumption, it is usually assumed, will be to increase urban food prices and hence the rate of inflation.

Agricultural taxes are thus needed in order to increase in a non-inflationary manner government revenues, savings, and capital formation —all of which are generally assumed to be necessary for economic growth. Heavier taxes on agriculture are needed even more than heavier taxes in general, both because of the sheer size of the agricultural sector and because of the desire not to reduce the rate of development by taxing the nonagricultural sector—presumably the progressive sector—disproportionately. Or, as W. Arthur Lewis put it in an influential book: "If it is desired to accelerate capital formation at a time when profits are still a small proportion of national income there is in practice no other way of doing this than to levy substantially upon agriculture, both because agriculture constitutes 50 to 60 percent or more of the national income, and also because levying upon other sectors is handicapped by the fact that it is desirable to have these other sectors expand as part of the process of economic growth."[6]

Many other authorities on development economics and taxation have echoed this emphasis on the triple function which *only* agricultural taxation can fulfill—to add to total savings, to increase the marketed surplus, and simultaneously to induce more efficient use of resources within the agricultural sector. There is similar near-unanimity that taxes on agricultural land are, if properly designed, the best way to achieve these goals.[7] Furthermore, quite apart from its economic merits or de-

the course of development has also recently been marshalled in Bruce F. Johnston, "Agriculture and Structural Transformation in Developing Countries: A Survey of Research," *Journal of Economic Literature* 8 (June 1970): 369-73.

6. W. Arthur Lewis, *The Theory of Economic Growth* (Homewood, Ill.: Richard D. Irwin, Inc., 1955), p. 231.

7. In addition to the earlier citations to Kaldor and Wald, see E. T. Mathew, *Agricultural Taxation and Economic Development in India* (London: Asia Publishing House, 1968), pp. 4-5; Robert B. Bangs, *Financing Economic Development* (Chicago: University of Chicago Press, 1968), pp. 127-28; Ursula K. Hicks, *Development from Below* (Oxford: At the Clarendon Press, 1961), pp. 321-22; and Stephen R. Lewis, Jr., "Agricultural Taxation in a Developing Economy," p. 460.

merits, inadequate taxation of the agricultural sector has also often been attacked as violating the traditional fiscal criterion of equity.[8] Wald, for example, has argued strongly in the Latin American context that much heavier taxation of well-to-do landowners is needed both to prevent the undermining of public confidence in the fairness of the tax system and to help enforce desired land redistribution and improved land use in general.[9] The only way to cure the many ills of the present economic system, development and fiscal specialists alike thus seem to agree, is by increasing taxes on the agricultural sector.

The Argument from Development Theory

This persuasive case for heavy agricultural taxation as an essential ingredient of development policy rests on several key arguments. One is that the process of economic development is everywhere inherently similar in important respects. Therefore, there are universally desirable characteristics of the tax system, viewed as an instrument of developmental policy. The underlying economic reasoning for this view appears in turn to derive from two simple propositions. The first is the conventional chain of reasoning that economic growth requires increased capital investment, more investment requires more saving, and higher taxes are needed to provide the saving. The second is that the expansion of the industrial sector (which is identified with economic growth) requires the transfer of substantial resources out of the agricultural sector. The general applicability of both these arguments may be questioned.

The developing world is ill-described by the simple Harrod-Domar growth model which underlies the usual fiscal prescription for higher taxes to raise savings and hence growth rates. Indeed, every link in the traditional chain of reasoning—that growth requires investment, investment requires saving, and taxes are needed to provide the saving—is weak. Increased investment, it appears, is neither sufficient nor, in some cases, necessary for growth: imports may not only be an additional requisite to permit the investment, but they may even, by permitting full operation of existing capacity, allow substantial economic expansion without investment. Similarly, increased saving alone may (in countries where such an import constraint is significant, as it seems to be in much of Latin America) lead not to an increase in the growth rate but to unemployment and underutilized capacity. Finally, higher taxes may reduce rather than increase total saving, depending on the source of the taxes and, most important, the pattern of government expenditures. It thus

8. The best example is afforded by the excellent study of Ved P. Gandhi, *Tax Burden on Indian Agriculture* (Cambridge, Mass.: Harvard University Law School, 1966); see also Mathew, *Agricultural Taxation*, chaps. 3-4.

9. Wald, "Reform of Agricultural Taxation," pp. 326, 329-30.

cannot be simply *assumed* that the circumstances of every country are sufficiently alike that the same medicine—higher taxes—can be prescribed without individual diagnosis of the particular circumstances of each case.[10]

The Dualistic Model

The argument for heavier agricultural taxation on the grounds that heavier taxes are needed, and that agriculture will have to provide much of the needed tax revenue because it is the largest sector of the economy, thus requires careful study in order to determine whether it is applicable in any particular country. The same is true of the special arguments for agricultural taxation already alluded to, which are derived from the principal advance so far made on the Harrod-Domar growth model—namely, the dualistic, or two-sector, model of the development process.

In essence, this approach views economic development as a structural transformation of the economy from a "traditional" one—where economic activity is predominantly in subsistence agriculture—to a "modern" one, in which the nonagricultural (especially the industrial) sector is the most important. This view clearly receives much support from the historical experience of the developed countries. But many influential writers on economic development have gone much further than this and, as Johnston writes, have really taken "the position that structural transformation should be viewed not merely as a consequence of development but as *a process that should be deliberately fostered by policy measures* to accelerate development and to ensure that low-income, preindustrial societies will succeed in realizing their goals of achieving self-sustained growth."[11]

The best-known formal development of this line of thought is the work of Fei and Ranis.[12] The approach taken in this formal analysis is to

10. Extended argument along the lines of this paragraph may be found in Richard M. Bird, *Taxation and Development: Lessons from Colombian Experience* (Cambridge, Mass.: Harvard University Press, 1970), chaps. 1-2, and "Optimal Tax Policy for a Developing Country: The Case of Colombia," *Finanzarchiv* (N.F.), Band 29, Heft 1 (February 1970): 30-53.

11. Johnston, "Agriculture and Structural Transformation," p. 374; emphasis added.

12. See J. C. H. Fei and G. Ranis, *Development of the Labor Surplus Economy* (Homewood, Ill.: Richard D. Irwin, Inc., 1964), and, especially, Fei and Ranis, "Agrarianism, Dualism, and Economic Development," in I. Adelman and E. Thorbecke, eds., *The Theory and Design of Economic Development* (Baltimore: Johns Hopkins University Press, 1966), pp. 3-41. Many additional references to the literature, and some necessary qualifications to the brief summary possible here, may be found in Johnston's recent review article, as well as in John W. Mellor, "Toward a Theory of Agricultural Development," in Southworth and Johnston, eds., *Agricultural Development and Economic Growth*, pp. 21-60.

divide the less-developed countries into two groups: the agrarian and the dualistic. The agrarian economy—much of present-day Africa, for example—is said to be characterized by the overwhelming preponderance of traditional agricultural pursuits, with nonagricultural activities largely restricted to artisan and service activities. The developmental problem in such societies is to generate and utilize effectively what Fei and Ranis label "slacks" in the dominant agricultural sector, especially in the form of agricultural produce not required for the maintenance of traditional consumption patterns. Whether such agricultural surpluses will lead in agrarian economics to increased per capita consumption by farmers in general, to more luxurious living by the wealthy, to expansion of nonproductive activities outside of agriculture, or to some other result, depends of course on such institutional factors as the existing class structure, tenure arrangements, and the prevailing structure of public revenues and expenditures.

The distinguishing feature of the dualistic economy, which is also poor and heavily agricultural, is the existence of a commercialized industrial sector which provides an alternative outlet for the agricultural surplus—though presumably the extent to which this outlet is utilized continues to depend on the same institutional factors. The developmental problem is how to increase real fixed capital in the industrial sector, while at the same time increasing the productivity of agricultural labor in order to free the labor needed by expanding industry. A crucial assumption in the Fei-Ranis analysis is thus that "physical capital plays a relatively less important role in agriculture; the labor-intensive adoption of new techniques, the application of fertilizer, and the like are considerably more important. *Thus the net flow of capital resources in the course of dualistic growth is out of agriculture and into industry.*"[13] The influence of this analysis in the agricultural tax discussion, even outside the limited range of "surplus labor" Asian countries for which it was originally intended, is clear in such general remarks as the following by Stephen Lewis, author of a balanced recent appraisal of agricultural taxation: "Since agriculture is the predominant sector and since the non-agricultural sectors will grow relative to agriculture, there is at least an *a priori* case that investment resources for the non-agricultural sectors must come in the first instance from agriculture. In other words, the agricultural sector must make *some* net contribution to the rest of the economy."[14]

13. Fei and Ranis, "Agrarianism, Dualism, and Economic Development," p. 24; emphasis in original. A similar assumed asymmetry in the production functions of the agricultural and industrial sectors is crucial to the model proposed in Bruce F. Johnston and John W. Mellor, "The Role of Agriculture in Economic Development," *American Economic Review* 51 (September 1961): 570, and to most other two-sector models.

14. Stephen R. Lewis, Jr., "Agricultural Taxation in a Developing Economy," p. 460; emphasis in original.

The Importance of "Slack"

The transfer of resources out of agriculture prescribed on the basis of this model will not, it is argued, hamper increases in agricultural productivity. On the contrary, it may even *stimulate* agricultural productivity, if it is clear to agricultural decision makers that the proceeds from increased productivity can be used to acquire ownership of industry or consumer goods. Turning the intersectoral terms of trade against agriculture through such means as heavy agricultural taxes may thus paradoxically increase agricultural productivity, owing to the ensuing increased attractiveness of industry as a result of the presumed investment of the transferred surplus. This stress on the opportunities to invest agricultural surpluses productively in industry is usually supported by reference to Japanese experience.[15] But the point to be emphasized is that the key underlying assumption is that there exists "slack," or unutilized, potential in the agricultural sector which can be mobilized through the combined stick-carrot approach of heavier taxes and more attractive uses of funds outside of agriculture. Exactly this reasoning underlies the usual economic case for heavier agricultural taxes.

Those who stress that limited domestic resources (e.g., saving) are the main obstacle to growth tend to assume that once the capital is made available, the right development-generating decisions will automatically be forthcoming. This is the traditional view of the role of fiscal policy in development. The same attitude is readily detectable in the discussion on agricultural taxation, where it is almost always simply *assumed* that causation flows in this direction, so that higher agricultural taxes will automatically bring about the desirable structural transformation of the economy. Indeed, tax and development experts apparently agree that it is only through the fiscal philosopher's stone of heavy agricultural taxation that presently poor, predominantly agricultural countries can be transmuted into something rarer and finer.

The conventional dual-sector analysis has thus often been taken to imply two policy conclusions regardless of the circumstances of the country in question. The first is that there can and *should* be a flow of capital from agriculture to industry in the earlier stages of development, a transfer preferably effectuated through heavy land taxes. The second is that the preoccupation with mobilizing and transferring this "agricultural surplus" (capital, food, labor) has implicitly led many to assume that in almost all cases a surplus *can* be extracted from agriculture without paying much attention to the needs of the agricultural sector itself. This neglect has been justified by the belief that the agricultural production function is such that output can be expanded without additional inputs

15. See Fei and Ranis, "Agrarianism, Dualism, and Economic Development," pp. 38-39, and Johnston and Mellor, "The Role of Agriculture," pp. 470-71.

of resources from the nonagricultural sector; indeed, it is usually argued that there exist substantial unutilized (or underutilized) resources in the agricultural sector—in Asia mainly labor, in Latin America perhaps land —which can be readily brought into use as a result of increased tax pressure.

Heavy land taxes will not only perform this necessary task of transferring resources out of agriculture, but they will, miraculously, do so without imposing any real long-term burden on the agricultural sector itself: "The increased tax burden will make the farmer work hard and recover the slack by making better use of presently-unutilized resources, including his own labor and other investable resources, government-provided technical knowledge, irrigation facilities, and fertilizers."[16] In a modern version of what Seligman called the "transformation" of taxation into more efficient production,[17] it is argued that where there is "slack" in the agricultural sector, taxation may not only mobilize surplus food, but may actually induce its creation. As Gandhi put this case with respect to India: "The average farmer in India will have to be made aware of these potentialities (and taxation may act as a lever) so that he picks up the slack and enriches his own life as well as the life of the nation. . . . Providing that slack exists, increasing the tax burden on the average farmer would force him to increase production. In the initial years there may be some element of real burden involved, but in due course, the additional taxation will be paid out of increased productivity resulting from the utilization of slack."[18] In the Latin American context these views are usually expressed more in relation to the underutilized land resources held by the wealthy than with respect to the work effort of the average farmer, but the underlying reasoning would appear to be the same. Even the most careful writers on agricultural taxation have thus generally accepted—albeit usually after expressing some doubts—that the simple dual-sector model sets forth the correct guidelines within which to design agricultural tax policy for all countries.

The Argument from Ethics

Finally, in addition to their many developmental virtues—producing revenues, increasing the marketed surplus, increasing effort and output through penalizing the underemployment or inefficient utilization of resources within agriculture, and moving farmers into the commercialized

16. Gandhi, *Tax Burden*, p. 171—where (again!) Japan is the cited example of this process.

17. E. R. A. Seligman, *The Shifting and Incidence of Taxation,* 5th ed. (New York: Columbia University Press, 1927), reprinted (New York: Augustus M. Kelley, 1969), pp. 5-8.

18. Gandhi, *Tax Burden*, pp. 163-64.

monetary sector—there is a strong equity case for heavy taxes on agricultural land in many countries. This case may be made in terms of both vertical and horizontal equity. Heavy land taxes will not only force large landowners in many instances to sell off some of their lands but they will also, by reducing land prices, permit lower-income agriculturists to acquire them. Besides this potential direct redistributive effect, only through heavy land taxes can rich landowners be made to pay their fair share of the taxes anyway—and without some such contribution to the fisc the necessary social cement of "fair shares" may be too weak to hold the elements of society together.

Studies of sectoral "tax burdens" extend this line of thought to the agricultural sector as a whole and argue that in the name of equity agriculture is usually "too lightly" taxed and needs to contribute more to the public revenues. The underlying assumption here is that some ethical principle such as "horizontal equity" (equal treatment of equals) is simply *assumed* to be of such power and cogency that the desirability, even the necessity, of the recommended policy change cannot be questioned by men of good will.[19] This is clearly a value judgment, though probably a widely accepted one, and as such is neither refutable nor demonstrable by economic analysis.

The approach to agricultural taxation as a question of the "tax-paying capacity" of the agricultural sector is often ingenious and may sometimes provide essential information for the formulation of tax policy. But it is basically misconceived if it is viewed as providing an objective guide to the appropriate tax policy in any country. First, there are very substantial difficulties in measuring both sectoral "capacity" to pay taxes and the "burden" of existing taxes. These problems are much more than statistical. "Tax-burden" tables, for example, even apart from the inevitably disputatious nature of the assumptions needed to construct them, cannot really yield any useful information about the distribution of the tax burden because the basic assumption underlying the exercise— that the pretax distribution of income would be the same if the tax system did not exist—is palpably false.[20] Second, with respect to the appropriate tax treatment of individuals, presumably the only subjects of taxation for whom equity questions are relevant, this aggregative approach obviously provides no answers. Third, the appropriate taxation to be levied on the agricultural sector as a whole ought, in principle, to be decided in accordance with one's appraisal of the dynamics of development in a particular country at a particular time, irrespective of the outcome

19. Gandhi, *Tax Burden*, pp. 12-13, provides a particularly clear example of the approach, but it also underlies many other recommendations in this field—for example, Wald's.

20. See Carl S. Shoup, *Public Finance* (Chicago: Aldine Publishing Company, 1969), p. 11.

of fundamentally meaningless static comparisons of tax "capacity" and "burden." Empirical studies of the "tax capacity" and "tax burden" of the agricultural sector, while they certainly provide useful ammunition in political arguments, would therefore appear to have a low priority in developing an appropriate aggregate tax policy for agriculture, except perhaps insofar as they are focused on quantifying existing intersectoral flows of resources.

Some Revisionist Views on Agricultural Development

To a striking extent, both the underlying development model and the accompanying tax policy recommendations outlined above appear to rest on a conventional interpretation of Japanese economic development in the latter half of the nineteenth century—that, to put it crudely, the nonagricultural sector is the engine of growth and tax revenues from agriculture the necessary fuel. Indeed, it is perhaps not too much to say that most authors' approaches to the general problem of determining the appropriate level and structure of agricultural taxation appear to be determined to a large extent by the part of the developing world with which they are most familiar. Those who think they are arguing from general development theory are in fact usually arguing from a particular interpretation of Japanese economic history. Those more "practical" men who stress the political obstacles tend to derive their knowledge from India or Latin America, while the African scholars form a (not necessarily harmonious) group of their own. The views of all are too often characterized by misplaced aggregation and the undue generalization of oversimplified models of particular experience.

The point may be illustrated by a brief look at the oft-cited Japanese experience in the latter part of the nineteenth century (the Meiji era). The general view is clearly that Meiji fiscal policy was a great success: "Meiji fiscal policy was able to raise large amounts of funds internally to finance the enormous expenditures required for the development and modernization of the economy. It did this mainly by taxing heavily the agricultural sector, without interfering with the healthy growth of the sector."[21] The thesis is thus that a rapid growth in agricultural productivity with little capital investment provided a surplus that could be used for capital formation elsewhere and that through the land tax—which provided over 70 percent of total government revenues and took 10-20 percent of agricultural income[22]—the state was able to rechannel this

---

21. Harry T. Oshima, "Meiji Fiscal Policy and Agricultural Progress," in William W. Lockwood, ed., *The State and Economic Enterprise in Japan* (Princeton, N.J.: Princeton University Press, 1965), p. 353.

22. Approximate figures; for precise data see Oshima, "Meiji Fiscal Policy," pp. 358-60.

"surplus" to industrial activities without hurting the growth of agricultural productivity.

In fact, there are several important contentious points in this conventional interpretation. First, there may not really have been much of a net outflow of resources from the farm sector in Meiji Japan anyway.[23] Second, while the tax system clearly transferred a good deal out of agriculture to the public sector, much of this appears to have been wasted from the point of view of development, largely in military expenditures.[24] Third, recorded agricultural productivity was based largely on land tax records and there is evidence of substantial initial underestimation of agricultural production for tax purposes, so that the rate of productivity growth was probably lower than was at one time thought.[25] Finally, there is growing sympathy for the view that "the extraction of large sums of money from the farm population was generally detrimental to the healthy development of agriculture, especially as so much was used relatively unproductively for military purposes."[26] Even if there was a net resource flow out of agriculture and agriculture continued to grow under its heavy tax load, this result, it has been argued, was due to the exceptionally favorable initial conditions in Meiji Japan and cannot serve as a lesson for present-day developing countries.[27]

The lesson of history is thus that there is no one lesson, either from Japan or elsewhere, which is readily applicable to developing countries in general. Each historical instance appears on close examination to be a special case, complex and unique in many important respects.[28] This, perhaps, is the real lesson of historical experience for present-day policy makers.

Limitations of Model Building

Facts can never defeat a model, however, no matter how often it is demonstrated that the policy implications emerging from the model were in

23. See Shigeru Ishikawa, *Economic Development in Asian Perspective* (Tokyo: Kinokuniya Bookstore Co. Ltd., 1967), pp. 318-20.

24. Oshima, "Meiji Fiscal Policy," pp. 372-80.

25. James I. Nakamura, *Agricultural Production and the Economic Development of Japan 1873-1922* (Princeton, N.J.: Princeton University Press, 1966). Nakamura's estimate of the degree of underestimation is itself considered exaggerated by other scholars (e.g., Henry Rosovsky, "Rumbles in the Ricefields: Professor Nakamura vs. the Official Statistics," *Journal of Asian Studies* 26 [1967-68]: 347-60), but no one would now accept the official figures uncritically, as was done in the era when the dualistic models were formulated.

26. Oshima, "Meiji Fiscal Policy," p. 354.

27. Ishikawa, *Economic Development in Asian Perspective*, p. 347.

28. For corroboration, see the cases of Germany and Britain in David S. Landes, "Japan and Europe: Contrasts in Industrialization," in William W. Lockwood, ed., *The State and Economic Enterprise in Japan* (Princeton, N.J.: Princeton University Press, 1965), pp. 93-182, and the various experiences outlined in E. L. Jones and S. J. Woolf, eds., *Agrarian Change and Economic Development: The Historical Problems* (London: Methuen & Co. Ltd., 1969).

fact arbitrarily built into its original assumptions and that the assumptions are unrealistic in the case at hand. One reason for the resilience of models in the face of contrary facts is that, despite the dangers of such paradigmatic reasoning, considerable simplification is indeed essential in order to help sort out our thinking on so complex and diverse a question as the role of agricultural taxation in developing economies.

Many of the arguments about the necessary and desirable nature of agricultural development reduce to the view that this or that characteristic of the agricultural sector will alter in a particular way as income levels rise. If these characteristics are interpreted as having analytic rather than merely descriptive significance, the basic question on the role of agricultural taxation then hinges on the extent to which the transformation from, to use Clifton Wharton's terms,[29] static Stage I to dynamic Stage III requires, permits, or is hurt by policies aimed at transferring resources out of agriculture. A secondary difference concerns the extent to which specific taxes (resource-transferring policies) can help or hinder agricultural development policies. Too often have implicit assumptions concerning these factors shaped, consciously or otherwise, writing on agricultural taxation. It is therefore crucial to be clear about the underlying model of the development process before proceeding to policy recommendations.

All "growth stage" models may of course be criticized as lacking in analytical power and operational relevance.[30] Nevertheless, such frameworks have proved useful in attempting through generalized approximations of reality to delimit the crucial variables relevant for developmental policy. Unfortunately, a wide range of the characteristics emphasized by such models may usually be found in different countries—and, indeed, even within the same country, where a primitive group of mountain farmers may be only a few miles away from a group of capital-intensive dairy farmers serving an urban market.

The policy recommendations emerging from any *general* model of the interconnections between agricultural and industrial development will thus either be so empty as to be useless ("both are good") or else in fact a special case applicable to, at most, a relatively limited group of countries ("tax agriculture heavily"). Whether the net flow of resources should be to or from the agricultural sector, for example—the most crucial question in designing agricultural tax policy—depends entirely upon the particular circumstances of the country in question: its social and institutional structure, its technological and market prospects and possi-

29. Clifton R. Wharton, Jr., *Research on Agricultural Development in Southeast Asia* (New York: Agricultural Development Council, Inc., 1963), p. 11.

30. For a critique of such models in a different sphere, see Richard M. Bird, "Wagner's 'Law' of Expanding State Activity," *Public Finance/Finances Publiques* 26, no. 1 (1971).

bilities, the relative size and productivity of the agricultural and industrial sectors, and so on and on. No general policy prescription can or should be expected to fit all circumstances. Paradigms serve an essential function in helping sort out our thinking on such complex analytical questions as the role of agricultural taxation in development, but, when applied uncritically to yield policy recommendations in concrete cases, they are more likely to hinder than to guide correct action. The relevant question is always: what combination of policies is needed to obtain our objectives in this particular situation?

The appropriate treatment of agriculture is thus not a subject about which one can make very useful recommendations in abstraction from particular real-world situations—especially since, in addition to the difficulties of determining the appropriate theoretical framework to apply, the nature of agricultural policy is such that it, even more than other aspects of development policy, must always be closely geared to local conditions. Countries differ in many respects—for instance, the share of agriculture in output, in exports, in the labor force, and in the provision of public revenues, as well as in income distribution, crop diversification, the state of public education, the capability of administration, etc. The appropriate agricultural tax policy must take all these and many other factors into account. The only useful position for a fiscal economist who, like most of us, cannot know everything, is thus one of agnostic pragmatism on the great issues and eclectic piecemeal theorizing on the small. This view is developed at a little more length in the conclusion. First, however, it is worth saying a little more about the nature and implications for tax policy of some of the "revisionist" views on agriculture's role in development.

Agriculture's Role in Development

One of agriculture's main developmental functions in the conventional model is to supply labor to the industrial sector. Tax policy may affect the flow of labor out of agriculture in several ways. The most basic is by affecting the rate of population growth. While one can think of a number of conceivable effects of fiscal measures on population growth, only two seem worth mentioning here: (a) the income effect of heavier taxes may discourage families from having more children (even if offset in part by some "personalization" of the tax to allow for family circumstances);[31] and (b) taxes specific to the agricultural sector may make

31. Haskell P. Wald, *The Taxation of Agricultural Land in Underdeveloped Economies* (Cambridge, Mass.: Harvard University Press, 1959), pp. 206-7, suggests such personalization of land taxes. Some have suggested the opposite sort of "personalization," i.e., discriminatory taxation of children; see references in Gunnar Myrdal, *Asian Drama*, vol. 2 (New York: Pantheon Books, 1969), p. 1502 n. But these suggestions have been adopted nowhere, nor do they seem likely to be.

migration to urban areas marginally more attractive and, once in urban areas, it is generally expected that birth rates will tend to decline. Both of these arguments may of course be countered. If, for example, the tax proceeds are spent in the rural areas, death rates may fall even more than birth rates so that the rate of population growth increases. Further, even if the surplus is extracted completely from the agricultural sector by taxes, the increased tax pressure may lead families to have *more* rather than fewer children, insofar as children are an investment rather than a consumption good. The effect of urbanization on birth rates is also questionable.[32] Any effects on birth rates would take years to affect the labor force, of course, and are probably too minute and uncertain in the first place to be worth any more time.

Looking more specifically at migration, recent work has suggested that rural migration can be explained to a large extent by the probability of obtaining employment and the magnitude of the rural-urban wage differential.[33] The effect of heavy agricultural taxes on this magnitude depends on their incidence and hence is not clear. If, for example, the principal result of these taxes is to lower the price of food eaten by urban consumers, migration will presumably be stimulated. If the result is to lower the price of wage goods for rural workers, the effect may be the opposite. In general, any tax measures which make rural life less attractive relative to urban life—as most sectorally discriminating taxes are likely to, especially when, as is usually envisioned, the proceeds are mainly spent in urban areas—will tend to induce more migration. This result would apparently be contemplated with equanimity by those who adhere to the crude labor-transfer model.[34] But in view of the increasing awareness of the social and political problems arising from the flow of rural migrants adding to the open unemployment in congested urban slums, one may perhaps doubt whether a tax "push" of this sort is really needed in most developing countries at the present time.

Questions have also been raised on the other side of the labor transfer argument: will the increases in agricultural productivity which all agree are needed for development require more or less labor than is at present employed in this sector? The accepted view, until recently, has been that an increase in agricultural productivity will in all likelihood largely be accomplished by a reduction of labor inputs. To quote

32. For an early discussion of these and other interactions between economic and population growth, see Richard M. Bird, "Crecimiento de la población y desarrollo económico," *Desarrollo Económico* 1 (julio-setiembre 1961): 17-42.

33. See the interesting model of Michael P. Todaro, "A Model of Labor Migration and Urban Unemployment in Less Developed Countries," *American Economic Review* 59 (March 1969): 138-48; see also John R. Harris and Michael P. Todaro, "Migration, Unemployment and Development: A Two-Sector Analysis," *American Economic Review* 60 (March 1970): 126-42.

34. See, for example, Wald, *Taxation of Agricultural Land,* p. 94.

Johnston and Mellor: "Reduction of the farm labor force is a necessary condition for establishing factor proportions that yield returns to labor in agriculture that are more or less in accord with returns to labor in other sectors. More concretely, insufficient movement out of agriculture will perpetuate, or lead to, excessively small farms and serious under-employment of labor as the proximate causes of substandard farm incomes."[35] Underlying this view, of course, is the assumption that the marginal product of labor in agriculture is zero or very close to zero in many less-developed countries. Few authorities on the subject now accept this, although one would never suspect as much from reading the taxation literature alone. The general and more plausible view is instead that the marginal product of agricultural labor is positive and that little if any redundant labor exists in agriculture.[36] As Johnston recently summed up the present status of the discussion, in a strikingly different fashion from his own views of ten years earlier: "Although economists commonly stress a trade-off between output and employment objectives, there do not appear to be inherent reasons for serious conflict between those objectives within agriculture."[37]

The de-emphasis on the role of agriculture as a supplier of manpower is supported by two other arguments. The first is the great importance of increased productive agricultural employment in itself. Not only is it important to increase the effective utilization of the present agricultural labor force, but it must be expected that the size of this labor force will be increasing steadily over the next decades in most countries. Further, Myrdal and others have argued that, at least in South Asia, the key to increased agricultural production is not *less* labor per unit of land but *more*: "If by a miracle the cultivators in South Asia could be induced to work more diligently, production would rise dramatically."[38] This approach agrees with the conventional argument that little if any extra capital is needed to increase output in agriculture because there is a good deal of "slack." The difference between the Myrdal and conventional views is that the former argues that the aspirations of peasants are limited—a sociological explanation of slack—while the latter suggests that rational response to economic incentives can be expected and is therefore optimistic as to the potential effects of taxation in eliciting favorable behavior from a developmental point of view.[39] The sociological approach, as the Myrdal quotation suggests, requires a "miracle" to achieve

35. Johnston and Mellor, "The Role of Agriculture," p. 590.

36. Impressive empirical documentation of this point has, for example, recently been assembled for India by Stanislaw Wellisz et al., "Resource Allocation in Traditional Agriculture: A Study of Andhra Pradesh," *Journal of Political Economy* 78 (August 1970): 655-84.

37. Johnston, "Agriculture and Structural Transformation," p. 392.

38. Myrdal, *Asian Drama*, vol. 2, p. 1294.

39. Cf. Gandhi, *Tax Burden*, pp. 151-53.

the desired result: hard as tax changes are to bring about in most countries, they would appear easier to incorporate into a development plan than miracles.

Perhaps in part because most of us are uncomfortable with miracles, but mostly as a result of increasing evidence, one view has gained increasing acceptance: that the responses of farmers everywhere to improvements in opportunities are economically rational. Instances where normal economic incentives seem not to work can usually, it appears, be explained away. For example, it has been argued that where the marketed surplus is observed not to rise in response to price increases, the explanation may lie not in economic irrationality on the part of agriculturists but rather in the tastes of the rural economy for the products of the manufacturing sector.[40] Improved variety, quality, and price of manufactured goods to suit rural needs may be what is needed to transfer the surplus. Rather than heavier taxes on agricultural output, lighter taxes on the *uses* of income might therefore, in some circumstances at least, be the way to increase the flow of food to urban consumers. Again, this argument urges that the analysis of agricultural taxes cannot be conducted in abstraction from the uses to be made of the proceeds. If, for example, the expenditures either facilitate marketing (farm-to-market roads) or increase the choice or reduce the price of incentive goods, the net effects on marketed surplus may be quite different from those when the proceeds go to raise urban wages—especially those of high cost servants—and hence the price of manufactured goods.

The problem of transferring capital out of the agricultural sector was discussed earlier. Analysis and experience on this crucial matter suggest that, while there may be a net inflow or net outflow from agriculture, a *gross* inflow to finance certain key projects is generally crucial to agricultural development.[41] Even if the capital is used for the development of the agricultural sector itself, the role of tax policy in mobilizing savings may therefore be vital. Taxing agriculture heavily to finance mainly agricultural investment, however, seems much more feasible than agriculture simply providing capital to other sectors, as in the traditional view.

Recent analysis has also directed increasing attention to the apparent necessity in many countries of increasing agricultural production, employment, and productivity in order to achieve the distributional and allocative objectives usually subsumed in the term "development." Agricultural development has increasing intrinsic as well as instrumental importance in this emerging view of the developmental process. No longer, for

40. Stephen Hymer and Stephen Resnick, "A Model of an Agrarian Economy with Nonagricultural Activities," *American Economic Review* 59 (September 1969): 493-506.

41. Bruce F. Johnston and John Cowrie, "The Seed-Fertilizer Revolution and Labor Force Absorption," *American Economic Review* 59 (September 1969): 579.

example, is it clear that "agriculture, as the dominant sector of an under-developed economy can and should make a net contribution to the capital required for overhead investment and expansion of secondary industry."[42] Instead, it is now argued by some that the principal immediate task of agricultural development in many, perhaps even most, developing countries is to raise the incomes and consumption of the large farm population itself and to provide employment on the farm for the increasing labor force.[43] President Nyerere of Tanzania recently expressed this point as follows: "Tanzania will continue to have a predominantly rural economy for a long time to come. As it is in the rural areas that people live and work, so it is in the rural areas that life must be improved. We have some industries now and they will continue to expand; but it would be grossly unrealistic to imagine that in the near future more than a small proportion of our people will live in towns and work in modern industrial enterprises."[44] Most people live in rural areas and will continue to do so for some years, so developmental policies cannot simply treat the well-being of most of the population as an instrument rather than an objective of policy. Implementing this view of agricultural policy obviously requires quite different tax policies than the more usual conception of agriculture as a sector to be mulcted of both men and money for the good of "the nation."

As already noted, the trend away from the "tax agriculture at all costs" school has been reinforced by the realization that extensive capital investment in agriculture may be needed in order to make technological innovations possible to accelerate the growth of the agricultural surplus. Indeed, in view of the rapid growth of the demand for food as income levels rise, a net flow of resources *into* agriculture may be necessary at early stages in some countries.[45] Even if this extreme position is not reached, the scope of the immediate increases in agricultural productivity potentially realizable in many countries from labor-intensive, capital-saving techniques now appears to be much lower than it did a few years ago to scholars heavily (albeit often unconsciously) influenced by what they conceived to be the experience of Meiji Japan.

The need to create institutional infrastructure (in transport and ed-

42. Johnston and Mellor, "The Role of Agriculture," p. 572. A decade later these same two authors would not make so categorical a statement: see the previous references to their respective review articles.

43. See Guy Hunter, *Modernizing Peasant Societies* (New York: Oxford University Press, 1969), pp. 10-11.

44. *Africa Report*, no. 6 (June 1967), reprinted in *Development Digest* 8, no. 4 (October 1970): 5. In line with this statement, Tanzania recently removed the principal direct taxes on the rural population (the personal tax and cesses) and replaced them by a general sales tax which presumably would be paid mostly by urban consumers.

45. See Johnston, "Agriculture and Structural Transformation," p. 383, and Ishikawa, *Economic Development in Asian Perspective*, chap. 4.

ucation, for instance) to invest in land development, and to devote much of industrial and importing capacity to the task of maintaining and improving the rate of growth of agricultural productivity, means in effect the closure of "the low cost route to agricultural development that seemed to be opened up by the dual economy models which have dominated much of the theoretical discussion of agricultural development during the last decade."[46] The possibility of a net flow of resources *from* agriculture to help the overall development effort thus turns out to depend very much, even in the long run, upon judicious and perhaps substantial investment *in* agriculture. These considerations become particularly important if one considers the present state of the public administration in many developing countries; the situation suggests that otherwise much of the outflow will be wasted from a developmental point of view by being absorbed by high industrial or service wages or other developmentally useless current governmental expenditure, while the taxes will hamper agricultural productivity—as Oshima has persuasively argued was true even in Meiji Japan, that paragon of land tax virtue.[47]

The importance of providing increased productive employment in agriculture was earlier emphasized as necessary to absorb the growing labor force and desirable as restraining the growth of social unrest in the burgeoning urban centers of developing countries. Furthermore, increased agricultural output consumed in the rural sector is, it was argued, necessary in some instances to ensure a fairer distribution of the gains from economic progress (and may itself, through improving nutrition, lead to some productivity gains). In addition, without rising incomes in the agricultural sector the expansion of industry may, in some countries, be limited by the size of the domestic market. It has recently been argued that this is the case in Nigeria, for example.[48] Others have suggested a somewhat similar situation may prevail in Colombia.[49] This question is a tangled one in both theory and practice, but it is certainly arguable that in some countries a good case can be made in terms of accelerating economic growth for expanding rural markets for simple consumer and producer goods, rather than contracting them through heavy agricultural taxes.[50]

These arguments are strengthened when agricultural exports are essential to provide the foreign exchange needed for developmental invest-

46. Yujiro Hayami and V. W. Ruttan, "Agricultural Productivity Differences among Countries," *American Economic Review* 60 (December 1970): 908.

47. Oshima, "Meiji Fiscal Policy," pp. 353-89.

48. See Carl K. Eicher, *Research on Agricultural Development in Five English-Speaking Countries in West Africa* (New York: Agricultural Development Council, Inc., 1970), pp. 19-29, for a summary of some relevant research.

49. Lauchlin Currie, *Accelerating Development* (New York: McGraw-Hill, 1966), pp. 25-27, 45, 200, and Bird, *Taxation and Development*, p. 17.

50. See Mellor, "Toward a Theory of Agricultural Development," pp. 35-36, and Hymer and Resnick, "Model of an Agrarian Economy."

ment, and heavy agricultural taxation may, by restraining agricultural output and marketing, actually reduce the availability of foreign exchange and hence lead to the early imposition of a foreign exchange constraint on development. In evaluating this argument, too much attention has been paid in the past to the admittedly gloomy long-run prospects for most agricultural exports and too little attention to their essential role *right now* in providing foreign exchange.[51] Even a temporary setback in agricultural exports in these circumstances—for example, through the adverse incentive effects of heavy agricultural taxation—may have long-lasting adverse effects on the economy.[52] There is a good deal of evidence on the specially sensitive responsiveness of cash export crops to price changes, so this danger is a real one.[53]

The Green Revolution

In the last year or two, the confused picture outlined to this point has been further confused by what is now known as the "Green Revolution."[54] Recent scientific breakthroughs in the development of new seed varieties of wheat and rice potentially mean that the food supply problems in many developing countries can be resolved—*if* the new seeds can be properly combined with fertilizer, irrigation, and other complementary investments. These conditions will not be easy to satisfy, since in many countries, as already noted, they may require substantial reorientation of both tax and spending policy. Furthermore, the change to more "modern" (i.e., standardized, homogeneous) farming practices increases the dangers of disastrous plagues of pests and crop diseases. Still more research is thus urgent, especially since the methods—chemical fertilizers, herbicides, pesticides, etc.—used both to launch the "revolution" and control its side effects are themselves increasingly being called into question on ecological grounds. Thus even as the old problems are resolved, new ones arise. Much the same is true with tax policy.

It is already clear, for example, that the gains from these innovations

51. An early recognition of the importance of this point may, however, be found in Johnston and Mellor, "The Role of Agriculture," p. 575.

52. See Bird, *Taxation and Development,* chap. 2, for a brief discussion of the upsetting effects of swings in foreign trade (however caused) on Colombia's development in the 1960s.

53. See the evidence summarized by Raj Krishna in Southworth and Johnston, eds., *Agricultural Development,* chap. 13, and Eicher, *Research on Agricultural Development.*

54. See Clifton R. Wharton, Jr., "The Green Revolution: Cornucopia or Pandora's Box?" *Foreign Affairs* (April 1969), pp. 464-76; Johnston and Cowrie, "The Seed-Fertilizer Revolution," pp. 569-82; and Johnston, "Agriculture and Structural Transformation," pp. 379-80.

are very unevenly distributed within the agricultural sector. The better-off farmers have both more capability and more opportunity to utilize the new technology, so that the immediate impact of the Green Revolution is often to accentuate inequality within the agricultural sector. The problems of tapping the presumably increased taxable capacity of agriculture may thus have changed in kind as well as degree. Not only may equity issues become increasingly important in areas undergoing this "revolution" owing to the resulting increased income disparities, but the problem of how to tax increased incomes without dampening incentives to productivity has been considerably sharpened.

Simultaneously with these problems on the revenue side, full utilization of the technological advances embodied in the new seeds requires substantial new investment in the agricultural sector. The problem of whether there should be a net outflow of resources from agriculture thus remains and may indeed be accentuated by these new developments, rather than resolved by them, as one might have predicted some years ago. Furthermore, the new techniques may—because of their nature as well as their distributional impact—encourage the use of more capital-intensive production techniques and hence tend to accentuate the employment and income distribution problems still more. "The new rice technology has added to the displacement of farm labourers [in South Asia]. The widespread use of one-man machines produced in Japan is driving unemployed peasants to the slum fringes of the cities. . . The rice revolution could contain the seeds of a revolution of another kind."[55] Since it seems clear that the innovations in question can in theory *create* rather than destroy employment, the fact that their net impact has in fact apparently been to displace labor points once again to their uneven distributional impact (as well as the distorted prices of capital and labor) as calling for policy action.[56] In general, then, the Green Revolution has created still more pressures on those who must design agricultural tax policy and has resolved none of the many problems which they already faced.[57] Necessity, it has been said, is the mother of invention: but so is invention the mother of necessity. The impact of the Green Revolution on agricultural problems and policies, including tax policies, once again suggests the truth of this dictum.

55. *The Economist* (April 4, 1970), p. 39.
56. Cf. Johnston, "Agriculture and Structural Transformation," pp. 380, 394. On the effects of tax policy on factor prices, see Bird, *Taxation and Development,* pp. 124-31.
57. For an interesting catalog of possible implications of the new agricultural innovations for tax policy, see Haskell P. Wald, "Where to Now? The Future for Research and the Possibilities for Fiscal Innovating in Development Policy," *Proceedings of the Sixty-Second Annual Conference on Taxation* (Columbus, Ohio: National Tax Association, 1970), pp. 691-703.

THE DESIGN OF AGRICULTURAL TAX POLICY

The theoretical discussion of the first part of this paper may be recapitulated as follows: the level and form of agricultural taxation appropriate for any particular country depends upon the initial conditions in that country and its developmental objectives and possibilities. The conventional argument that heavy agricultural taxes are always and everywhere an essential ingredient of development policy is derived from an oversimple model of agriculture's role in development and an unrealistic view of the feasible structure of agricultural taxation. It cannot, therefore, be lightly applied to any particular country without close examination of individual circumstances. Countries in which most of the population is agricultural, whose export earnings depend heavily upon agricultural exports, which are trying to develop through exploiting their internal markets for consumer goods, and which are in some sense politically responsive to the current well-being of the mass of the (rural) population, are much less well advised to attempt to tax agriculture heavily than are countries which can better afford, in both economic and political terms, to reduce incentives to agricultural productivity and to encourage migration to urban areas. Even in circumstances where heavy agricultural taxes are called for, it appears that as a rule a good proportion of the surplus thus generated will have to be reinvested in agriculture itself (even in cases where there is "slack" in one form or another which may potentially be utilized) if the rate of growth in agricultural productivity is to be maintained. The potentially more refined effects of various tax measures must take second place to these basic decisions on the appropriate tax level.

Latin American Practice

There appears to be no country in Latin America in which agriculture has been taxed heavily enough in recent years either to provide substantial resources for public developmental purposes or to affect significantly the allocation and distribution of resources within the agricultural sector.[58] The most effective taxation of agricultural land has probably been in Chile. Even there, however, it appears that no government has even enunciated an explicit policy as to the appropriate size and nature of agriculture's contribution to the development effort.[59] Some interesting

58. This section is a summary based on a more extensive review of agricultural taxation in selected Latin American countries, prepared for the United Nations, Department of Economic Affairs, Fiscal and Financial Branch, and to be published by them as part of a forthcoming study.

59. "One looks in vain for internally consistent policies and programs supporting conscious national strategies of agricultural development in Latin America."—Solon L. Barranclough, "Agricultural Policy and Land Reform," *Journal of Political Economy* 78, no. 4 (supplement, July/August 1970): 907.

experiments in land taxation have also been carried out in other countries, notably Jamaica, and others have been under study (for example, in Bolivia), but in general the record has been rather discouraging to advocates of more and better land taxes, with some Latin American countries, notably Venezuela (and Peru until recently), levying no tax on rural land at all, and others—Paraguay, Guatemala, Panama, Brazil, etc.—doing so only very unsuccessfully.

When the agricultural sector appears to be taxed moderately heavily, it has usually been by means of taxes on exports of agricultural products rather than through direct taxes on income or property. Examples are provided by coffee in Colombia and Central America, bananas in Ecuador and some Central American countries, and wool and meat in Uruguay. The administrative ease of taxing exports appears in these instances to have outweighed the usual political difficulties of taxing agriculture, whereas in the case of land taxes the considerable administrative complexity of the conventionally recommended approach has combined with the political problems to block the development of an effective tax system.

On economic grounds alone, however, heavier reliance upon taxes on agricultural land would seem the most desirable way to obtain increased public revenues from the agricultural sector for developmental purposes, for only through land taxes can developmentally desirable incentives be created within the agricultural sector while at the same time increasing its contribution to public revenues. Severe noneconomic constraints have, however, generally prevented governments from following this particular path to development, and it is hard to see increased land taxes realistically replacing export taxes as revenue producers in many countries in the near future. If it is desired to increase the short-run contributions of agriculture to the public treasury in Central America, for example, it is probably advisable in the first instance to improve and strengthen the export taxes rather than to pin one's hopes on levying heavy land taxes.

In the long run, of course, export taxes on agricultural products are not a promising fiscal instrument upon which to rely, in part because of their disincentive effects; so heavier taxes on agricultural land have much more merit, if political circumstances allow their use, and sufficient time and effort can be devoted to establishing the necessary legal and administrative framework. Latin American experience in this regard suggests that the most rewarding path to follow, if an agricultural land tax is to contribute much to development, would be to concentrate on establishing a solidly based simple property tax with meaningful rates, rather than through graduated rates of tax, special taxes on idle lands, and similar devices attempting to achieve primarily nonfiscal purposes.

In the past the inherent problems of levying heavy and effective land taxation has been complicated in Latin America by the propensity to attempt to achieve many complex nonfiscal purposes through the land tax—to bring idle lands into production, discriminate against absentee landowners, break up large landed estates, and so on and on. In each and every instance of these attempts, however, the relatively low nominal tax rates and the inadequacy of the basic property valuations have resulted in such low effective rates of tax that few, if any, of these nonfiscal objectives have actually been realized. These same factors, of course, lie behind the relatively low burden of agricultural land taxes characterizing Latin America today. The key role of land valuation in an effective land tax system thus emerges particularly clearly from Latin American experience.

Furthermore, as Daniel Holland has noted, the experience in Jamaica suggests strongly "the wisdom of choosing procedures that may be 'second best' in theory but 'first best' in practice. Basically, Jamaica was able to get off the ground because at a number of steps in the process where there was a choice between an unalterably correct or completely thorough procedure and one that fell short of perfection but could be basically satisfactory, Jamaica opted for the latter."[60] The evidence for this proposition in the long history of unsuccessful attempts at taxing agricultural land in Latin America is overwhelming. For progress to be made on this front, it is clear that the tendency to let the perfect be the enemy of the good must be overcome.

Any survey of agricultural taxation in developing countries raises several puzzling questions. Virtually all authorities seem to agree that a properly constructed tax on agricultural land is the most desirable way to mobilize and transfer the needed resources from the agricultural to the nonagricultural sectors of the economy, since only this tax can perform this task without affecting agricultural production too adversely. Yet nowhere, in Latin America or elsewhere, does the recommended form of land tax appear to be an important revenue-raiser—and certainly not one of increasing importance. Indeed, few countries appear to have effective land taxes of any sort, largely because of the almost universally weak valuation systems—systems which have, in many cases, remained weak despite decades of plans and programs supposedly designed to improve them. Where agricultural taxation effectively transfers resources (at least in gross terms) out of agriculture, this task is generally accomplished through taxes on agricultural exports or, occasionally (though not in Latin America), through other taxes on production. And even in these instances it appears that the importance of these revenue sources has been declining in recent years in most countries.

60. Daniel M. Holland, "A Study of Land Taxation in Jamaica," in Arthur P. Becker, ed., *Land and Building Taxes* (Madison, Wis.: University of Wisconsin Press, 1970), pp. 250-51.

The answers to this puzzle may lie mainly in the administrative and political factors mentioned below. There are also, however, a number of analytical and factual puzzles which confuse matters—for example, the incidence of export taxes and the virtually universal lack of information on the volume and pattern of savings and investment in the agricultural sector itself. When combined with the growing uncertainty of many as to the role that mobilization of resources from agriculture *should* play in development, these factors may play as great a role as politics in explaining the absence in most countries of a clear and coherent policy direction on the vital question of agriculture's appropriate contribution to development resources—and the corresponding presence in most developing countries of a confused and confusing mass of contradictory public policies affecting land use, agricultural production, and the distribution and allocation of agricultural resources.

Finally, the outstanding impression conveyed by a brief survey of (mostly) secondary studies of agricultural taxation in various Latin American countries is, apart from the weakness of some vital primary information, how little empirical work has really been done with the available information, despite twenty years of continual discussion of agricultural tax problems.[61] Furthermore, much of the existing empirical work appears to be concerned more with the "relative burden" of taxation on the agricultural and nonagricultural sectors, although the relevance of information of this nature for the design of agricultural taxation is, as argued earlier, far from clear.

Despite the tenuous nature of all these generalizations, one conclusion seems clear: as matters now stand, the direct taxation of agriculture in most of Latin America—as in almost all developing countries—contributes very little to the mobilization of resources for developmental purposes. Where much revenue is collected (as through some export taxes) the effects on agriculture itself are not likely to be desirable; where the effects are, at least in theory, desirable (as through well-ordered land taxes), little revenue is collected. No less-developed country today appears to be emulating the oft-cited experience of late-nineteenth-century Japan in relying on heavy agricultural land taxes as a prime source of revenues for development. Whether the reasons for this apparent regular pattern are political or otherwise, the prospects of a drastic change in this situation in the immediate future do not appear to be especially strong. From a developmental point of view, therefore, the

61. Almost none of the questions raised twenty years ago at the Harvard Conference on Agricultural Taxation and Economic Development have yet been answered; for example, see Haskell P. Wald and Joseph N. Froomkin, eds., *Papers and Proceedings of the Conference on Agricultural Taxation and Economic Development* (Cambridge, Mass., 1954), pp. 31-56, for an impressive list of problems requiring research. A very similar list was recently put forth by Wald, "Where to Now? The Future for Research," pp. 691-703.

results of a survey of the taxation of agriculture in Latin America must be considered somewhat depressing, certainly if one believes that agriculture *should* make a net contribution through the tax system to development elsewhere in the economy.

Although the theoretical argument of the first part of the paper was conducted without special reference to Latin America, all the questions raised there are of course equally relevant in the Latin American context, despite the fact that few if any countries appear to have considered them explicitly in shaping agricultural tax policy. The fact that few countries in Latin America appear to tax agriculture very heavily is thus unlikely to reflect very deep thought about the many and complex conceptual issues at stake. Three other explanations are commonly offered for this general failure to obtain much of a contribution for public revenues from the agricultural sector.

Feasibility Constraints on Tax Level

One explanation is "that insufficient recognition of the strategic role that agriculture can and should play in contributing to the capital requirements of economic development has been a factor in the failure to realize the potential for a higher rate of capital formulation."[62] In view of the lack of explicit discussion of these matters in many Latin American countries, there may be some truth in this proposition that the failure to tax agriculture reflects some such perceptual deficiency on the part of policy makers. On the other hand, they have been told about the conventional reasoning often enough by foreign advice-givers, so their failure to act on this advice may equally well reflect a different perception of the appropriate reality on their part. Yet again, to argue that "correct" knowledge will necessarily lead to "correct" action suggests a rather naive view of the policy process.

Few proponents of heavier taxes on agriculture have actually been this naive. Instead, they fall back on a second sort of explanation for the "inadequate" agricultural taxation characterizing most developing countries, not least in Latin America: "In many instances the hesitation to tax the agricultural sector is traceable to political factors, although administrative difficulties are generally cited as the explanation. *Either* the rural votes have to be safeguarded—a question of great significance in most democratic, underdeveloped countries in view of their massive rural sectors. *Or* the landed interests constitute an oligarchy powerful enough to block further taxation of the agricultural sector."[63]

62. Johnston and Mellor, "The Role of Agriculture," p. 579. Gandhi, *Tax Burden*, p. 8, appears to consider this an important factor even in India, where all these issues have been explicitly discussed for years.

63. Jagdish Bhagwati, *The Economics of Underdeveloped Countries* (New York: McGraw-Hill, 1966), p. 78; emphasis in original.

Nicholas Kaldor prefers to emphasize only the political power of the wealthy in his explanation of the failure of the underdeveloped countries to tax agriculture adequately, although he agrees in downgrading the importance of the administrative obstacle to effective agricultural taxation.[64] Many writers on Latin America would agree with him.

While there is certainly much merit in this view for some countries, attributing the widespread low level of direct taxation on agriculture *entirely* to a failure of political will is too simple. The administrative aspects of heavy agricultural land taxes, particularly those intended to exert positive incentive effects, require more careful consideration than they have normally received from their proponents. In fact, the inevitable administrative limitations in any developing country do appear to constitute a sufficiently formidable obstacle to the implementation of many of the more sophisticated recommendations (though not nearly so much to heavier taxation of agriculture in cruder forms) to explain in part the widespread absence of effective legislation of this sort. This point may be made clearer by a brief consideration of the possibilities of different *forms* of agricultural taxation.

Feasibility Constraints on Tax Form

The crucial importance of the particular interweaving of political, economic, and administrative conditions which characterizes each country in determining the feasibility of agricultural tax recommendations may be made clearer by looking at the likely fate of an "ideal" agricultural tax proposed by one of the leading writers in the field, Haskell Wald.

Wald's "ideal" tax plan requires that all agricultural land be classified and assessed in terms of its presumptive net income. As he points out: "To achieve this, two types of soil classifications are necessary: (1) in terms of inherent soil characteristics (i.e., scientific soil mapping to determine the 'soil profile'), and (2) in terms of economic use capabilities, as determined by potential water supply, climate, exposure to sunshine, topography, availability of farm implements, etc. Each delineated land area should be assigned a rating in accordance with its potential net income under average growing conditions and proper management, with appropriate allowances for distance from trading centers and other market factors."[65] The unreality of postulating the existence of this in-

64. Nicholas Kaldor, *Essays on Economic Policy*, vol. 1 (London: Gerald Duckworth & Co. Ltd., 1964), p. 18; see also "Will Underdeveloped Countries Learn to Tax?" ibid., pp. 263-65.

65. Haskell P. Wald, "Taxation of Agriculture in Developing Countries," in A. N. Agarwala and S. P. Singh, eds., *Accelerating Investment in Developing Economies* (Bombay: Oxford University Press, 1969), pp. 168-69. An even more horrific list of the "required" characteristics for the potential net income tax may be found in Jarach, *El impuesto a la renta normal potencial*, pp. 26-30.

formation as a prerequisite speaks for itself. Indeed, Wald himself noted, in what must be one of the most striking understatements in the literature on development finance: "The requirements for its successful implementation in all its phases are doubtless prohibitive for many countries. . . ."[66] Nevertheless, he suggests that this approach provides an appropriate target at which to aim.

The logic of this position may seem irrefutable. It has, however, frequently been refuted by the facts, the principal one of which is that in every country, *without exception,* in which grandiose plans of this sort have been proposed, they have failed to be realized. The uniformity of this experience of failure may suggest that something is wrong with the proposed solution. And so it appears to be. For if a country were capable of even attempting on a large scale the sorts of things Wald proposes, it would no longer be an underdeveloped country. And if it were not underdeveloped, it would presumably not need to rely on heavy agricultural taxation and on indirect and back-door attempts at effective income taxation through "personalized" land taxes. In short, the basic problem with Wald's proposed reform of the agricultural land tax to achieve better its fiscal ends (revenue, equity) is the same as with the many similar proposed reforms to achieve nonfiscal ends—that is, it really assumes away many of the problems with which it is allegedly designed to cope.

Writers who favor the extensive use of agricultural taxation for nonfiscal purposes occasionally recognize, usually with a note of surprise, that the many good things for which the legislation was enacted never seem to eventuate. But their analyses of the causes of this repeated failure —many instances of which may be noted in Latin America—leave much to be desired. One recent author, for example, attributes it to the difficulty producers have in understanding the incentive effects of tax structure and to the generally negative attitude most people have toward taxes—an attitude fostered by the "complexity, incoherence and lack of stability in the tax formulas which are passed" and by the inadequacy of the tax education program. When the taxes fail, as they usually do, "the failure may be attributed not to the tax itself but rather to the legal formulas adopted to carry out this particular law, which established, for example, exceedingly low rates or legal formulas which are too complicated, and which normally go hand-in-hand with a high percentage of tax evasion."[67] The problem with this approach is that it leaves out of account the political economy of taxation.

66. Wald, "Taxation of Agriculture," p. 169.
67. José M. Gimeno Sanz, "Taxation: Some Considerations Concerning Its Importance in the Economic Development of the Agricultural Sector," mimeographed (Santiago, Chile, 1970), pp. 13-15. See also José M. Gimeno Sanz, *La Tributación Agropecuaria,* 2 vols. (Santiago, Chile: Oficina de Planificación Agricola, 1970).

It is true, for example, that one reason why no incentive uses of agricultural taxes appear to have worked is that the legislation has almost always been poorly laid out and inadequately based on facts. As already suggested, an important reason in most countries is that the necessary precise information on soils and their capacity to produce income simply does not exist. Even more important, such proposals really have no political backing as a rule. These three points are not unconnected. Advocates of nonfiscal uses of agricultural taxation usually focus on the first point, dispose of the second by saying that one needs this information anyway "to design an adequate Agricultural Development Plan or an efficient Agrarian Reform,"[68] and simply ignore the third.

The administrative difficulty cannot be so easily disposed of, however. While it may not in fact be as hard to get a *rough* idea of the necessary information as has sometimes been said, it will *always* be rough—and therefore hard to use, even if the political environment permitted. Furthermore, the assumption apparent not only in this argument but in a great deal of the literature favoring the nonfiscal use of agricultural taxation, that the state not only can but must have the requisite detailed information, can bear little weight. (The additional argument that the now advanced countries have gotten along with wretched assessment systems so perhaps a good informational base is not so crucial, simply ignores the points that these countries have never tried to place much nonfiscal weight on their agricultural tax systems, and—more important —they have never had to place such *fiscal* weight on agriculture as many less developed countries, pressed by time and circumstance, now feel they must do.) Finally, it seems unlikely that it will be efficient to employ scarce administrative resources in administratively subtle schemes to avoid direct political conflict.

Considering further the political aspect, it is curious that the many writers who have proposed major tax changes largely on the grounds of their allegedly beneficial effects on economic incentives never appear to recognize the peculiar political setting that would have to prevail for these recommendations to be both feasible and effective. The common argument that heavier taxes on the potential output of agricultural land will induce landowners *either* to use land more productively *or* to get out of the land-owning business and sell to someone else who will do so rests, for example, on two quite implausible assumptions: first, that the government can administer the complex tax envisaged (i.e., it has all the relevant data and can effectively assess and enforce the correct tax levy), and second, that the only option facing landowners is to pay up or get out. The implausibility of the first was commented on above. The second has been less noticed: the problem here is that landowners have a third option—they can protest, or, in Hirschman's terminology, exercise the

68. Sanz, "Taxation: Some Considerations," p. 16.

"voice" instead of the "exit" option.[69] A possible interpretation of the failure to levy heavy taxes on agriculture in some countries is thus that landowners are able to utilize effectively the voice option—which one would suspect is lower in cost and more available to them in the usual case than the exit option on which the conventional argument depends so heavily—at an early stage and kill off such proposals before they are enacted. In other instances, the role of voice may be more crucial at a later stage, when it comes time actually to implement penalty tax legislation already on the books: Chile, Brazil, and Colombia, among many others in Latin America, offer examples. The most effective way to block reform legislation may often be to set up a body (or pass a law) charged with the reform task, but so crippled by its organization or structure that it cannot do it.

Linking Taxes and Expenditures

This stress on the importance of political as well as economic means of avoiding tax pressure is not meant simply to deplore the former and praise the latter. Rather, it adds considerable weight to the economic arguments adduced earlier for strategic investments in the agricultural sector as essential ingredients of development policy in many situations. The point now is different from the common argument—which is also sound—that in order to impose a tax successfully in most developing countries one must first demonstrate a good reason for spending the tax proceeds, preferably one which can be shown to benefit in some moderately direct way the prospective taxpayers. Properly designed earmarking and benefit financing are as useful and even essential with respect to agricultural taxation as anywhere else.[70]

Consideration of the role of voice in shaping the outcome of tax policy suggests an extra virtue for such policies in the present context, however: namely, opinion is likely to split the opposition to the new tax measures and hence make their introduction more feasible. It seems much less likely that attempts to demonstrate "unused taxable capacity" and the relative sectoral tax burden of agriculture will help much in this respect, since the landed interests (or just plain farmers) can unite in protest at attempts to justify additional taxation by this approach.

Strategy and Tactics of Tax Change

Both political and administrative constraints are thus crucial in shaping the feasible level and, especially, structure of agricultural tax policy. In most of Latin America, these considerations (and past experience) would

---

69. See Albert O. Hirschman, *Exit, Voice and Loyalty* (Cambridge, Mass.: Harvard University Press, 1970).

70. See, for example, the discussion in Bird, *Taxation and Development*, chap. 5.

appear to urge relatively simple taxes on agricultural land supplemented by as many benefit taxes and user charges as possible and backed up by careful research on the appropriate level of the net intersectoral flow of resources in the country in question. Attempts to go beyond this simple prescription and to resolve all of man's ills with gimmick-ridden personalized taxes on potential income are not only unlikely to come to pass but may also tend to block more feasible measures (which may sometimes be more, rather than less, drastic).

The most serious problem with most schemes for reforming agricultural taxation is that they are too perfect. Now, complexity may be a virtue rather than a vice—for example, when it is needed to cope with a complex economic situation or when it leapfrogs over problems—and perfection is presumably a desirable, though unattainable, quality. But attempts to achieve perfection in one blow through complexity seldom work. One reason is that they paint so vivid a picture of all the complicated problems that might conceivably be encountered that few political decision makers are willing to consider them seriously. And generally the politicians are right, for the only way they can cope in a difficult and changing world is to do what has to be done next and not to worry too much about taking into account all the possible consequences of their actions. Furthermore, we do not know what the "perfect" agricultural tax system is for any particular country with any certainty, nor, if we did, would it likely be useful to impose it all at once in a comprehensive all-or-nothing program. Rational, calculating man just does not work that way, and those concerned with improving agricultural tax policy might therefore be better advised, as a rule, to devote their efforts to the difficult enough task of getting a small, sound basis upon which to build the better world piece by piece.

This argument for gradual and piecemeal adjustment of the agricultural tax system from where it now is to where it "should" be for any particular country at a particular point in time—itself a notion fraught with technical and philosophic difficulties[71]—is based on both a theoretical argument and a political assessment. The latter is simply that any political system can absorb only so much policy change at any one time without serious fracture, particularly with respect to tax reform, which by its nature engenders few supporters and many opponents. Those whose tax burdens are lightened by the reform will take it as merely a delayed and inadequate recognition of their special circumstances, while those whose burdens are increased can never be persuaded that the increase is justified. Major changes in tax systems usually take place only as a result of acute crisis, such as wars, depressions, or revolutions. All-

71. Some of these are explored in Bird, "Optimal Tax Policy," and (in a very different context) "The Tax Kaleidoscope: Perspectives on Tax Reform in Canada," *Canadian Tax Journal* 18 (September/October 1970): 444-73.

or-nothing alternatives therefore make strategic sense only when one either expects or hopes for some radical change in the values of government in the near future. Whether a holistic or a piecemeal approach is more advisable as a tactical matter depends on the prevailing circumstances. Sometimes a more radical approach may make a less drastic but still radical approach more acceptable than it otherwise would be. But as a rule it would appear that dramatic breaks with the existing system are more likely to generate conflict than to produce acceptable solutions immediately. Attempts to achieve indirectly goals such as land reform that have been rejected directly are equally unlikely to get anywhere, as much Latin American evidence suggests.

There are also good theoretical reasons, apart from the limitations of the collective political digestion in most countries—unless one is willing to consider a broad and sweeping political change as either probable or necessary—to support a continued piecemeal approach to tax reform. One such reason is the effort involved in obtaining information and reaching a decision. Given man's finite intelligence, there is good reason to expect that introducing an element of "disjointedness" into the tax reform process by considering only a part of the system at a time will enable us in general to reach more satisfactory decisions, by placing the dimensions of the problem more within the limitations of our communicating and information-absorbing abilities.[72] Rationality is in fact generally aided by the subdivision of problems into manageable parts, so long as the relevant ramifications of changes throughout the economic and social system are taken adequately into account.

Furthermore, in practice, policy making is almost invariably a never-ending process of nibbles rather than a once-for-all resolution of some important issue. This sequential process has several important advantages: it gives our limited intelligences a reasonable chance to consider the effects of particular measures; it gives us a second chance to take remedial action if something does not work out quite the way we expected it to; and it allows us to incorporate into later measures feedback from the constituency our policy is intended to serve, thus focusing policy mainly on correcting perceived wrongs rather than on the much more controversial and difficult task of establishing future norms. It also permits the ready incorporation of adjustments to accommodate policy to shifting conditions and objectives.

This sequential approach to policy, far from being inherently deficient compared to the holistic, comprehensive approach favored by most

72. See Charles E. Lindblom, *The Policy-Making Process* (Englewood Cliffs, N.J.: Prentice-Hall, 1969). See also Herbert Simon, *Administrative Behavior,* 2nd ed. (New York: The Free Press, 1957) for similar ideas in a different context. A general philosophical argument against holistic planning of reforms may be found in K. R. Popper, *The Poverty of Historicism* (London: Routledge & Kegan Paul, 1957).

would-be reformers, may actually improve our chances of making good policy decisions in the face of the constantly changing interdependent complexity of social and economic realities. As Charles Lindblom has put it: ". . . analytical methods cannot be restricted to tidy scholarly procedures. The piecemealing, remedial incrementalist or satisficer may not look like an heroic figure. He is nevertheless a shrewd, resourceful problem-solver who is wrestling bravely with a universe he is wise enough to know is too big for him."[73] Unless, therefore, one has a very great deal of faith in the wisdom and foresight of any conceivable person or group, the piecemeal approach is not only the necessary tactical approach to implementing even large changes, but it is also, despite its untidiness, usually the only way we have to be even partly sure the changes we implement will be the "right" ones.

In the present context, this line of reasoning again supports the earlier stress on the importance of initiating and fostering the acceptable (e.g., simple, low-rate land taxes associated with some tangible benefit to at least some prospective taxpayers) rather than the perfect. It is of course quite possible that in particular countries objective analysis of the situation may suggest that drastic land redistribution—which usually means a revolution of some sort—is the only way to achieve professed social and economic goals.[74] Even so, there would seem to be nothing to gain (and perhaps something to lose—time) by attempting to achieve such revolutionary aims through reformist measures such as land taxes. Such indirect policies assume too much stupidity on the part of one segment of the polity (the landowners) and equally unwarranted capability on the part of another (the administration) to stand much chance of success.

Conclusion

The principal concern of this paper has not been to demonstrate how countries can mulct their agricultural sectors—and certainly not to argue that they should. Rather, its aim has been to illustrate the wide and often conflicting range of objectives and instruments conceivably open to those concerned with agricultural tax policy. The conclusions are not particularly encouraging to those who believe in the general applicability of simple developmental models or in the possibilities of technical end runs around the political difficulties and administrative weaknesses hampering agricultural tax policy in all countries. Although the problem is a subtle and complex one, varying from country to country, a general approach—quite different in tone from that usually offered in papers with titles similar to this one—has been tentatively ventured: the road to heavier agri-

---

73. Lindblom, *Policy-Making Process,* p. 27.
74. See Edmundo Flores, "Issues of Land Reform," *Journal of Political Economy* 68, no. 4, part 2 (July/August 1970): 890-905.

cultural taxation in general (if desired) and more effective agricultural land taxes in particular lies in simplicity, even crudity, of both valuation technique and tax structure, coupled with appropriate expenditure policy, rather than in the panacea of personalized taxes on presumptive agricultural income.

Acknowledgment.—The author is most grateful for the research support extended by the Harvard Law School International Tax Program in connection with a study of agricultural land taxation in developing countries, now in preparation.

Comment—George E. Lent

BIRD poses two fundamental questions with particular reference to agricultural taxation: is heavier taxation of agriculture a necessary condition for economic development, and is taxation of potential income of agricultural land the best way to tax agriculture? His reexamination of the first issue seriously questions the conventional wisdom and makes a constructive reevaluation of the proper role of tax policy in a developing economy. The second question is answered in the context of a tax reform strategy of the "second best" which offers much sound advice.

THE DUAL ECONOMY THESIS

Bird challenges the commonly accepted view that a net transfer of resources from agriculture is an indispensable condition for industrialization of the economy, and that tax policy should be used as an instrument for this transformation. He is careful, however, to emphasize the mutual interaction of agricultural and industrial development and the need to take a pragmatic view of the comparative requirements of each under different conditions and at different stages of development.

It is true that some fiscal economists, drawing on the questionable evidence of the Meiji period, have concluded that Japan's land tax was a key factor in effecting a transfer of resources from agriculture to industry. This view, however, finds little support in the work of Fei and Ranis, who have presented perhaps the most formal model of a dual economy. While they acknowledge the role of the land tax in financing the social and economic overheads in the early Meiji period,[1] they attach far greater importance to the "connectedness" between the agricultural and industrial sectors, which facilitated direct investment of farmers in decentralized rural industries, close to the soil. Reacting to the intersectoral terms of

1. Irma Adelman and Erik Thorbecke, eds., *The Theory and Design of Economic Development* (Baltimore: Johns Hopkins University Press, 1966), p. 39.

trade and the changing relative returns on investment, landowners channeled their savings into the emerging industries.

I believe Bird is on sound ground in rejecting the hypothesis that
agricultural tax policy should under all conditions be dictated by the
objective of transferring resources from the agricultural to the industrial
sector. Under some conditions agricultural development itself must be
served through large expenditures on infrastructure for irrigation and
highways, as well as by private capital investment.

It would have been very illuminating if Bird had applied his thesis
more directly to the Latin American scene, where we find a wide range
of dualism in the economy. Some countries, especially in Central America,
are only just emerging from a predominantly agricultural economy. Many
Latin American countries, however, do not appear to conform to the condition usually assumed in the model of a dual economy, where agriculture is the dominant sector as it was in Meiji Japan. Although the population is predominantly rural in most countries, the following table shows
that agriculture in the more-developed countries of Latin America accounts for a relatively minor share of gross domestic product.

TABLE 1

VALUE-ADDED BY AGRICULTURE AS A PERCENT OF GDP

	1959	1968
Venezuela	6.5[a]	7.0
Chile	11.1[a]	8.1[b]
Mexico	16.3	13.3
Argentina	19.9	15.4[b]
Peru	26.5[c]	20.0[cd]
Brazil	22.6	22.6[b]
Colombia	34.3	29.9[b]

SOURCE: *National Accounts of Less Developed Countries,*
1959-68, OECD, Paris, June 1970.
[a]1960.
[b]1967.
[c]Percent of national income.
[d]1966.

In 1968, for example, it contributed only 7 percent in Venezuela and 8
percent in Chile. Only in Colombia, with a percentage of 29.9, did it exceed one-quarter of the GDP. In all of these countries, with the exception of Brazil, the share of agriculture has declined since 1959. Agricultural output has of course been increasing in absolute terms to meet the
needs of expanding population. In these countries, however, industrial
capital is supplied predominantly from nonagricultural resources, including capital imports (indeed, much capital is transferred abroad). This
development can be seen clearly in the rapid industrialization of countries
such as Mexico, the value of whose agricultural output increased from

22.5 billion pesos in 1959 to 31.5 billion pesos in 1967, at 1959 prices, but whose share of total GDP declined from 16.3 percent to 13.3 percent.

At their present stage of development, it cannot be inferred that the tax policies of Latin American countries should be guided by the objective of transferring resources from the agricultural to the industrial sector. Indeed, industrialization probably has been proceeding in most of these countries under the reverse conditions, with agriculture contributing proportionately less in tax revenue than its share of GDP. It is not easy to confirm this opinion statistically because of the difficulty of ascertaining the incidence of various duties on imports, sales taxes, or even income taxes. Several years ago I made careful estimates for Ecuador which indicated that the agricultural sector contributed about 27.5 percent of all government tax revenue, against a 37.9 percent share of GDP. In some countries—especially in Central America—duties on exports of primary products, income taxes, property taxes, import duties, and sales taxes may well equal or exceed the share of agriculture in GDP. But because of the generally low ratios of taxes to GDP in these countries, the net transfer, if any, is bound to be relatively small. Moreover, as Bird points out, a large part of government expenditures is devoted to rural infrastructure and agricultural improvements, and in some countries export and other taxes are earmarked for this purpose. Because of the many complex factors involved it would be exceedingly difficult, if not impossible, to show any correlation between the pace of industrialization and agricultural tax policies.

TAXATION OF AGRICULTURE

I turn now to the other fundamental question posed: is taxation of potential income of the agricultural sector the best way to tax agriculture? In the context of Bird's paper, this bears on the most feasible approach to the taxation of agricultural land.

First, we should consider alternative methods of reaching agricultural income. The technique most generally found in Latin America is a tax on agricultural exports. Undoubtedly this is the most practicable method of exacting a contribution from the farming sector, because of the ease of administration through customs. (A similar result is achieved through the use of multiple exchange rates administered by the central bank.) In other than exceptional circumstances, however, it is difficult to defend export taxes because of their disincentive effects on the production of export commodities and balance of trade. Moreover, such taxes discriminate in favor of other commodities produced for the domestic market. However, where there is an international commodity agreement, as in the case of coffee, they may usefully supplement direct controls on production. And, properly designed, they also serve a desirable purpose in siphoning off excess purchasing power that may arise from a boom in commodity prices or a devaluation of the currency. Under usual conditions, however, export taxes can best be defended as a substitute for an income tax where a great number of small producers make it impracticable to assess and collect it equitably. An export tax may also be used as a technique for advance collection of an income tax on farmers, as in Peru and Uruguay.

In principle, an income tax based on reported income is a more equitable instrument for taxing farmers, but it is effectively limited to larger plantations, concessions, and exporters that maintain adequate records. It is employed with some success in a number of Latin American countries, but in others farmers are exempted and its potential has not been fully realized. It is of interest that Paraguay has just reformed its income tax law and plans to substitute an income tax for the export tax previously assessed on cattle growers. In a few other countries the income tax is integrated with export taxes or with a net wealth tax. However, a tax on reported net income not only fails to reach the mass of small- and intermediate-scale farmers, but it does not tap the income potential of large landowners and others that is represented by idle or underutilized land.

This brings us to the substance of Bird's paper on the taxation of potential income represented by the ownership of land. Anyone who has observed the present state of land taxation in developing countries is bound to agree with his observation that the record is a dismal one, not only in Latin America but also in other parts of the world. This sad state is relieved in the Latin American and Caribbean areas by recent progress in Chile, Jamaica, Puerto Rico, and perhaps a few other countries. Some countries have not adopted a tax on agricultural land—e.g., Bolivia, Dominican Republic, Haiti, Peru, and Venezuela. Others have a land tax in name only, based on self-declarations or on assessments that reflect nominal values established many years ago.

It is virtually impossible, on the basis of published data, to ascertain the amount of revenue derived from agricultural land taxes where they are applied, and there is a strong presumption that it is greatly exceeded by the taxes on urban property. Nevertheless, it is of interest that in El Salvador taxes on net wealth, including the value of agricultural land, amounted in 1968 to 7.3 percent of total government tax revenue; net wealth taxes contributed 8.3 percent in Nicaragua, and property taxes 5.5 percent in Costa Rica. Available data also show that real estate taxes amount to over 4 percent of total tax revenue in Colombia, Paraguay, and Jamaica.

If the process of industrialization is to continue to absorb an increasing share of the resources of Latin American countries, agricultural productivity must be improved in order to assure an expanding output. There appears to be sufficient "slack" in the rural economy to permit an expansion of both. This is evidenced both in the increasingly serious problem of rural unemployment and in the extensive unused and underutilized arable land areas. I believe that more intensive land taxation can and should be instituted as one instrument that will assist in implementing the transformation to a more industrialized economy by encouraging more effective use of land and labor. Other measures are of course also needed to facilitate the process, including colonization, land reform, and provision of agricultural credit facilities.

In principle, a fixed annual charge placed on land provides an incentive to increase output. This is the well-recognized income effect of taxation. If the fixed charge on the larger idle tracts is high enough, it will induce better utilization through more intensive cultivation, lease, or sale of part of the land, and thereby help absorb the growing rural labor force. Aside from its allocative effects, such a tax also serves to improve the equity of the tax system.

A land tax may be based either on the value of the land or a fixed amount per unit of area depending on its potential yield. The choice of methods rests largely on the availability of the relevant data necessary for implementation of the tax. Jamaica apparently has found sufficient reliable records of sales to warrant a valuation approach; but even when sales prices are reported, they are suspect because of the levy of other taxes on transfer of property, etc. Land values in Uruguay are capitalized annual rentals as determined by a sampling of lease contracts. Bolivia, on the other hand, plans to assess land by reference to its presumed yield; for this purpose it classifies land into eleven different soil types, according to use as pasture or for crops, and by size of holdings. Chile has attempted by elaborate techniques to determine values per hectare for each of twelve qualities of land in each township, adjusted for locational factors. I believe that any of these techniques may serve the purpose, and what might be practicable in one country is not necessarily the most feasible in another, depending on the conditions of tenure, availability of necessary data, and administrative capability.

The almost universal neglect of taxes on land value is attributable to a variety of factors, which have been summarized by Bird and others: the composition of political power, landowners' distrust of the government, and administrative incompetence. I am perhaps more optimistic than he that these obstacles can be overcome and that agricultural land taxes can be greatly strengthened if governments are convinced of the important role they can play in economic development. Evidence of this is seen in Jamaica, Chile, Nicaragua, and El Salvador. Unfortunately, the balance of political power in many Latin American countries is too unstable to get legislative support for such a tax program even when the administration is convinced of its desirability.

There are many technical requirements for the successful implementation of a land tax system. These are delineated by the United Nations in its excellent Manual of Land Tax Administration and I will not repeat them here. However, I should like to point out some of the essential conditions for progress in this area.

Land registry.—The first prerequisite is a land registry system, which identifies all parcels of land in the country and is supported by adequate land maps. This not only fixes boundaries but also identifies ownership and provides for transfer of title. The necessity of preparing such a registry in Bolivia has delayed the introduction of its land tax.

Fixing annual assessment.—The most critical and difficult phase of land tax procedure is the determination of relative assessment of land of different yield or value, depending on the system used. Compliance with the tax—taxpayer morale—rests fundamentally on how accurately the assessments reflect differential values or yields of different properties and distribute the burden in an equitable fashion.

I have become convinced that centralized direction and control, if not actual administration, of the cadastre is essential to accomplish this. Except in federal systems of government, the cadastre should be under the supervision of the central government. It is sufficiently removed from local pressures to prepare objective valuations and should be sufficiently manned with trained technicians to apply uniform standards throughout the country. Although largely for political reasons the Catastro administration of Uruguay has failed in the past to maintain current values, its organization could serve as a model for other governments. The Chilean example is also very impressive.

I believe that there is no substitute for administratively determined assessments. Self-assessment, as practiced in several Central American and South American countries, has been a failure. There has been much debate over market-enforced self-assessment, but I am convinced that the merits claimed for it are illusory.[2] Not only would it seriously undermine rights in private property and be of questionable legality, but, if enforced, it would strike unevenly and penalize the unwary who would be uninformed of changing property values if no guidelines were provided. Moreover, its effectiveness would depend on whether the sanctions—i.e., sale of the property—was a credible threat. The poor record of property tax enforcement in Latin American countries provides no basis for such credibility. In my view, the government would abdicate its responsibility if such a system were instituted.

2. See John D. Strasma, "Market-Enforced Self-Assessment for Real Estate Taxes," *Bulletin for International Fiscal Documentation* 19 (1965): 353-63, 397-414, and Daniel M. Holland and William M. Vaughn, "An Evaluation of Self-Assessment Under a Property Tax" in Arthur D. Lynn, ed., *The Property Tax and Its Administration* (Madison, Wis.: University of Wisconsin Press, 1969), pp. 79-118.

Keeping values current.—Failure to update property values is one of the greatest weaknesses of the property tax. Neglect of periodic revaluations has impaired its elasticity as a revenue source, diluted its effectiveness as an incentive, and compounded its inequities. Annual indexing of assessments based on changes in market values of crops, as practiced in Chile, is essential in an inflationary economy. Quadrennial or quinquennial revaluations are indispensable in a growing economy.

Collection.—If the property tax revenue is allocated to local governments, it may be desirable to provide for local collection (although it is centrally collected in Uruguay). Property tax delinquency is endemic throughout Latin America, and more effective collection methods need to be devised. Sending notices of tax due, quarterly or semiannual payments, convenient facilities for payment, publicity, and penalties enforced for delinquencies are some of the techniques found to be fruitful. Collection by agents on a commission basis, or tax farming, should be abolished.

It should be acknowledged that a tax on land value (or potential yield) is one of the most complex and difficult taxes to administer properly. The success of its implementation turns basically on the soundness and fairness of the cadastre itself. While the establishment of a proper cadastre may take several years and involve a sizable investment, this investment will repay itself many times in enhanced revenues and serve as well many other useful purposes, not the least of which is the implementation of taxes on the transfer of property, net wealth taxes, and inheritance taxes. Most important, it requires constant vigilance to keep it up to date.

Discussion

N. KALDOR: It is evident from what Lent says that there are some countries like Ecuador, Paraguay, and Chile that have made a serious attempt at land taxation in a narrow sense of providing government revenue. Of course, in almost all of the Latin American countries agriculture is in some sense heavily "taxed" through adverse terms of trade. This is a form of taxation which has unfavorable effects on economic growth. The highly adverse terms of trade imposed on agriculture by the general economic policies of Latin American governments have been a major factor in all sorts of problems.

As for taxation of agriculture through *direct* taxes or land taxes, based on potential output or presumed income from land, Bird seems to apply the facts of North America to the very different conditions of Latin

America. Canada and the United States are rather special countries in the sense that agriculture is largely a matter of farming by farmers who are owner-cultivators and absentee land ownership is not a prominent feature. But in Latin America circumstances are very different. The cultivators receive only a modest share of the net output of agriculture. A large share, the surplus, is extracted from them by landlords who are passive and who monetize their income, but this monetized income does not serve any very useful social purpose. In fact, it was the accepted view in the nineteenth century, following the theories of Ricardo, that the income accruing as rent to the landlords is a passive element which is spent in an unproductive manner. Because land is a safe and permanent source of income (actually of a growing income, since land values and land rents are always rising), landowners need not save at all. It is the entrepreneurs, the businessmen, the profit earners who use their incomes productively in investment; the landlords spend their incomes on consumption. From what I know of a country like Chile, the very large landowners do not even live in Chile. They mostly live in Paris and spend their incomes from Chilean land, which not only means unproductive expenditure but also contributes to the balance-of-payments problem.

To the question of why these people are not taxed, an answer is that in the past they have been taxed, at least in the countries of the Middle East and in Asia and Japan. The 10 percent tax on land based on assessments of the value of land is an ancient form of revenue going back many centuries and was almost the sole source of revenue for many governments. These land taxes were completely eroded in the last fifty years due to the failure to make the normal quinquennial cadastral reassessments. On account of inflation, the land values on which the tax is now based have become purely nominal, so that while the tax may be nominally 10 percent, in fact it amounts to a fraction of 1 percent of the true annual value of the land.

The issue is, how can these taxes be revived? In a world in which the price mechanism is perfectly functioning, all the factors affecting potential yield should be accurately reflected in the market value of the land. In a perfect market and under perfect competition, land values take into account all the factors affecting the potential fertility of the soil— the sunshine, locational advantages, etc. All one would have to do is tax land values on an annual basis, i.e., the amount the land would fetch on the open market. Of course, markets are not perfect in this sense, and to ascertain the true potential yield in practice is a difficult business. In the nineteenth century British revenue officials in India fixed a reasonable market value for the land, a cadastral value, by taking into account all the numerous factors that a property surveyor would take into account in arriving at a valuation. The valuation so arrived at would stand for five years, and after five years the job had to be done again. This was kept up throughout the nineteenth century. But in Latin America, for administrative and political reasons this appeared to be a very difficult thing to do, at least until recently, and hence was not done. I agree with Lent that it ought to be done. Experience with this method of assessment shows that even when the initial cadastral valuation is successfully made, it is very difficult to keep it up to date. One alternative, to which Bird did not refer, is a scheme worked out by A. C. Harberger and myself at the Santiago Conference in 1962, later developed more fully by John Strasma,[1] based on a method of self-assessment that makes use of the market but does not depend upon forced sales of land. I do not agree that this scheme is subject to the kind of strictures that Lent made at the end of his remarks concerning the use of the market for self-assessment.

W. BAER: Having lived in Brazil I cannot accept the typical latifundia model of Latin American agriculture. One could apply this model to northeast Brazil, but not to the huge area of southern Brazil (the states of Rio Grande do Sul, Santa Catarina, Paraná, São Paulo, and the southern part of Minas Gerais). In these states, one can find many family-owned farms and the whole structure of agriculture is quite different from, say, the agricultural conditions in the Peruvian valleys. The appropriate types of land reform, changes in land distribution, or modernization of agriculture are quite different from what one would recommend after studying Central America or the Andean countries.

One problem found in areas such as southern Brazil with its many small farms (not minifundia, but often fairly efficient small farms) is the monopoly element in the system of agricultural produce distribution, which prevents fluctuations in prices from being passed on to the producer. In other words, a problem of agricultural modernization in this case is how to tax the middleman, or what to do about the agricultural distribution system.

R. THORN: Many people have expressed the idea that there will be a transfer of income from the agricultural sector to the industrial sector. It may very well be true, as Lent points out, that in some countries the agricultural sector is already paying more in taxes than the benefits it is receiving from the government. But it is also generally receiving very low benefits. In addition, even though the share of national income originating in agriculture might be low, the number of people engaged in agriculture is often very high. If we think of all that needs to be done in agriculture, the only reasonable question is what percentage of the necessary expenditures on the development of the agricultural population (including expenditures on the health and education of people in the rural sector as part of total expenditures on agriculture) will be paid by the

---

1. John D. Strasma, "Market-Enforced Self-Assessment for Real Estate Taxes," *Bulletin for International Fiscal Documentation* 19 (1965): 353-63, 397-414.

agricultural sector itself. I see little possibility in the near future in any Latin American country of net transfers taking place from the agricultural sector to the industrial sector.

Agriculture is one sector in which local taxation might be successful because a large part of the benefits would be local. Needed improvements in the agricultural sector are more easily locally identified, and thus it may be possible to finance a good share of these expenditures at the local level.

I agree with Lent that whether taxation is on the value of the land or is a fixed amount depending on potential yield is a matter of minor importance, because the possibility of these taxes directly stimulating production is not great. The major value of these taxes is to enable the government to acquire resources and pump them back into the agricultural sector, so that it can begin to make the contribution to economic growth it has thus far failed to do in most of Latin America.

J. LEVIN: I should like to discuss two points, the first of which has already been touched upon. There is a sharp distinction to be made between types of agriculture in Latin America. One type is that of export agriculture—coffee, in many cases—in which there is indeed a sectoral transfer of resources from agriculture to industrial development. In the case of Colombia, coffee exports have been subsidizing a fixed, and therefore in real terms declining, price of petroleum products within the country. In the case of Brazil, coffee export taxes go into a sterilized account which offsets bank credit expansion. Thus, when considering the taxation of agriculture in Latin America, we already have in mind a distinction between these traditional export types of agriculture, which are taxed, and other types of agriculture. In some cases, these other agricultural crops fall into the category of new exports or nontraditional exports or minor exports and receive the subsidies which go to stimulate such exports.

Second, with the adoption of land reform and other such direct measures there has been a general shift in approach away from taxation to resource transfers by other means. There is a generally unfavorable view of the transfer of resources through taxation, but the transfer of resources is taking place through other mechanisms. There is, for example, a very thin line between taxation and the enforcement of reserve requirements on banks for certain types of credit allocation. Mexican practice is a prime example of this. The end result—shifting resources to what are considered priority uses—is much the same as with open taxation.

R. MUSGRAVE: Bird's discussion is very interesting, but I would have preferred to see him examine the role of various forms of land taxation in relation to the specific objectives which such taxation might have, e.g., raising revenue, increasing the output of agriculture, land reform, and so forth. This is an interesting analytical issue which has not been dealt with sufficiently. I hope that Bird and others will deal with such matters as the significance of assessing land value as against income; dealing with actual versus presumptive bases; relating tax rates to size of acreage, rate of return, size of return; using various forms of progression, and so forth.

6

Expenditure Policy for Development

RICHARD A. MUSGRAVE

HAVING worked mainly on the revenue side of development finance, I thought this a welcome opportunity to take a look at the other side of the coin. Tax experts, after all, operate on an act of faith: while taxes may be imposed in a more or less equitable fashion, and with more or less desirable effects, their raison d'être is to finance public services. If the tax reformer exhorts developing countries to increase their tax effort, as he is wont to do, this is done on the presumption that resources to be withdrawn from the private sector will be used more effectively on the public side.

What, then, is the validity of this presumption? In exploring this question, one is struck by the dearth of material on the role of public expenditures in economic development. While there are numerous studies dealing with the role of taxation and the properties of a good tax structure, there is little comparable material on the expenditure side. The reason perhaps is that the expenditure problem is inherently more difficult. Where the tax doctor can fall back on a few standard rules, no similar prescriptions are available for expenditure policy. As to taxes, we all agree that the burden should be distributed in an equitable fashion, that disturbing effects should be minimized, that certain corrective or incentive effects on the private sector may be generated, and that allowance should be made for the effects of alternative taxes on saving, investment, and the balance of payments. Granting that ideas about an equitable burden distribution differ and that the techniques of generating incentive effects remain controversial, these rules nevertheless go far in suggesting measures which can be considered an improvement of the tax structure.

On the expenditure side, there are no corresponding principles. The proper questions may be asked, but the answers are hard to come by. The two basic questions are (a) what the proper level of public expenditures should be at various stages of economic development, and (b) what

171

constitutes an optimal expenditure composition at each stage. These two issues are largely interdependent, since the overall expenditure level must be derived from the need for particular items. Yet the constraint imposed by the country's taxable capacity is a further variable which acts directly upon the overall expenditure level. Unfortunately, it is not evident on what basis the need for particular services is to be judged. Is it to be thought of in terms of consumer preferences between social and private goods, or is it to be related to an overriding objective of economic growth or industrialization? Moreover, what emphasis should be given to the distributional implications of fiscal measures? These and related questions must be answered before conclusions on an optimal expenditure structure can be drawn.

THE OVERALL LEVEL OF EXPENDITURES

Beginning with the appropriate overall share of public expenditures, let us see first what the facts have been. This may be viewed in terms of a worldwide pattern or for Latin American countries only.

Worldwide Sample

Various studies have shown that the ratio of public expenditures (or tax revenue) to GNP rises with rising per capita income. This seems to hold true on both a time series and a cross-section basis. If we trace the expenditure to GNP ratio historically over the last seventy-five years, we find that this ratio has exhibited a more or less steady upward trend in most developed countries, such as the United Kingdom, United States, Germany, and so forth. Since this was also a period of sustained rise in per capita income, there is a suggestion (though not proof) that the former had been a function of the latter.

A similar result is obtained from a cross-section comparison among countries with different per capita incomes but for the same period. Regressing the size of the public sector (as measured by the expenditure or, with essentially similar results, the tax to GNP ratio) with per capita income for a worldwide sample of some forty countries, we find a strongly positive relationship. Thus, predicted revenue as percent of GNP rises from 16 at a per capita income of about $250 to 24 at an income of $1,000, and 34 at $2,000.[1] The evidence is similar if we use an index of

---

1. See Richard A. Musgrave, *Fiscal Systems* (New Haven: Yale University Press, 1969), p. 112, where a sample based on the mid-fifties was used. The text ratios are based on this equation:

$$T/GNP = \underset{(10.530)}{.1365} + \underset{(6.4360)}{.0001076Y_c} \quad R^2 = .52.$$

A better fit for the tax to GNP ratio was obtained from a logarithmic function:

$$T/GNP = e^{\underset{(-14.90)}{-3.6896}} Y^{\underset{(8.1373)}{.3369}} \quad R^2 = .64.$$

industrialization in lieu of per capita income. This is as may be expected, since the share of GNP originating in industry is correlated positively with per capita income. Similarly, a negative coefficient is obtained if income originating in agriculture is the independent variable.

In all, it appears that both historical and cross-section approaches sustain the proposition that the share of the public sector increases with per capita income. The cross-section evidence is, however, subject to an important qualification. While a reasonably good regression fit is obtained for the sample as a whole, including low- as well as high-income countries, the fit is much poorer if the sample is divided between low- and high-income countries. While Wagner's Law holds if we compare the average low-income country (with per capita income of, say, $500 or less) with the average high-income country (with per capita income of, say, $1,200 or more) there is little evidence for its operation within each subgroup. Thus, no significant relationship prevails if one limits the sample to countries with incomes below, say, $400. Since the crucial problem of development is in this range, it is difficult to generalize on expenditure behavior.

Turning to the place of Latin American countries in the worldwide picture, it is interesting to note that their performance typically shows a less-than-average tax to GNP ratio. This holds for our sample of forty countries, as well as for a large sample of eighty-two countries, using data for the mid-sixties.[2] It appears from the latter that tax revenue as a percent of GNP for Latin American countries was below the predicted value for eleven countries, while only eight countries showed a percent in excess of the predicted value. The shortfall was highest for Mexico, Colombia, and El Salvador, while the excess was largest for Brazil and Chile.

Latin American Sample

If the comparison is limited to Latin American countries, and we use per capita income, industrialization, and openness as explanatory variables, the results given in Table 1 are obtained.[3] The relation to per capita income is shown in Chart 1.

While the overall fit is less good than for the worldwide sample, this reflects the previously noted phenomenon of clustering and the fact that the Latin America sample consists of relatively low-income countries. Nevertheless, there remains some positive relationship between per capita

---

2. The underlying regression predicts the tax to GNP ratio as a function of per capita income, the degree of industrialization, and a measure of openness of the economy. See G. S. Sahota, "Empirical Standards to Appraise the Allocation of Resources among Social Goods," manuscript, Table 3.

3. Based on data from sample by G. S. Sahota, *Empirical Standards.*

income and the tax to GNP ratio. Also, it is interesting to note that adding the degree of industrialization as an explanatory variable improves the fit, raising the R^2 from 0.38 to 0.41. Industrialization facilities taxation and/or higher expenditures facilitate industrialization. Openness enters with a negative sign and is not a significant factor in explaining the revenue to GNP ratio. There is little relationship between openness and

TABLE 1

DETERMINANTS OF PUBLIC SECTOR SHARE IN LATIN AMERICA[a]

Variables
x_1 = revenue as a percent of GNP
x_2 = per capita income
x_3 = value-added by industry as percent of GNP
x_4 = imports as percent of GNP

I	$x_1 =$	9.37166 (2.03004) 4.6	$+$	$0.015266x_2$ (0.00489) 3.1					$R^2 =$	0.3780
II	$x_1 =$	9.11383 (2.06341) 4.4	$+$	$0.012399x_2$ (0.00588) 2.1	$+$	$0.06077x_3$ (0.06809) 0.89			$R^2 =$	0.4093
III	$x_1 =$	9.68569 (2.68264) 3.6	$+$	$0.015403x_2$ (0.00510) 3.0	$-$	$0.0100087x_4$ (0.05343) -0.19			$R^2 =$	0.3794
IV	$x_1 =$	9.16476 (2.77865) 3.3	$+$	$0.01244x_2$ (0.0062399) 2.0	$+$	$0.060397x_3$ (0.071691) 0.84	$-$	$0.015272x_4$ (0.054882) -0.29 $R^2 =$ 0.4094		

[a]Includes sample of 18 Latin American countries, 1966 (see Appendix Table). Brazil is excluded. Addition of Brazil greatly reduces the fit, with equations I and II reading as follows:

I*	$x_1 =$	11.0759 (2.6098) 4.21	$+$	$0.01259x_2$ (0.00689) 2.0			$R^2 =$	0.1858
II*	$x_1 =$	10.4677 (2.61313) 4.0	$+$	$0.0077508x_2$ (0.00738) 1.0	$+$	$0.10767x_3$ (0.08607) 1.3	$R^2 =$	0.2584

per capita income (except for Venezuela and Uruguay), the tax-handle aspects of trade (easier collectability of customs) not being a significant factor in generating a higher revenue ratio.

The performance of various countries may again be assessed by comparing the actual with the predicted ratios. The results are shown in column 6 of the Appendix Table.[4] As before, we find Brazil to be greatly in excess of the predicted value, followed at some distance by Chile and Argentina, the Dominican Republic, Ecuador, and Peru. Uruguay, Pan-

4. The predicted values are based on equation II,* Table 1, with Brazil included.

CHART 1

<u>Revenue to GNP Ratio and Per Capita Income, 1966[a]</u>

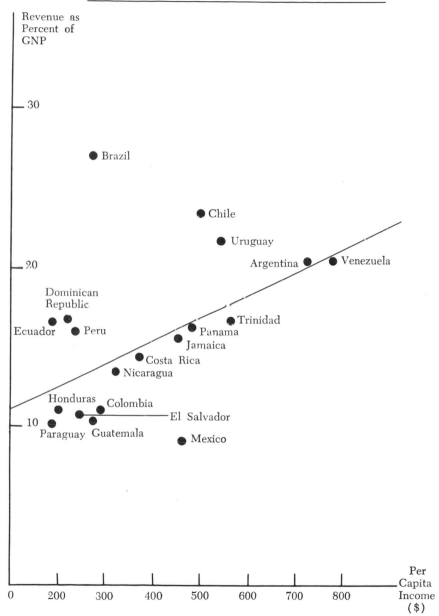

[a]For data see Appendix Table, columns 1 and 2. The equation for the regression line is given in equation I°, Table 1.

ama, Trinidad, and Jamaica are also above the line. At the other extreme we have Mexico, which falls greatly below, followed at some distance by Colombia, Guatemala, El Salvador, Venezuela, and Honduras. Costa Rica and Nicaragua are also below the line.[5]

Implications

These facts are interesting, but what do they imply for policy purposes? Should coincidence of predicted and actual behavior be interpreted as a sign of "correct" fiscal performance, with Brazil and Mexico equally unsatisfactory deviants, if on opposite sides of the regression line? Or should one say that the predicted value, based on average behavior, indicates a minimum ratio which should be attained, with an excess an additional gain? Posing the question in this form invites the response that no general rules can be laid down, "because the circumstances of each country differ." This homily is always true, but it is not where the matter can rest. While differences exist, there are similarities as well.[6] Moreover, certain relevant differences, such as industrialization, openness, and other variables, are accounted for already in the regression analysis.

The fact that several countries at the below-$300-per-capita-income level have revenues well above 15 percent is evidence that countries at 10 percent would have found a higher level within the range of their fiscal capabilities. The more difficult question is whether they *should* have made use of this capability. This poses the question of how much of its resources a country at various levels of income *should* devote to public as against private uses. This depends on preferences, policy objectives, and political organization. Some communities may prefer private goods to social goods and where there are options, such as in education, may choose to provide such services by a private rather than a public route. Others may have the opposite preferences. But granting all this, there are also some basic economic questions to be asked.

THE ECONOMICS OF EXPENDITURE GROWTH

From the economist's point of view, the central question may be posed as follows: let us suppose that resources are used efficiently, including the allocation between private and social as well as consumer and cap-

5. A number of similar and related investigations are available. For the latest study and literature references, see Charles Montrie, Kenneth G. Fedor, and Harlan Davis, "Tax Progress Within the Framework of the Alliance for Progress: A Comparative Evaluation," *National Tax Journal* (September 1970). See also J. R. Lotz and E. R. Morss, "Measuring Tax Effort in Developing Countries," *IMF Staff Papers* (November 1967).

6. It should be noted that defense expenditures are not a major factor in explaining differences in the revenue to GNP ratios among Latin American countries. Such expenditures range from less than 1 to 3 percent of GNP and mostly absorb less than 10 percent of revenue. There is no significant relationship between the defense to GNP and revenue to GNP ratios.

ital goods. Private goods, for this purpose, are defined as goods whose benefits are largely internal so that they can be provided for by individual purchase at the market. Social goods, in turn, are goods whose benefits are largely external so that their provision must be determined through the political process and implemented through the budget. This does not mean or, in any case, need not mean public production. Budgetary provision for social goods may involve public purchases of privately produced goods, just as publicly owned enterprises may produce and sell private goods at the market. Our discussion of the size of the public sector therefore relates to public provision for social goods and not to the scope of public ownership. Defined in terms of social goods share, the size of the public sector thus differs from that defined in terms of public production, a point which is of particular importance for developing countries and mixed political systems.

Our distinction between private and social goods applies to both consumer and capital goods. The question whether, given efficient resource use, the public purchase to GNP ratio should rise with per capita income, may thus be divided into asking: (a) whether the importance of externality-intensive relative to private-type consumer goods rises with per capita income, and (b) whether the importance of externality-type capital goods relative to private-type capital goods increases as per capita income rises. In addition to these allocational considerations, the efficient size of the public sector depends on the further question (c) whether the need for transfer payments should be expected to rise or fall with per capita income.

These three issues, which determine both the appropriate level and the composition of expenditures, will now be considered. I am aware, of course, that the size of the public sector cannot be explained purely on this basis. Historical, political, and social factors enter as well. Nevertheless, it is useful, especially in the development context, to pose the problem in these terms.

Consumer Goods

At the low level of per capita income which prevails in most developing countries, the bulk of consumption goes to furnish the bare necessities, leaving little space for goods of a nonessential kind. This does not mean, however, that there is no need for social goods. Certain basic public services have to be rendered, including municipal outlays for civil administration, protection, sanitation, and so forth. Such services are no less necessary than the basic items of private consumption. As income rises, part of the gain will generate increasing demand for such services, but it may well be that the demand for an ample supply of private goods (food, clothing, housing) expands more sharply. This will be the case especially in view of the demonstration effects generated by the example of developed countries. Because of this, there is little reason to expect that the income elasticity of demand for public consumer goods should be in excess of unity over this low per capita income range. Later, as consumption rises into the luxury range, there will be an increasing demand for complementary public goods, suggesting an increased share of the latter in expanded consumption. Speculation of this sort suggests a flat and, in any case, hardly rising share of public consumption during the earlier stages of development, with perhaps more rapid expansion in the public share later on.

Two specific points may be added, however, which may change this pattern. First, it should be noted that the consumption pattern at any given average per capita income depends greatly upon the distribution of income. In the growth context, this pattern depends on the distribution of the increment in income or the fruits of economic growth. I would not be surprised to find that an unequally distributed increment will call for a larger share of public consumption expenditures than an equally distributed income growth.

Second, the need for increased public services may be affected greatly by the process of urbanization. If, as tends to be the case, income growth is associated with urbanization, it is also likely to call for an increased need for public services. This follows because urban living requires more services to be rendered in public form than does rural living, be it because of economies of scale, external costs generated by private provision, or for other reasons. This applies both with regard to current (consumption) and to capital outlays, the latter being especially important during a phase of rapid urban expansion. Growing urban expenditure requirements may well be the decisive factor in the Latin American picture, calling for a more than proportional growth of public services in the present development stage.

Capital Goods

The investment part of the problem is somewhat easier to handle, at least in conceptual terms. The basic question here is whether the supply of externality-intensive types of investment is of particular importance at early stages of economic development.

This would seem to be the case, because the building up of an infrastructure dominates investment activity at this stage. The construction of transportation facilities, provision for irrigation, regional development projects—all involve substantial degrees of external benefits which cannot be accounted for properly by private calculus. As industry develops, these needs become less important and a larger share of capital formation comes to be in the form of plant and equipment expenditures which can be undertaken more readily by private firms. Considerations of this sort suggest that public capital expenditures may well occupy a larger share in the earlier development phase (though not the earliest) and then show a relative decline as a higher level of income is reached.

Supposing this pattern to be correct, there is the further question of how large a share of resources is to be allocated to total (public plus private) capital formation. If capital formation is low at lower levels of per capita income, public investment may be a smaller fraction of GNP even though it occupies a relatively large share in total investment. Since economic development implies a rising investment share in GNP, this again suggests that we may expect, initially at least, a rising ratio of public investment.

One crucial factor is the treatment of human investment. While I have been dissatisfied in the context of high-income countries with the preoccupation of U.S. economists with the effects of taxation on earnings, rather than with the role of educational investment as acquisition of a durable consumer good, earnings effects are undoubtedly of major importance for economic development. Industrialization cannot be carried out without a labor force which possesses the technical know-how needed to operate the equipment. As may be expected, studies have shown the rate of return on investment in education to be very high, higher in many cases than investment in so-called real assets.[7]

It is absurd, therefore, to limit the concept of investment and public capital formation to the latter category. Education as well as brick and mortar should be counted, with schoolteachers' wages included no less than the structures in which they teach. The concept of public capital formation and saving underlying the model budgetary practices of the United Nations are, I believe, very misleading and should be changed.

Public investment, formally, includes not only externality-intensive investments which must be provided for publicly, but in many instances the government also engages in investment activities which might be undertaken privately. This may be so for lack of entrepreneurial talent in the private sector, or because the necessary amount of capital cannot be assembled privately in the absence of broad capital markets, or because public operation of such enterprises is preferred on social and political grounds. Prestige considerations, such as the presumed value of operating a steel industry (whether profitable or not) may be another factor.

It is interesting, therefore, to see how the size of the public sector (as defined previously in terms of the tax or expenditure ratio to GNP) relates to the importance of public investment activity. As shown in the Appendix Table (column 7), the ratio of investment to GNP varies

---

7. See Marcelo Selowsky, "On the Measurement of Education's Contribution to Growth," *The Quarterly Journal of Economics* (August 1969).

widely, with five countries in our sample having ratios between 12 and 14 percent; six, between 14 and 20 percent; and four, 20 percent and above. At the same time (see column 8), there is no pronounced relation between this ratio and the share of public capital formation in total investment. Some countries with about medium investment to GNP ratios, such as Brazil and Chile, have a very high public share, while others with a higher investment ratio have a low public share. We find, however, some tendency for high tax ratio countries to have a high public investment share. This is the case especially for Brazil and Chile, though not for Uruguay and Argentina. This suggests that the size of the public

APPENDIX TABLE

	x_1 T as % of GNP (1)	x_2 Y in $ (2)	x_3 V as % of GNP (3)	x_4 M as % of GNP (4)	T° as % of GNP (5)	(1)–(5) (6)	I as % of GNP (7)	GI as % of I (8)
Brazil	26.9	269	28	16.5	15.6	11.3	16.5	44.8
Chile	23.3	474	26	22.5	16.9	6.4	17.9	45.3
Uruguay	21.8	531	63	22.7	21.4	0.4	13.6	7.2
Argentina	20.1	705	15	15.3	17.5	2.6	20.0	12.2
Venezuela	20.1	744	60	60.0	22.7	−2.6	21.4	39.6
Dominican Republic	16.9	220	17	34.1	14.0	2.9	12.1	23.7
Trinidad	16.7	541	13	70.3	16.1	0.6	n.a.	n.a.
Ecuador	16.5	188	17	27.9	13.8	2.7	14.5	26.7
Panama	16.1	451	16	41.6	15.7	0.4	19.4	15.7
Peru	16.0	228	18	34.7	14.2	1.8	20.7	23.4
Jamaica	15.6	427	15	58.4	15.4	0.2	n.a.	n.a.
Costa Rica	14.3	362	15	45.9	14.9	−0.6	16.4	23.9
Nicaragua	13.5	311	13	45.4	14.3	−0.8	17.0	26.6
Colombia	11.0	285	22	19.2	15.0	−4.0	19.7	18.6
Honduras	11.0	199	15	44.6	13.6	−2.6	14.3	19.6
El Salvador	10.4	240	15	48.0	13.9	−3.5	13.1	27.6
Guatemala	10.3	265	14	28.1	14.0	−3.7	12.3	18.2
Paraguay	10.2	189	15	21.3	13.5	−3.3	12.9	22.8
Mexico	9.0	460	29	14.4	17.2	−8.2	20.0	11.9

SYMBOLS: T, revenue; Y, per capita income; V, value-added by industry; M, imports; I, total investment; GI, government investment; T°/GNP, predicted ratio.
SOURCES: Columns 1, 2, 3, 4—see G. S. Sahota, "Empirical Standards to Appraise the Allocation of Resources Among Social Goods," unpublished manuscript, Table 3; based on U.N. *Statistical Yearbook* (1968) and *Yearbook of National Accounts* (1968); in determining T°/GNP, attempt is made to exclude nontax revenue but to include all levels of government; data for 1966. Column 5—projected value of T°/GNP based on regression on Y and V/GNP for 19 countries. Columns 7, 8—see Charles Montrie, Kenneth G. Fedor, and Harlan Davis, "Tax Performance Within the Framework of the Alliance for Progress: A Comparative Evaluation," *National Tax Journal* (September 1970): 332; only central government included.

sector may be as indicative of differences in organization as of differences in the division of resources between social and private goods.

Transfers

It remains to consider the role of transfer payments. Returning to the historical view of developed countries, it is evident that the last fifty years have shown both a rapidly rising per capita income and a rapidly rising share of this income being subject to redistribution through the tax-transfer mechanism. In large part, this reflects the social and political trends toward the welfare state during this period, but it may also suggest that wealthier countries can afford (on incentive or other grounds) to devote a larger share of their income to redistribution. In the developing countries, the level of transfer payments is already substantial, even though per capita income is still very low. Nevertheless, transfer payments are still growing, and frequently in forms which benefit particular groups and contribute to economic rigidities rather than to assuring greater security and a more equal distribution of income for the population as a whole.

Income distribution in most Latin American countries is exceedingly unequal, and I believe that a substantial correction of this situation is prerequisite to orderly social and economic development. The role of expenditure policy in remedying this situation is of vital importance. Where tax policy has been relatively unsuccessful, can expenditure policy be expected to do a better job?

An important contribution can be made on the expenditure side, but transfer payments are not the answer. To be sure, the potential amount of redistribution of consumption is not negligible. As distinct from developed countries, the share of the wealthy in total consumption is quite substantial. Thus, the upper 10 percent of income recipients typically absorb, say, 45 percent of total consumption and the upper 5 percent absorb over 25 percent. Redistribution of consumption toward the poor could thus be a significant factor in raising their consumption levels. But it is not easily accomplished. The results of highly progressive income taxation may be to reduce saving and to induce capital outflow. Taxation of luxury consumption (be it by excises on luxuries or a progressive spending tax) is more promising. But even then the resulting average level of consumption at the lower-income levels would remain very low. The better approach, therefore, is to divert high incomes now flowing into excess consumption toward capital formation and to assure that the resulting gains from growth are widely shared. This involves not only progressive consumption taxes, but also a proper direction of investment. A substantial share of human investment in particular may be directed so as to upgrade skills of the low-income groups.

Moreover, distributional as well as efficiency objectives will be served by directing investment into more labor-intensive types of technology. Students of economic development are concerned increasingly with the prospect of increasing unemployment as well as lagging income growth. As technology becomes increasingly labor-saving and the growth of capital stock is directed into such channels, the capital-labor ratio rises rapidly and the growth of employment is retarded. This might be the most efficient use of capital if attention is directed at rising per capita income only, but such is too narrow a view. The prospect of rising unemployment is disturbing because it suggests further deterioration of the social situation. To meet the problem, tax measures might be taken to encourage labor-intensive technology; but beyond this, expenditures on research should be helpful in encouraging the development of new technologies, designed to meet the needs of low-income and labor-abundant economies rather than those of high-income and labor-scarce economies.

INSTRUMENTS OF EXPENDITURE POLICY

I now leave the discussion of expenditure development and turn to some of the instruments for expenditure planning.

Governmental Organization

Attention must be paid to the relation (or lack thereof) between finance ministries and planning agencies. While the former typically has the function of budget preparation in a narrow sense, the economic issues of expenditure planning (to the extent that they are dealt with at all) are typically the responsibility of the planning agency. Finance ministers and heads of planning agencies do not readily cooperate, so that there tends to be little relationship among tax, budget, and expenditure policies, and no effective coordination with overall economic policy making. Expenditure, and especially investment planning, is clearly a basic part of development policy, but so is the tax side of the picture. Neither can be determined intelligently without reference to the maintenance of internal and external balance by monetary and fiscal policies. Given the typical lack of cooperation between finance ministers and planning agencies, a coordinating council is badly needed to rationalize policy making.

Another aspect of governmental organization which is of major importance for expenditure planning involves the country's vertical fiscal structure. The proper degree of fiscal centralization or decentralization in a developing as well as a developed country is a function not only of economic efficiency, but depends in large degree upon historical factors and the strength of regional interests. Nevertheless, in developing as in developed countries, there remains some degree of freedom in securing a more efficient pattern of organization. A distinction should be drawn between the more highly developed municipalities, usually in the form of metropolitan areas, and the large number of small local units which are frequently incompetent to conduct efficient fiscal administration of either tax or expenditure measures. Governmental reorganization which grants considerable discretion to selected larger municipal units, while extending central control over the smaller localities, will thus be helpful in improving fiscal performance.

Cost-Benefit Analysis

I finally turn to the use of cost-benefit analysis as a technique by which expenditure priorities can be set. Much has been written about investment criteria and I will here only touch on those aspects of this technique which are of special importance in the development context.

Cost-benefit analysis is at its best in the evaluation of specific projects. It is less well-suited to designing the general strategies of development policy, such as the relative weights to be assigned to industrial and agricultural development or the choice between regional development patterns. Nevertheless, cost-benefit analysis is useful even in this connection, if only by forcing the consideration of alternatives in more explicit form and by encouraging an attempt to evaluate results.

In one important respect, cost-benefit analysis is more readily usable in the context of developing countries. In developed countries, the projects in question frequently deal with provision of ultimate consumer goods (such as the pleasures of visiting a park or the gain from improved health due to anti-air-pollution measures) which by their nature as social goods cannot be evaluated by the market. Yet some evaluation of the final product is needed to measure the present value of the returns. Without an evaluation of benefits, only a cost-effectiveness type of analysis, evaluating alternative methods of providing the same service, can be applied. This difficulty is avoided, or largely so, in development projects such as transportation or irrigation, where the return may be measured by its effects on the cost of outputs which in turn are sold in the market. Development investment is essentially investment in intermediate goods and as such it lends itself more readily to evaluation.

As against this advantage, there are other features of developing economies which render application of cost-benefit analysis more difficut. In order to evaluate a project, its true social costs and gains must be entered. Even where such costs and benefits can be discussed in terms of market prices, these prices may not reflect true social value. Hence, shadow prices which express the proper social cost or benefit must be substituted. In the Latin American setting in particular, this is of importance in connection with the influence of factors such as overvalued exchange rates which understate the true cost of capital equipment and an overvalued cost of labor. Both distortions render capital too cheap relative to labor, and thus contribute to the previously noted problem of labor-saving technology and unemployment. Other price distortions, resulting from market imperfections, lack of mobility, and so forth, pose similar difficulties. In evaluating the benefits of a particular project as well as in determining the opportunity cost of foregoing private projects, prices which allow for these distortions must be used. The design of government projects in particular should allow for these adjustments.

Similar problems arise in the context of dynamic development planning, where the set of prices applicable when the project is planned may be surpassed by a new set which prevails for most of the project's useful life. Similarly, the product prices and costs applicable for any one project in isolation may differ from those which become appropriate if an entire development plan is considered.

Next, there is the need to allow for secondary or indirect effects which are not reflected in the immediate market costs or prices to which the product is directly related. These effects may be of particular importance for development planning. The project may give rise to a complex set of forward and backward linkages which are of major importance to the overall picture of economic development. The conclusion to be drawn from this is that the cost-benefit technique cannot be applied adequately as an isolated project-by-project procedure, but that it must be applied as an integral part of overall development planning.

Matters of distribution, as noted before, are an important aspect of development planning. In recent years there has been an increasing tendency for writers on cost-benefit analysis to include distributional weights in the objective function. While I have been skeptical of this as a general practice for a country such as the United States—where the distributional objectives can and should be met more directly by tax-transfer measures such as a negative income tax or by education programs—I feel differently about it in the context of Latin American development planning. Available resources are too limited in many cases to sustain both redistribution and growth policies. The solution, therefore, has to be through a redistribution-oriented growth policy. This is of importance especially with regard to investment in education and health, but it arises also with regard to housing and municipal investment. Going further, it may have important bearing on the promotion of industry versus agriculture and on the choice of techniques in each case. Nor can the desire for some degree of balance in the rate of development among regions be ruled out of court. The economist's verdict that people should move is all well and good, but historical and political factors cannot be overlooked entirely. There is thus a good case for including distributional considerations (on both the benefit and cost sides) into the cost-benefit calculus for economic development, but it is important that this be done explicitly and uniformly over projects, lest the distributional adjustment be allowed to cover up elements of bias in the planning process.

Determination of the proper discount rate finally remains a major issue for project evaluation in development planning. The literature, delighted with the analytics of the problem, has dealt with this issue at great length. Concern has been with (a) whether the social rate of discount to be used in project analysis should be set below the private rate, and (b) if the latter is used, how it is to be determined. In the context of development planning, much is to be said for the social-rate approach. Determination of a private market rate is difficult without a developed capital market and it is complicated further by the presence of inflation. Moreover, private saving is so limited and concentrated in a small sector of the population that the market rate can hardly be taken as a valid measure of the community's time preference over the asset life. Nor can the level of investment in the private sector be taken as optimal. The private rate of return, therefore, can hardly serve as a measure of the true social return, even if a single private rate could be determined. In addition, there would be reasons in a developing economy for setting the social below the private rate even if these imperfections did not exist.

We can conclude, therefore, that development planning—and project evaluation in particular—must postulate what is to be considered the social discount rate for purposes of public policy. Or, putting it differently and perhaps more realistically, an acceptable minimum consumption path must be postulated and the discount rate derived therefrom. This, of course, must be done within the constraints of available resources and the maintenance of both internal and external balance.

Conclusion

When I first contemplated this paper, I had the vision of ending up with a neat table with rows showing major expenditure categories (such as development, education, health and welfare, and social security) and columns showing various levels of per capita income. In each cell, I would then enter a target expenditure to GNP ratio. Such a table would provide a standard against which the expenditure performance of a particular country could be assessed and the structure of its expenditure development could be planned. Unfortunately, we do not have the data (except for the total expenditure to GNP ratios) to do this even in terms of actual figures, not to speak of their normative evaluation. While some data for central governments are available, the expenditures of lower-level governments are not. Yet these must be included to obtain a meaningful picture. Hopefully, researchers will provide such data in the not too distant future.

This spade work must then be followed by the more difficult task of establishing what might be considered optimal expenditure structures. Allowing for the growth contribution of various expenditure categories and for legitimate differences in preference patterns among countries, this is a difficult road to travel; but there is no reason why some progress should not be made. In the meantime, the tax planner will have to continue acting on faith, or else limit himself to dealing with tax structure at whatever overall level of revenue is set for him.

Comment—Ifigenia M. de Navarrete

I want to congratulate Musgrave on his paper, and I do not find any strong points of disagreement. Hence, I shall concentrate my comments on those points on which I perhaps feel more strongly than he does. I would like especially to emphasize certain aspects of the relationship between fiscal and development policies.

THE IMPORTANCE OF EXPENDITURE POLICY

Musgrave claims that fiscal theorists have worked more on the tax structure side than on expenditure policy. It seems to me that one cannot talk of an ideal tax structure for any stage of development. In public economics, the issue of highest priority is *not* the level of taxation or even the tax structure itself, but the functions of government and hence the level and structure of public expenditure, that is, the command over real resources and their alternative uses. This issue has been clearly understood by Latin American politicians who, in real-world economics, have used the expenditure power of government to promote development. The tax structure has been neglected and consequently has remained old-fashioned, regressive, and inefficient. This has led to deficit financing and an enormous increase in the public debt, mainly foreign-held.

The next issue would then be *how* to finance the required level of public expenditure. One could even disregard taxes altogether if it were not that the effects of such a procedure might seriously harm economic policy objectives. Hence, taxes remain the main source of revenue and "tax whatever you can" is the up-to-date golden rule to apply in development, where growing needs tend to surpass revenue and goods and services provided by the government have a higher priority than private goods and services whose consumption must be sacrificed in order to satisfy government demand. However, logic advises that taxes must fall on those sectors, regions, or individuals that possess taxable capacity.

The second golden rule of taxation is to build up an excellent and loyal staff of public officials able to detect fiscal capacity, devise measures to absorb it, and measure its economic effects on resource allocation, growth potential, and income distribution.

In practice, however, public expenditure has not been altogether independently determined. Its level has been constrained by deficient tax systems, which have helped to concentrate income, strengthen the status quo, and retard the transformation toward a more equitable society.

THE ECONOMICS OF PUBLIC EXPENDITURE

As Musgrave points out, analysis of the level and structure of public expenditure does not belong in the realm of market economics and marginal analysis, but in the much wider field of political economy. Public economics does not have a rigorous resource allocation framework with the same intellectual attraction as the neoclassical system of price determination and market equilibrium. A general equilibrium system for public economics still remains to be constructed.

Further research work is needed in the area of the mixed economy, where one part of the resources is allocated according to market demand and another, increasing share according to social and political demands. Empirical and quantitative research is also urgent in measuring with technical precision the concepts of social costs and benefits as opposed to private costs and profits. Private goods are those whose utility functions are mainly internal to the individual, so that the level of demand is determined by the relationship between marginal utility and the respective price. Social goods are those whose utility functions produce external as well as internal utility. Since they can have a social as well as a market demand, the distinction between private and social goods is not the same in all societies. The nature of social goods and the amount provided are a function of the prevailing economic system, the stage of development, the level of income per capita, the distribution of income and wealth, the degree of urbanization, and other structural factors.

Private goods would be mostly consumer or final demand goods. In the social goods category would fall those goods whose social demand would be greater than market supply *at prevailing market prices or factor costs,* so that total demand could not be satisfied *at the level and quality deemed appropriate for a particular society.* Such is the case of education, medical service, health, nutrition, public housing, etc. So I fully agree with Musgrave that their provision must be determined through the political process and implemented through the public budget.

THE POLITICAL ECONOMY OF PUBLIC EXPENDITURE

One of the most significant economic events of the postwar period has been the expansion of the public sector in both developed and less-developed countries, more so in the more industrialized ones. It seems to me that a very significant factor that would correlate with the level of public expenditure (in addition to the level of income) would be the level of "political development"—if we could measure it. It is very likely that the higher the political participation of the population, the higher the rate of public investment (because of local pressures) and current social expenditure. Take, as examples, Chile and Uruguay with high public expenditure rates and Mexico, Colombia, and El Salvador, where political development has lagged and which have the lowest tax burdens in Latin America. (Of course, we should also take into consideration and adjust for military expenditures.) We need more interdisciplinary research when dealing with large units such as governments or corporations, because economic policy is greatly influenced by power pressure factors. A low level of political development also helps to explain the uneven income distributions typical of many Latin American countries. Granted that we want a more democratic society, the strategy of development ought to serve this objective; and the greater the inequality of income, the greater the need for both social consumption and public investment.

There is an evident need for a strong social and employment policy in developing countries. The objective of employment ought to become integrated with public investment in the planning mechanism. To date, most Latin American development plans are nothing but public investment plans with sources of finance attached to them, depending on the degree of agreement between the minister of finance and the minister of planning.

THE STRUCTURE OF PUBLIC EXPENDITURE

In an illuminating article written some time ago,[1] Martin and Lewis demonstrated by empirical research that the level and structure of public expenditures depended on not only the level of income per capita but also the social and political philosophy of the government about what the size of the public sector ought to be. Following them, several studies were made in Mexico and I did one myself a few years later.[2] The first strategic variable in development is still investment. As income and output grow, the investment coefficient increases. In Mexico, around 8-9 percent of GDP was devoted to investment in the late thirties; this proportion increased to 20 percent in the sixties and has remained so for the past several years. When the development process started, public investment represented about half of total investment. As private investment responded, public investment diminished proportionately and stabilized at

1. A. Martin and W. A. Lewis, "Patterns of Public Revenue and Expenditure," *The Manchester School of Economic and Social Studies* 24 (September 1956): 203-44.

2. I. M. de Navarrete, "El Financiamiento de la Educación Pública en México," *Investigación Económica* 18, no. 69 (1958): 21-55.

around 40 percent in the early sixties. Then, the government began to be criticized because its current expenditures were too high and because of waste and inefficiency. It was also argued that the private sector ought to fulfill a greater share. For example, it was said: why create another source of corruption with public housing? As a result, the government provided a financial apparatus to be used by private companies. When the satisfaction of social needs is turned over to the private sector, public investment decreases. This happened in Mexico, and now public investment is down to around 30 percent of total investment.

Hence, I disagree with Musgrave that the best way to redistribute income is not through transfers or progressive taxation because the result may be to reduce savings or induce a capital outflow. Nor can I agree with his conclusion that a better approach would be to divert high incomes now flowing into excess consumption into capital formation and then assure that the resulting gains from growth are widely shared. This seems to me contradictory, since how does one share if not through the tax-expenditure mechanism? In addition, progressive taxation on income, wealth, and expenditure can coexist with tax incentives on investment. Private investment can be stimulated by public investment that creates external economies; and total savings will not decrease if public savings increase. Musgrave's recommendations can even be self-defeating, since they could stimulate capital-intensive production techniques, decrease labor employment, and increase the concentration of income even if the rate of growth were to remain constant.

Estimates of the cost of providing adequate education, medical care, social security, and urban infrastructure in Mexico—based upon the amount of real resources available, i.e., the supply of teachers, doctors, nurses, social workers, hospitals, etc.—would indicate a yearly expenditure of around 10 percent of GDP; public investment would require 8 percent, and administrative services 4 percent, so that total government expenditure would amount to 21-22 percent of GDP, the figure cited by Martin and Lewis years before. Mexico has been spending about half this amount, only 10-11 percent of GDP.[3]

A final word on waste. We seem very worried about waste and corruption in the public sector. I would only like to point out that waste and corruption in the private sector are sometimes worse.

Comment—Frederic L. Pryor

MUSGRAVE carries out three tasks in his paper on public expenditure policies in Latin America. First, he places the aggregate amount of public

---

3. The whole public sector, public enterprises included, spends about 18 percent of GDP now.

expenditures in various Latin American nations in both a world and a regional perspective; second, he analyzes on a theoretical plane several different expenditure components; and finally, he presents some useful prescriptions for expenditure policy making. The first two tasks are exercises in positive economics; the third, in normative economics. I would like to focus my remarks primarily on his positive analysis with only a few sidelong glances at normative considerations.

Following the theoretical structure of his book *Fiscal Systems*,[1] Musgrave distinguishes three major expenditure components: current expenditures for goods and services, transfers, and investment. Although I am not sure that this is the most useful way of dividing public expenditures for analysis, it is a method quite amenable to empirical research. Although considerable data on these aggregates are available and several comparative studies focusing on Latin American public expenditures are to appear in the future,[2] neither Musgrave nor I could incorporate these into our remarks in a highly formal manner (e.g., through regression calculations); in this comment such data are incorporated only informally and a number of suggestions for future research are presented. Let us now examine each of the three expenditure categories.

The most crucial distinction within current governmental expenditures for goods and services is between expenditures for military and civilian purposes. Turning to Musgrave's Chart 1 showing the relationship between the ratio of tax revenue to the GNP (which is a proxy variable for the ratio of total governmental expenditures to the GNP) and per capita income, it appears that almost every country with a greater tax to GNP ratio than predicted has a much higher ratio of defense expenditures to GNP than countries falling below the line. Average military expenditures as a percentage of GNP for countries above the line are roughly 2.5 percent; and for countries below the line, 1.3 percent.[3] Depending on one's notion of causation, several explanations are possible. From the expenditure side, one might argue that the degree of substitution between military and civilian expenditures is quite low in Latin

1. Richard A. Musgrave, *Fiscal Systems* (New Haven: Yale University Press, 1969).

2. In the ECLA publication *Statistical Bulletin for Latin America* (*Boletín Estadístico de America Latina*), expenditure breakdowns according to a number of classifications are given for most countries. In addition, a number of Ph.D. theses on public expenditures in various Latin American nations following the Peacock-Wiseman definitional schema have been written; and a summary report for six nations by Irving Goffman and Dennis Mahar has appeared, "The Growth of Public Expenditures in Selected Developing Nations: Six Caribbean Countries, 1940-1965," *Public Finance/Finances publiques* 26, no. 1 (1971). Finally, I have been informed that the World Bank has completed an extensive study that, unfortunately, has not been released.

3. The data come from United States Arms Control and Disarmament Agency, *World Military Expenditures 1969* (Washington, D.C.: Government Printing Office, 1969), Table 2, and refer to 1967.

America so that greater military expenditures would raise the total amount of public expenditures; from the tax side, one might argue that revenues over and above those needed to finance a basic minimum of public expenditures were placed in the military. Although determination of the exact relationship between total tax revenues, total public expenditures, and total military expenditures requires much more detailed research, it should be clear that omission of this military factor in the analysis of aggregate governmental expenditures or governmental expenditures on current goods and services may lead to misinterpretations of the reported regression results. It should be emphasized that other factors—e.g., higher welfare expenditures, higher rates of inflation, or higher losses by public enterprises—might also influence the aggregate ratio of government expenditures to the GNP, and mechanisms similar to those proposed for defense expenditures may operate. Although the aggregate results presented by Musgrave in Table 1 are quite interesting, a detailed explanation requires an empirical analysis of a number of factors including various expenditure components.

In analyzing current governmental expenditures for current goods and services, Musgrave puts forward a fascinating hypothesis: greater income inequality leads to a larger share of public consumption expenditures in the GNP in order to compensate for certain inequities. This proposition seems based on certain normative considerations (i.e., there should be such compensation) that may not carry over to the realm of positive economics. That is, a government dominated by a small oligarchy that receives a large share of national income may not feel it necessary to tax itself in any manner to provide transfers to some of the poor; governmental action may parallel rather than alleviate the bad effects of a maldistribution of income. In any case, the proposition can be empirically tested and, although I hope that Musgrave is correct, my reading of Latin American politics leads me to suspect the reverse.

Several issues regarding governmental transfer expenditures require comment. Musgrave's fear that economic development is, or could be, retarded if tax revenues are channeled into transfers (rather than investments) focuses on a question for which much research is needed. At the present time governmental transfer expenditures appear low in Latin America, with the ratio of such transfers to total governmental current expenditures (current expenditures on goods and services plus transfers plus subsidies) less than 25 percent in all nations except Chile and Uruguay (and, indeed, less than 15 percent in most nations).[4] In more than half of the nations, transfer expenditures are less than governmental savings, a relationship that is reversed in developed economies. Although

4. These data are for 1966 and 1967 and come from ECLA, *Statistical Bulletin for Latin America,* and United Nations, *Yearbook of National Income Statistics,* various issues.

we cannot really know if the extent of such transfer expenditures is out of line with other nations that have similar levels of development until systematic comparisons are made, I suspect that this is not the case. Unless considerable political changes (i.e., changes in the political strengths of various income groups) occur in Latin America, it does not seem likely that excessive transfer payments will prove to be a very important barrier to development for the next decade.

It can also be argued that certain types of transfer expenditures—namely, subsidies to business—may actually encourage rather than retard economic growth. Of course, it should be added that subsidies can also encourage irrational and wasteful uses of resources. I hope not to appear unduly cynical, but it seems likely that such "antidevelopmental subsidies" are probably much greater in value than "prodevelopmental subsidies" in a number of Latin American nations, particularly in light of Baer's comments, in his paper in this volume, about chronic deficits run by public enterprises in particular nations. Some idea of the relative importance of such subsidies can be gained from the information that subsidies constitute more than 10 percent of current governmental expenditures in Chile and Uruguay and more than 5 percent in at least four more nations.[5] Only much more research can reveal whether such subsidies actually encourage or hinder economic development.

In his discussion of capital expenditures Musgrave raises a vital issue: the degree of substitution between public and private investment expenditures. In some Latin American nations this seems to be quite low and the effect of public investment is to raise overall investment and, presumably, the growth rate; in other countries such substitution seems to be high, so that total investment does not seem affected and the growth rate may actually be lower if less profitable investments are chosen by the government. The degree of substitution between these two sources of investments depends partly on the direction of governmental investment (whether such investment is complementary or competitive with private investment), partly on the degree to which capital outflows and foreign investments in the nation are regulated, and partly on particular institutional factors in the capital markets. I have never seen a systematic empirical comparative analysis of such issues, a lacuna in the development literature on Latin America that seems inexcusable.

Musgrave proffers several extremely useful prescriptions for the ways in which decisions about public expenditures should be made. For the purpose of analysis, however, it seems profitable to place such prescriptions in a broader context of the developmental strategy pursued by the government. By developmental strategy I mean the basic policy decisions about development (e.g., transportation policies, import substitution versus export development, the choice of capital- or labor-intensive tech-

5. Ibid.

nologies, the degree to which particular regions are chosen for development, and so forth), the institutions through which these policies are implemented, and the particular instruments chosen to realize each goal. The types of necessary information, the types of expenditure controls, and the manner of administration depend vitally upon the development strategy, and until the latter is specified we cannot really make very detailed prescriptions about policies for the administration of public expenditures. It has been a disappointment to me that the conference papers did not focus more upon such global questions of developmental strategy so that the fiscal and expenditure analysis that most of us are pursuing could have been placed in greater perspective.

Discussion

A. CHURCHILL: At the World Bank we have been working for some time on this question of the determination of the level of expenditures and why some countries have different patterns than others. I would like to suggest a slightly different format than the one proposed by Musgrave.

Taking countries with, say, per capita income somewhere between $800 and $1,000 (which would classify as developed countries) and making appropriate corrections for activities some countries put in the private sector and others put in the public sector, the pattern of expenditures as a percentage of GNP appears remarkably similar. Countries with somewhere around $1,000 per capita income spend roughly the same amount of GNP on transportation, the same amount on welfare; it varies a little bit, but not as much as at the lower end of the income scale.

Looking at the underdeveloped countries, particularly those below $600 per capita income, one country at, say, $200 per capita income may spend 8 percent of its GNP on education, but another may spend 1 percent; on transportation one country may spend 10 percent, another may spend 2 percent. That is, there is tremendous variation. If one tries any kind of cross-section analysis below about $600 per capita income, one winds up with no significant relationships. But *within* a country, on a time series basis one can explain some of the changes in expenditures. It seems to be true that the pattern of expenditures can be viewed as a capital stock adjustment, which depends on what a country starts off with and how fast it wants to get to its objectives. It also depends on the social and political system whether it arrives at these goals rapidly or slowly. In a given country, transportation may start with expenditures equal to 1 or 2 percent of GNP and then follow an irregular path over time, eventually reaching a point common to most developed countries. Education may follow a completely different path. The paths which countries may choose appear to be quite varied, depending on the political situation, the income distribution, or the kind of transport—if it is a big country or a little country or whether it has lakes or mountains.

This is all very discouraging for the formulation of general theory. *Within* a country one can sometimes predict with a degree of accuracy the particular path followed by a particular type of expenditure. But, I am afraid we have not reached the point yet of constructing a general positive theory.

D. TRUETT: Musgrave refers to the "optimal" expenditure composition. Obviously, this must be some sort of general equilibrium concept, which I submit is a will-o'-the-wisp. There is no hope of finding this in the structurally imperfect economy of an underdeveloped country. I think Musgrave realizes this, at least implicitly, when he later abandons the concept in order to pursue the subject of the application of benefit-cost analysis to investment projects, which is a well-known *partial* equilibrium tool.

Musgrave also uses the term "instruments of expenditure policy." I would like to inject the term "instrumentalism" at this point, for which credit is given John Dewey. Instrumentalism is a philosophical approach in which solutions are sought to specific existential problems, with ends-in-view or current standards of valuation that are in no way final but themselves are derived from the problem under consideration and its context. It thus involves a continuous yet scientific empirical process of trial-and-error judgment carried on in a dynamic setting.[1] As Navarrete emphasized, the central issue is to determine the *objectives* of expenditure policy. Instruments are sterile unless we know the context in which they are to be used. The concept "optimal expenditure policy" is an analytically positive construct, which exists in spite of its context, or without any context at all for that matter. The institutional structure, I think, predominates in the utilization of the instrumentalist approach and, in this view, "grand schemes" are not operational but what has been labeled "mutual adjustment planning" is. With the latter approach, continuous alteration of instruments and objectives takes place in a dynamic policy context.[2] Thus, the expenditure structure and the tax structure evolve in the context of specific developmental objectives and an optimal program is never the case.

V. TANZI: First, I would like to call attention to Chart 1 and point out that practically all the countries above the line are countries with inflation and all those below the line are countries with stable prices. I

1. John Dewey, *The Quest for Certainty* (New York: G. P. Putnam's Sons, 1929), and *Experience and Nature,* 2nd ed. (New York: W. W. Norton and Co., Inc., 1929).

2. A good exposition on this approach is: Robert J. Shafer, *Mexico: Mutual Adjustment Planning* (Syracuse, N.Y.: Syracuse University Press, 1966).

raise this point because inflation probably has something to do with the difference between purchasing power parities and the official rate of exchange. In dealing with Latin America, it may be improper to use official rates of exchange in making the type of comparison shown in Chart 1. If we changed from official rates of exchange to purchasing power parities, the distribution of countries might be somewhat different. In connection with the distribution of income, Musgrave states that an unequal income distribution probably increases the share of public expenditure to GNP. Again, the countries above the line include Uruguay and Argentina, which seem to have a better distribution than the rest of Latin America.

Second, I would like to call attention to a study I did for the London Institute of Economic Affairs[3] dealing with the OECD countries, in which I tried to correlate certain types of public expenditures to GNP. Expenditures on goods and services in the OECD countries were correlated with GNP. However, when I broke this down between defense and non-defense expenditures, and here I am supporting Pryor, it turned out that defense was the one category which was very income-elastic; the other types of expenditures were hardly related to GNP at all. What I called social expenditures, which include mostly transfers to families, welfare payments, and so forth, were not at all related to GNP. Social and political factors played very much more of a role in determining these latter expenditures.

R. THORN: A study I did supports Navarrete's and Tanzi's remarks in that social expenditures seem to explain a great deal of the extreme variation in government expenditures among various countries.[4] I do not think this can be explained via some kind of econometric model without political inputs. Each country must decide how it is going to solve its social-political equation. In Latin America we have had many attempted solutions. I notice that the three countries farthest above the regression line are all countries with very high social expenditures as well as high military expenditures: Brazil, Chile, and Uruguay. Two of them are among the most successful Latin American democracies, Chile and Uruguay. Mexico falls way below the line, again largely because of its low social expenditures; it is way behind the others but it has not suffered the ill consequences. My study seems to indicate that countries that are very low in their relative level of social expenditures tend toward political instability, but Mexico has found a political equation that for the moment has prevented instability; I do not know if it can continue to do so in the future.

3. Vito Tanzi, J. B. Bracewell-Milnes, and D. R. Myddelton, *Taxation: A Radical Approach* (London: Institute of Economic Affairs, 1970).
4. Richard S. Thorn, "The Evolution of Public Finances During Economic Development," *The Manchester School of Economic and Social Studies* (January 1967).

My own studies indicate that investment expenditures are highly variable relative to other forms of government expenditure. Investment expenditures often seem to be the residual item in the budget, absorbing a major portion of fluctuations in government income.

The question Musgrave asks is perhaps not the right one. I think the question we should be asking is, what is the trade-off between social expenditures and growth? Perhaps economic growth could have achieved many of the objectives which were achieved via increased social expenditures largely through transfer payments. Maybe many Latin American countries chose the wrong course, in the sense that they could have achieved a greater improvement in social welfare by concentrating on economic growth rather than on increased social expenditures.

J. MORRALL: An important conclusion Musgrave reaches about Latin America based on specifically empirical research requires closer examination. He states that the performance of the Latin American countries typically shows a less than average tax to GNP ratio. This conclusion is based on a regression equation for eighty-two countries that finds a positive relationship between tax revenue as a percent of GNP and per capita income, and that shows eleven Latin American countries lying below the regression line and only eight above. Unfortunately, Musgrave does not present the full eighty-two-country data, which is necessary for an adequate examination of this significant finding. If we turn to his Chart 1, a regression line based only on Latin American data is presented. This nineteen-country regression line is likely to be approximately the same as the eighty-two-country regression line, because here twelve countries lie below and seven above the line. However, this is not crucial to the following point, which is mainly illustrative. (In any case, the positions of the countries relative to each other would be the same.) A more appropriate statistical test than simply counting the countries above and below the regression line to determine whether the fiscal effort of Latin American countries is significantly different from that of the other countries would be to count the countries above and below a confidence interval around the regression line of, say, one standard deviation. The standard deviation for the constant term in Musgrave's equation I* is 2.6, and when this is applied to Chart 1 we find that only two countries lie below the confidence interval, Guatemala and Mexico, while six countries lie above the confidence interval. Such evidence would lead to a conclusion opposite to Musgrave's, i.e., that the Latin American countries typically show a greater than average tax (and thus expenditure) effort. Since Musgrave does not present the data for all eighty-two countries, we therefore cannot be sure of the correct "conclusion," but certainly broad generalizations made without the appropriate statistical tests can be misleading. The danger also arises that such conclusions, once reached, can quickly lead to ex post rationalizations of the findings, as has already been demonstrated by the preceding discussion on this point.

E. Morss: More research is needed on the relationship between taxes and expenditures on two specific subjects. First, more knowledge is needed on the income redistributional effects of expenditures and taxes taken together. Musgrave and Daicoff did the pathbreaking study on this subject for Michigan back in the fifties, and Gillespie did a more comprehensive study including federal, state, and local U.S. governments later. Second, Stanley Please of the World Bank and others have argued that higher taxes in developing countries go to more consumption expenditures, and that the net effect is to reduce the overall level of investment. I and others have done work suggesting that this is not the case, but the subject is clearly far from resolved.

I am quite skeptical about the usefulness of further cross-sectional work on the changing structure of government expenditures as a country develops until we have better and more uniform measures of expenditures by function. Thus, we must be very careful in interpreting the data in Chart 1 on still another ground. If one compares Brazil and Mexico, one sees that Brazil is far above the regression line and Mexico is far below it. One of the major reasons for this result is the fact that Brazilian public enterprises run tremendous deficits while Mexican public enterprises pretty well balance their books.

Concerning the point raised about military expenditures, I coauthored a study that examined military expenditures as a percentage of GNP.[5] We looked at countries in which this ratio was high, expecting to find that in these countries either taxes would be relatively high or prices would be rising relatively faster. It turned out that taxes were slightly higher, but not so much higher as to prevent inflation. But, there was no inflation either. So we backed into the conclusion that, in cases in which military expenditures are relatively high, other expenditures are held down. This fits with the idea that the ratio of government expenditures to GNP is a constant as per capita income rises up to about the $800 level. One reason that the tax to GNP ratio rises as per capita income rises, but the government expenditures to GNP ratio does not, is that foreign aid decreases as per capita income rises.

R. Musgrave: As against the case for a purely empirical view, let me plead once again for a systematic *theoretical* approach to the matter of expenditure development. Theories can be presented and can be disposed of, but one must have a theory. Whether it be a socialist system or a market system, one must have some notions about what constitutes an efficient resource allocation, which must involve the division of the product

5. J. R. Lotz and E. R. Morss, "A Study of Military Expenditures," *Revista di diritto finanziario e scienze della finanze* (December 1969).

between social and private use. (Of course, the problem of resource allocation is also a function of the state of income distribution, which determines demand, but more about this later.) There *is* a valid distinction between social and private goods based on the weight of externality-type versus internalized-type benefits and costs. This is a technological phenomenon, not an ideological phenomenon. It therefore poses much the same kind of problem under socialism as it does in a market system. The question, then, is what happens to the efficient product mix—with regard to the division between social and private goods—as the economy grows? What happens to the composition of the bundle of investment goods which are needed at various stages of development and to the bundle of desired consumer goods as income rises?

In a sense this is asking for a normative theory, i.e., how *should* the mix of output change? But, it is also trying to assert a positive theory, i.e., that actual development is, to some degree at least, related to this efficient pattern. Of course, demands are partly endogenous and not wholly exogenous, and preference patterns depend on many things. Yet there is a preference pattern and the notion of efficient allocation is not discarded even if we allow for these endogenous elements. Thus the problem has a double focus—that of asking what would be efficient, and that of testing the actual pattern in relation thereto.

Such a theory of optimal expenditure composition differs from optimal tax structure theory in several regards. The optimal tax structure, as it evolves over time, is largely a function of economic institutions. For example, if 99 percent of all output is agricultural, then land taxation is bound to be of great importance; but this importance shrinks as the share of agricultural output falls in the course of development. As the structure of income-generating types of property changes, so does the tax system. Tax structure theory is a theory of tax base adaptation to changing institutions, whereas the key in expenditure development theory is how the division of total output (within the investment goods and the consumption goods categories) changes between goods that are primarily of the externality type and others primarily of the internality type. The problem is very complex, but this framework gives at least a way of going at it.

I recognize that these considerations only relate to the mix of real output and omit the problems of income distribution and the role of fiscal policy in income redistribution as development proceeds. These latter considerations are more difficult to include in this kind of economic analysis, for several obvious reasons. The allocation problem is a matter of efficiency analysis only and lends itself more readily to traditional tools, while the distribution issue is not of this sort. The changing role of distribution policy reflects changes in the social welfare function, the political structure, and many other things. The fact that per capita income rises with development has a bearing on the problem, but many other factors are involved as well.

The theory of expenditure structure development thus differs from that of tax structure development, but are the two linked? When one talks about optimal allocation, one deals with the use of resources and their opportunity costs. Therefore, both taxes and expenditures are in the picture. While the tax side is determined by institutional, technical, and political factors, the reality of "taxable capacity" places some constraints on the expenditure side. What can be accomplished on the expenditure side, therefore, is a function of not only the "efficient product mix" approach, but also the limitations which the tax side imposes in a particular institutional context.

The theoretical framework here suggested is rather more ambitious than the Peacock-Wiseman proposition that people are more hesitant to raise taxes than they are eager to reduce them. While this proposition is helpful, it is not an *economic* theory of expenditure development. My feeling is that the wartime effects wash out over time, and that in the long run much the same pattern would result with or without the observed wartime expenditure peaks. However this may be, a more complex and broadly gauged theoretical framework is needed. While no clear analytical framework for fiscal and development theory is available at this point in time, there are at least some hypotheses to be tested, and I hope those working in this area will try to do so.

7

Recentralization: The Budgetary Dilemma
in the Economic Development
of Mexico, Bolivia, and Costa Rica

JAMES W. WILKIE

THE purpose of this study is to suggest that public expenditure[1] growth in some Latin American countries involves a fundamental problem regarding presidential power and the nature of state policy. Because (a) central governments have been subject to political difficulties and long-term programs often have been affected by the abuse of presidential authority, and/or because (b) decentralized government agencies have been judged more efficient to develop and carry out modernization policy, one may note that in at least three countries of Latin America the power of the central government has been increasingly restricted to social and administrative matters.

With the rise of an autonomous sector designed to carry out economic policy in such countries as Mexico, Bolivia, and Costa Rica, important centralized activity of the state has been delimited to be outside the sphere of politics. Thus an institutional framework tends to grow which is not necessarily responsive to changing interest groups and which by its very nature may prevent planning and/or policy change. In this regard, fiscal policy for industrialization, for example, may have serious implications for political stability, the base upon which economic development rests.

DECENTRALIZATION

Until only recently, Latin American governments have been concerned generally with limiting the role of the chief executive. After independence, so many presidents came to abuse their authority that the organizers of

1. "Public expenditure" is here defined as (a) all central government expenditure and (b) all decentralized outlay, including public enterprises and mixed public and private corporations in addition to governmental commissions, institutes, independent agencies, etc. The subtotals for (a) and (b) give a consolidated financial statement. For purposes of this work, financial analysis generally is limited to expenditure (in contrast to taxation) policy; and analysis is taken up in terms of political (in contrast to strictly economic) aspects of investigation. Since the paper deals with budget-

government in many Latin American countries sought to strengthen legislative and judicial functions at the expense of the executive branch of government. Beginning in 1911 with José Batlle y Ordóñez's Uruguayan model in this hemisphere, a number of states have experimented with the creation of decentralized agencies which are intended to operate autonomously, much like a private business. Theoretically, such corporations allow apolitical *técnicos* (highly specialized professionals)[2] to develop long-range plans which are immune from the vagaries of politics. If such agencies are not self-financing, they may be empowered to negotiate their own loans and credits; and in return for interim central government subsidies, the decentralized sector often is expected eventually to generate a profit from the use of national resources in order to provide funds for expanded central government activity. In this manner, national resources are used for national rather than private or foreign profit.

With the advent of the Alliance for Progress in the 1960s, the United States virtually forced some Latin American nations to develop rational budgetary plans in order that assistance might be channeled to avoid duplication, to prevent programs from working at cross-purposes, and to martial priorities.[3] Perhaps it is ironic that the United States would ask the Latin Americans to formulate overall blueprints lacking in the United States itself, but even the U.S. Congress assented to the Alliance's requirements for the creation of governmental agencies which could develop

---

ary problems, it is intended to discuss apparent bottlenecks and difficulties rather than to stress successes in Latin American state policy. Although much of the data presented here is not strictly comparable from country to country, every effort has been made to adjust data where necessary.

2. The term *"técnicos"* often has been translated to mean "economic technicians" (as in Raymond Vernon, *The Dilemma of Mexico's Development: The Roles of the Public and Private Sectors* [Cambridge, Mass.: Harvard University Press, 1963], pp. 136-38). The term here is used more broadly to refer to specially educated persons (*licenciados, ingenieros, economistas, arquitectos*, etc.) who attempt to develop complicated public policy without primary regard for political considerations. *Técnicos* are employed in central as well as decentralized agencies, but generally they have more latitude in the latter, which may be less dominated by political appointees. Nevertheless, one may not assume that *técnicos* operate efficiently in contrast to politicians. Not only do both move about within and between the central and decentral spheres, but also both are confronted with multilayered administrative departments, many of which are staffed by persons appointed under previous leaders or by timeservers who have acquired some sort of tenure. Furthermore, all *técnicos* do not necessarily have the same ideological outlook, let alone agree on the appropriateness of alternatives with regard, for example, to monetary policy as it effects economic growth rates.

3. With regard to a country in which consolidated accounting antedated the 1961 Alliance for Progress, it is interesting to note that by laws of 1959 and 1960, Colombian autonomous agencies have been obligated to submit their budgets to the finance ministry as an annex to the central budget. In 1962 apparently 43.4 percent of public sector expenditure was decentralized, according to the Joint Tax Program of the Organization of American States and the Inter-American Development Bank, *Fiscal Survey of Colombia* (Baltimore: Johns Hopkins University Press, 1965), p. 231.

plans. Though the rise of "uncontrollable expenditure" in the United States (especially in social welfare trust funds) has meant that American presidents have decreasing discretionary power to influence public sector expenditures, the upshot of Alliance programs has been to encourage Latin American countries to bring their own decentralized sectors under executive control.

Not all Latin American countries face the dilemma posed by the growth of decentralized budgetary expenditure. Table 1 shows that among the six countries for which this writer has summary data,[4] decentralized expenditure amounts to less than one-third of public expenditure in Argentina as well as Venezuela. In contrast, about half or more of public expenditures are decentralized in Mexico, Bolivia, Costa Rica, and Brazil, the latter being highest of all. (The U.S. case is discussed below in special terms.)

The present study is limited to a comparative analysis of public expenditure in Mexico, Bolivia, and Costa Rica in order to assess the role of governmental policy as ascertained by this investigator's field research in three diverse countries which face the similar problem of attempting to expand presidential power. The view developed here is that while recentralization of economic development may be desirable in order to overcome many problems, the political and social ramifications of such policy merit extended discussion.

SELECTED CASE STUDIES

Of the three countries studied here,[5] each has had an important revolution and each is now attempting to reform the pattern of government and budgetary policy which emerged in earlier years. Mexico's experience began in 1910 with a political upheaval lasting until 1930. During the 1930s Lázaro Cárdenas developed a policy of social action in his country's revolution when he emphasized immediate benefits for the masses. From 1940 to 1960 Mexico was engaged in an industrial revolution, a program actually beginning during the Cárdenas period. Since 1960, Mexico's leaders have claimed to develop a balanced revolution by diverting federal funds from economic expenditure into social outlay.

In this regard, much discussion as to whether the Mexican Revolution

4. Most countries do not yet have the means either to develop or publish a consolidated statement. Problems of comparability in such countries are occasioned by the fact that accounts may be shown on a gross or net basis and in rare cases amortization of the debt may not be included in totals. Also, accounting may be incomplete because, according to problems of definition, some decentralized agencies may not be included in calculations. Without exhaustive investigation in Argentina, Brazil, and Venezuela, for example, it is not possible to assess the comparability of data for these countries.

5. Because of space limitations, generalizations are made at the usual risk of oversimplification, but it is hoped that this problem has been kept to a minimum.

TABLE 1

RELATIVE BUDGETARY POWER OF CENTRALIZED AND DECENTRALIZED[a]
SUBSECTORS OF PUBLIC EXPENDITURE IN SIX LATIN AMERICAN
COUNTRIES AND THE UNITED STATES

Country	Year	Total Amount (100.0%)[b]	Centralized (%)[c]	Decentralized (%)[c]
Argentina	1962	240 million	87.0	13.0
Bolivia[c,d]	1970	6,066 million	27.8	72.2
Brazil[d]	1965	9,956 million	24.7	75.3
Costa Rica[e]	1968	1,535 million	51.2	48.9
Mexico	1967	79,451 million	51.4	48.6
Venezuela	1967	12,685 million	67.8	32.2
United States	1967[e]	432,429 million[f]	86.9	13.1

[a]Decentralized subsector includes public enterprises, mixed public and private corporations, governmental commissions, institutes, independent agencies, etc.
[b]In local currency at current prices; *includes debt amortization as well as interest payments* (see text for discussion).
[c]May double-count some or all transfers from one subsector to the other.
[d]Projected outlay in contrast to actual expenditure.
[e]Fiscal year 1966-67.
[f]Includes $274.2 billion debt amortization and $12.6 billion interest.

SOURCES: Argentina, Secretaría de Estado de Hacienda de la Nación, *Memoria, 1962,* pp. 14-16, 103; Bolivia, Ministerio de Finanzas, *Presupuesto General de la Nación, 1970; Gobierno Nacional Central,* p. 2; Brazil, Ministério do Planejamento e Coordenação Econômica, *Consolidação Orçamentária do Governo Féderal, 1965,* p. 16; Costa Rican Comptroller General's Office; Mexican Comptroller General's Office; Venezuela, Banco Central, *Informe Económico, 1968,* pp. A114, A121; and United States, Bureau of the Census, *Statistical Abstract, 1970,* p. 378, and (for $274,172 million debt amortization) Treasury Department, *Annual Report, 1967,* p. 593.

is dead or alive after sixty years misses the point that the Mexican government and the Partido Revolucionario Institucional (PRI) have successfully continued to justify the holding of power in the name of an open-ended institutional framework which develops new approaches for changing times.[6] Beginning with President Plutarco Calles (1924-28)[7] executives began to establish decentralized agencies to conduct economic affairs of the state; such policy reached a peak during the era of President Adolfo López Mateos (1958-64). Under his successor, however, the executive branch of government fully realized that it had created a system over which it had little or no control; and President Gustavo Díaz

6. For further discussion see James W. Wilkie, *The Mexican Revolution: Federal Expenditure and Social Change Since 1910,* 2nd ed., (Berkeley: University of California Press, 1970), and James W. Wilkie and Edna Monzón de Wilkie, *México Visto en el Siglo XX; Entrevistas de Historia Oral: Ramón Beteta, Marte R. Gómez, Manuel Gómez Morín, Vicente Lombardo Toledano, Miguel Palomar y Vizcarra, Emilio Portes Gil, Jesús Silva Herzog.* Distributed by Cuadernos Americanos for the Instituto Mexicano de Investigaciones Económicas (Mexico, D.F., 1969).

7. President Porfirio Díaz actually began such policy by arranging for the government to begin purchase of railways.

Ordaz (1964-70) developed a series of presidential decrees designed to reorganize the government framework and to give the Ministry of the Presidency real as well as theoretical power over national development.

Bolivia underwent a sweeping revolution after 1952 when Víctor Paz Estenssoro led his Movimiento Nacionalista Revolucionario (MNR) to power. Paz hoped to prevent future violence by following the Mexican example of developing an institutionalized revolution, a program he began to introduce especially during his second term in the presidency, 1960-64. However, he was overthrown in November shortly after beginning his third term in office.[8] During the MNR's twelve consecutive years in the presidency (Hernán Siles Zuazo filled the term 1956-60), a number of important decentralized agencies were created as part of a tradition already established by prerevolutionary governments. Post-MNR presidents brought decentralization to a peak, and only in the 1970s did a reaction against such a framework come in the form of an administrative reorganization. Though the military-dominated governments after 1964 had claimed to be developing the MNR revolution in a "purified" form free from political considerations, this issue did not prove to be convincing because administrative problems were compounded as the central government gave up more and more power to autonomous agencies. Not until 1970 did a group of central government *técnicos* propose specific actions to end near-total chaos in governmental planning. These *técnicos* claimed that their policy represented a new and viable alternative to MNR policy which influenced the 1950s and 1960s.

Costa Rica's revolution came in 1948 when José Figueres, an apolitical farmer and industrialist, was joined by Padre Benjamín Núñez's labor-oriented Catholic groups in a successful attempt to overthrow the pro-Communist government of President Teodoro Picado. As Figueres has noted, in 1948 he was interested specifically in following the Uruguayan model of state decentralization in order to limit the power of the president; and with a new basis for state action implanted, Figueres turned over his office to the duly elected opposition.[9]

By 1953, however, Figueres felt that he should return to the presidency in order to establish the principles of his new Partido Liberación Nacional (PLN), principles which implicitly if not explicitly favored the development of Costa Rica's middle class. During his presidency for the

8. For a concise history of Bolivian affairs since the 1930s, see James W. Wilkie, *The Bolivian Revolution and U.S. Aid Since 1952: Financial Background and Context of Political Decisions* (Los Angeles: Latin American Center, University of California, 1969).

9. Views developed here on Costa Rican affairs are taken from tape-recorded conversations with José Figueres by James W. Wilkie, Albert L. Michaels, and Edna Monzón de Wilkie in Oral History Interviews (Buffalo and Columbus, 1968); the Uruguayan model (and the 1933 Tennessee Valley Authority example) are discussed by Father Benjamín Núñez in James W. Wilkie, Albert L. Michaels, and Edna Monzón de Wilkie, Oral History Interviews (Guatemala City, 16 July 1970).

period 1953-58 he followed his earlier program of decentralization, a process continued by the opposition which alternated in power with the PLN during the 1960s.

Not until Figueres prepared to return to power for the term 1970-74 did he realize that he had established a system over which he lacked control. Thus at the very time that he wished the presidency to assume state power in order to follow up his middle-class revolution of 1948 with a "revolution for the masses," he found that the form of government he had instituted was not flexible enough to meet the demands of a new era.

Country comparisons given in Table 2 portray differences among Mexico, Bolivia, and Costa Rica and provide a comparison with the United States, the most influential country in each of the three nations' affairs. In relation to total population and total GNP of the United States, the selected countries located in North, Central, and South America appear small. In terms of GNP per capita, Mexico and Costa Rica have a better position than Bolivia, but neither compares favorably with the United States.[10]

Surprisingly, public expenditure per capita in the three Latin American countries is within the same range (and this observation also holds for the amount of decentralized outlay). Expenditure of approximately $140 per capita is only about one-sixteenth of the expenditure per capita in the United States, which explains to some degree why public sector policy in the former countries often does not appear to have much impact on the masses. If the decentralized portion of this amount is deducted, funds over which the president has relative control decrease to $71, $55, and $74 per capita in Mexico, Bolivia, and Costa Rica, respectively, compared to $1,887 in the United States.

Actually, the controllable figure for the United States is inflated because of special factors, especially programs resulting from legislation which often stipulates rates to be paid and conditions of eligibility for beneficiaries. Such problems are particularly true for the following decentralized and/or open-ended programs: social security payments, unemployment coverage, farm price supports, public assistance grants, and veterans' benefits.[11] In 1967, built-in costs for relatively uncontrollable programs including debt amortization and interest payments made up over 90 percent of total U.S. civilian outlays.[12]

10. In relation to territory, however, population density in Costa Rica and Mexico exceeds that for the United States, a factor which might indicate that those countries do not necessarily need more population as much as they need to develop the quality of life for the population already in existence.

11. United States, *Budget, 1971*, p. 42. It should be noted, however, that since 1945 independent federal corporations must secure their funds from congressional appropriations, like any other governmental agency, and unexpended balances revert to a general fund.

12. United States, *Budget, 1969*, p. 15; and U.S. Treasury Department, *Annual*

TABLE 2

Country Comparisons: Mexico, Bolivia, Costa Rica, and the United States

Indicator	Mexico (1967)	Bolivia (1970)	Costa Rica (1968)	United States (1967)
1. Population (million)	45.7	3.8	1.6	199.1
2. Total hectares (million)	197.3	109.0	5.1	936.3
3. Density (1 as a percent of 2)	23	3	31	21
4. GNP (million dollars)[a]	24,112	911[b]	747	803,914
5. GNP per capita (dollars)[a]	528	240	467	4,037
6. Public expenditure[c] (million dollars)[a]	6,362	511	232	432,429
7. Public expenditure per capita (dollars)[a]	139	134	145	2,172
8. Decentralized expenditure per capita (dollars)[a]	68	79	71	285
9. Public expenditure as a percent of GNP	26.4	56.1	31.1	53.8
10. Income tax collections (million dollars)[a]	809	18	15	95,497
11. Income tax as a percent of public expenditure	12.7	3.5	6.5	22.1
12. Income tax as a percent of GNP	3.4	2.0	2.0	11.9

[a]Nondeflated.

[b]Provisional 1969 data.

[c]Public expenditure = centralized plus decentralized outlay.

SOURCES: 1. UCLA *Statistical Abstract of Latin America, 1967* (Los Angeles: Latin American Center, University of California), p. 57. 2. Ibid., p. 52. 3. Calculated. 4. UCLA *Statistical Abstract of Latin America, 1968*, p. 241; Bolivia, Ministerio de Planificación y Coordinación, *Revista de Planificación y Desarrollo 1* (1970): 3; Costa Rica, Banco Central, *Estadísticas Económicas, 1963-1968*, p. 11. 5. Calculated. 6. Calculated from Table 1 with exchange rates given in UCLA *Statistical Abstract of Latin America, 1967*, p. 189, and *Bank of London and South America Review 4* (1970): 527. 7. Calculated. 8. Calculated from Table 1. 9. Calculated. 10. Mexican Comptroller General's Office; Bolivia, Ministerio de Finanzas, *Presupuesto General de la Nación, 1970*, p. 9 (second series of pagination); Costa Rica, Dirección General de Estadística, *Anuario Estadístico, 1968*, p. 305; United States, *Budget, 1971*, p. 585. 11-12. Calculated.

Though debt amortization is excluded from some types of functional analysis of expenditure (as in the U.S. government's budgetary analysis), it is included here to make U.S. figures comparable to Latin American data. Latin American governments customarily include debt redemptions in their budgets in order to show that they are meeting national and international obligations, as well as to reveal the proportion of governmental fund-raising activity required for repayment of previously expended loans.[13]

FUNCTIONAL ANALYSIS

Functional analysis for public expenditure in Mexico, Bolivia, Costa Rica, and the United States is presented in Table 3. Since it is necessary to distinguish between centralized and decentralized analysis as well as to develop a consolidated view of expenditure which helps us to understand the total impact of public activity in relation to political decisions, in effect Table 3 is concerned with presenting alternative views of reality.

Though it would be helpful to examine the historical nature of these realities, data for the decentralized and consolidated budgets, as we have seen, are only available for the late 1960s. Mexico was the first of the four countries to attempt to integrate the decentralized sector into a unified budget, beginning to expand coverage of data in 1965. Bolivia adopted its consolidated budget only in 1970; and Costa Rica had not solved its problems by the onset of the 1970s. The United States began to develop its consolidated budget in the fiscal year 1969 by providing reorganized data for the period of the 1960s. Thus with some adaptation

---

Report, 1967, p. 593. If debt amortization is excluded from analysis, in 1967 the uncontrollable amount was about 61 percent. The comparable estimation for 1971 was 69 percent (see United States, *Budget, 1971*, p. 42).

13. In contrast to many Latin American countries which are dependent upon foreign loans, in the United States 95 percent of the public debt is domestically held (D. J. and A. F. Ott, *Federal Budget Policy*, 2nd ed. (Washington, D.C.: Brookings Institution, 1969), p. 109. Thus, debt transactions exclusive of interest payments are omitted from the U.S. government budgetary analysis on the grounds that borrowing and repayment involve exchange of assets and are neither receipts nor expenditures. It could be argued, however, that debt redemption should be included in U.S. government analysis in order to show the extent of obligations falling due in any given year. In societies which live on credit, provision for meeting obligations becomes an important part of state policy, depending, for example, on inflationary and deflationary conditions. Such policy may influence the capital market of funds available for public and private financial activity (including new borrowing); and it may be argued that funds used for debt repayments will be spent differently by the private sector than if they are not repaid and are spent by the public sector. With regard to arguments for including in the budget loans *by* the government (as distinguished from loans *to* the government discussed above), cf. Wilfred Lewis, Jr., ed., *Budget Concepts for Economic Analysis* (Washington, D.C.: Brookings Institution, 1968), part 1. The matter of debt problems will be raised in further detail in the last two sections of this paper.

TABLE 3

FUNCTIONAL ANALYSIS[a] OF PUBLIC EXPENDITURE IN MEXICO, BOLIVIA,
COSTA RICA, AND THE UNITED STATES

	Mexico (1967)	Bolivia (1970)	Costa Rica (1968)	U.S. (1967)
Centralized	$40,853[b]	$1,684	$786	$381[c,e]
Economic	37.6%	26.1%	16.5%	2.8%
Social	20.3	30.9	38.9	2.4
Administrative	42.1	43.0	44.6	94.8
Decentralized	$38,599[d]	$4,382	$749	$62[c,e]
Economic	75.5%	86.8%	40.4%	19.6%
Social	19.5	8.7	57.2	67.5
Administrative	5.0	4.5	2.4	12.9
Consolidated	$79,452[d]	$6,066	$1,535	$432[e]
Economic	55.4%	69.9%	28.2%	4.8%
Social	22.7	14.9	47.8	11.0
Administrative	21.9	15.2	24.0	84.2

[a]*Economic functions* include communication and transport; development and conservation of natural resources; and development, promotion, and regulation of industry. *Social functions* include educational and cultural services; and health, labor affairs, public assistance, and medical services. *Administrative functions* include general administration; military outlay; pensions; and debt amortization and interest. For more detailed definitions see James W. Wilkie, *The Mexican Revolution: Federal Expenditure and Social Change Since 1910*, 2nd ed. (Berkeley: University of California Press, 1970), p. 13, and *The Bolivian Revolution and U.S. Aid Since 1952: Financial Background and Context of Political Decisions* (Los Angeles: Latin American Center, University of California, 1969), pp. 65-67.
[b]In millions of local currency (except U.S., in billions); totals equal 100.0%.
[c]U.S. projected in contrast to actual outlay; actual functional analysis not available for conversion to consolidated account (the "international" subfunction is divided here according to economic, social, and administrative activities; "space research and technology" is considered an economic activity). No deductions for interfund transfers.
[d]Functional analysis prepared by the Mexican Comptroller General's Office.
[e]The consolidated account is calculated on a different basis than that used for the subsectors, which the government has not revised for its new concepts; thus subtotals do not add to $432 billion.
SOURCES: Mexican and Costa Rican percentages are adapted from data provided by the comptroller generals' offices in Mexico City and San José. Bolivian data are from Bolivia, Ministerio de Finanzas, *Presupuesto General de la Nación, 1970*, pp. 9-11, 13-14. U.S. percentages are adapted from *Budget, 1968*, pp. 333-67 and 456-61; *Budget, 1971*, pp. 587-91; and Treasury Department, *Annual Report, 1967*, p. 593.

for comparability, consolidated data are available only in the contemporary period.[14]

In 1967, Mexico's central government was proportionally more active in economic affairs than any of the countries under discussion. With almost 38 percent of expenditure centered on economic matters, it retained

14. Bolivia has some consolidated figures dating from the early 1960s, but centralized and decentralized aspects are not always clear. Cf. Bolivia, Dirección General

direct control which was relatively quite high. In this manner, combined socioadministrative matters came to only about 62 percent of outlay.

In Costa Rica (1968) and Bolivia (1970), social expenditure of the central government reached (or was scheduled to reach in the latter case) a secondary position in relation to administrative outlay, which has traditionally been highest in all, except Mexico during the period of its industrial revolution.[15] Bolivian and Costa Rican socioadministrative outlay came to about 74 percent and 84 percent, respectively. Though these figures were higher than in Mexico, they were low compared to central government activity in the United States.

Using the criteria of functional expenditure developed in this paper, U.S. central government activity for 1967 cannot even be said to be socioadministrative in nature; rather, it was dominated by nonsocial and noneconomic outlays in which defense (18 percent), debt amortization (72 percent), and debt interest (3 percent) helped administrative activity to reach almost 95 percent of centralized expenditure.[16]

With regard to decentralized expenditure, Mexico and Bolivia have concentrated economic activity in this sphere; Costa Rica has emphasized social affairs, in spite of the fact that its social portion of centralized outlay reached about 39 percent (the highest of any country discussed here). In comparison, the U.S. decentralized sector exceeded even Costa Rica's decentralized social activity.

The consolidated result for Mexico and Bolivia shows a basic economic orientation, compared to Costa Rican and U.S. budgets, which are generally concerned with socioadministrative activity. Similarities between policy in the three Latin American countries, however, are revealed in the fact that the general economic impact of consolidated outlays is much greater than that imputed from only analyzing the centralized activity for which presidents are directly responsible.

What are the implications for statecraft if economic affairs are increasingly delimited to be outside of politics? And what are the prospects of incorporating decentralized or autonomous agencies into state planning in order to prevent new kinds of challenges to central government authority? Whereas in the past regionalism was considered to be

---

de Estadística y Censos, *Boletín Estadístico* 93 (1967): 1-3; and U.S. Agency for International Development/Bolivia, *Estadísticas Económicas* 11 (1970): 39. For historical series on central government expenditure in Mexico (1910-63) and Bolivia (1930-66) see James W. Wilkie's works cited in Tables 4 and 9. A summary of Costa Rican data is given in Table 13. Because of adjustments of data for comparability, methods developed here may differ slightly from functional analysis prepared, beginning in recent years, by each government.

15. See Table 4.

16. In terms of analysis which omits amortization of the debt from accounts, in 1967 interest amounted to 13 percent and defense to 69 percent of central government outlay. In the U.S. consolidated analysis, however, the totals were 8 percent and 44 percent, respectively. See United States, *Budget, 1971*, pp. 587, 591-92.

the major threat to central government political power, it appears that today the threat to a strong presidency comes from the rise of agencies which in effect constitute states within states. This development represents a new and more sophisticated challenge to central authority than existed when leaders struggled over federal and confederational issues of government. The problem involves various aspects of central government effectiveness and assumptions about the role of the decentralized sector in each of the three Latin American countries.

MEXICO

The Mexican central government has never been very effective in estimating its income and expenditures; and perhaps this has accounted for political success. In a country where the division of the revenue pie is not clear to ministries which compete for funds, governmental options are left open for pragmatic action. Thus a voracious military lost relative power in Mexico, for example, as it was subject to budgetary legerdemain. The central government provided the absolute amount of funds promised to the military; but as budgets expanded over projections, the generals received a declining proportion of actual expenditure compared to the percentage propagandized in the projected budget.[17] Between 1949 and 1969, the central government underestimated its income by an average of 55 percent each year. Only once since 1949 did estimates come close to actual collections (in 1953 the government collected only 9 percent more than projected). In all but four other cases, collections ran between 41 and 200 percent of estimations; and in those four cases, growth was at about one-third higher than planned. The greatest problem in government estimates came in the early 1960s when planning was deficient by an average of 76 percent, the most serious underestimation coming in 1965 when the decentralized sector was integrated into consolidated accounting.[18]

The record of the decentralized sector since 1965, when data are available, is much better than that of the central government. Between 1965 and 1969 total collections ran only an average of 21 percent higher than estimates.[19] Though in 1966, 1967, and 1968 planning was relatively accurate, in 1969 revenue was underestimated by over 20 percent; and in 1965 income was underestimated by nearly 50 percent.

The pattern of Mexican central government expenditure for the period from 1947 to 1969 is shown in Table 4. Presidents Adolfo López Mateos and Gustavo Díaz Ordaz functionally expended actual total cen-

17. Wilkie, *Mexican Revolution*, pp. 100-106.
18. Mexico, Contaduría de la Federación, Cuenta Pública, "Estado Analítico de Ingresos" (yearly).
19. Ibid.

tral government funds the same way, although the latter projected to spend almost as much for social as economic development. Both of the presidents reduced the share of the budget devoted to economic affairs, emphasizing new social outlay necessitated by the shift from industrial to balanced revolution. In the meantime, funds spent on general administration increased (in spite of projections) to gain renewed support from a bureaucracy which felt that it had not received benefits commensurate with other sectors of society. Such action was apparently appropriate for

TABLE 4

Average Percentage of Mexican Central Government Budgetary Expenditure by Type of Emphasis and Presidential Term

Years	President	Projected No. of Years in Average	Total = 100.0%[a]		
			Economic	Social	Admin.
1947-52	Alemán	6	39.2	18.6	42.2
1953-58	Ruiz Cortines	6	43.8	20.4	35.8
1959-64	López Mateos	6	38.9	31.6	29.5
1965-69	Díaz Ordaz	5	38.1	37.4	24.5
		Actual			
1947-52	Alemán	6	51.9	13.3	34.8
1953-58	Ruiz Cortines	6	52.7	14.4	32.9
1959-64	López Mateos	6	39.1	19.5	41.4
1965-68	Díaz Ordaz	4	40.3	20.6	39.1

[a]For definition of functional emphasis, see Table 3, note a.
Sources: Wilkie, *Mexican Revolution*, p. 32; Mexico, Secretaría de Hacienda y Crédito Público, *Presupuesto General de Egresos de la Federación*, yearly; and Mexico, Contaduría de la Federación, *Cuenta Pública*, yearly. For analysis which omits debt amortization, see Clark W. Reynolds, *The Mexican Economy: Twentieth-Century Structure and Growth* (New Haven: Yale University Press, 1970), p. 291; Reynolds gives Mexican government functional categories which are slightly different from those developed in this study.

stability, as the PRI has faced electoral problems in the Federal District, the seat of greatly centralized government.[20]

The growth and importance of Mexican decentralized capital investment in projected public sector outlays (see Table 5) shows that since the late 1940s the central government increasingly has lost influence in this aspect of national development. The same situation was true in 1925 before active central government policy was stimulated by President Calles. And when Cárdenas assumed the presidency in 1934, growth of central government expenditure further eclipsed outlays of decentralized investment (then limited to the Mexican National Railways), which de-

20. See James W. Wilkie, "New Hypotheses for Statistical Research in Recent Mexican History," *Latin American Research Review* 6:2 (Summer 1971): 3-17.

clined to less than 30 percent. With Cárdenas's expropriation of the foreign-owned oil industry in 1938, however, the decentralized sector received new impetus, a capacity for growth that came to fruition under President Alemán, who emphasized increased investment in decentralized electrical power development as well as in railways.[21]

Actual capital investment figures (in contrast to projections since 1939) are not available except for the recent presidency of Gustavo Díaz Ordaz,[22] and the data are not broken down as to centralized or decentralized outlay. Though these data (given in Table 6) do not tell us the impact of central government policy, the fact that they exist at all indicates

TABLE 5

DECENTRALIZED MEXICAN INVESTMENT AS A PERCENTAGE OF TOTAL PUBLIC SECTOR
INVESTMENT, 1925-70 (PROJECTED DATA BASED UPON INCOMPLETE REPORTING)[a]

Year	%	Year	%	Year	%
1925	54.9	1941	33.8	1957	53.7
1926	44.1	1942	31.2	1958	57.3
1927	44.3	1943	32.4	1959	56.1
1928	41.4	1944	37.9	1960	66.8
1929	41.8	1945	44.1	1961	64.8
1930	40.8	1946	40.8	1962	65.7
1931	36.3	1947	48.1	1963	60.7
1932	41.1	1948	48.3	1964	61.3
1933	37.6	1949	53.4	1965	66.5
1934	35.7	1950	58.0	1966	66.4
1935	29.9	1951	50.7	1967	62.7
1936	28.6	1952	49.7	1968	62.4
1937	28.6	1953	53.5	1969	64.2
1938	28.8	1954	54.6	1970	63.8
1939	42.9	1955	56.5		
1940	49.3	1956	55.7		

[a]Data for 1925-38 are for actual expenditures.
SOURCES: Mexico, Dirección de Inversiones Públicas, *Inversión Pública Federal, 1925-1963*, pp. 33-40, 111, and *Inversión Pública Federal, 1964-1965-1966*, Tables 2, 12, 18; and sources for Table 6.

that for the first time the central government is not only able to gauge the real role of public sector policy, but also to determine this role as it affects Mexico's thirty-two political entities. Of the total 87,007 million pesos invested between 1965 and 1969, 25.1 percent was social in nature, with only 2.2 percent of the total being devoted to administrative functions. Thus, 72.7 percent went into economic investment, including 10.3 percent devoted to agricultural, ranching, and fishing programs.

21. It is interesting to note that Presidents Cárdenas and Avila Camacho projected capital investment in agricultural affairs at about the same share (20 percent) as President Alemán; see Mexico, Dirección de Inversiones Públicas, *México: Inversion Pública Federal, 1925-1963*, pp. 55-57.

22. For projected regional figures, 1939-63, see ibid., passim; and for 1959-66, see Wilkie, "New Hypotheses for Statistical Research," Table 3.

TABLE 6

MEXICAN PUBLIC SECTOR CAPITAL INVESTMENT BY ENTITY, 1965-69,
COMPARED TO POPULATION IN 1970

	Actual Expenditure			
	Total Amount(%)[a]	Industrial Share(%)[b]	Transport and Communication Share(%)[c]	Population 1970(%)[d]
Total Mexico	100.0	100.0	100.0	100.0
Aguascalientes	.6	.2	1.3	.7
Baja California	2.0	1.1	3.1	1.8
Baja Calif. Terr.	.9	.2	2.4	.3
Campeche	.7	.3	1.9	.5
Coahuila	3.7	4.6	2.8	2.3
Colima	.6	.3	1.6	.5
Chiapas	1.8	2.1	2.7	3.3
Chihuahua	3.9	3.7	6.5	3.3
Distrito Federal	24.5	8.2	10.9	14.3
Durango	1.4	.7	1.4	1.9
Guanajuato	3.8	5.7	4.4	4.7
Guerrero	2.0	2.2	2.2	3.3
Hidalgo	1.5	1.3	2.2	2.5
Jalisco	2.6	2.3	4.6	6.8
México	3.8	4.4	5.3	7.9
Michoacán	1.8	1.1	3.2	4.8
Morelos	.8	.4	1.3	1.3
Nayarit	.5	.4	1.0	1.1
Nuevo León	2.2	3.1	2.3	3.5
Oaxaca	2.0	2.4	2.4	4.2
Puebla	1.7	2.0	2.1	5.2
Querétaro	1.3	.4	3.7	1.0
Quintana Roo	.4	.1	1.0	.2
San Luis Potosí	1.2	1.0	2.6	2.7
Sinaloa	4.3	1.1	6.6	2.6
Sonora	2.2	1.3	4.0	2.3
Tabasco	5.6	10.9	2.4	1.6
Tamaulipas	7.9	13.8	3.0	3.0
Tlaxcala	.3	.2	.6	.9
Veracruz	12.2	23.4	8.2	7.9
Yucatán	1.2	.8	1.5	1.6
Zacatecas	.6	.3	.8	2.0

[a]87,007 million pesos; total includes social (25.1%), agricultural/ranching/forestry (10.3%), and administrative/defense (2.2%) investments not shown separately here.
[b]34,719 million pesos equals 39.9% of total amount.
[c]19,593 million pesos equals 22.5% of total amount.
[d]48,225,238.
SOURCES: This actual investment data has been provided by Mexico's Dirección de Planeación Sectorial y Regional in the Ministry of the Presidency, subsequently published as México Dirección de Inversiones Públicas, *Inversión Pública Federal, 1965-1970*, p. 174. Cf. Emilio Múgica Montoya, coordinator, *Programa de Desarrollo Económico y Social de México, 1966-1970* (Mexico, D.F.: Comisión Intersectorial, Secretaría de la Presidencia, Secretaría de Hacienda y Crédito Público, n.d.) for an analysis of projections (295 pages plus appendix), unfortunately printed only for extremely limited distribution. Population data are from Dirección General de Estadística, *IX Censo General de Población, 1970, Resumen General Abreviado*.

With regard to industrial development (39.9 percent of total investment), almost one-quarter was allocated to the state of Veracruz (23.4 percent); Tamaulipas (13.8 percent) and Tabasco (10.9 percent) also received greater shares than the Federal District (8.2 percent), which has traditionally been Mexico's industrial center. In the four cases, investment was divided about equally between oil and electrical development in all but the Federal District, where investment was dedicated to outlays for iron and steel development.

Infrastructural investments in transport and communications (22.5 percent of total public investment) were not so concentrated as the industrial growth they are designed to support. Only the Federal District with 10.9 percent (an amount which includes the construction of a subway system) and Veracruz with 8.2 percent had relatively high amounts. In spite of criticism concerning the construction of Mexico City's subway (some intellectuals believe that the money might have been better spent for rural development), the relationship of investment to population was fairly well balanced under Díaz Ordaz.

Where critics of Mexican centralization of the Federal District can make their best case today lies outside the sphere of industrial policy. Since the population in the capital is located in the narrow confines of a valley and apparently is most susceptible to political mobilization, two-thirds of the public sector's heavy emphasis on social expenditure was located there. This emphasis weighted the total effect of public sector expenditure toward the Federal District; if social outlay is subtracted from total investment in Table 6, the Federal District's share in investment declines from about one-quarter to 10.8 percent. Thus disaggregation of total amounts leads to a very different view than that presented in official partial summaries.[23]

That the central government has gained this new capacity to assess development is impressive. With the tremendous growth of decentralized agencies and the confusion as to their legal status, the government of Díaz Ordaz showed real organizational talent in even compiling the figures given in Table 6. That the central government would eventually have to undertake this task became increasingly evident after 1940.[24] Of

23. For example, see Mexico, Secretaría de la Presidencia, *Sexto Informe que rinde al H. Congreso de la Unión el C. Presidente de la República Gustavo Díaz Ordaz, 1970*, Anexos 1-4.

24. On Mexican planning in general, see William P. Glade, Jr., "Las Empresas Gubernamentales Descentralizadas," *Problemas Agrícolas e Industriales de México* 11 (1969): 1; Miguel S. Wionczek, "Incomplete Formal Planning: Mexico," in Everett E. Hagen, ed., *Planning Economic Development* (Homewood, Ill.: Richard D. Irwin, 1963), pp. 150-82; Robert J. Shafer, *Mexico: Mutual Adjustment Planning* (Syracuse, N.Y.: Syracuse University Press, 1966); Clark W. Reynolds, *The Mexican Economy: Twentieth-Century Structure and Growth* (New Haven: Yale University Press, 1970); and Roger D. Hansen, *The Politics of Mexican Development* (Baltimore: Johns Hopkins University Press, 1971).

the nearly three hundred decentralized agencies for which the Ministry of National Patrimony could give information in a 1964 directory,[25] six were founded by Porfirio Díaz; three by Alvaro Obregón; five by Calles; eight during the era from 1929 to 1934; twenty by Cárdenas; forty-five by Manuel Avila Camacho; fifty-four by Alemán; fifty-three by Ruiz Cortines; and seventy-nine by López Mateos.[26]

Priorities of expenditure in the public sector are presented in Table 7 with some reservation. Not only is the data becoming more complete only in recent years, but periods in the series alternate between projected and actual data. Nevertheless, it is apparent that centralized and decentralized government investment in industry gained slowly. As suggested above, the government did not conceive its role to lie in industrial development until the very late 1930s, and the concept grew slowly after heavy initial outlay in 1940. Not until the mid-1950s did the public sector devote as much as one-third of capital investment to the industrial sector, and the 40 percent mark was not reached until the 1960s.

In the meantime, the public sector conceived its role to lie mainly in the development of communications and transportation systems. Even though infrastructural investment declined between 1925 and 1970 from 93.9 percent to 21.5 percent, the growth of outlay in real terms (adjusted for inflation) means that it was gaining many more pesos per capita than during the 1920s and 1930s when three-quarters of public capital investment was devoted to communications and transportation. In 1938, for example, this category received (in real terms) twenty-two pesos per capita, an amount that reached forty-one pesos by 1968.[27]

Whereas in the past many observers have felt that Mexico's modern industrial growth depends upon the development of markets in rural

25. Mexico, Secretaría del Patrimonio Nacional, *Directorio General de Organismos Descentralizados, Empresas de Participación Estatal, Establecimientos Públicos, Comisiones, Juntas e Institutos Dependientes del Gobierno Federal, 1964,* preámbulo. The Directory noted, however, that its listing was incomplete because of lack of available data as well as deficiency in juridical classification of the agencies.

26. It would be presumptuous to say that the number of agencies created by presidential period as given here is complete. Not only are 21 agencies listed without date of formation, but also there is no indication of their original dates of creation prior to the latest reorganization. The 1969 Mexican government *Manual* which gives the latter information, however, only offers data on less than 100 of the almost 250 agencies which it lists. Such confusion indicates that even by 1970 Mexican government information on what constitutes the decentralized sector still left much to be desired and that national planning is far from complete. See Mexico, Secretaría de la Presidencia, *Manual de Organización del Gobierno Federal, 1969-1970.* Cf. David Ibarra, "Mercados, Desarrollo y Política Económica: Perspectivas de la Economía de México," in *El Perfil de México en 1980,* 2 vols. (Mexico, D.F.: Siglo XXI, 1970), 1: 192-97, for a useful alternative but incomplete list of decentralized agencies.

27. Calculated from Mexico City's 1939 wholesale price index converted to 1950 terms, and from population estimates also supplied by the Dirección General de Estadística. (Between 1938 and 1968, in current prices, Mexico's total public investment increased from 198 million pesos to 20,447 million pesos, according to the sources for Table 7.)

areas (thus necessitating capital investment in the rural sector),[28] the terms of debate appear to have changed in a way that few have foreseen (or in a way that few realize). Though investment priorities (Table 7) saw outlay for agriculture (including irrigation, ranching, and forestry) usually exceed expenditure for industry until 1947, after that date the reverse was true. But even more importantly, investment in the agricultural sector has lost out to expenditure on social welfare. Indications that

TABLE 7

AVERAGE MEXICAN CENTRALIZED AND DECENTRALIZED PUBLIC SECTOR
INVESTMENT PRIORITIES BY PRESIDENTIAL PERIOD 1925-70[a]

Years	President	No. of Years in Average	Industry	Communications/ Transportation (%)	Agriculture/ Ranching/ Forestry (%)	Social Welfare (%)
1925-28	Calles	4	—[b]	79.1	20.1	5.8
1929	Portes Gil	1	—	73.5	10.2	16.3
1930-32	Ortiz Rubio	3	—	76.6	11.5	11.9
1933-34	Rodríguez	2	—	75.9	11.0	13.1
1935-40	Cárdenas	6	5.1	66.3	18.1	9.6
1941-46	Avila Camacho	6	10.6	59.1	16.9	11.6
1947-52	Alemán	6	22.0	43.0	20.1	13.6
1953-58	Ruiz Cortines	6	32.4	37.2	14.9	13.8
1959-64	López Mateos	6	34.6	29.9	9.8	22.4
1965-70	Díaz Ordaz	6	40.3	22.4	10.5	24.7

[a]Excludes administration-defense category not listed separately; readers should note problematic nature of data in which actual and projected figures are used according to availability in order to construct time series. Actual outlay is given for 1925-38, and 1965-69. Projected investment is presented for 1939-64 and 1970.
[b]Indicates zero or less than .5%.
SOURCES: 1925-63 data are from Mexico, Dirección de Inversiones Públicas, *Mexico: Inversión Pública Federal, 1925-1963*, pp. 19, 53-58, 119. Data for 1964 are from *Inversión Pública Federal, 1964-1965-1966*, mimeographed (1967). Data for 1965-70 are from sources in Table 6 (cf. Mexico, Secretaría de la Presidencia, *Sexto Informe que rinde al H. Congreso de la Unión el C. Presidente de la República Gustavo Díaz, 1970*, p. 97, which gives higher totals with some percentage differences but which is incomplete because no total regional distribution is presented).

social development might be considered more important than outlay for agricultural development came in 1929, 1930, 1931, 1933, 1934, and 1952; and since 1956 social welfare functions consistently have been thought to be more important than agricultural growth. Thus the de facto issue does not now appear to be whether agricultural development has priority in the process of national modernization, but how great a percentage of investment funds should be allocated to improving the quality of life needed to modernize society. As suggested above, the Federal District

28. See, for example, Sanford A. Mosk, *Industrial Revolution in Mexico* (Berkeley: University of California Press, 1950).

has received the greatest share of social welfare expenditure; and in 1965, for example, when President Díaz Ordaz announced that the capital city was authorized to receive only 10 percent of total investment funds,[29] the actual figure came to almost double that amount.[30]

In spite of problems in coordinating centralized and decentralized activity discussed above, the Mexican economy and its industrialization have continued to make major yearly gains. Table 8 shows that for the 1960s, the average increase per year for real GDP was 7.1 percent. The subtotal for industry was even higher, averaging 8.9 percent, with the manufacturing sector equalling that growth rate.

TABLE 8

PERCENTAGE GROWTH OF MEXICO'S REAL GROSS DOMESTIC PRODUCT AND INDUSTRIAL OUTPUT (BASED ON 1960 PRICES)

Year	GDP(%)	Industry	
		Total(%)[a]	Manufacturing(%)[b]
1961	4.9	5.3	5.5
1962	4.7	5.5	4.6
1963	8.0	9.8	9.2
1964	11.7	15.7	17.4
1965	6.5	7.3	9.5
1966	6.9	9.6	9.4
1967	6.3	8.7	6.8
1968	8.1	10.0	10.1
1969[c]	7.3	8.3	8.0

[a]Includes mining, petroleum, manufacturing, construction, and electricity.
[b]Included in industrial total.
[c]Preliminary.
SOURCE: *El Mercado de Valores* (30 November 1970), p. 700.

In suggesting at the outset that a lack of planning has given the Mexican government political successes, perhaps one may hypothesize at this point that the Mexican economy is so healthy that disarticulation of state policy may at times be positive. Because this idea is both controversial and complicated, it will be reserved for discussion after the cases of Bolivia and Costa Rica have been examined. In any case, it is related to a number of dilemmas facing development problems in Latin America.

BOLIVIA

If Mexican governmental disarticulation has been an implicit threat to the power of the presidency, the Bolivian situation is even more critical. Although theoretically central governments maintain control over decen-

29. "Primer Informe de Gobierno [del] Presidente Gustavo Díaz Ordaz," *El Día* (2 September 1965), suplemento, p. 2.
30. Calculated from sources for Table 6.

tralized agencies through appointment of directors, as a matter of practice influence (let alone control) generally is possible only by overcoming great difficulties. If agencies do not use standardized accounting practices, interagency comparability is impossible. In addition, agency role vis-à-vis the central government is hard to ascertain because audits are rarely undertaken and a director infrequently knows the extent of his own agency's activities. Thus the agency becomes a state within a state precisely because the central government has given up power without realizing what it has done. (It should be noted also that often it is difficult for the chief executive to find out what his own central government is actually doing, let alone determine the activity of autonomous agencies.)

The Bolivian problem of governmental disarticulation is compounded by several factors, not the least of which is that there is even less statistical information than for Mexico. First, the president of Bolivia has been hampered in his planning activities by the congressional prerogative of earmarking taxes, a problem which Mexican presidents do not face. By 1964, when earmarked taxes were omitted from the budget in order to eliminate accounts not subject to audit, they made up 36.5 percent of gross expenditure.[31] Second, budgets are generally not prepared at the beginning of the year but long after de facto decisions have been made (the 1970 budget, for example, did not appear until August). Third, functional analysis of public sector finances has been confused by lack of data on the relative power of the president compared to autonomous agencies.

Whereas data published by the Bolivian planning ministry in 1966 show the central government as controlling over 70 percent of public sector expenditure,[32] revised data provided by the U.S. Agency for International Development (USAID) in Bolivia reveal otherwise.[33] Between 1963 and 1969, when some reliable data are available, the central government expended the following shares of public sector outlay, respectively: 26 percent, 26 percent, 31 percent, 33 percent, 33 percent, 33 percent, and 32 percent. Furthermore, the first detailed analysis of consolidated accounting (resumed in Table 1 above) indicates that the central government role in 1970 might be as low as about 28 percent.

Although no functional analysis is available which would offer an actual view of public sector investment priorities for any year and for each region of the country, the historical trend presented in Table 9 shows that central government outlay in the era financially dominated by Víctor Paz Estenssoro (1945-69) gave the central government a small role in economic development.

31. Earmarked taxes are excluded from analysis here; see Wilkie, *Bolivian Revolution*, p. 52.
32. Bolivia, Secretaría Nacional de Planificación y Coordinación, *Bolivia en Cifras, 1966*, p. 6.
33. USAID/Bolivia, *Estadísticas Económicas* 11 (1970): 39.

Bolivia's recent history of central government expenditure revolves around the policy of Paz Estenssoro. Paz made a financial revolution during 1945 and part of 1946 when he served as minister of finance. His policy of emphasizing social outlay at the expense of economic expenditures carried through in subsequent years until his MNR gained power in the revolution of 1952. Although economic emphasis gained somewhat, it was still far below the pattern set during the period from 1942 to 1944 by President Peñaranda. Paz's downfall in 1964 did not change the pattern he set in 1945.

TABLE 9

AVERAGE ACTUAL PERCENTAGE OF BOLIVIAN CENTRAL GOVERNMENT BUDGETARY
EXPENDITURE BY TYPE OF EMPHASIS AND ERA

| | | | Total = 100.0% | | |
Time Span	Era	Years	Economic	Social	Administrative
1942-44	Pre-Paz[a]	3	26.8	20.8	52.4
1945-51	Post-Paz[b]	7	10.5	28.4	61.1
1952-64	MNR[c]	13	15.0	34.6	50.4
1965-69	Post-MNR[d]	5	13.1	36.0	50.9
1970-	Técnicos[e]	1	26.1[f]	30.9[f]	43.0[f]

[a]Encompasses parts of Peñaranda and Villarroel presidencies.
[b]Encompasses epoch initiated by Paz Estenssoro's period (1 January 1945–19 July 1946) as minister of finance under President Villarroel; and includes Hertzog and Urriolagoitia presidencies.
[c]Encompasses Paz and Siles Zuazo presidencies.
[d]Encompasses Ovando, Barrientos, and Siles Salinas presidencies. Because the Bolivian government attempted a budgetary reorganization during 1965-66, this author was concerned that long-standing data for time-series analysis might be disrupted (see Wilkie, *Bolivian Revolution*, p. 18). The reorganization, which involved the maintenance of data on cards according to programs, has since been abandoned and the time series for activity by ministry reconstituted. These data have been adjusted here in order to make post-MNR functional budgetary analysis consistent with data through the MNR period.
[e]Encompasses Ovando, Miranda (one day), and Torres presidencies.
[f]Projected in contrast to actual outlay.
SOURCES: Wilkie, *Bolivian Revolution*, p. 21; Balances, Departamento de Contabilidad, Tesorería Nacional; and Bolivia, Ministerio de Finanzas, *Presupuesto General de la Nación, 1970.* See also James W. Wilkie, "Public Expenditure Since 1952," in James M. Malloy and Richard S. Thorn, eds., *Beyond the Revolution: Bolivia Since 1952* (Pittsburgh, Penn.: University of Pittsburgh Press, 1971).

Only in the budget for 1970 does one note a projected shift from social outlay to a more balanced policy. If the *técnicos* (many of whom were formed during the MNR period) have their way, the central government would begin to assume direct control over economic development. In the past, this control was delegated to USAID and a proliferation of autonomous agencies.

As discussed elsewhere, USAID never lived up to its promises. During the 1950s much aid was needed for direct budgetary supports which could keep the Paz government from being overcome by radical labor-left leaders and Communists. Even during the 1960s, when USAID attempted to switch to economic development (in spite of Alliance for Progress calls for social outlay), a shift toward economic projects by USAID was offset by new noneconomic programs conducted in Peace Corps and military assistance operations.[34]

Bolivian economic affairs, then, were decentralized among autonomous agencies, most of which operated with losses. The central government found that it not only could not count on anticipated agency profits from tin, transport, and oil, for example, but also that often it would *have* to subsidize a series of unprofitable ventures.

Given the confused growth of agencies shown in Table 10, it is no wonder that in 1970 Bolivian *técnicos* could claim that only through a governmental reorganization could the central government rationally develop the country's potential.[35] Although the MNR government established a Ministry of Planning and Coordination in 1963, like many such ministries in Latin America it found coordination to be an excruciating process. As the *técnicos* noted of the existing system in 1970: "With regard to planning, the situation is chaotic. In spite of the existence of a planning agency headed by an official of ministerial rank, the other ministers and directors of decentralized agencies generally make their own plans (or simply do not plan at all but fall back on their daily routine). Consequently, the coordination of planning as well as execution and evaluation of planning is virtually nonexistent. . . ."[36]

The *técnicos* went on to note: "The administrative function is carried out in a process which is extremely complex and costly. The existing rudimentary systems require 173 different operations for simple payment of one budgetary item; permission to pass merchandise through customs requires more than 87 steps; and even a simple request for annual vacation in a decentralized agency . . . means 59 operations before the employee can obtain his final authorization.

"But there are even worse examples of defective bureaucratic processes. In one ministry, for example, it has been discovered that 59 different operations are necessary to receive a letter and file it with a response. And as a corollary of these examples, the process for granting a mining concession in Bolivia, a country dedicated to mining, requires 250 steps."[37]

34. James W. Wilkie, "Public Expenditure Since 1952," in James M. Malloy and Richard S. Thorn, eds., *Beyond the Revolution: Bolivia Since 1952* (Pittsburgh: University of Pittsburgh Press, 1971), Table 3.

35. [José Ortiz Mercado, coordinator], *Estrategia Socio-Económica del Desarrollo Nacional, 1971-1991*, 2 vols. (La Paz: Ministerio de Planificación y Coordinación, 1970).

36. Ibid., 1: 116-17.

37. Ibid., 1: 117.

These revealing statements do much to puncture the myth of state planning propagandized by recent Bolivian governments. At first, Bolivian leaders (following examples of other Latin American countries) believed that by simply establishing a Ministry of Planning and Coordination, disarticulation between the centralized and decentralized agencies (as well as between agencies within each sector) could be resolved. However,

TABLE 10

GROWTH OF BOLIVIAN PUBLIC SECTOR AGENCIES SINCE 1952

Agency	Pre-1952 Agencies	1952-63[a]	1963-69[a]	Total by 1970
Government/administration/defense	8	0	7	15
Agriculture/ranching	3	3	5	11
Mines/petroleum	2	3	1	6
Industry/commerce	1	6	2	9
Energy	0	2	0	2
Public works/communi-cation/transport	7	2	10	19
Finances	8	0	1	9
Education/culture	4	4	3	11
Social welfare	7	3	8	18
Housing	0	2	1	3
Health	2	0	3	5
Total	42	25	41	108

[a]It is interesting to note that one recent observer claims that the MNR was not really revolutionary because it represented an "elitist life style." According to James M. Malloy, *Bolivia, The Uncompleted Revolution* (Pittsburgh, Penn.: University of Pittsburgh Press, 1970), pp. 306-7, one of the reasons Paz Estenssoro fell from power in 1964 was because he "felt the need to create a new technocratic elite which could truly lead the country to development"; thus he "paid less and less attention to party affairs."

Ironically, as seen in this table, post-MNR governments fragmented state power by creating so many new decentralized agencies that the *técnicos* now seek to clean up the confusion through recentralization. If the popular sector, however, has its way with the current president of Bolivia, Juan José Torres, decentralization apparently will be developed with a vengeance, with students, workers, miners, and peasants taking control from the *técnicos*.

SOURCE: [José Ortiz Mercado, coordinator], *Estrategia Socio-Económica del Desarrollo Nacional, 1971-1991*, 2 vols. (La Paz: Ministerio de Planificación, 1970), 1:115c.

Bolivia's *técnicos* have pointed out explicitly why mere coordination does not work: "For the last thirty years the government has been asystematically creating an excessive number of decentralized agencies, with an average of one agency each three years. Since 1965 the average has been three agencies per year without attention to *scientific principles* of administration. Under a false concept of the meaning of 'autonomy' or 'autarky,' this growth has provoked a breaking away of agencies from the nucleus of governmental control. This phenomenon must be attributed fundamentally to the absence of juridical norms concerning the concept of [centralized-decentralized relations which are] neither defined scientifically nor juridically in the country's legislation. In the final analysis, [relations are affected by personal influence which central government officials are able to exert over directors of decentralized agencies]."[38] In short, Bolivia is only now finding out what Mexico has fully discovered in the last ten years: coordination without a budgetary control is a vague term without much meaning for effective state planning.

But if the Bolivian central government has been so inept at managing the affairs of a "revolutionary" society, how can one account for a dramatic growth in GDP during the 1960s?

As shown in Table 11, total real GDP averaged a yearly gain of 5.0 percent between 1959 and 1969. Industrial growth showed surprising strength after 1962, and it would appear that the attempts by Paz and Barrientos to encourage private sector investment were handsomely rewarded. As in the Mexican case of the 1960s, the manufacturing subtotal grew at the same average as the total for industry (6.8 percent a year), although the Mexican average was several percentage points higher. Internal warfare set off by the Che Guevara movement did not appear to affect the growth of GDP, but that may be because the figures themselves are questionable.[39]

If the Bolivian *técnicos* are critical of the state's role in national development, their position is important from two points of view. In the first place, it is clear that they consider the role of the *técnico* to be the most important influence and the indispensable, vital basis for the rational direction of their society. The tone of their work is one of omniscience. If they are given their due place in the power structure the program is simple: "The new Administration and its newly formed bureaucracy must be based upon three basic precepts: (a) loyalty to the society which it serves; (b) passion for responsibility to public service; and (c) permanent intellectual and professional growth.

"As opposed to the private sector, the public sector increasingly utilizes new technologies, principally with regard to research on economics, finance, and production. But this positive State contribution to the development of productive forces until now has not been systematically and organically carried out. Rather, [it has responded in many cases to

38. Ibid., 1: 114-16.
39. Nevertheless, during the 1960s most observers were convinced that the Bolivian economy made great strides forward, regardless of problems in measurement. Utilizing a variety of analyses touching on qualitative aspects of development, a consensus emerged that Bolivia was beginning to overcome its historical backwardness. See, for example, Malloy and Thorn, *Beyond the Revolution;* Dwight B. Heath, Charles J. Erasmus, and Hans C. Buechler, *Land Reform and Social Revolution in Bolivia* (New York: Praeger, 1969); and Cornelius H. Zondag, *The Bolivian Economy, 1952-65: The Revolution and Its Aftermath* (New York: Praeger, 1966).

urgent or arbitrary decisions made by international or foreign agencies].
The new bureaucracy must participate in the new mission which the State
has in modern society."[40]

Furthermore, the *técnicos* noted that there are two positions concerning the role of the public sector, the first of which they do not deny but
seek to correct: "The first position stems from the idea that the State is a
'bad administrator,' and it condemns direct state intervention in the economic life of the country, [assigning it the supplementary role of main-
taining] . . . 'tranquility and public order.' The result is a curious mixture
of neoeconomic liberalism and political absolutism. The other position,

TABLE 11

PERCENTAGE GROWTH OF BOLIVIA'S REAL GROSS DOMESTIC PRODUCT AND
INDUSTRIAL OUTPUT (BASED ON 1958 PRICES)

| Year | GDP(%) | Industry | |
		Total(%)[a]	Manufacturing(%)[b]
1959	− .3	4.0	− 1.8
1960	4.3	2.2	9.7
1961	2.1	− 1.5	.2
1962	5.6	10.1	10.7
1963	6.4	9.9	6.6
1964	4.8	6.5	8.9
1965	6.9	11.3	9.8
1966	7.0	8.8	12.3
1967	6.3	12.8	3.2
1968	7.2	7.7	6.3
1969[c]	4.8	3.5	8.9

[a]Includes mining, petroleum, manufacturing, construction, and electricity.
[b]Included in industrial total.
[c]Preliminary.
SOURCE: Bolivia, Ministerio de Planificación y Coordinación, *Revista de Planificación y Desarrollo; Cuentas Nacionales, 1950-1969* 1 (1970): 7. For a devastating
criticism of the ministry's method for arriving at the above figures, see Laurence
Whitehead, "Basic Data in Poor Countries: The Bolivian Case," *Bulletin of the
Oxford University Institute of Economics and Statistics* 31 (1969): 205-27.

sustained in the present strategy for development [postulates that the
State] . . . must fulfill a directive, innovative, and entrepreneurial function
[so as to create economic development. Such growth will be produced
to the extent that masses are mobilized in a system of planning which
adapts to our national characteristics and which] substitutes 'the rules of
the free market,' with the common effort directed toward pre-fixed rationally planned goals."[41]

That the Bolivian *técnicos* should develop a detailed strategy for

40. [Ortiz Mercado], *Estrategia Socio-Económica del Desarrollo Nacional,
1971-1991,* 1: 126.
41. Ibid., 1: 128.

national development is admirable, but in the analysis of their country they have omitted four important factors. First, they have assumed that the plan will be carried out in an apolitical vacuum, an assumption belied by the fact that between 6 October and 7 October 1970, the presidency changed hands at least three times. Second, baseline analyses for projected growth in all fields are woefully inadequate; and few historical studies are available which would show whether or not there is a reservoir of experience which would provide a realistic stimulus for change. Third, the fact that the decentralized sector has advantages in hiring better-qualified personnel means that generally the least attractive bureaucrats go into the central government. Fourth, financial considerations are absent from planning.[42] For these reasons, any hope that the *técnicos* might be able to carry out their plan is very remote indeed.

In sum, it is interesting to note that in spite of ambitious plans for the 1970s, Bolivian government politicians in general have been concerned in the past about the lack of high-level manpower capable of conducting the country's public affairs. Because of the country's high rate of illiteracy (almost 69 percent in 1950, the date of the last population census),[43] and because of continued problems in educational development, the common stereotype places Bolivia among the countries in Latin America which suffer from disadvantages which the more-developed countries such as Costa Rica do not face.

COSTA RICA

Costa Rica has long been described as a land of literate, middle-class, rural folk who have solved many problems in their society by employing more schoolteachers than soldiers. In this view, Costa Rica does not suffer from the ills of its Latin American neighbors because it has (1) equitably-sized landholdings (in contrast to latifundia) and (2) deeply rooted democratic traditions which make a "model political system [with] . . . governmental agencies that operate independently of presidential control."[44] Unfortunately, this stereotyped description does not appear to be as accurate as previously supposed; and it is being reevaluated by the country's current chief executive, José Figueres, who himself was greatly responsible for setting up the so-called "model."

When José Figueres led a movement in 1948 to overthrow a Communist-oriented government, he set out to establish a system in which the chief executive would have little power. In his view, the cen-

---

42. Ibid., 2: 503-41.
43. UCLA *Statistical Abstract of Latin America, 1962*, p. 25.
44. Joseph A. Ellis, *Latin America: Its Peoples and Institutions* (New York: Bruce, 1971), pp. 204-5.

tralized government would provide for peace, stability, and honesty in which the private sector would prosper. His solution to this problem was to expand state ownership and control beyond the traditional areas of insurance and railways to include banking, electric power, public housing, communications, and agricultural enterprises. Of the nearly 130 decentralized agencies in Costa Rica,[45] only 9 agencies are listed as having been founded prior to the Figueres revolution.[46]

Even as Figueres took much economic activity out of the political arena, he encouraged the development of private entrepreneurship and the growth of a free market economy, two elements of Costa Rican life which had led to his own business success. In short, he sought to create a mixed-capitalistic system (or, as he would have termed it in his earlier days, a "mixed-socialistic system") in which the central government would not play a dominant role.

By creating a series of autonomous agencies, his system would permit long-term planning and political considerations would be reduced to a minimum by appointing directing boards with staggered terms overlapping with alternate presidential periods. In this manner, no political party could control any agency, unless it could win successive terms in the presidency; and to date this has not happened since the Figueres revolution. In contrast to the Mexican PRI and the Bolivian MNR, the Costa Rican PLN has never been able to gain one-party domination.

The importance of decentralized sector expenditures as compared to total centralized outlay is given in Table 12. Although these data include problems of definition and possible double-counting of intersectoral transfers, they do give some indication of the relative power of the autonomous agencies since 1950. Clearly they suggest that if state planning is to be carried out, consistent series must be developed which take into account the problems of definition and transfers.

With regard to the decentralized sector, the percentage share of year-to-year outlay dedicated to economic activities shows amounts that are less than 50 percent after 1959. These figures include capital and current outlay, the latter being as important for the purposes of political analysis as the former for economic interpretation. Without an adequate organizational framework (including, for example, budgeting for qualified administration, project guidance, and auditing), the success of capital investment outlays remains very much in doubt.[47] As suggested in Table

45. Costa Rica, Dirección General de Estadística y Censos, *Anuario Estadístico* (1968), pp. 306-7.
46. See the incomplete *Manual de Organización de la Administración Pública de Costa Rica,* published in 1962 by the Costa Rican Ministerio de Economía y Hacienda. Cf. Universidad de Costa Rica, *El Desarrollo Económico de Costa Rica,* vol. 4, and *Sector Público de la Economía Costarricense* (1962), pp. 27-28.
47. Costa Rican problems in supervising the expenditure of decentralized agencies are discussed in the section "Budgetary Controls."

3, then, the decentralized economic impact on Costa Rica in recent years has not been as great as the PLN itself originally might have hoped.

In addition to developing decentralized government, Figueres attempted to restrict the chief executive even further (and specifically to prevent the corruption in government which the civil war sought to overthrow in 1948). Thus, Figueres capped what was essentially a revolution in public administration by creating a comptroller general's office to con-

TABLE 12

COMPARISON OF COSTA RICAN CENTRALIZED AND DECENTRALIZED
ACTUAL EXPENDITURE, 1950-68

Year	Centralized	Decentralized	
	Actual Outlay (in Million Colones)[a]	Actual Outlay (in Million Colones)[a]	Percent Devoted to Economic Functions[b]
1950[c]	136.1	96.5[c]	78.2[c]
1951	144.2	96.0	76.1
1952	190.4	112.4	75.8
1953	222.1	155.3	77.9
1954	244.0	156.4	74.3
1955	303.8	201.8	72.8
1956	297.4	266.2	77.8
1957	325.9	266.5	73.0
1958	341.5	298.6	74.8
1959[d]	350.2	252.6[d]	41.1[d]
1960	376.1	255.8	45.1
1961	408.2	294.2	46.0
1962	437.7	377.3	46.4
1963	477.7	414.9	47.1
1964	531.2	449.5	50.4
1965	569.5	586.7	51.8
1966	675.7	582.3	43.1
1967	747.6	633.5	44.3
1968	785.7	749.0	40.4

[a]In current prices; may double-count intersectoral transfers, thus accounting for some of discrepancy discussed in notes c and d below.
[b]Functions of the National Insurance Institute are here divided equally between economic, social, and administrative outlay.
[c]1950-58 decentralized series may be incomplete, depending upon treatment of semiautonomous public agencies. See also note a above.
[d]1959-68 decentralized series appears to be more complete than 1950-58 series (see also note a above), except cf. Costa Rica, Dirección General de Estadística y Censos, Anuario Estadístico, 1968, pp. 306-7, for example, which gives higher amount for 1968 depending upon how "decentralized sector" is defined. For a very different definition of this sector, see classification system developed by the Central Bank of Costa Rica.
SOURCES: Centralized figures are from account books of the Costa Rican Comptroller General's Office; series is consistent for entire period, 1950-58. Decentralized data for 1950-58 are from Universidad de Costa Rica, El Desarrollo Económico de Costa Rica, vol. 4, Sector Público de la Economía Costarricence (1962), pp. 96-97. Data for 1959-68 were provided by the Department of Budgetary Control of the Comptroller General's Office.

trol central government expenditure. In short, he would strictly limit the budgetary power of the presidency. In fact, however, the comptroller general (named by the legislative assembly for an *eight-year* term)[48] has come to rival the president's budgetary power, because without his consent funds cannot be transferred from one account to another; and he has power to exercise some budgetary controls (including audits) over the decentralized sector.[49] In contrast to Mexico, where presidential discretionary power over central government funds is absolute, the Costa Rican presidency is limited much as the Bolivian chief executive who has to contend with earmarked taxes, except that the Costa Rican president is also limited by the comptroller general as well as by the decentralized sector.

Given the above limitations on the Costa Rican presidency, one can appreciate the decreasing economic leverage of the executive office as shown in Table 13. Prior to the Figueres revolution of 1948, presidents spent over one-third of the central government budget on economic matters. President Rafael Angel Calderón Guardia, "the protector of the masses," actually devoted about 47 percent of the budget to economic development, mainly by reducing administrative expenses to an all-time low. It was during the "eight-year period" of Calderón Guardia and his protegé Teodoro Picado that "corruption" reached unprecedented levels in Costa Rican history, allegedly through favoritism in the letting of contracts for economic development.[50]

In 1948 the cost of the civil war meant a shift in expenditures. Economic outlay declined as the share of administrative expenses increased to cover the cost of the civil war. Since the Figueres group personally had financed the overthrow of the Picado government at considerable cost, difficulty, and risk, it was reimbursed for expenses by the new government.[51]

The last year of notably high central government economic expenditures was 1949. Most of the 49 percent economic share in expenditure involved the nationalization of the banking system and the refunding of

---

48. Though the PLN has controlled the legislative assembly since 1953 (see Henry Wells, "The 1970 Election in Costa Rica," *World Affairs* 133 [1970]: 13-28, especially p. 15), an eight-year appointment for the comptroller general makes him independent for all practical purposes; he cannot be removed from office except by a two-thirds vote of all legislative members (see Costa Rica, Asamblea Legislativa, *Ley Orgánica de la Contraloría General de la República* [1968], pp. 10-12).

49. Ibid., passim.

50. In Oral History Interviews with Wilkie, Michaels, and Wilkie, José Figueres (Buffalo, 23 March 1968) has stressed the issues of corruption as well as Communism as reasons for generating the revolution of 1948.

51. For a justification and an accounting, see Movimiento Liberación Nacional, *Los Pagos de la Guerra de Liberación Nacional* (San José: Editorial Liberación Nacional, 1953). The Figueres group apparently intended to use some of this repayment to overthrow other dictators in the Caribbean, but was frustrated by internal problems of organizing a new government while defending the country against incursions from Nicaragua.

TABLE 13

AVERAGE ACTUAL PERCENTAGE OF COSTA RICAN CENTRAL GOVERNMENT BUDGETARY
EXPENDITURE BY TYPE OF EMPHASIS AND PRESIDENTIAL TERM

Term[a]	President	No. Years in Average	Total = 100.0%[b]		
			Economic	Social	Administrative
1929-32	Gonzáles Víquez	4	33.3	18.0	48.7
1933-36	Jiménez Oreamuno	4	33.8	18.9	47.3
1937-40	Cortés	4	37.7	22.5	39.8
1941-44	Calderón Guardia	4	46.6	20.4	33.0
1945-47	Picado	3	35.6	24.5	39.9
1948[c]	Picado/León Herrera/				
	Figueres	1	23.4	23.8	52.8
1949	Figueres	1	49.3	16.4	34.3
1950-53	Ulate	4	28.6	25.3	46.1
1954-58	Figueres	5	23.4	30.2	46.4
1959-62	Echandi	4	17.9	36.0	46.1
1963-66	Orlich	4	18.5	35.2	46.3
1967-68[d]	Trejos	2	16.7	37.5	45.8

[a]Terms of budgetary control do not coincide exactly with periods in the presidency (for example, with regard to the 5-year period, Figueres served from 8 November 1953 to 8 May 1958).

[b]For definition of functional emphasis see Table 3, note a; total includes extraordinary outlay such as Inter-American Highway funds (1942-46) and expenditure outside the budget (as in 1956 and 1962).

[c]Disaggregation of *subvención* and *afectaciones especiales* categories (for which no actual breakdown is available for 1948) is based upon percentage distribution of projected outlay. Data for year include extraordinary expenses of civil war.

[d]The 1967-68 Costa Rican governmental functional classification, for example, differs from official data reorganized here for comparability with Mexican and Bolivian figures. Thus the Costa Rican Comptroller General's Office calculates shares for economic, social, and administrative outlay as 18.1%, 44.4%, and 37.5%, respectively. Much of the difference is accounted for by the government classification of its retirement fund (5.3%) as a social expenditure, which in analysis here is included as an administrative outlay. See Costa Rica, Contraloría General de la Nación, *Liquidación del Presupuesto del Gobierno Central, 1967*, p. 13A; and *1968*, Table 6.

SOURCE: Adapted from account books of the Costa Rican Comptroller General's Office.

the national debt. Once these one-shot measures were undertaken, and the process of creating decentralized agencies was undertaken in earnest,[52] the central government's share in economic functions began to decline steadily.

Under presidents of the 1950s, the share in economic outlay finally fell below 20 percent, a figure which declined to about 17 percent by the late 1960s. In short, we may see in Costa Rica the evolution of what may

52. Among the older decentralized agencies, the State Liquor Factory was phased out of central government subventions by 1947 and the railroads ten years later. Figueres's 10 percent levy on capital holdings in 1949 permitted nationalization of the banks, not only increasing economic outlay but also the absolute amount of funds spent that year; in 1949 the central government spent 208.6 million colones, compared to 114.9 million in 1948 and 136.1 million in 1950.

be called the "socioadministrative state," a system in which the central government tends to concentrate on social and administrative matters. Although theoretically a decentralized sector will manage economic affairs, as in Costa Rica, the decentralized sector itself may tend to function in ways which are only partially economic. Thus, a situation can arise in which state power is segmented with no direction or order in economic affairs.

By the late 1960s Figueres and his PLN were becoming aware of the above problems. Furthermore, Figueres began to feel that the revolution of 1948 mainly had benefited the middle sector of Costa Rican society, in spite of all the PLN's talk over the years of helping the country's masses. Figueres felt that problems of population growth, urbanization, and a decline in prices for the country's coffee and banana exports meant new challenges to government. Not only did these problems (which had not been entirely foreseen in 1948) overshadow the old issues of "corruption" and "Communism" over which the civil war had been fought, but academic investigations of Costa Rican life suggested that old stereotypes were never true. Thus, the meaning of Costa Rica's high literacy rate was called into question;[53] and a student of land problems surprisingly suggested that Costa Rica needs *land reform* in order to overcome problems of latifundia.[54] The left wing of the PLN, led by Father Benjamín Núñez, set forth a document suggesting ways to remedy the ills of Costa Rica's problems, especially including rising unemployment.[55]

Although Figueres did not accept all of these criticisms, he campaigned for the presidency in 1969 in terms of the new problems (as well as recalling the glories of 1948). Fully aware that he had created a presidency which possessed little direct effectiveness, he confronted the issue of reorganizing his own system so that he would have the power to face new problems. In sum, the governmental structure created after 1948 was one which was intended to decentralize the state; by 1970 the PLN felt the need to recentralize governmental affairs.

Yet while Costa Ricans discussed aspects of a new negative image of their country, and as old stereotypes fell by the wayside in critical reexamination of the national situation, the growth of GDP and industrial output yielded a counter-image. Table 14 shows that although growth of GDP was highly erratic, the average for the period from 1958 to 1968 was

53. Rafael Cortés, *Panorama de la Educación después de Noventa y Cinco Años de Educación Gratuita y Obligatoria* (San José: Universidad de Costa Rica, 1967), quoted by Father Benjamín Núñez in Oral History Interviews with Wilkie, Michaels, and Wilkie (Columbus, 21 April 1968).

54. See José Manuel Salazar, *Tierras y Colonización en Costa Rica* (San José: Universidad de Costa Rica, 1962). This work, written as a thesis, was an important factor leading to the establishment of Costa Rica's Instituto de Tierras y Colonización in 1962.

55. *Patio de Agua: Manifiesto Democrático para una Revolución Social* (San José: Impresos Urgentes, 1968).

6.1 percent. As in Mexico and Bolivia, the average for industrial output was equal to growth in the manufacturing sector, but the 9.1 percent average was higher than either of the other two countries.

One could well ask whether or not either of the above images of Costa Rica is accurate. First, with regard to national problems, Costa Ricans have followed with great interest the collapse of the Uruguayan

TABLE 14

PERCENTAGE OF REAL GROWTH OF COSTA RICA'S GROSS DOMESTIC PRODUCT AND ITS INDUSTRIAL OUTPUT, 1958-68 (BASED ON 1936 COLONES)

Year	GDP(%)	Total(%)[a]	Manufacturing, Mining, and Quarrying(%)[b]
		Industry	
1958	2.8	9.6	7.4
1959	5.5	8.6	4.2
1960	8.0	7.7	13.0
1961	2.7	2.0	–2.3
1962	9.6	13.9	14.4
1963	5.8	12.2	13.7
1964	2.3	1.9	7.3
1965	10.6	10.9	7.7
1966	7.0	10.4	11.1
1967	5.1	9.6	12.3
1968	7.8	13.7	11.7

[a]Includes manufacturing, mining, quarrying, construction, and electricity; mining and quarrying have been very minor to date.
[b]Unfortunately for comparability with other countries, manufacturing is lumped together with mining and quarrying; this amount is included in the total for industry.
SOURCES: Calculations for growth of GDP are made from data in Costa Rica, Banco Central, *Memoria Anual–1967* 1:169; and *Estadísticas Económicas, 1963 a 1968*, p. 12. Standard colones are calculated with San José wholesale price index provided by the Banco Central de Costa Rica; with regard to price index see the Bank's *Ajuste del Indice de Precios al por Mayor* (1966).

model for development.[56] Whereas once that country was characterized as "the portrait of a democracy" and as "the Switzerland of Latin America," today it is beset not so much by rural-urban problems (as an eminent political scientist predicted little over fifteen years ago)[57] but by a system of decentralization which investigators do not know much about and which politicians cannot control. Thus even the political recentralization of the Uruguayan central government (which was accomplished in 1966 by the abolishment of a nine-man presidency in favor of a one-man

56. Between the mid-1950s and mid-1960s, Uruguay's average yearly growth of GNP in constant prices was only .1 percent, with the period 1961-66 showing an average yearly decrease of –.1 percent. See U.S. Agency for International Development, *A.I.D. Economic Data Book: Latin America, 1967,* p. 9.
57. Russell H. Fitzgibbon, *Uruguay: Portrait of a Democracy: An Informal Survey of the Switzerland of Latin America* (London: Allen and Unwin, 1956).

presidency) can resolve few problems, because most of the state's economic activity and high levels of consumption remain beyond central government control.

Because of Uruguay's problems, some Costa Ricans have suggested that their country might find itself in the same situation due to similarities in smallness of size, limited production possibilities, heavy social expenditure, and decentralization of government. Thus Father Benjamín Núñez, leader of the PLN left wing, has stated: "I recommend that a small and underdeveloped country like Costa Rica should choose the road of poverty to become some day a rich country. We cannot pretend to have the standard of living of capitalistically developed nations. The standards of our living conditions must be defined *not* according to the American way of life, but instead, according to our *own* way of life, dictated by our environment, our national resources, our own technical development and our own historical evolution. The problem is that the capitalist world, the developed world, has sold to the under-developed countries like Costa Rica the idea that in order to be well-developed, they must have, from the start, the standards of living that the U.S. has reached after a long process of capitalization."[58] Although Núñez's opinion might seem extreme, it reflects an important view that Costa Rican life needs reorientation, regardless of apparent economic growth.

Second, with regard to the image of increasing economic development, perhaps the growth of GDP in Costa Rica (and/or Bolivia and Mexico) is part of a political imperative. If the economy does not show growth, the party in power cannot long continue to justify its holding of power. In this sense, those decentralized agencies that are charged with calculating GDP figures share common ground with political leaders. Since economic change is usually measured by central bank officials or planning agency officers, they themselves are at least partially responsible for the success or failure of highly visible policy. All too often, then, there is no independent evaluation of economic progress; and in this one case, at least, some officials of the centralized and decentralized sectors may find that their interests coincide in emphasizing positive rather than negative factors in analysis.

These and other matters are subsumed under some basic dilemmas which arise from the relations between two governmental sectors. One sector is responsible directly to the people through the elective process; the other sector is independent from either the people or their elected representatives. It is to these issues that we now must turn after examining centralized and decentralized relations in three countries of Latin America.

58. Father Benjamín Núñez, in Wilkie, Michaels, and Wilkie, Oral History Interviews (Columbus, 22 April 1968).

PROBLEMS OF GOVERNMENT

As seen in the above analysis of three Latin American countries, the budgetary dilemma in economic development is complex. Not only is economic development dependent upon the role of *técnicos* capable of making crucial decisions concerning the allocation and management of funds, but the *técnicos* in decentralized agencies may be in a position to challenge subtly the authority of the central government in many ways.

First, if the central government turns over its economic powers to decentralized agencies, its own *técnicos* remain in a position which is relatively powerless. If economic expenditure plays a more dynamic role in national development than social and administrative outlay, the president has little leverage to change the direction of his country's affairs. Though we have seen that social expenditure is vital to national development, its results cannot be implemented with rapidity.

Second, although it may seem efficient to create new agencies which fall outside the realm of traditional bureaucratic sloth and inefficiency, the best personnel may well abandon central government structures in order to gain the freedom, recognition, and perquisites granted to employees of the decentralized agencies. Needless to say, the central government is thus weakened by a decline in the quality of its manpower as well as in its budgetary powers.

Third, if two systems of government exist and only the centralized portion is directly responsible to the elective process, one might well ask who wants to serve at the pleasure of the public. Most of the decisions made at the decentralized level are obscure and remote to the man in the street, who does not understand, for example, rediscount rates, credit allocations, import substitution policies, or subsidies and guarantees to mixed public and private corporations. The cases which do tend to be understood by the general public involve instances such as increase in bus fares or the clashes of student group with student group (and subsequently with the police). In those cases the careers of the centralized government officials are jeopardized. Thus, it would be logical for many political leaders as well as *técnicos* to prefer to enter the relative safety of decentralized service, which is not necessarily responsible to public complaints, demands, or whims.

Fourth, decentralized sectors have been set up to encourage long-term development. By taking such planning out of the hands of politicians, who may change with relative frequency, *técnicos* may make commitments for periods which extend throughout several presidencies. Clearly, such action is necessary for efficient expenditure of funds and to coordinate the phased development of complicated projects. Nevertheless, what happens to the wishes of the electorate should they decide upon a change in the order of national priorities? Not only may the central government lack the discretionary funds to redirect national life, but also it may have to support decentralized agencies which are not financially self-supporting. While this latter aspect may give some leverage to the central government, decentralized projects are often governed by rules and regulations set down by the very international agencies which the central government does not want to alienate because of its own scarce resources and/or pending new agreements. In addition, if the *técnicos* of a national decentralized agency find themselves frustrated or blocked in their plans, they often find it convenient to use their international connections to move into an international development agency, further depleting the stock of manpower necessary to administer the affairs of the developing country.

Fifth, if central governments are to assert their authority over the entire public sector, they must revamp the central government bureaucracy so that it is as qualified as its competitor. Even if the central government were able to overcome the "law of bureaucracy" which requires the creation of new agencies because it may be impossible or too expensive to reform administratively the existing organization (although some agencies may have outlived their usefulness), decentralized officials may rebel at losing their independent standard of operation. In any case, expanded social outlay for education of qualified central government manpower would cut into the public expenditure pie.

Sixth, because decentralized agencies take their tasks seriously, they may find that they must develop their own standards and procedures which are not compatible with those of a national bureaucracy. This means that in many cases these agencies cannot be directly compared or even that audit of expenditure cannot be undertaken on a comparative basis.

Seventh, with the development of consolidated accounts, one might suppose that central governments can rationally plan development. Yet the exact opposite may be true: consolidated figures may merely show how funds are being expended, only giving the impression that the result was preprogrammed. In this manner, presentation of data on diffuse and uncoordinated plans may appear to give spurious coherence to government operations.

Eighth, if the development of consolidated analysis precedes actual fusion of the decentralized agencies into the central government proper, one might expect to gain some partial insights into the effects of consolidation. This would be true especially in the three countries under analysis here, because each has attempted to regain control over the decentralized sector (as will be discussed further below). Thus, on the one hand, whereas one might suppose that the consolidated budget allows planning ministries to coordinate policy and reduce expenditures in one sector as they raise outlays in the other, such might not be the case, as in Bolivia.

On the other hand, however, there are indications that the Mexican case has succeeded where Bolivia has failed. In the meantime, Costa Rica has offered a confused middle ground.

Elsewhere I have described Bolivia's status as that of a "frozen revolution";[59] that is, central government activity long has emphasized socio-administrative outlay. In short, the central government has not been able to gain much control over the economically oriented decentralized sector, and it remains to be seen whether or not the *técnicos'* plans for administrative reforms and a 1970 budgetary shift to give the central government more economic importance can be accomplished in the midst of political chaos.

The Mexican case is somewhat different. As I suggested in another study,[60] central government deemphasis of economic outlay after about 1960 may have been made possible by the growth of decentralized economic activity. In this manner, the Mexican *central* government could take a more direct *social* action in its own budgetary activity. If the growth of decentralized outlay in absolute terms for the period from 1965 to 1969 is any indication of expansion under President López Mateos (1959-64) when no total data are available, one could surmise that such growth would relieve the central government of the need to continue high levels of economic expenditure. As a matter of fact, about 90 percent of the capital investment projected by the decentralized sector for the period from 1959 to 1963 was scheduled for economic development.[61]

In the Costa Rican case, it would appear that not only has the central government continued to deemphasize economic expenditure (Table 13), but also that the decentralized government has failed to take up the slack, mainly because the latter sector has become as heavily involved (if not more involved) with social and administrative affairs as with economic activities (Table 12). Though the series prior to and after 1959 are divergent because of definition of the decentralized agencies, one could say that Costa Rica appears to be reacting to unplanned developments rather than attempting to guide the course of events.

Ninth, though politicians are often presumed to pervade the inefficient centralized sphere of government and are posed against *técnicos* mainly located in the efficient decentralized agencies, actually the latter entities are often managed by political appointees who, even with the help of *técnicos*, may not be able to determine the full range and impact of their agencies. The full-fledged *técnico* may not be interested in preserving the autonomy of the decentralized sector but in integrating centralized and decentralized government so that his talents of rationally

59. Wilkie, *Bolivian Revolution*, p. 41.
60. Wilkie, *Mexican Revolution*, p. 273.
61. Mexico, Dirección de Inversiones Públicas, *México: Inversión Pública Federal, 1925-1963*, pp. 111-18.

organizing the *whole* state may be best brought to bear, as projected in the Bolivian case discussed above. In any event, the *técnico's* influence may not stem from actually holding power, but in simply being the man who presents alternative courses of action to those who make decisions.[62]

BUDGETARY CONTROLS

As suggested throughout this study, Bolivia, Costa Rica, and Mexico increasingly have sought to bring the decentralized sector under presidential control. That the Bolivians had achieved little success by 1970 is attested in the following quote: "Until 1965 the budget included only authorizations for central government outlay. The decentralized sector approved its own budgets. . . . Since that date, a consolidated budget has been worked out with all the budgets of the decentralized sector being approved by the central government.

"Nevertheless, above all, the result has been only formal, because the Ministry of Finance has resources of information and mechanisms to audit only central government programs. [With regard to the decentralized sector], in practice the budget does not even constitute a limit on expenditures; and also it is not even known whether or not programs have been carried out as planned. . . ."[63]

Presumably the Bolivian solution to this problem is akin to that of Costa Rica. According to a Costa Rican reform of 30 May 1968, the Constitution of 1949 was revised to permit autonomous agencies to enjoy only the right of administrative independence, with loss of the privilege of making their own policy.[64] The presidency itself set up the mechanism for making policy and controlling public investments.[65] In the meantime, however, the Comptroller General's Office reported in 1967 that "the inevitable limitation of personnel prevents a complete and permanent control of public administration; therefore it is possible only to make selective and periodic checks [of certain institutions]."[66]

Attempts to integrate planning of the entire public sector in Mexico have a longer history, much of which has been described ably by others.[67]

---

62. This view of the *técnico's* power to influence decisions through the choice of technical alternatives is stressed by Vernon, *Dilemma of Mexico's Development,* p. 137.

63. [Ortiz Mercado], *Estrategia Socio-Económica del Desarrollo Nacional, 1971-1991,* 1: 47. Departments and municipalities have their own budgets and also are excluded from audit by the central government.

64. Cf. Article 188 in Costa Rica, Asamblea Legislativa, *Constitución de la República de Costa Rica (7 de noviembre de 1949),* 1967 ed., rev. 1968 ed.

65. See, for example, Costa Rica, Oficina de Planificación, *Informe sobre el Control del Programa de Inversiones Públicas* (1965).

66. Costa Rica, Contraloría General de la República, *Memoria Anual, 1968,* 1-B.

67. See note 24.

Suffice it to say here that the first Mexican plan for national investment was created by the Nacional Financiera for the period from 1953 to 1960, but that not until 1958 was the Ministry of the Presidency charged with full powers of planning.[68] Although since 1965 the Mexican Comptroller General's Office has integrated the income and outflow of decentralized funds into public expenditure accounts, that office does not have the funds or personnel necessary to audit the decentralized agencies, hence in all but a few cases it must accept each agency's own report at face value. Also, as in Bolivia and Costa Rica, before full policy control will be possible the agencies themselves will have to adapt standardized accounting procedures.

A constant flow of regulations from the Mexican presidency has attempted to close gaps in the centralized government's control over the decentralized sector, one of the most recent being a proposal by President Luis Echeverría Alvarez. Within seventeen days of taking office, he sent to the Chamber of Deputies a projected Law for the Central Government Control of the Decentralized Sector. This law was designed to oversee personnel and financing of the agencies, as well as to establish a permanent registry of investments and profits, especially in mixed public and private corporations in which the state has minority share in control of operations.[69] Further, with regard to decentralized entities in which the state has majority share in direction, the 1971 federal budget specifically prohibits those agencies from applying for, obtaining, or accepting any credits or liabilities for whatever purpose or from whatever source without first obtaining permission from the Ministry of Finance.[70]

RECENTRALIZATION

That the process of recentralization of government in Mexico, Bolivia, and Costa Rica has gotten under way is of historical importance. In a sense, nineteenth-century economic development in Latin America was an aberration after the extremely centralized control exercised by Spain and Portugal over their colonies in the New World. Though this control was often more theoretical than real, Latin American countries did have to find ways within "the system" in order to evade unworkable policy. During the nineteenth century, theoretically the state abdicated its inherited right to control economic life, even though many traditional limits on the free movement of goods continued, especially as related to geographical battles over centralism versus federalism.

68. See Mexico, Comisión de Administración Pública, Secretaría de la Presidencia, *Prontuario de Disposiciones Jurídicas para las Secretarías y Departamentos de Estado, 1970,* and *Manual de Organización del Gobierno Federal, 1969-1970.*
69. *Tiempo* (Mexico City, 28 December 1970), p. 5.
70. *El Mercado de Valores* (Mexico City, 4 January 1971). The approved new law is given ibid. (11 January 1971).

With the onset of the twentieth century, the power of central governments generally came to be constitutionally established in order to provide a focus for national integration. Though even today regional caudillos continue to exist in Bolivia[71]—and strong men continue to dominate Mexican states—the geographical-constitutional issue of central versus regional control pales beside the new administrative issue of who will control national funds.

Given state taxation powers and the fact that the state is the greatest source of employment, especially in countries which have limited economic activity, the power to spend funds and offer jobs becomes crucial in political battles, often to the exclusion of any ideology whatsoever. In this light, it is understandable why Mexico, Bolivia, and Costa Rica would attempt to limit presidential authority (including abuse involving nepotism and cronyism) by decentralization of decisions.[72]

Since economic growth, as shown in the development of GDP for Mexico (Table 8), Bolivia (Table 11), and Costa Rica (Table 14), continued in spite of decentralization of the political economy, the theoretical implications have interesting ramifications. One can argue (A) that efficiently coordinated and controlled government would have permitted (and will permit in the future) growth to proceed at even greater rates than in the past. Conversely, one could assert that (B) growth has been possible precisely because decentralization has prevented the central government from organizing a monolithic state which would have completely disrupted the free market. These arguments require some extended explication.

Argument A.—In the first instance, arguments for recentralization have led central governments to wonder about the extent of their role (direct and/or indirect) in national affairs, traditionally measured in terms of governmental activity as a percentage of GDP.[73] Table 15 partially answers this question by presenting the limited data available for the three countries under consideration. Apparently the role of the Mexican central government since 1950 has ranged as high as 10 to 15 percent. Though these percentages may not appear to be very high, it may be noted that no other single element of society has such influence. Thus the central government sets a tone within which national development takes place and within which the private sector must operate. Furthermore,

71. James M. Malloy, *Bolivia: The Uncompleted Revolution* (Pittsburgh: University of Pittsburgh Press, 1970), p. 291. However, Carlos Serrate, an MNR leader, has maintained in Oral History Interviews with Wilkie and Wilkie (Los Angeles, 1971) that Malloy's views in this case are greatly exaggerated.

72. Unfortunately, however, nepotism and cronyism appear to have been nourished by decentralization—there have been not only more jobs to bequeath but fewer checks on activities.

73. For a view indicating that the economic measure of GDP should be supplemented by the development of measures for social modernization, see the Poverty Index offered in Wilkie, *Mexican Revolution*, part 2.

TABLE 15

Public Expenditure as a Percentage of Gross Domestic Product, 1950-68[a]
(In Current Prices)

Year	Mexico Central	Mexico Decentral	Mexico Total	Bolivia Central	Bolivia Decentral	Bolivia Total	Costa Rica Central	Costa Rica Decentral	Costa Rica Total
1950	7.9	b	b	4.3	b	b	10.2	7.3[c]	17.5[c]
1951	8.6	b	b	5.0	b	b	9.9	6.6	16.5
1952	10.8	b	b	3.7	b	b	11.8	6.9	18.8
1953	8.8	b	b	2.4	b	b	12.4	8.7	21.1
1954	10.7	b	b	2.3	b	b	12.6	8.0	20.6
1955	10.1	b	b	1.7	b	b	14.5	9.6	24.1
1956	10.3	b	b	2.8	b	b	13.9	12.4	26.3
1957	9.9	b	b	9.0	b	b	13.7	11.2	24.9
1958	10.7	b	b	10.0	b	b	13.9	12.1	26.0
1959	10.5	b	b	9.2	b	b	13.6	9.8[c]	23.4[c]
1960	13.4	b	b	7.9	b	b	13.6	9.3	22.9
1961	12.5	b	b	8.5	b	b	14.0	10.1	24.1
1962	11.5	b	b	8.5	b	b	14.9	11.9	26.8
1963	10.4	b	b	8.8	25.5	34.3	13.8	12.0	25.8
1964	12.2	b	b	8.9	26.0	34.9	14.8	12.5	27.3
1965	14.6	10.8	25.4	10.6	24.2	34.8	14.4	14.9	29.3
1966	11.6	12.7	24.3	10.2	21.8	32.0	16.0	13.7	29.7
1967	13.3	12.6	25.9	10.2	21.4	31.6	16.3	13.8	30.1
1968	12.1	12.5	24.6	10.0	20.1	30.1	15.8	15.1	30.9

[a]Figures here are not exactly comparable to data in Table 2 because of differences in definitions and sources.

[b]No data available.

[c]For problems of discontinuity in series, see Table 12 notes.

Sources: For Mexico, a new presentation of GDP figures in market prices since 1950 is given in Leopoldo Solís, *La Realidad Económica Mexicana: Retrovisión y Perspectivas* (Mexico, D.F.: Siglo XXI, 1970), p. 700. Thus, percentages can be calculated without the problem of accounting for unexplained GDP deflation methods; decentral and central expenditures used in calculations are from sources given in Table 4. For Bolivia, a new presentation of GDP figures in market prices since 1950 is presented in the Bolivian source for Table 11. Percentages can be for the first time also calculated without the problem of variation in deflators between GDP and expenditure; expenditures used in calculations are from sources in Table 9 and USAID/Bolivia, *Estadísticas Económicas* 11 (1970): 39. For Costa Rica, data on GDP are from sources in Table 14, and United Nations, *Statistical Bulletin for Latin America* 2:1 (1965), p. 36. Data on expenditures are from Tables 12 and 13.

these percentages finance operations in which the central government's power is multiplied by its licensing of business, controlling imports, and subsidizing of development, for example, as well as taxing the private sector selectively in order to encourage the growth of certain industries, depending upon geographic considerations.[74]

The importance of the Mexican decentralized sector can be shown only for the period since 1965. Since it has ranged from about 11 percent to 13 percent of GDP, we may suppose that such figures date from at least the early 1960s, growing to those levels during the 1950s.[75] Given the importance of the decentralized sector, it is no wonder that both politicians and *técnicos* have displayed extraordinary interest in expanding their authority directly over this sector in order to enhance central government influence.

The Bolivian case presents an interesting bit of irony. While MNR officials unanimously condemned the tremendous inflation which threatened to topple their government, Table 15 shows that stopping the inflation finally gave the central government some importance as a percentage of GDP figures. With the onset of drastic stabilization policies in 1957, the central government percentage of GDP dramatically increased to 9 percent, a figure which on the average held up through 1968. Prior to 1957 the MNR percentage never went over 4 percent, and in 1955 it dropped below 2 percent.

As Table 15 shows, the importance of the Bolivian decentralized sector is manifest, although apparently it has steadily declined from over 25 percent to about 20 percent in relation to GDP. If the *técnicos* had their way, however, they would expand state power to closely control that sector. Because apparently the percentage of Bolivia's total public sector expenditure has never exceeded about 35 percent of GDP, planned expansion of the public sector's importance to over 50 percent of GNP (Table 2)[76] may seem implausible. This difference may only seem to be further evidence that Bolivia's *técnicos* do not take into account the reality of their country's affairs; but if projected administrative and budgetary reforms are carried out in the 1970s as planned, they may reveal a greater extent of decentralized activity than hitherto has been recognized. In any case, the *técnicos* are proposing nothing short of an administrative

74. If recentralization is effectively consummated, the central government will become even more important as it mobilizes the fragmented resources of the decentralized sector to enhance its position as the single most visible and influential organized element of society. For further analysis in this regard, see discussion of Table 15 and the last section of this paper.

75. Roberto Anguiano Equihua, *Las Finanzas del Sector Público en México* (Mexico, D.F.: Universidad Nacional Autónoma de México, 1968), sheds no light on the growth of decentralized expenditure. To resolve the question, investigation would have to be made in the accounts of each agency.

76. With regard to Table 2, it is estimated that Bolivia's GNP is 98 percent of GDP.

revolution which may well delimit the sphere of the private sector as the importance of the public sector grows with rapidity. Whether such a revolution can be undertaken successfully remains to be seen.

Only Costa Rica has a long-term series for the importance of the decentralized sector. Even with its limitations (see Table 15, note b), one can infer that the decentralized sector gained near parity with central government activity by 1956. Thus the total but fragmented public-sector impact in Costa Rica reached at least 25 percent during the period 1955-64, after which the amount increased to about 30 percent of GDP. Clearly, if the PLN were to "guide" national development to make a new revolution for the masses, it would have to engage in active recentralization of affairs.

Though in Argument A one could hypothesize that increased central government controls and integration of the entire public sector would spur new development,[77] it is possible to develop another theory concerning the growth of government influence. This hypothesis is related to the expansion of credit, specifically as reflected in payments on the public debt.

Examination of Table 16 shows that, in comparative terms, Mexico has dedicated a much greater share of its central government outlay to amortizing the public debt (as well as paying interest) than either Costa Rica or Bolivia.[78] In a sense, the fact that any country can devote extremely high amounts of its centrally controlled funds simply to provide a revolving fund to finance governmental activity offers an index (however imperfect) of national and international confidence in such state policy.[79] With regard to Mexico, not since the era of Porfirio Díaz has such a large percentage of central government funding been allocated to payment of the public debt. In 1961 López Mateos surpassed Díaz's 32.3 percent share for 1900-1901, but by then Mexico's debt was basically domestically held.[80]

This hypothesis on the expansion of governmental credit is not meant to suggest that Mexico has entered into a neo-Porfirian era, but that the government has been able to expand the scope of its activity by expanding the amount of domestic funds it has available. Thus, a high percentage

77. Cf. Vernon, *Dilemma of Mexico's Development*, chap. 7; he contends that Mexico may have run out of traditional stimuli (such as exports of raw materials and imports of tourists) which have helped the country over economic growth hurdles in the past.

78. For broad aspects of and bibliography for financial intermediation not discussed here, see Dwight S. Brothers and Leopoldo Solís, *Mexican Financial Development* (Austin: University of Texas Press, 1966).

79. See note 13.

80. Whereas in 1911 only about 24 percent of Mexico's federal debts were domestically held (Jan Bazant, *Historia de la Deuda Exterior de México, 1823-1946* [Mexico, D.F.: Colegio de México, 1968], p. 169), about 98 percent were domestically held in 1961 (Wilkie, *Mexican Revolution*, p. 301).

of budgetary repayment does not necessarily mean that the country has lost control of its financial decisions. Although these figures do not tell us a complete story because debts of noncentral government agencies are excluded,[81] unless officially accepted as federal obligations by the Mexican Congress, they do suggest that the Mexican investor has gained a great deal of confidence in his central government.

Perhaps the goal of a developing country such as Mexico is to build

TABLE 16

PUBLIC DEBT PAYMENTS AS A PERCENTAGE OF ACTUAL CENTRAL GOVERNMENT EXPENDITURE, 1947-69 (INCLUDES AMORTIZATION AND INTEREST)

Year	Mexico(%)	Bolivia(%)	Costa Rica(%)
1947	15.6	3.6	12.8
1948	16.0	3.4	11.2
1949	14.2	.8	13.2
1950	16.0	4.7	27.3
1951	16.5	2.9	18.9
1952	13.8	1.6	14.3
1953	14.7	.9	12.3
1954	13.3	.9	11.7
1955	20.1	2.3	14.0
1956	16.0	1.5	13.7
1957	17.6	2.6	15.3
1958	15.6	4.1	13.9
1959	22.0	5.0	12.1
1960	27.3	4.0	11.1
1961	36.2	2.5	12.6
1962	27.2	4.6	12.1
1963	17.1	4.3	11.2
1964	24.4	5.0	15.1
1965	26.9	3.1	16.0
1966	21.5	6.1	17.7
1967	28.9	10.4	16.5
1968	21.7	11.0	16.5
1969	20.3[a]	8.8	18.3

[a]Preliminary.
SOURCES: Tables 4, 9, and 13, respectively; and Costa Rica, Ministerio de Hacienda, *Memoria Anual, 1969*, pp. 122-23, part B.

up such a large debt service that, like the United States, it can remove amortization of the debt from functional analysis in the budget. In this manner, a huge debt will give the central government leeway to initiate new programs, considering only interest on the debt in functional analysis of expenditure. If this be the case, Mexico is much further on the road to such a policy than its neighbors. The cases for Bolivia and Costa Rica

81. However, data in Joseph S. La Cascia, *Capital Formulation and Economic Development in Mexico* (New York: Praeger, 1969), pp. 34-35, indicate that indebtedness of the country's decentralized enterprises also was about 98 percent domestically held in 1961.

are not as clear-cut, mainly because of a lack of data on capital investment. Nevertheless, it is apparent in Table 16 that Bolivia's debt payments
were very low until the late 1960s and that Costa Rican percentages have
not kept pace with the Mexican figures. Costa Rica's high figure for 1950
involved payments which established the creditability of the post-1948
governments.

Argument B.—If one could claim that recentralization would permit
greater growth than at present, conversely one could argue that growth
has been possible because decentralization has done much to prevent the
establishment of an inefficient monolithic state. Because the decentralized
sector is removed from the political arena and may be unresponsive to
changing calls for new policy, its very existence may prevent the development of hasty action by those politicians who work with técnicos in the
central government to pose as leaders of a new faith—in this case, faith
in technical answers to all problems.

It would be misleading to suggest that all técnicos think alike (or
that there is something akin to a "union of técnicos"); and one should not
think that all of them would even begin to concur with the ideas for
social and economic management of society expressed by the Bolivian
técnicos quoted above. Thus, even though demagogic political leaders in
a country such as Bolivia may from time to time gain political power with
the idea of implementing a master plan, they will find it very difficult
to get far because they do not really control the state. They will find
themselves checked not only by various levels of técnicos (as well as by
politicians in their own government who would be difficult to deal with
in any case), but they will also find themselves blocked by the multi-
variate decentralized agencies which hold the country's economic power.

If the decentralized agency argument has political validity in an unstable country such as Bolivia, it also has relevance in a one-party state
such as Mexico. Since the Mexican Congress is virtually an arm of the
president and of the official party, meaningful battles over the nature and
direction of society rarely take place in the legislative sphere. Because
the decentralized sector has its own bureaucracies with their own special-
interest constituencies throughout the country, however, the decentralized system allows a good deal of ideological interplay; and the fact that
agencies often work at cross-purposes provides an escape valve for political pressures.

Although Costa Rican politics have neither been chaotic (as in Bolivia) nor one-party in nature (as in Bolivia and Mexico), in one sense
decentralization has provided a neutral framework to resolve political
differences. Shielded from the glare of publicity, board members of opposing political parties have been able to work out solutions to national
problems without fanfare or rancorous debate.[82] To sum up this argument,

82. This argument is drawn from Father Benjamín Núñez's Oral History Inter-

it may be said that decentralization prevents the implementation of any monolithic policy, thus helping to prevent the emergence of a totalitarian government as well as permitting both the private and public sectors to find a way around unrealistic policy.[83]

CONCLUSIONS

The issue of centralized versus decentralized government has perplexed many Latin American countries and has created a series of dilemmas, many of which are only imperfectly understood. The dilemmas involve the question of who will control the state's funds and how the funds will be spent. Obviously the assignment of expenditure priorities may be confused by fragmented state power. If the central government is to be socioadministrative in nature, in contrast to an economically oriented decentralized sector, then societies may lack that strong leadership which itself has been a problem because leaders have often abused their power or attempted to make it monolithic.

As discussed in this study, three different cases show very different practices and results in the process of decentralization and recentralization. Whereas the Bolivian central government almost completely surrendered its economic development goals to decentralized agencies generating much of their own income, it created a diffuse system which the Ministry of Planning would now like to make monolithic. In the Costa Rican case, the central government decided to set up social as well as economic functions on an apolitical, "businesslike" basis. To avoid this extreme fragmentation of state policy, Costa Rica will apparently adopt the type of controls which are also emerging in Mexico and are projected for Bolivia.

Under the new plan of recentralization, decentralized agencies will be permitted only administrative autonomy, with policy subject to overall state plans developed under the aegis of the central government.[84] In

---

views with Wilkie, Michaels, and Wilkie (Guatemala City, 16 July 1970). Father Núñez was a member of the board of directors of Costa Rica's Instituto Nacional de Vivienda y Urbanismo for over a decade, serving as president of the board during much of that time.

83. Ironically, a master plan for Cuba apparently has failed (and authoritarianism has been made inefficient), in part because of Fidel Castro's desire to decentralize the decision-making process. One may hypothesize that when his government decided to (a) institute on-the-job worker participation in decisions, (b) introduce moral in contrast to material incentives, and (c) implement financial "self-budgeting" of government, Castro himself laid the groundwork for a system he could not fathom, let alone control. Cf. Roberto M. Bernardo, *The Theory of Moral Incentives in Cuba* (University, Ala.: University of Alabama Press, 1971).

84. For a philosophical justification of such a plan, see Wilburg Jiménez Castro, *Los Dilemas de la Descentralización Funcional: Un Análisis de la Autonomía Institucional Pública* (San José: Escuela Superior de Administración Pública América Central, 1965).

effect, this compromise means that the autonomous sector will retain its elite bureaucratic status, but will lose its policy-making power. The dilemma here is obvious: how can a decentralized agency be autonomous if it cannot make its own decisions?

An even worse dilemma is suggested by the fact that the result of this compromise requires state funding of two bureaucracies, with the central government employees remaining in a position of inferiority. In this manner, there will continue to be a great disparity between (a) failure in management of social affairs (the social security and medical programs run by many Latin American governments offer a vivid example of this problem, not to mention the inability of governments to cope with problems of education, etc.), and (b) success in management of economic development (graphically measured in terms of GDP, miles of road construction, etc.). After comparing the efficiency of the economic agencies to the productivity of social agencies (decentralized as well as centralized) which deal with the masses, one may well ask how long the public will put up with the gross inefficiency in social services. It is interesting to note that a major cause of Mexican revolution in 1910 stemmed from the fact that the social and political opportunities of the Porfirio Díaz era did not keep up with the great economic growth for which the government was responsible. Thus, upheaval occurred when the aspiring middle classes joined forces with the masses, who had been exposed to the idea of a better way of life.

Even as it becomes possible to distinguish between the funds over which the central government does or does not have control, the president and his planning ministers also must make a distinction between understanding (a) the role of the public sector and (b) methods of actually reallocating expenditures to determine how state funds will be functionally spent.

As pointed out in the case of the United States, mere incorporation of the decentralized sector accounts into a consolidated system with central expenditures may actually confuse the manner in which policy is made. Whereas the president of the United States now better knows the *effect* of public sector expenditure, the extent of those funds subject to his *control* is not always clear. Because the decentralized sector in the United States contains trust funds and/or earmarked funds to operate decentralized agencies, the president may actually know more about the impact of policy but less how to manipulate policy to change that impact.[85]

85. It is noteworthy that in 1971 President Nixon's Advisory Council on Executive Organization found that U.S. federal regulatory agencies are "not sufficiently accountable for their actions to either the Congress or the President because of the degree of their independence and remoteness in practice from the constitutional branches of government." The council has recommended that these agencies be stripped of their autonomy and given cabinet-level status, with presidential appoint-

The same problem is equally relevant in Latin American countries which have incorporated major income-producing entities (such as tin mines, oil production, etc.) into the public sector. Thus, mere consolidation of accounts does not necessarily help the chief executive decide how to allocate funds, because most of the public enterprise finances are beyond his control—such funds not going into the pool of money over which the president has discretionary authority. Consolidated accounts as presented to the public in Mexico (and the United States),[86] for example, now tend to give a picture of greater presidential power than actually exists. In an ideal situation, however, leaders and citizens should know what money the president can be held accountable for in manipulating financial resources to resolve unforeseen problems as new needs arise with changing times. Such a budgetary presentation would make clear within the consolidated account the extent and function of centralized and decentralized subtotals by geographical region.

Costa Rican problems perhaps best represent the dilemma which Latin American leaders face in resolving needs for long-range planning versus the need for adapting governmental actions to unforeseen developments and desires of new generations to influence their own times. Thus Costa Rican President José Figueres is in a unique position to answer a key question facing many Latin American countries: how does one organize government so that it can respond to the needs (real or imagined) of changing times? Over twenty years ago, Figueres faced a problem which involved the creation of institutions to meet the demands of that time. Given Costa Rica's needs of 1948, the decentralized system seemed most appropriate. But given Figueres's desire *today* to use state power in a new way, the system he set up for long-term planning is not necessarily responsive (even with reform) to his four-year mandate to effect change for the masses in Costa Rican life. This dilemma, then, is political, social, and economic. The needs of the centralized and decentralized sectors are different and may be irreconcilable.

With regard to images of state policy, to the cynic (or to the "realist") political needs are not meaningful in countries where the masses cannot be really aware of complex issues built into problems of economic development in the face of expanding populations. In this view, political "needs" are imposed on the populace by leaders, the masses being inarticulate and unable to express themselves effectively. To follow this line of argument further, the masses may not be able to identify with such "needs" even after they have been explained by leaders from outside their

---

ments subject to Senate confirmation, in order that various agencies set up over the course of this century might operate more in step with present-day needs. *Los Angeles Times* (12 February 1971).

86. Although, as we saw in the second section of this paper, the U.S. budget does try to give a gross picture on the amount of "uncontrollable funds," cf. Table 3, notes c and e, for limitations on the functional understanding of U.S. expenditure.

milieu. In the latter case, one-party rule is often seen to be the answer to problems of political instability, with the government generating support for many of its programs through its vast bureaucracy or through what may be called the "fiesta system" involving "spontaneous manifestations" which are sponsored by the government.

If such government is to be effective, often it is better that the bureaucracy as well as the populace know as little about what is really happening as is feasible. Thus, in Mexico, public debates over whether one-quarter of the central government *projected* budget should be devoted to education[87] serve to confuse the real issue that educators *actually* will be lucky to get half that share. While such policy may be harmful to education, it has helped to keep the share of military budgets down; in the latter case, it is wise for the Mexican government not to reveal its real intentions in the budget. Hence, the policy of perhaps deliberately underestimating central government income is understandable. Also, this helps to explain why the Comptroller General's Office keeps two sets of books: both contain the same basic data on expenditures, but the red-bound yearly volume lacks analytical information carried only in the dark-bound volume, circulation of which is highly restricted.[88]

In taking into account developments in Mexico, Bolivia, and Costa Rica, I am struck by the fact that in each country great changes were made in public administration and in the way different social classes shared in the benefits of new government orientations. Yet in each country there are degrees of preoccupation about the future of economic growth. With rising populations and the possibility of inflation, each of the three countries is concerned with providing a greater share of benefits to the masses.

Since all three countries look to industrialization (or to greater industrialization) as a major impetus to economic development, they face a common dilemma. Industrialization requires educated manpower; and if developing countries are to compete in a world which uses ever more modern technical processes, jobs tend to be eliminated. Unfortunately, all three of the countries under discussion need to develop labor-intensive projects which provide jobs for their expanding populations. If the countries follow the former path, they may be able to reduce an increasing gap between the developed and developing nations, but only at the risk of social upheaval—none of the three countries has the affluence to support unemployment caused by industrialization. Of course, these countries can continue in a traditional life which involves underemployment and labor-intensive employment, but such a course does not solve the problem of development.

87. See Wilkie, *Mexican Revolution*, p. 164, note 5.

88. For an example of data which are thus not generally available, see data on origin of income-tax payments by state in Wilkie, "New Hypotheses for Statistical Research in Recent Mexican History."

If recentralization is to be undertaken, perhaps governments which follow such a debatable policy need officials who promise little but simply attempt to resolve dilemmas with the full realization that their answers will only be temporary and only create new problems. Among the imperfect systems described in this study, Mexico appears to emerge as a model for recentralization. In spite of problems, Mexican *técnicos* in the whole public sector have faced the problem of precisely defining and supervising the decentralized sector; and they have attempted to eliminate double-counting of transfer funds as well as to develop standardized accounting procedures. And most importantly, they have recently developed data to understand the functional impact of outlay on the various regions of Mexico.

If the old geographical issues of rural versus urban development and constitutional issues of centralism versus federalism have been downgraded by the problem of financial centralization and decentralization,[89] the issue of the one-party versus multi-party state may also be affected until the matter of recentralization of state policy is resolved. In the final analysis, the question of who controls the government (or whether leaders represent the elite, middle classes, or masses) is not as important as how the leaders decide to budget their scarce resources. The broader problem is not in obtaining power, but in deciding what to do once political "victory" has been won.

Acknowledgment.—Research funds to make this study possible were provided by the University of Florida; University of California, Los Angeles; Ohio State University; and Historical Research Foundation. The author is indebted to Edna Monzón de Wilkie for assistance in field work and in preparation of this study. Gratitude is also extended to David T. Geithman for a careful critique of ideas presented here; to Waldo W. Wilkie for aid in completing calculation of data; and to Lyle C. Brown for editorial advice.

Comment—Fuat Andic

IT is difficult to comment upon Wilkie's paper, for it contains interesting information and observations and reaches controversial conclusions. It steers along the confluence of turbulent waters of history, political science, public administration, sociology, and economics. Anyone who reads this extensive paper will be struck by the interdisciplinary nature of its con-

89. For discussion of Mexico City's importance in the centralization of financial, administrative, and cultural affairs, see James W. Wilkie, "La Ciudad de México como Imán de la Población Económicamente Activa, 1930-1965," in Bernardo García Martínez et al., eds., *Historia y Sociedad en el Mundo de Habla Española: Homenaje a José Miranda* (Mexico, D.F.: El Colegio de México, 1970), pp. 379-95.

tent. My ignorance in these fields is of varying degrees. But sometimes ignorance creates courage, and it is with this courage that I make certain general remarks which touch upon fields other than economics. I am fully aware of the controversial technical and statistical aspects of the paper; however, I shall restrict my comments to general conceptual issues only.

First, let me emphasize the two most interesting issues presented in the paper, beginning with the issue of centralization versus decentralization as exemplified by three Latin American countries. This separation of public authority is based, more or less, on the following functional concept.

The centralized government is responsible, as the cases presented show, in various degrees for social and administrative expenditures and decentralized agencies are mainly responsible for economic expenditures. This has come to be historically so, as evidenced by the statistics, however shaky their foundation may be. This separation of the decision-making power has wide-ranging implications in the sense that it is very much beyond the scope of fiscal policy for industrialization, but encompasses the entire process of decision making for development as such. It is this decision-making process which will determine the degree of success or failure of economic growth.

The second important issue is the upsurge of a new type of creature, the so-called *técnico*. While on the one hand the *técnicos* are in fact created by this separation of decision-making process between centralized and decentralized agencies, they in turn lend themselves to the perpetuation of this division by eroding the human resource base of the centralized government: *técnicos* have moved from the centralized to the decentralized sector, or into international agencies.

The conclusion that Wilkie reaches is that for a better functioning of the public sector and for possibilities of coordinated planning and policy change, it is absolutely essential that a *re*centralization take place with a full integration of central and decentral governments.

Let us turn for a moment to the first point: why is there a separation between centralized and decentralized public sector entities? Who are they? It is considerably easier to understand what constitutes the centralized sector: the president and the cabinet, who are mainly responsible for administrative expenditures as well as capital outlays basically of social nature (although I would argue that educational expenditures in countries where human capital formation is very deficient are not really social, but economic, outlays). In any case, the centralized sector is considerably more homogeneous than the decentralized.

The decentralized sector is very heterogeneous: it includes agencies for planning and research as well as mixed enterprises which operate as private firms. According to Wilkie, it is this sector which is responsible for decisions on economic activities and it is this sector which has been purposely left out of the control of the central government or the president.

Questions arise as to whether in effect they are outside the control of the executive power. My belief is that in the ultimate analysis they are not as outside the executive power as may appear at first inspection. What is relevant, however, is that through time, for historical, social, and economic reasons they have become a government within the government.

Turning to the second point: who is the *técnico*? How does he come about? Why does he go to the decentralized sector rather than stay within the centralized? Are we really faced with a phenomenon similar to what Burnham called in 1941 a "managerial revolution," i.e. (borrowing his concept), a "*técnico* revolution"? Are they really becoming a class of governors and decision makers? The answer to these questions requires a precise definition of the *técnico* and determination of the role of *técnicos* within the society.

Unfortunately, the paper does not provide satisfactory answers. It does not even give an operational definition of the *técnico*. There is a functional definition—"highly specialized professional"; but there is another one concerning attitudes towards power—"the man who presents alternative courses of action to those who make decisions." This latter I find rather unsatisfactory, for obviously—as the three historical cases show—the *técnicos* are interested in alternative courses of action as well as in normative decision making.

The interesting question is: why are the *técnicos* in the decentralized agencies? Wilkie says that there are not enough to go around. This is not a sufficient explanation. The point is that they do not go around except in one direction. My feeling is that they go to decentralized agencies because they find it impossible to work within the centralized, established bureaucracy where mediocrity prevails and most of the civil servants are lawyers. In fact, tongue in cheek, one can say that there is a positive correlation between the predominance of lawyers in decision making and underdevelopment. This may or may not be the case in the three countries under study, but it is so in others with which I am more familiar. At least some *técnicos*, not to say most, are foreign-trained economists, engineers, etc., who return to their native countries with an altogether different *Weltanschauung*, and the basic incompatibility is obvious. While they are pushed out by the centralized sector, they are pulled in by the decentralized one, where they become problematic for the centralized government.

This brings me to my comments on the conceptual essence of Wilkie's paper. There are really two issues involved: one is the need for the political power group to determine the national priorities of public expenditure; the other is the need for *técnicos* to show the alternatives for the attainment of the objectives and priorities and to implement them. The *recentralization* argument really hinges upon the following considerations, and I hope I am not putting my words into Wilkie's mouth. In the whole development planning process, a set of targets is determined politically by the political decision maker. This is the well-known social welfare function of the Tinbergen-Theil analysis of development planning. It is nothing else but a statement of the policy objectives. It is the duty of the *técnicos* to convert these objectives into quantitative targets and derive instruments of policy: fiscal, social, economic, etc. I gather from the paper, perhaps reading between the lines, that the central government feels that it is losing the power of determining the social welfare function, and that the *técnico* is assuming the role of this determination —as well as serving in the role of *técnico* for carrying out the implementation. He is therefore controlling national funds, which in fact goes very much against the raison d'être of the *técnico*. Therefore, one can conclude that at least the three countries under consideration have suffered instead of gained from the decentralization process.

Comment—Suphan Andic

I would like to make only methodological comments: two of minor importance (minor in that they would not change the essential core of the paper) and one which I think is of major relevance.

First, in the paper there is an unwarranted comparison between the Latin American economies and the United States. It gives the content and relative size of programs uncontrollable by the U.S. president. The question is: can one really compare the uncontrollable part of U.S. expenditures with those of Mexico, Costa Rica, and Bolivia? Are not the nature and type of these expenditures very different in the north and south (or center) of the continent? Wilkie gives the content of such expenditures to be social security payments, farm price supports, welfare payments, interest on public debt, veterans' benefits, etc., which do not all necessarily have their counterparts in the three countries concerned, let alone in all Latin American countries. Moreover, as expounded in the paper the decentralized sector in the three countries is very amorphous and vague: there are government commissions, institutes, as well as reputedly profit-motivated public and private enterprises in various economic activities such as mining, oil drilling, refining, etc. There is the additional point: are not many of these so-called uncontrollable expenditures in the United States financed out of sources enacted by the U.S. Congress and signed by the president? It seems to me that a crucial division exists: on the one hand, there is the determination of the sources to be used for given expenditures, the priorities for which are determined in the legislature (such as the recent raising of the social security tax and the ceiling salary on which it is assessed, and changes in benefits). On the other hand, there is the determination of the agency which will spend and administer such funds.

A second disagreement I have is with the statement that per capita public expenditure in the three Latin American countries is only one-sixteenth the expenditure per capita in the United States, followed by the phrase "which explains to some degree why public sector policy in the former countries often does not appear to have much impact on the masses." First of all, to use average concepts is misleading, and I am sure Wilkie will agree with me on that. Using *his* statistics, however, the ratio of per capita public expenditure to per capita GDP is even higher in Bolivia (56 percent) than in the United States (53 percent). I do agree with Wilkie's statement, not because per capita expenditures are one-sixteenth of those of the United States, but because there is a regressive redistributive element in the structure of the budget with respect to taxation as well as expenditures. Although there is no clear-cut statement as to what decentralized expenditures are *specifically* included in any of the three countries, it is clear from the general definition given in note a of Table 1 that these include public enterprises such as electricity, telephone, oil companies, etc. Considering that a large portion of the population do not have telephones, electricity, or very often water in their houses and that such enterprises operate with losses and are highly subsidized (as evidenced by the discussion of Baer's paper in this volume), it would not be surprising that such public expenditures benefit the relatively wealthy, bypassing the masses. In this connection, it is absolutely essential to know who pays for the financing of these expenditures and who benefits from them. Moreover, considering that the income tax is such a low percentage of GDP and public expenditures, I would judge the expenditures to have a regressive redistributive effect.

This brings me to my major point: a question of statistical methodology relevant for the nonstatistical analysis. Nowhere in the paper is there an explanation of the concept of expenditure included in the decentralized subsector. Are these expenditures gross or net? If they are gross, there would be a substantial amount of double-counting in terms of transfers from one agency to another and interindustry purchases, since to conform to GDP concepts, purchases by the tin mines of electricity produced by a public enterprise, for example, would have to be excluded.

I tend to agree with Wilkie that to arrive at a meaningful consolidated account of the centralized and decentralized sectors, it is essential to have a true integrated fusion between the two; however, I do not think we can begin to measure the size of the public sector and derive conclusions from the statistics *if* the statistics are based on shaky grounds. It seems to me that whatever the dialectical interrelationships might be between the factors which explain the decentralization and recentralization tendencies, to be able to detect such tendencies it is absolutely essential to know what exactly is the public sector and what exactly is its size. This cannot be known unless a precise definition of the sectors is provided and a statistical methodology is devised and applied consistently, for purposes of comparison, to the wealth of data available on the three countries—i.e., unless one constructs a consolidated account of the public sector. Consolidated account does not mean, as Wilkie understands it, the indication of the president's discretionary authority over the pool of money, but if correctly constructed represents the "true" magnitude of the national resources which are channeled through the public sector, centralized or decentralized. Only then can a complete picture be obtained of the expenditures by public authorities, each expenditure being included only once in the aggregate, transfers between different public authorities and between different accounts of one public authority having been eliminated. If public enterprises are conceived as forming part of governmental activities, as is the case in the present paper, their activities are to be included in the estimates to the extent of expenditure on capital account. Expenditure on current account should, of course, be excluded to the extent it is offset by current revenue. Thus, only the net balance of current expenditure and total capital expenditure should be given. There is also the problem of separating expenditure items of a purely financial nature, such as the repayment of debt. Such a separation does not mean that an accounting should not be given of purely financial transactions, which obviously are of great significance in finding out the intersectoral flow of such funds and thus reaching policy decisions of economic and political nature. (The U.N. Manual should come in very handy in erecting the entire statistical structure.)

I should like to add that Wilkie's paper is necessary but not sufficient for constructing a theory of public sector growth in developing countries.

Comment—Dennis J. Mahar

ONE of the common laments among persons interested in the public finances of Latin America concerns the paucity of information on the decentralization of national government. Delving into this morass has discouraged all but a few hardy souls, mainly because of the difficulties in gathering data often scattered among hundreds of agencies jealously guarding their respective autonomies. Definitional problems also plague the researcher in this field, especially with respect to "mixed corporations" operating on the profit motive, producing and selling products to the general public. (Are they part of the public sector or the private sector?) Wilkie's paper thus comes as a welcome effort in an area which has become too important to relegate to a footnote or two in a treatise on the public sector. That this effort comes to us from a historian may also cast some light on the relative intellectual courage of the academic disciplines.

My comments are of three types. First, I would like to make a few general observations about the relative merits and drawbacks of decentralization (a process which I prefer to call "decentralized centralization," in order to avoid confusion with the redistribution of revenue sources and/or functions from higher to lower levels of government) and the counter trend of "recentralization." Second, I would like to add a few comments about these phenomena based on my own research in Brazil. Finally, I would like to point out some possible drawbacks in Wilkie's statistical presentation.

In theory, the transfer of certain social and economic functions from the central government to autonomous agencies would seem to be an ideal solution to problems of long-term development in the milieu of an unstable executive branch. By delegating responsibility to the *técnicos*, socioeconomic development may thus proceed untrammeled by purely political considerations. In practice, however, such laudable benefits may be eclipsed by concomitant drawbacks.

Once the process of "decentralization" is started it seems to gather a momentum of its own. In some instances it appears that any new function amenable to public provision and/or control is immediately given autarky status. Thus the decentralized sector grows like Topsy, with the leeway for discretionary action by the chief executive subsequently growing smaller and smaller. Furthermore, the agencies established often seek to assert their own importance by expanding personnel (via Parkinson's Law?) and show a stubborn resistance to their dissolution when changing conditions render their services less important. (This latter tendency, however, is not confined to autonomous agencies in Latin America—witness the "tea tasters" controversy in the United States.)

The primary danger involved in the decentralization of national government is not so much that it dilutes the power of the president (although this may produce serious difficulties in the promotion of national planning), but that it provides a "back-door" method of greatly enlarging and fragmenting the public sector. As mentioned above, it often becomes extremely difficult to dissolve these "states within states" (to borrow Wilkie's term) once they are created. Thus after a period of rapid decentralization, a country finds itself with a Frankenstein which is very difficult to destroy, i.e., hundreds of autonomous agencies competing for revenues (with each other and with the national and subnational governments), duplicating functions, and possessing no real common goal other than self-preservation and/or some dim concept of "national development."

A solution to the dilemma presented by the process of "decentralization" is by no means clear. "Recentralization" is one possible answer, although I see no obvious reason why a central government should necessarily be better equipped to supervise tasks formerly carried out autonomously. The growth of consolidated budgeting is to me a more hopeful sign, although Wilkie rightly points out that all-encompassing budgets do not necessarily give a chief executive a clearer picture of his discretionary options (but should this be one of their major purposes anyway?).

TABLE 1

SOME INDICATORS OF DECENTRALIZATION IN THE BRAZILIAN PUBLIC SECTOR,[a]
SELECTED YEARS, 1939-63 (PERCENTAGES)

Year	(1)	(2)	(3)	(4)	(5)
1939	—	2	4	5	0
1947	2.0	12	22	20	30
1950	2.9	15	26	23	34
1955	3.5	18	34	33	39
1960	4.7	20	37	32	58
1965	5.7	24	42	39	61
1968	7.6	31	54	52	69

[a]Excluding "mixed" corporations (companhias mistas).
COLUMNS IN TABLE: (1) total expenditures of the autarkies (autarquias) as a percentage of GDP; (2) total expenditures of the autarkies as a percentage of total public sector expenditures; (3) total expenditures of the autarkies as a percentage of total expenditures at the national level; (4) current expenditures of the autarkies as a percentage of total current expenditures at the national level; (5) capital expenditures of the autarkies as a percentage of total capital expenditures at the national level.
SOURCE: Conjuntura Economica (October 1970).

I do think, however, that at least knowing where the money is going, even though the range of presidential powers is not appreciably clarified, is a great improvement over the previous situation of ignorance on both counts. What is probably needed are greater checks over the creation of new autonomous agencies, mergers of agencies performing similar functions, and the introduction of rudimentary program budgeting and planning-programming-budgeting (PPB) systems. In most cases, however, these latter techniques must remain in the dreaming stage for many years to come.

The process of decentralization in Brazil has, by Wilkie's own accounting (see his Table 1), proceeded further than in either Mexico, Bolivia, or Costa Rica. The following table offers additional evidence of this phenomenon. Each of the five indicators of decentralization has moved in the same direction, i.e., toward a greater importance of the decentralized sector relative to GDP, the total public sector, and the central government. Due to lack of suitable data it was impossible to include the expenditures of the "mixed" corporations. (Apparently someone thinks they should be considered as part of the private sector, since they are included in this section in the national accounts.) Had they been encompassed in my table, the concept of the "decentralized sector" would have been greatly expanded. In a consolidated budget of the public sector prepared by the Fiscal Studies Center of the Getúlio Vargas Foundation, it is shown that the "mixed" corporations were spending an amount close to the total of the central government and autarkys combined by 1964.[1]

The initial impetus for the establishment of a decentralized sector in Brazil came in the 1930s when Getúlio Vargas created a number of autarkies (*autarquias*) for the purpose of regulating the production and prices of certain agricultural commodities (coffee, sugar, cacao, etc.) hard hit by the depression. This action by Vargas can probably be attributed to an effort on his part to appease powerful regional interest groups. Vargas (in the role of *o pai do povo*) also established a social security system, at this time organized as an autarky. During the war years emphasis shifted to the public sponsorship of basic industry and infrastructure. Between 1941 and 1945, the Brazilian government created five mixed corporations (*companhias mistas*) involved in the production of iron and steel, hydroelectric energy, caustic soda, and aircraft engines. The intent behind these actions had definite nationalistic overtones. (Note Baer's paper on this point.)

Decentralization of the public sector accelerated in the postwar years, especially after the mid-1950s. By the early 1960s, autarkies and mixed corporations were operating in almost every sector of the Brazilian economy, including transportation, communication, banking and credit, regional development, electric energy, commodity controls, iron and steel, petroleum, etc. It is likely that the growth of the public sector also began reaching the point of diminishing returns in these years. Although many of the decentralized entities performed admirably, others (e.g., the railroads) experienced huge operating deficits requiring inflationary subsidies from the central government. Furthermore, the central government became increasingly constrained in its budgetary action by the proliferation of revenues earmarked for distribution to the decentralized sector. Rational planning also became far more difficult as more economic and social functions fell outside the sphere of central authority.

In the last few years some reforms have been attempted, although expenditures of the decentralized sector have continued to grow in both absolute and relative terms. There have been efforts by the Fiscal Studies

1. *Revista Brasileira de Economia* (June-September 1966), p. 60.

Center of the Getúlio Vargas Foundation and the Ministry of Planning to formulate consolidated budgets with expenditures organized in functional categories, but this work is still incomplete. The central government has also reduced the volume of earmarked revenues, although considerable amounts of resources are still collected and expended through extrabudgetary funds. In addition, some minor autarkies have been merged and/or absorbed by other decentralized agencies, e.g., the institutes of pine and maté were recently absorbed by the forestry development institute. All of the above are probably steps in the right direction and may be a prelude to a policy of "recentralization." However, even with the strong executive branch Brazil now possesses, diminishing the power of the firmly entrenched decentralized agencies will be a very difficult policy to carry out.

In my concluding comments, I would like to point out what I consider to be some rather important drawbacks in Wilkie's presentation of government expenditure data. Due to the problems of data collection in developing countries, these suggestions are admittedly easier said than done, but I do think they warrant some attention. Without further research, the outcome of these suggested revisions is unclear, although they might alter some of the paper's conclusions.

A potentially important drawback of Wilkie's presentation is that only some (or none—it is not clear from the paper) of the government expenditure data are net of intersectoral transfers and/or subsidies. Presumably, the central governments of Mexico, Bolivia, and Costa Rica subsidize at least some of the decentralized agencies to a greater or lesser degree (the opposite case, i.e., the decentralized agencies subsidizing the central government, seems far less likely). If these intersectoral transfers are quantitatively significant, then both the overall size of the public sector and the size of the central government relative to the decentralized subsector will be greatly overstated. Wilkie is apparently aware of this double-counting problem and has inserted several caveats to this effect in the paper's footnotes, but since he gives us little information on the relative degree of intersectoral transfers in these case studies, we are left with imprecise intercountry comparisons.

A second problem arises in Wilkie's functional analysis. To me, his analysis in terms of only three expenditure categories, i.e., economic, social, and administrative, is simplistic and not very revealing. In particular, I am bothered by Wilkie's equation of control over expenditures in his "economic" function to control over economic development. This judgment ignores the distinct possibility that public expenditures on human resources, e.g., education and health, may do more to hasten the process of national development than expenditures on physical resources, e.g., communication, transportation, conservation, industrial promotion, etc. Thus, the argument that central governments in these three countries have lost control over development expenditures because their functions have become more "socioadministrative" in nature is not verified by the data presented in the paper. More detail needs to be included on the relative importance of the subfunctions, e.g., education versus social security, and the type of expenditures emphasized within subfunctions, e.g., primary and secondary education versus university education.

Although the functional categories developed for Mexico, Bolivia, and Costa Rica are less than ideal for analytical purposes, their application to U.S. data for purposes of comparison is unreasonable. A case in point is the use of debt amortization payments in the U.S. public expenditure data. As Wilkie points out in note 13, amortization payments represent only an exchange of assets and as such have little economic significance. By their inclusion in aggregate expenditure one arrives at a completely misleading picture of the economic impact of the U.S. national government (shown in Table 2 as spending an amount equivalent to 53.8 percent of the GNP). A much better case can be made for including debt amortization payments in the public expenditures of a developing country, especially if a large part of the debt is foreign-held. I am not convinced, however, that they should be arbitrarily inserted in the "administrative" functional category. If the debt was originally incurred for financing some development-related project, perhaps amortization and interest payments should be included in the "economic" functional category.

Discussion

I. NAVARRETE: Wilkie's point about the lack of presidential control in my view is not accurate for Mexico. What is true is that the finance ministry sometimes cannot control all expenditures to its liking and stories are spread among foreign advisors and foreign *técnicos*. The president and the political structure in fact hold strong control over the whole public sector. Sometimes the public sector, especially the decentralized agencies, must respond to social and political demands which do not fit exactly with the economic or financial interpretations of the finance minister. From a broader point of view, this is advantageous for development, since it is not uncommon that finance ministers tend to support conservative policies and are opposed to planning, which generally implies greater public expenditure and less monetary control.

Wilkie is also incorrect, in my view, on the planning and coordination mechanism in Mexico. All public agencies must have their investment programs authorized and their financing sources are well looked into. But thus far, planning is limited to public investment and its sources of financing. Moreover, it is true that planning is not a "democratic" process but is still a sort of technocratic planning. By "democratic" planning, I mean a process whereby objectives would be widely discussed, every organized group given an opportunity to be heard, a consensus formed for their acceptance, and the process of implementation integrated with state and local governments, professionals, intellectuals, technicians, the private business sector. Public investment programs, however, are efficiently carried out in Mexico and with quite good control.

Concerning the increased power of the *técnicos* in presenting alternatives to those who make decisions, many times the *técnicos* are successful because they justify the *politicians'* choice. It would help the professionals and intellectuals to open lines of communication among themselves and also with the general public and middle classes and thereby be responsive to wider groups in a more democratic way, rather than only be heard by the president or the finance minister.

A. CHURCHILL: At one time or another I have worked on the public accounts of all three of these countries. To choose these three countries and then hope to get anything in common out of a comparison surprises me, because the decentralized public sectors in all three are quite different phenomena. One thing they do have in common, which explains much of their growth in this century, is simply their social security institutions. In all three of these countries, recent expenditure growth has been in the social security institutions. One might therefore ask about the government's control over the social security institution. In Bolivia the social security institution is very much under the thumb of the government and is in a position of doing what it is told. Costa Rica's social security institution relies largely on transfers from the central government and also must do very much what it is told. In Mexico, which has the largest social security institution of the three, the institution is also in a position of receiving fairly substantial transfers from the central government.

But, except for the social security institutions, the decentralized sector in Costa Rica is a collection of small institutions which do not receive much money from any source. In Mexico, if one deducts CONASUPO, the price support agency, and PEMEX, not much remains except the railroads, which again receive large subsidies from the central government. In Bolivia, the decentralized sector consists largely of COMIBOL and the petroleum company. (Incidentally, the size of the figures in Wilkie's paper for Bolivia is very surprising. The public sector in Bolivia is insignificant; if one eliminates elements like sales of petroleum and minerals, public expenditures total something under 10 percent of total GNP.)

The only similarities I see are COMIBOL and the petroleum institution in Bolivia and PEMEX in Mexico. These have large sources of funds outside government. Admittedly, they both work within the political

system, but they are largely out of the hands of the finance minister because they do not receive any money from his office. To lump all these
agencies and countries together and extract any trends I find an almost
impossible task.

H. HINRICHS: A study by the World Bank shows that during the 1950s
and 1960s government revenues grew more rapidly than GNP for most
less-developed countries, but *current* government expenditures were
growing much more rapidly than revenues. Thus, public sector savings
were falling in many cases, and expenditures related to the size of
bureaucracies and government employment were growing much more
rapidly than had been anticipated.

The theory of expenditure decentralization from a developmental
strategy point of view takes as basic gospel that resources should be allocated to the best entrepreneurs, those who can maximize the marginal
social and economic product desired from these resources, be they found
in the private sector or in mixed enterprises or in government at the local,
state, or national level. Thus, it follows that one cannot form any general
theories as to who should manage resources; it depends upon where the
best entrepreneurs are located. Consequently, for Mexico, Costa Rica,
and Bolivia, three very dissimilar countries, I do not see how one can
argue that expenditures should be recentralized.

J. LEVIN: I am pleased and surprised to see a substantial paper on
the attempts to decentralize and split away the power of the president in
Latin America. Some previous analyses have referred to the existence of
decentralized agencies as a form of feudalism. In terms of a structure of
government in which substantial power came to reside in decentralized
agencies which could resist attempts to erode that power, the use of the
term feudalism has some merit. In the literature on public administration,
the growth of decentralized agencies in Latin America has been ascribed
to the existence of external preaudit by the Controller General's Office,
an arm of the legislature, which in Latin American budgetary systems of
the past fifty years was given the right to scrutinize each expenditure before it was made. According to some accounts, decentralized agencies
were created to escape this scrutiny.

It is interesting now to see expenditure recentralization ascribed to
an emphasis on development. In a number of other instances, I have
seen the counter-influence taking place: in order to spur development,
many new decentralized entities were created. Sometimes this occurred
through the influence of external agencies interested in keeping their
financial assistance outside the budget and free of legislative allocation
and control, and in some cases this movement took place as part of the
Alliance for Progress. What developed domestically is equally interesting. While external agencies pressed for development expenditures to take
place outside the budget through decentralized agencies, the national

governments were unwilling to lose all control. The result, in some cases, was the growth of planning agencies which assumed control over expenditures of the decentralized agencies outside the budget. Thus, there is one system of control within the budget and a different system of control outside the budget located in the planning department, which may possess the power to approve the budgets or projects or capital expenditures of the decentralized agencies.

One of the disadvantages created by the decentralized agencies is the difficulty they present for current evaluation of what is actually happening in government. Anyone who has tried to make out consolidated government sector accounts, or even accounts for the central government alone, runs across an important problem of timing. Many development programs are spelled out in terms of the development expenditures of the central government; unfortunately, these expenditures formally take place when the central government makes a transfer to the decentralized agencies. There may be a considerable lag, which occurs because the decentralized agencies in many countries are incapable of expending money when they get it. Thus, the most significant—and secret—information comes to be the bank deposits of the decentralized agencies, which reveal the magnitude of this lag. There has also been an influence in recent years for central control of the decentralized agencies arising from the need for greater control of cash management.

V. TANZI: What disturbs me about Wilkie's paper is the neoclassical bias I find in it. The theory of public finance tells us that if one gives the budget over to the central government, it will allocate expenditures in such a way that, at the margin, the marginal product of each type of expenditure will be the same. That is obviously very nice for situations in which governments act rationally and are not subject to strong political pressures. Is this the situation in Latin America? I doubt it. Let me illustrate this point. I remember having a discussion with the minister of planning of Brazil, a Yale-educated economist, and I asked him why earmarking is used so extensively in Brazil. His answer was simply that one must earmark revenues to insulate public investment from political pressures. Otherwise, the extra money will just be "wasted" on additional wages and salaries. The basic point is that, if a government increases revenues in Latin America today, this revenue will probably go merely toward current expenditure increases of the type that are not very helpful for development purposes. To insulate extra revenue from this type of political pressure, one must earmark it, and earmarking revenue implies decentralization.

J. WILKIE: I am not proposing either recentralization or decentralization as a matter of policy. Rather, I am attempting to call attention to the fact that the process of recentralization *is under way* in at least three countries. This process will no doubt continue in Latin America whether one approves or disapproves of such a policy and whether the countries are similar or dissimilar.

With regard to the view that the countries investigated are very dissimilar (a comment which may imply that my study is thus invalidated), such a statement reveals little understanding of the nature of comparative studies in general. In short, we do not necessarily study countries because they have similar characteristics (it is highly doubtful that many countries are very similar anyway), but analysis is generally undertaken to show how different countries with dissimilar economies, cultures, and traditions resolve similar problems.

In attempting to define the scope of the executive as opposed to the decentralized sector of governmental activity, obviously we have the problem of eliminating double-counting of transfer expenditures in order to determine the relative budgetary role of centralized and decentralized agencies. This is precisely one problem that the governments of Mexico, Bolivia, and Costa Rica are trying to resolve through the development of more precise budgetary procedures and definitions. To show how this problem has not been solved, I point out in Table 12 of my study that Costa Rican time series data for the growth of decentralized expenditures are remarkably inconsistent. Data for the period of 1950-58 appear to have little relation to data for the epoch 1959-68, probably because of changes in definition of what constitutes the decentralized sector, as well as methodology in counting intersectoral transfers. Also, as I have noted elsewhere, various officers of the Costa Rican central government are in disagreement about how many decentralized agencies even exist.[1]

Those who believe that transfer payments have been "minimal" might take into account the following governmental estimations for transfers by the central government in 1970: Costa Rica, 22.3 percent; Bolivia, 14.1 percent; Mexico, 16.3 percent.[2] The total for Mexico was 22.8 percent in 1963.[3] In my analyses of expenditures, I disaggregate these transfers by function and count them as part of central government expenditures on the rationale that they are part of (and would not be possible without) central government activity.

In reply to Navarrete's statements, I do not say that Mexico's planning has been a complete failure; in fact, I go out of my way to say that the central government under President Díaz Ordaz gained new and impressive capacity to assess development in two ways. For the first time

1. James W. Wilkie, "On Methodology and the Use of Historical Statistics," *Latin American Research Review* 5:1 (Spring 1970): 91.

2. Projected figures are from Costa Rica, Contraloría General, *Memoria Anual, 1970: Informe Financiero del Sector Público,* part 3, Table 4; Bolivia, Ministerio de Finanzas, *Presupuesto General de la Nación* (1970), p. 6; and Mexico, *El Mercado de Valores* (December 15, 1969), p. 868.

3. Mexico, Secretaría de Hacienda y Crédito Público, *Presupuesto General,* (1963), p. 4.

in Mexican history we not only know the *actual* (in contrast to *projected*) figures on capital investment, but we know the geographic distribution of these expenditures. These are feats which few other countries can boast.

While some of us would like to distinguish between developmental and nondevelopmental expenditures (as opposed to social, economic, and administrative categories), such a distinction would be very difficult to make. This is especially a problem with governmental payrolls, where salaries tend to be counted as current (or nondevelopmental) rather than capital (or developmental) expenditures. Unless a way could be worked out to reclassify, for example, teachers' salaries as a developmental outlay, the scheme would break down. At any rate, I cannot see many Latin American governments revamping their functional (let alone administrative) budgetary analysis to develop such a sophisticated approach in the near future.

Finally, in suggesting that three Latin American countries have only begun the process of recentralization, I do not attempt to offer a definitive study but to sketch the outlines of a little-recognized problem. The drive for recentralization marks an important turning point in the history of the twentieth century, and the topic of recentralization may well be vital to our understanding of future Latin American economic development.

8

The Role of Government Enterprises
in Latin America's Industrialization

WERNER BAER

IN Latin America the direct participation of government in economic activity has rarely occurred, because of ideological convictions of the governing classes about the role of the state in the productive process. Prior to the Great Depression of the thirties Latin American governments had played a relatively passive role in their economies—leaving the development of exports, of most infrastructure projects, and of industries to the private sector. Often the latter received special government help— e.g., subsidies to railroads, favorable rates for public utilities, etc. Thus, the state acted as a "stage-setter" rather than direct participant.

But the Great Depression of the thirties and the Second World War "forced a reluctant review of the role of government in national economies. Government agencies intervened in the market to purchase agricultural, ranching, and mining output, to regulate exports or dispose of surplus, to supervise the volume and composition of imports, and to control the level and rates of exchange. . . ."[1] Also because of the shortage of imported manufactured goods due to balance-of-payments problems, import-substitution industries were developed to relieve shortages.[2] To promote industrialization, many Latin American governments "assisted directly and indirectly the maintenance and expansion of established units, financed the creation of new ones, and provided all the solicited levels of protection in the form of tariffs and exchange and import controls. . . ."[3]

In this review I will first survey conditions and motives which have led governments to take an increasingly direct part in productive activi-

1. Stanley J. Stein and Barbara H. Stein, *The Colonial Heritage of Latin America* (New York: Oxford University Press, 1969), pp. 191-92.
2. For a survey of import-substitution industrialization, see Werner Baer, "Import Substitution Industrialization in Latin America: Experience and Interpretations," *Latin American Research Review* (Fall 1971); see also Joseph Grunwald, "Some Reflections on Latin American Industrialization Policy," *Journal of Political Economy* (July/August 1970).
3. Stein and Stein, *Colonial Heritage*, p. 192.

ties since the thirties. This will be followed by an analysis of the relative impact of these activities on the economies as a whole. I shall then discuss the behavior of government firms as compared to private firms. Finally, I shall speculate on the future of the directly productive government sector as Latin American economies face the problems of the post-import-substitution industrialization era of the seventies.

CIRCUMSTANCES WHICH HAVE LED TO GOVERNMENT PARTICIPATION IN PRODUCTIVE ENTERPRISES

I shall begin by summarizing the ways in which government productive enterprises were created and have grown in four of Latin America's major countries.

Argentina

Direct government activities became significant under the Perón regime,[4] whose aim it was to make the state the predominant power in the nation's economic life. The government created a state fleet in 1944 (thus adding to an already existing state tanker fleet, created in the twenties, and a state merchant marine, founded in 1941) and in the late forties expanded it by nationalizing some private lines. In 1944 the government also expanded its role in the financial field by establishing the state industrial bank, which became the sole source of medium and long-term credit for small and medium-sized manufacturing firms. A little later the central bank was fully nationalized and the government expanded its participation in the insurance business.

In the same period the Argentine government expropriated the large grain elevator companies of Buenos Aires and La Plata and in 1946 this action was extended by the creation of the Argentine Institute for Promotion of Trade (IAPI), whose chief initial function was to handle all wheat exports. Soon thereafter IAPI expanded into the export of other staples, especially meat. It also moved into the importing field and in the early fifties over 60 percent of the country's exports and 20 percent of its imports were handled by this agency. In its first years IAPI made huge

---

4. Carlos Díaz-Alejandro has stated that it would not be accurate to characterize the pre-1930 economy as purely laissez-faire. He maintains that "State interventions in economic matters is considered legitimate in the Latin and Spanish traditions, and while some 'liberals' who dominated the Argentine government fought this ancient custom, attachment to laissez-faire was neither very deep nor widespread, even in the pre-1930 halcyon days." He points to the fact that already in the early part of the century the Argentinian government was active in banking and oil extraction. "The Argentine State and Economic Growth: A Historical Review," in *Government and Economic Development,* Gustav Ranis, ed. (New Haven: Yale University Press, 1971).

profits and became a major source of financing government programs.[5]

The mid-forties also saw the nationalization of foreign-owned public utilities—the British-owned gas company of Buenos Aires, a number of subsidiaries of American and Foreign Power Company, the telephone system, and the railroads. By the end of the forties, "the major traditional foreign equity interests in the economy (exclusive of meat-packing concerns) had been liquidated."[6]

Many have questioned the economic wisdom of the Perónist nationalization sprees and their aftereffects—for example, the price policies of IAPI toward agriculture which worked to the detriment of that sector, the using up of the country's foreign exchange reserves to buy out foreign-owned public utilities. These actions were motivated by nationalist considerations and by the desire for "subjugating economic interests (though not economic forces) to the power of the state."[7] Although the latter objective was attained in part, the exhaustion of foreign reserves and increasing foreign indebtedness diluted the achievement of economic independence.

Direct public participation in industrial production most often occurred because of a combination of circumstances which had not been anticipated. In 1947 the National Administration of State Industries was created to operate expropriated companies which had belonged to owners from Axis power countries. These firms operated mainly in the metallurgical, electrical, textile, pharmaceutical, and chemical fields, and were administered by the armed forces, which had started a number of other industries. The air force operated in such areas as motorcycle production, cars and trucks, parts for airplanes, etc. The army ran about sixteen factories and two small blast furnaces. Few of these firms, however, functioned on a significant commercial basis.

The largest direct industrial operation of the Argentine state was in the field of steel production. SOMISA was founded as a mixed company (80 percent of the shares owned by the government) in 1949. It built a large integrated steel plant at San Nicolas. The justification for this government enterprise was that private capital was not available on the scale required for a large integrated steel operation and that such a firm was necessary to encourage derivative metal-using industries, mostly established by the private sector. Construction on the plant was started only in 1955 and production commenced in 1961.

Government control and participation have been dominant in oil extraction and petroleum refining ever since petroleum was discovered at Comodoro Rivadavia in 1907. In 1922 the government established the

---

5. William P. Glade, Jr., *The Latin American Economies: A Study of Their Institutional Evolution* (New York: Van Nostrand, 1969), pp. 423-25.

6. Ibid., p. 426.

7. Ibid.

state oil fields, Yacimientos Petroliferos Fiscales (YPF), for development of the petroleum deposits. All petroleum reserves became the property of the state. In the mid-sixties YPF administered close to 70 percent of total output and controlled about 60 percent of refinery capacity and 55 percent of the domestic market for refined products. Private domestic and foreign firms may submit bids to YPF for drilling and service contracts and some continue to operate in refining and marketing.

After the overthrow of Perón in 1955 there occurred some retrenchment in the government sector. Many state firms were sold to private groups and most expansion of manufacturing activity was attributable to the private sector. One notable exception was steel. Private foreign capital was also encouraged and contracts were signed with foreign oil companies for the exploration, drilling, and transportation of oil for YPF. Some of these policies caused substantial nationalist criticisms and were partially the causes of considerable political troubles in the late fifties and sixties.[8]

Brazil

Until the late thirties direct involvement of the state in productive activities was almost nonexistent. The creation of the state steel company (Companhia Siderurgica Nacional) in the late thirties was a "residual" event, i.e., it took place after all attempts to get local and foreign private capital to build an integrated steel mill had failed. Later state expansion in the steel industry was of a similar residual nature. For example, the integrated plants of COSIPA and USIMINAS began as mixed private/local government enterprises. The cost of the projects, however, was so immense that only by equity participation of the state development bank (BNDE) was it possible to complete the projects. At the time these steel mills were completed, the BNDE was majority shareholder in each of the firms.[9]

The state petroleum company (Petrobras) came into being in the early fifties as a result of nationalist pressures to keep exploration and subsoil ownership out of the hands of foreign companies. It monopolizes petroleum exploration, controls and operates about 84 percent of all refining, and has a small proportion of the consumer gasoline market. Through its Companhia Nacional de Alcalis the Brazilian government has a monopoly on domestic production of caustic soda.

Since the Second World War the Brazilian government has acquired the country's railroads, run most coastal and river transport systems, and administered most of the country's major ports.

The Brazilian government's role in the banking and credit sector is

8. Díaz-Alejandro, "Argentine State and Economic Growth."
9. For details see Werner Baer, *The Development of the Brazilian Steel Industry* (Nashville, Tenn.: Vanderbilt University Press, 1969).

also substantial. The Banco do Brasil (a government bank) received more than 22 percent of the country's bank deposits in 1969 and was responsible for a similarly large amount of current credit. The Banco do Brasil was also the country's chief source of rural credit. Also, through the development bank (BNDE), special banks (like the Banco do Nordeste, the National Housing Bank [BNH], etc.), and numerous federal government savings banks, the government controls a major portion of long-term and housing credits. By 1969 all federal, regional, and state banking entities received over 60 percent of all deposits.[10]

Most of the country's power-generating facilities built in the fifties and sixties were provided by government firms, some owned by the federal government and some by state governments.[11]

Without excluding private domestic or foreign firms, the government company Companhia Vale do Rio Doce has become Brazil's leading mineral exporter, shipping about 80 percent of Brazil's iron ore exports. Private foreign and domestic capital have options on exporting iron ore from lands they own, but little export capacity had been developed at this writing. Manganese exports, however, are mainly in the hands of private concerns. It should be noted that the Companhia Vale do Rio Doce was formed as a result of pressures from nationalist groups in the state of Minas Gerais who were concerned about foreign control of natural resources.

Government companies also operate in the fields of insurance, warehousing, and storage. The government even owned an automobile manufacturing concern—Fabrica Nacional de Motores—which, after years of operating at considerable losses, was sold in the late sixties to Alfa Romeo, from which it had been operating under license.

Chile

In Chile direct government participation in economic activity dates back to the 1920s, when laws establishing social insurance programs were passed. The many institutions which these programs encompassed included the operation of hospitals, food and clothing stores, the country's largest vaccine-producing firm, and the largest pharmaceutical enterprises. Much of the money of these programs was also invested in stocks of industrial enterprises.

In the twenties the Chilean government also increased its participation in the banking and finance fields. The Mortgage Credit Institute (Caja de Credito Hipotecario) and the National Savings Bank (Caja

10. *Mundo Economico* (Julho-Agôsto 1970), p. 43.
11. For a detailed study of the Brazilian government's increasing participation in the power sector, see Judith Tendler, *Electric Power in Brazil: Entrepreneurship in the Public Sector* (Cambridge, Mass.: Harvard University Press, 1968).

Nacional de Ahorros) had already been created in 1855 and 1910, respectively. These institutions were complemented by the creation of a number of government banks specializing in certain sectors. These state banks provided credit to agriculture, mining, and industry, and for development of specific regions of the country and specific sectors.

The Chilean government also moved into the insurance field at an early stage and in 1933 the State Insurance Institute was created to monopolize fire and casualty insurance for government and semipublic agencies.

The most dramatic intervention of the Chilean state came with the creation of the Chilean Development Corporation (CORFO).[12] Although it was established in 1939 in order to cope with the aftereffects of a devastating earthquake, it served "as a powerful autonomous fiscal organization to implement [the government's] development program."[13] Over the years CORFO became involved in project, regional, and even national economic planning. It also participated in the execution of plans and projects. In areas where private capital had not ventured (or had not ventured on a sufficient scale) CORFO organized firms and operated them as state enterprises. Some of the latter were subsequently sold wholly or in part to private investors. Through its operations CORFO had a considerable impact on the Chilean economy. It has been estimated, for example, that in the period 1939-54 it controlled over 30 percent of investment in machinery and equipment, more than one-fourth of public investment, and close to 20 percent of gross domestic investment.[14] CORFO became involved in a great variety of different sectors. It participated in the national electric enterprise, the national petroleum company, a copper rolling and wiring plant, beet-sugar refineries, a national hotel corporation, an agricultural machinery and equipment company, the largest rubber-manufacturing plant, and the national steel mill.

CORFO's funds came from taxes levied specifically to finance its activities, from general government contributions, from credits of the central bank, and from external credits.[15] In the latter capacity CORFO also acted as a financial intermediary between foreign creditors and Chilean investors. Gradually CORFO also generated internal funds from commissions, interest, dividends, etc. Over the years the importance of internal funds grew, amounting to 20 percent of investment funds in 1951 and 40 percent by the end of the fifties.[16]

12. For a review of CORFO's activities, see Markos Mamalakis, "An Analysis of the Financial and Investment Activities of the Chilean Development Corporation: 1939-1964," *The Journal of Development Studies* (January 1969).
13. Ibid., p. 118.
14. Ibid.
15. Ibid., p. 120.
16. Ibid., p. 126.

Mexico

Despite its revolutionary experience in the early part of the century, the Mexican government's direct intervention in the economy was fairly similar to that of other governments in Latin America. In the late thirties the railways were completely nationalized. At about the same time the Federal Electricity Commission was created and thereafter the state continuously expanded in that field. In 1960, with the government's purchase of all remaining privately owned power companies, the state firm had a complete power monopoly. Also, in 1938, with the expropriation of the foreign-owned petroleum industry, the Mexican government acquired a monopoly in the exploration, refining, and distribution of the products of that industry. This monopoly was exercised by the giant state firm PEMEX.

By the twenties the Mexican government had already moved directly into the financial sector. The Banco de México was set up as a central bank in 1925. Shortly thereafter state-operated sectoral banks were created, and over the following decades an array of government banks were established to cover all types of credits. In the thirties the Mexican government also entered into the marketing field, not only as a regulator, but also as an active participant.

The greatest direct participation of the Mexican government in the economy has been through the Nacional Financiera S.A. (NAFIN), which was founded in 1934 but became an important developmental institution only in the 1940s. NAFIN is a publicly owned institution (90 percent of its shares are held by the government). Like Chile's CORFO, NAFIN has acted as promoter and financier of corporations. In the early sixties NAFIN "was creditor, investor, and guarantor for 533 business enterprises of all kinds; it held stock in 60 industrial firms; and it was majority stockholder in 13 firms producing steel, textiles, motion pictures, plywood, fertilizers, electrical energy, sugar, lumber and refrigerated meats. At the end of 1961 . . . Nacional Financiera's loans were nearly half as large as those of all private credit institutions, and they accounted for more than one third of total lending by Mexico's public credit institutions."[17]

The reasons for NAFIN entering various fields of economic activities have been varied—the government might simply ask it to enter a field, it might help a debt-ridden firm, it might agree to accept stocks as repayment of loans, etc. The government has been the prime mover in getting NAFIN to invest in infrastructure, the manufacture of railroad cars, automobiles, coke, chemicals, and fertilizer. The private sector conceived and

17. Calvin P. Blair, "Nacional Financiera: Entrepreneurship in a Mixed Economy," *Public Policy and Private Enterprise in Mexico*, Raymond Vernon, ed. (Cambridge, Mass.: Harvard University Press, 1964), p. 194.

began most other projects, in a number of which NAFIN is now a majority shareholder.[18]

Other Countries

One finds similar patterns of direct governmental intervention in the economy in many other Latin American countries. In Peru, for example, the government-owned Banco Industrial has been engaged in promotion of and participation in various industrial enterprises. The Peruvian government has also created firms in petroleum, fertilizer, and steel production. The Colombian government founded many industries through its Instituto de Fomento Industrial;[19] most of these were gradually sold to the private sector. The Venezuelan Corporación Venezolana de Fomento (CVF), founded in 1946, has also engaged in activities similar to CORFO and NAFIN.[20]

According to calculations made by Brandenburg in the early sixties, out of the thirty-two largest enterprises in Colombia, ten were fully owned by the government and included such fields as railways, finance, various public utility firms, and petrochemicals. For Venezuela, Brandenburg found that twelve out of the thirty largest corporations were in government hands, including public utilities, steel, chemicals, sugar refining, tourism, airlines, and shipping.[21]

THE ROLE OF GOVERNMENT ENTERPRISE

It should be clear from this brief country-by-country review that ideological considerations about the role of the state in the economy have rarely, if ever, been important in the growth of Latin American state enterprises. A combination of circumstances has forced an increasingly direct participation of the state in economic activities. These circumstances can be classified into three principal categories—the growth and industrialization policies of the state, nationalism, and welfare statism. Although these categories overlap, i.e., the motivations for the growth of state enterprises are mixed, I shall for convenience briefly outline them separately.

18. Ibid., p. 236.
19. This institute has set up about thirty large enterprises since the late forties, including the Planta Colombiana de Soda, Industria Colombiana de Llantas, Acerias Paz del Rio, Cementos Boyaca, Celulosa y Papel de Colombia, and Forjas de Colombia. See "Industrial Development in Latin America," *Economic Bulletin for Latin America* (Second Half of 1969), p. 50.
20. United Nations, *El proceso de industrialización en America Latina* (New York, 1965), pp. 182-85.
21. Frank Brandenburg, *The Development of Latin American Private Enterprise* (Washington, D.C.: National Planning Association, May 1964), pp. 60, 65.

Growth and Industrialization Policies

With the dearth of entrepreneurial capacity and the inability of the private sector to save sums for projects requiring large investment outlays, the state was often forced to enter into certain activities. This was especially the case in an industry such as steel, and in certain other types of heavy industries and public utilities. In some countries the state entered only after it was clear that neither domestic private nor foreign private capital was willing to enter into certain fields of activities which were deemed essential to the industrialization of the country.[22] In such cases, the role of the government enterprise was to act as a stimulant and/or complement to the development of an industrial structure. For example, the establishment of government steel plants was deemed essential to spur on the development of metal and metal-using industries.

It is of interest to note that in almost all countries the majority of government firms were mixed companies in which the government (either directly or indirectly) controlled the majority of the shares. In many cases it was the stated intention of the government to turn the firms over to private enterprise through sales of shares. In some instances this occurred (for example, in Chile and Colombia), while in other cases circumstances never permitted such an event. Implied in this attitude was a vision of the state entering productive activities only on a temporary basis, setting up facilities which would be gradually taken over by private groups. This has been labeled by some as "transitory socialism," a necessary stage in the process of industrialization.

Nationalism

The urge to industrialize was, in part, based on nationalist desires for greater economic independence from the traditional industrial centers of the world. Most governments, however, faced a dilemma. They wanted to maximize the insulation of their economies from the vicissitudes of the international market and to maximize domestic control over natural

22. Most experienced observers feel this to have been a most important reason for the development of state enterprises. For example, Raymond Vernon states, "From time to time in the development of any country, there arises a near-indispensable demand for some single, indivisible production unit on a scale so large or in a field so unfamiliar as to exceed either the risk-taking proclivities of the private sector or its capacity to mobilize the capital for the venture . . ." (*Public Policy and Private Enterprise*, p. 7). Similar observations have been made by Victor L. Urquidi, "Fiscal Policy in Latin America's Economic Development," in *Fiscal Policy for Economic Growth in Latin America*, published for the Joint Tax Program (Baltimore: Johns Hopkins University Press, 1965), p. 15. For an analysis of the extent to which militarist and reformist types of regimes are responsible for sizable increases in the direct economic activities of the state, see Charles W. Anderson, *Politics and Economic Change in Latin America* (Princeton, N.J.: D. Van Nostrand Company, Inc., 1967), pp. 327-29.

and capital resources. However, due to capital and entrepreneurial scarcities, industrialization forced most Latin American countries to rely on foreign savings and know-how.

What we observe in most Latin American countries is a compromise situation, in which a large portion of the manufacturing sector has been left to domestic and foreign private capital; but the state reserved for itself sectors that were felt to be too central and sensitive to be in foreign hands, and the private domestic sector did not have the capital or the entrepreneurial abilities to take charge. This explains the state's involvement in petroleum, mining, and public utilities.[23]

Welfare Statism and Miscellaneous Events

Latin America's network of infrastructure (railroads, power and gas systems, telephone systems, etc.) was developed in large part by private foreign enterprises. These had been attracted by the promise of high returns, as a result of both special subsidies in the construction period and favorable rate structures.

The growth of more populist and development-oriented regimes resulted in policies less favorable to public utilities. Rates were increasingly controlled by the states and used to serve (or subsidize) the urban population and the growing industrial sector. The situation was especially serious in inflationary economies where public utility rates were often not allowed to rise with the general price level.[24] As a result, private utilities made few efforts to modernize and expand their capital stock and in many cases the existing stock was allowed to fall into disrepair. The resulting decline in the service of public utilities brought increasing pressure on governments to resolve this situation. In some cases the government nationalized the utilities (usually with compensation to the companies), while in other cases government companies were formed to provide the increased services which the private foreign companies were unwilling and/or unable to supply. In such cases the government's share of public utility services increased rapidly and soon became dominant.

There can be little doubt, however, that government take-over of public utilities was also motivated by nationalism. Many governments felt that public utilities were too critical in the economic structure of the country to be left to foreign corporations. This should not be too difficult

23. I am fully aware that "nationalism" itself could be considered an ideology. However, in the context of this paper I am using the term in a narrow sense concerning the relative roles of the state and private enterprise in the economy.

24. For some case studies see W. Baer, I. Kerstenetzky, and M. H. Simonsen, "Transportation and Inflation: A Study of Irrational Policy-Making in Brazil," *Economic Development and Cultural Change* (January 1965); Judith Tendler, *Electric Power in Brazil*, pp. 50, 209-10; and Robert T. Brown, "The Railroad Decision in Chile," in Gary Fromm, ed., *Transport Investment and Economic Development* (Washington, D.C.: Brookings Institution, 1965).

to understand. Due to their natural-monopoly nature, many developed countries have nationalized or regulated public utilities. Thus a natural monopoly in the hands of foreigners in less-developed countries is even more susceptible to nationalization. As indicated above, in a number of cases government take-over was facilitated at the end of World War II because indebted countries like the United Kingdom were anxious to liquidate their investments.

It is interesting to note, however, that where the state came into the possession of directly productive firms because of special circumstances (e.g., the confiscation of German firms in Argentina), many were sold

TABLE 1

SHARE OF PUBLIC SECTOR IN THE GROSS DOMESTIC
PRODUCT OF SELECTED COUNTRIES[a]

	1955(%)	1966(%)		1961(%)
Argentina	27	28	U.S.	30.2
Brazil	24	33		
Colombia	20	21	W. Germany	39.2
Mexico	15	22		
Chile	23	35	U.K.	34.5
Peru	19	21		
Venezuela	28	26	Sweden	23.9

[a]Includes all government expenditures and investment of public enterprises
SOURCES: United Nations, *Estudio Económico de America Latina 1968*, (New York, 1969), p. 109; Richard A. Musgrave, *Fiscal Systems* (New Haven: Yale University Press, 1969), p. 41.

again to the private sector. This was especially the case of smaller productive concerns which had little strategic importance in the economy and for which the state had little managerial personnel to spare.

IMPACT OF GOVERNMENT FIRMS ON THE ECONOMY

It is evident from the data in Table 1 that the weight of the public sector in Latin American countries is considerable and in some cases is similar to that of Western European countries and the United States. For some countries data are available on the distribution of public investment expenditures according to government organs. This is shown in Table 2. It will be noted that for Brazil in 1966, over 35 percent of public investment was attributable to public enterprises. Although the contribution of Chilean public enterprises to public investment amounted to only 25 percent, the sum of Chile's public enterprises and autonomous agencies investment gives an even larger proportion than the comparable proportion for Brazil. Some of the autonomous agencies are in fact government enterprises; that is, they function as government entities rather than mixed enterprises, where the government is the major shareholder.

Another interesting measure of the relative importance of the public sector is shown in Table 3. Public fixed investment as a proportion of total investment became dominant in Brazil and Chile in the mid-sixties and represented a very sizable proportion in the other countries shown in part a of the table. Much government investment, however, goes into such projects as schools and hospitals. I was able to get a further breakdown for only some countries. Part b of Table 3 gives a special breakdown of Brazilian investments according to three subdivisions—private, public, and publicly owned firms. One notes a steady rise in the importance of the last from the late forties to the mid-sixties. Finally, in part c of the table one notes a more than tripling of the proportion of investment of Mexican government firms as a proportion of total direct government expenditures.

TABLE 2

DISTRIBUTION OF PUBLIC INVESTMENT EXPENDITURES
IN SELECTED LATIN AMERICAN COUNTRIES, 1966

	Central Govt. (%)	States (%)	Municipal Govts. (%)	Autonomous Agencies (%)	Public Enterprises (%)	Total (%)
Brazil	12.0	8.8	10.1	33.8	35.3	100.0
Colombia	20.5	3.3	24.2	52.0		100.0
Chile	28.6			46.3	25.1	100.0
Mexico	34.0	10.8		55.2		100.0
Peru	40.3			29.3	30.4	100.0

SOURCE: United Nations, *Estudio Económico,* p. 113.

Some other measurements might provide additional insights into the relative importance of government enterprises. Table 4 shows the proportion of the ten, twenty, and thirty largest firms in each country which are government, private, and foreign-controlled. The predominance of government firms in the largest enterprises is striking.

It is also of interest to note that the only Latin American firms listed in *Fortune*'s yearly survey of the 200 largest industrial enterprises outside the United States are the three state petroleum enterprises Pemex (which ranked 66 by sales and had 71,788 employees), Petrobras (86, with 34,101 employees) and Argentina's YPF (125, with 34,160 employees). Only one Latin American bank was listed among the 50 largest outside the United States and that was the Banco do Brasil, which ranked 18, with 42,457 employees, and whose assets were growing at a faster yearly rate than any of the other banks listed.[25]

25. *Fortune* (August 1970).

GOALS AND PERFORMANCE OF GOVERNMENT FIRMS

In order to judge the performance of government firms one has to come to some agreement about their goals. Depending on what the latter are, these firms could either get high or low grades in evaluation of their performances.

One could use the standard criteria employed to evaluate private firms' performances—efficiency in the use of factors of production and profitability. Profits in a private firm should be large enough to provide

TABLE 3

(a) PUBLIC FIXED INVESTMENT AS A PROPORTION OF TOTAL FIXED
INVESTMENT FOR SELECTED LATIN AMERICAN COUNTRIES

	1960-62(%)	1964-66(%)
Argentina	22.4	28.5
Brazil	34.5	61.8
Chile	59.5	66.5
Mexico	32.7	31.3
Venezuela	43.7	39.6

SOURCE: United Nations, *Economic Survey of Latin America, 1967* (New York, 1000), p. 101.

(b) BRAZIL: INVESTMENT OF PUBLICLY OWNED FIRMS[a] AND OF THE PUBLIC
SECTOR AS A PROPORTION OF TOTAL INVESTMENT

	1947-53(%)	1954-59(%)	1960-65(%)
Public sector	25	28	34
Publicly owned firms	3	7	17
Private sector	72	65	49
Total	100	100	100

SOURCE: Arnoldo de Oliveira Werneck, "As Atividades Empresariais do Governo Federal no Brasil," *Revista Brasileira de Economia* (July-September 1969), p. 106.
[a]Publicly owned firms are enterprises owned by the federal government.

(c) MEXICO: INVESTMENT OF WHOLLY OR PARTIALLY OWNED GOVERNMENT
FIRMS AS A PROPORTION OF TOTAL DIRECT EXPENDITURE OF
GOVERNMENT ON CURRENT AND CAPITAL ACCOUNT

1939	13.6%
1950	25.5%
1960	35.3%
1962	37.4%

SOURCE: Clark W. Reynolds, *The Mexican Economy: Twentieth Century Structure and Growth* (New Haven: Yale University Press, 1970), chap. 6, Table 2.

some funds for remuneration of shareholders and maybe for part of expansion plans.[26]

As can be seen in Table 5, many publicly owned firms in Latin America do not meet the basic criteria of a private firm. The data in the table were obtained from sixty-four public enterprises around the world, of which twenty-four were in Latin America.[27] All corporations taken together had surpluses on their current operations, the smallest surpluses occurring in Latin America. It will be noted, however, that railways were in deficit even for current operations; this was also the case with "Other Transport" for Latin America, and also with "Other Industry" in both Latin America and other parts of the world.[28] When one includes depreciation charges, all sectors combined show a deficit and only the petroleum, electricity, and communications sectors remain with some

TABLE 4

PERCENTAGE DISTRIBUTION OF OWNERSHIP OF LARGEST ENTERPRISES
IN 6 LATIN AMERICAN COUNTRIES IN 1963[a]

	Top 10		Top 20		Top 30	
	A	B	A	B	A	B
Government	78.2	82.7	68.1	71.7	62.4	65.8
Latin American private	10.5	11.5	18.1	19.3	21.2	22.4
Foreign private	11.3	5.8	13.8	9.0	16.4	11.8
Total	100.0	100.0	100.0	100.0	100.0	100.0

[a]Unweighted average of top 10, 20, and 30 firms. Size of firms determined by capital and reserves. (A) includes Chilean copper and nitrate exporters; (B) excludes latter. Countries involved: Argentina, Brazil, Chile, Colombia, Mexico, and Venezuela.
SOURCE: Frank Brandenburg, *The Development of Latin American Private Enterprise* (Washington, D.C.: National Planning Association, May 1964), p. 66.

surpluses. Finally, when new investments are included, all sectors show substantial deficits. This means that only through government transfers (i.e., subsidies) or loans were these state firms able to cover their depreciation and new investment needs (and in the case of transportation in Latin America, subsidies were needed even to cover current expenditures).

26. The following section draws in part on the material and some ideas found in Laurence Whitehead, "Public Sector Activities," in Keith Griffin, ed., *Financing Development in Latin America* (London: Macmillan & Co., 1971).
27. The table is based on a study made by the International Monetary Fund and published in its journal—Andrew H. Gantt II and Giuseppe Dutto, "Financial Performance of Government-Owned Corporations in Less Developed Countries," *IMF Staff Papers* (March 1968). Table 5 is based on data found in this article and put together into one table by Whitehead, "Public Sector Activities."
28. "Other Industry" includes firms like the Argentine State Coal Corporations, the Bolivian Tin Mining Corporation, the Colombian State Paz Del Rio Steel Mill, etc. For discussions of railroad deficits see Baer, Kerstenetzky, and Simonsen, "Transportation and Inflation," and Alan Abouchar, "Inflation and Transportation Policy in Brazil," *Economic Development and Cultural Change* (October 1969).

TABLE 5

Average Financing Needs of 64 Public Enterprises in Underdeveloped Countries[a]

	Number of Enterprises	(A) Surplus on Current Operations	(B) Surplus after Depreciation	(C) New Investment	(D) Surplus After All Investment (B−C)	(E) Government Transfers
Railways						
Latin America	4	−57.1	−84.1	5.3	−89.4	90.6
All	12	−13.5	−40.5	0.5	−41.0	35.3
Other transport						
Latin America	4	−3.8	−33.8	16.4	−50.2	44.5
All	11	+10.9	−19.1	0.2	−19.3	17.8
Petrol						
Latin America	5	+43.3	+23.3	50.0	−26.7	−1.6
All	7	+33.8	+13.8	36.9	−23.1	−0.7
Electricity						
Latin America	3	+21.0	0.0	93.2	−93.2	59.6
All	13	+27.2	+6.2	108.2	−102.0	33.7
Communications						
Latin America	2	+26.7	+6.7	31.6	−24.9	14.5
All	8	+5.7	−14.3	17.7	−32.0	28.6
Other industry						
Latin America	6	−6.6	−30.6	24.5	−55.1	45.7
All	13	−6.3	−30.3	107.8	−138.1	63.3
All sectors						
Latin America	24	+2.1	−21.9	34.4	−56.3	42.3
All	64	+8.0	−16.0	50.3	−66.3	32.9

[a]In percentage of enterprise activity, where activity = ½ (revenue + expenditure).
Source: *IMF Staff Papers* (March 1968), pp. 108, 110, 111, 113, 115; new investment in column C is the excess of total investment (given on p. 111) over depreciation (the difference between column A and column B).

The poor performance of railways can be explained by pricing and employment policies. In countries like Argentina, Brazil, and Chile, rail rates were allowed to lag behind the general price level in order to put a brake on price rises and in order to protect the government from the ire of railroad users. Although it was not unknown to governments that the inflation-restraining pricing policies of railroads were usually more than offset by inflation-inducing railroad subsidies, the latter were less immediately noticeable to the public.

Most Latin American railroads also operate under conditions of overemployment. For political and social reasons governments have been reluctant to allow railroads to lay off the large disguisedly unemployed labor force.

Only three sectors were able to cover depreciation needs in Latin America. "Other Industry," which means mainly directly productive industries like steel, coal, and mining, were not able to cover depreciation. However, this latter sample contained no Brazilian or Mexican firms. Some of them earned enough to cover both depreciation and some new investments. For example, a study of Brazilian public enterprises in the period 1956-60 revealed that directly productive industrial enterprises not only were profitable, but their profits grew at twice the rate of the wage bill. Thus, in 1960 the profits of state industries were large enough to exceed the deficit of the state transport sector.[29] It is clear from the evidence available, however, that no sector could finance a substantial portion of its investment needs.

One should not forget, of course, that usually the private sector is eager to take over the more lucrative industries, while it is wary of acquiring the more "lumpy" basic industries and infrastructural enterprises. This was observed especially in those countries where the government (or its development corporation) initiated firms with the hope of transferring them eventually to the private sector. As might be expected, only the more lucrative enterprises were taken over from the government.[30] Thus, many countries find themselves in a situation where the private sector "controls most of the lucrative opportunities in manufacturing, while public enterprise undertakes the 'lumpy' infrastructural investments needed to create a suitable environment for the private sector."[31]

What are the implications of this performance? Could one conclude that since state firms are inefficient and use prejudicial pricing policies

29. Annibal Villela, "As empresas do governo federal e sua importancia na economia nacional—1956/60," *Revista Brasileira de Economia* (Março do 1962).

30. United Nations, *El proceso de industrialización en America Latina*, p. 127. If lucrative public enterprises are easily transferred to the private sector, then Victor Urquidi's suggestion that "there is no reason based on fiscal policy to prevent cross-financing among industrial or other enterprises concerning the [public] sector" is not feasible. "Fiscal Policy in Latin America's Economic Development," p. 17.

31. Whitehead, "Public Sector Activities."

and are thus in constant need of government subsidies, they should be transferred to the private sector? Has their performance hindered economic growth and industrialization?

Many state firms are not allowed to function like private firms because the owner, i.e., the government, considers them as cogs in the overall economic policy machinery of the government. Under what circumstances would it be desirable for the government to have its firms charge prices which result in losses?

First of all, pricing prejudicial to the profit position of a firm might be followed for efficiency reasons. The government could require its firms to price on a marginal cost basis, which could result in a number of firms working below average cost. A host of questions would then arise about the transfer of funds from firms which show a profit because their marginal cost is higher-than-average cost or from other sectors of the economy to the deficit firms.

Second, pricing in a manner prejudicial to achieving a surplus adequate to cover current expenditures, depreciation, and expansion of the firm may be quite consistent with certain broader distributional goals of the government—e.g., providing cheap transportation to the urban masses and to industry, cheap power or steel to the industrial sector, etc. Uneconomic employment policies of railroads in Argentina and Brazil might be consistent with the general efforts of these governments to cope with a redundant urban labor supply.

A third reason for subsidized pricing policies could be the government's desire to create external economies. These can result in the industrial growth stimulated by government rate policies.

If for these reasons government firms have to rely on subsidies to cover current, depreciation, and some expansion costs, an evaluation of the situation can only be made according to some distributional criteria —who benefits from the low prices and who pays for the subsidies? Who benefits from external economies? What proportion of the benefits of low prices of electricity and transport go to the mass of urban workers and what proportion to private firms in terms of lower input prices? Who benefits from lower steel prices?

Such considerations should be confronted with a different point of view which has been most clearly stated by Stolper:[32] "Private business can go broke rapidly, whereas in government-owned enterprises the taxpayer can be drawn upon to make up for losses almost indefinitely. Thus in socialized industries the mechanism is lacking which converts a private loss into a public gain, and if heavy losses occur within a framework of government ownership, the economy gets more and more boxed into a situation in which further growth becomes impossible. The case

32. Wolfgang F. Stolper, *Planning Without Facts* (Cambridge, Mass.: Harvard University Press, 1966), p. 278.

against government ownership would be substantially weakened if socialism were to invent the equivalent to bankruptcy."

Stolper's dilemma could be partially answered in considering who pays for the subsidies. What classes, for instance, will bear the burden of taxes which are used to raise funds for the subsidies? There is a limit to taxing the lower-income groups and there is a limit to taxing the private productive sector. One authority has stated the case most succinctly when considering the functioning of a mixed economy: ". . . public investment and private investment are simultaneously complementary and contradictory. Theoretically, a point may be reached where taxation to finance public enterprises, added to taxation imposed for general revenue purposes, is so high that the incentives for private investment are completely eliminated. In such a situation, the government presumably has the alternative of reducing both taxation and public investment to a point where private incentives become operative again or of going over to a fully socialized economy."[33] The same can be said for fund-raising through taxation in order to subsidize deficitary government enterprises. Of course, subsidies can be paid by running government deficits. This has been a common way of facing the problem in a number of Latin American countries. In the fifties and sixties government budgetary deficits in Argentina, Brazil, and Chile were often caused by the need to subsidize government enterprises (especially railroads) and these deficits in turn were responsible for periods of extremely high rates of inflation. The inflationary route was often taken to avoid making direct or explicit distributional decisions as to who would bear the burden of the subsidies. But even this route has its limits—i.e., there is a limit to the degree of inflation which a country can tolerate. The stabilization programs following high rates of inflation have usually witnessed determined efforts by governments to rationalize (i.e., increase the efficiency) of the operations of government firms and to institute more realistic prices.

The larger the subsidies, the more will a state enterprise become a fiscal instrument of the government. In fact, one could introduce a system of gradations—there are state firms which are allowed to operate like private firms (maximizing internal efficiency and charging prices commensurate with costs and with expansion plans, e.g., the Brazilian Companhia Vale do Rio Doce, and some of the Latin American steel firms), while others have to operate with all sorts of government constraints. The latter, of course, consist in large part of public utilities. However, even directly productive state enterprises have been known to follow policies dictated by outside considerations. For example, in Brazil at times government firms, such as steel, were forced not to raise prices as part of the government's stabilization plans.

33. A. H. Hanson, *Public Enterprise and Economic Development* (London: Routledge and Kegan Paul, Ltd., 1969), p. 190.

CONCLUSIONS

In this review we have shown how, as a cause and by-product of industrialization in the last three to four decades, government enterprises have become an important sector of the Latin American economies. The industrialization ambitions of most governments necessitated the entrance of the government into areas where no domestic private or even foreign enterprises would venture. In some cases nationalist considerations prevented foreign private enterprises from entering certain fields of activities. In still other cases (especially public utilities) government controls prevented private groups from entering or enlarging facilities. The fields which government entered were, however, important complements to other areas in which private enterprise predominated.[34]

The performance of government enterprises has left a lot to be desired when judged by the criteria applied to private firms. Some cannot cover even their current expenditures, while almost all need substantial outside funds for expansion purposes. This is often due to the broader goals of government in running its firms—subsidy prices to the public for various products and services, employment absorption, etc. One thus has to use broader social criteria in evaluating performance. However, I would agree with Díaz-Alejandro that "accepting a variety of goals, however, does not justify every public measure."[35] There has to be a limit to the deficits which a public enterprise can run if a mixed system is to be continued—i.e., there are taxation limits or inflationary limits beyond which such a system would be unable to continue to function adequately.

Acknowledgment.—I wish to thank Andrea Maneschi and William O. Thweatt for many helpful suggestions.

Comment—Donald L. Huddle

BAER'S review paper summarizes some of the major reasons behind the growth in the Latin American public enterprise sector and demonstrates that sector's impact in terms of rising public investments. He discusses

34. A recent article by Frederic L. Pryor provides some interesting insights into the motivations for, the extent and pattern of, public ownership in developed countries. The motivations for nationalization in those countries do not always completely overlap with those which have prevailed in Latin America. Pryor's findings show, however, that "the relatively highest nationalization ratios occur in the utilities and in the transportation and communication sectors, while the relatively lowest ratios appear in the agriculture, forestry and fishing and in the commerce and finance sectors." See "The Extent and Pattern of Public Ownership in Developed Economies," *Weltwirtschaftliches Archiv*, Band 104, Heft 2 (1970), pp. 175-76. With the exception of finance, this pattern is also quite evident in Latin America.

35. Díaz-Alejandro, "The Argentine State and Economic Growth."

performance criteria and concludes, somewhat agnostically, that the life of one who must evaluate public enterprise is not simple due to the wide variety of goals pursued. The question of what weights to attach to such goals is indeed difficult, if not in principle, then certainly in practice.

I cannot hope to resolve these challenging issues here. Much has been done and will have to continue to be done on a case-by-case basis, although varying degrees of similarity will occur for one industry across regions and countries. For instance, utilities, communications, and transportation are believed to involve such economies of scale and large optimum size that public ownership is to be expected so as to neutralize the resulting market power; public ownership can also be anticipated for industries that are said to be vital to rapid progress, e.g., fuel, power, transport, and iron and steel.

To answer definitively the questions posed regarding the impact, goal satisfying, and efficiency of public enterprise in industrialization, better-quality and more comparable, disaggregated data are needed. We would like to have, both in total and per sector, the percentage of assets owned by government over time. But we must proceed more intuitively, as has Baer, with the data at hand.

There can be no disagreement with the finding that public enterprises have played an important and expanding role in the Latin American industrializations since the 1930s. All of the data confirm this, including the growth rates of government and publicly run sectors since 1945, shown in Table 1.

As industrialization has proceeded rapidly, so has public enterprise flourished. On this subject, however, data are open to misinterpretation. One example is in Baer's Table 3, where he shows the government's proportion of total fixed investment for Latin American countries. Without data showing absolute investment levels, such figures can lead to incorrect conclusions; for instance, Brazil's proportion increased from 34.5 percent in 1960-62 to 61.8 percent in 1964-66, a truly astounding increase in the public share, but it does not seem so bizarre when the deep recession and investment slump are recognized. All of the percentages in Baer's Tables 1-3 would be more meaningful if absolute figures or indices were also included.

The hypothesis that deep and heavy industrialization has been strongly associated with more widespread and capital-intensive public enterprise seems reasonable to me. But I do not believe it has been well established. In any case, the sphere of public enterprise has been by no means unlimited. What in the 1930s was originally a concentration on a few large-scale projects to improve infrastructure or to establish basic industry has fanned out into petroleum, iron and steel, and even chemicals, but the great bulk of public activity is still in the more traditional mining, transportation, power, and communications sectors.

TABLE 1

GROWTH RATES OF GOVERNMENT AND PUBLICLY OWNED ENTERPRISES
BY SECTOR (PERCENT PER YEAR)

Sector	1945-60	1960-65
Government	4.0	3.0
Minerals	6.9	4.0
Transport and communications	5.7	8.5
Electricity, gas, and water	—	10.5
Industry	5.9	5.5

SOURCE: Economic Commission for Latin America, *Economic Survey of Latin America* (1965), p. 19, Table 7.

With all this said, I wonder if the fact of being public or private is of such great importance. Granted that, as Stolper states in *Planning Without Facts*, we should invent the equivalent of bankruptcy for the public sector, we may have to reinvent it also for the large-scale private sector. A recent study by ECLA reported (see Table 2) the relationship between large-scale manufacturing in selected Latin American countries and the United States. In all cases, except in Mexico, between 50 percent and 70 percent of total value-added in manufacturing came from as few as 2 percent and no more than 6.5 percent of the total number of factories, whereas in the United States less than 80 percent of total value-added came from almost 15 percent of the factories. Given that the employment shares and installed capacity shares were commensurate with the value-added shares, one wonders about the real difference between state and private enterprise, especially where taxes may finance the operation

TABLE 2

SELECTED LATIN AMERICAN COUNTRIES AND THE UNITED STATES:
SHARE OF LARGE-SCALE INDUSTRY IN MANUFACTURING

	(1) Number of Factories as % of All Factories[a]	(2) % of Total Value-Added in Manufacturing	(3) Ratio of (2) to (1)
Brazil	6.5	68.0	10.5
Central America	4.6	48.7	10.5
Chile	6.3	68.8	10.9
Colombia	6.0	70.6	11.8
Mexico	13.3	76.5	5.8
Paraguay	1.9	48.6	25.6
Venezuela	2.6	59.5	22.9
United States	14.8	79.4	5.4

[a]Factories of 100 or more employees.
SOURCE: Columns 1 and 2, United Nations, *Economic Bulletin for Latin America* 14, no. 2 (1969): 17, Table 8.

and/or investments of a public enterprise and where taxes (or inflationary finance) may also finance the operation and/or investments of private firms via low interest loans, subsidies, protection, state business contracts, etc. The very concept of "efficiency" in such instances is elusive, and I think has been so in Latin American instances. We do need to know the incidence of benefits and costs of government enterprise operation. Baer appropriately asks: who benefits from low prices, who pays the subsidies, and who benefits (or is harmed) by externalities, etc.? However, he stops a bit short. I believe the expenditures-benefits cannot be separated from the taxation-incidence. This is a simultaneous, mutually determinable process, which is most complex to ferret out both in principle and in practice. Work on this problem seems most important.

Let me also stress that the dichotomy thus far has omitted an important characterization, namely that a firm may be private but not national—it may be foreign. The "foreignness" of a firm is of more than passing importance, for not only do foreign firms tend to be large, but they also tend to account for a very sizable proportion of manufacturing growth, in at least the Brazilian case if not others. Estimates by Morley and Smith showed a market share of foreign private business in total manufacturing of 33.5 percent (as compared to only a 6.1 percent share by the Brazilian government).[1] The foreign firms were large, comprising nineteen of twenty-four large firms in transport equipment, seventeen of twenty-two in chemicals, etc.; in fact, industry-wide only thirty-one of the hundred largest firms were controlled by Brazilian private industry, while four were government controlled and sixty-five were foreign.

A glance at summary data for all of Latin America for various resource areas plus steel (Table 3) shows an overall picture not so different from the above pattern. Except in steel production (integrated mills) and petroleum in several countries, the domination is by foreign interests and not either by the state or by local private firms.

Thus, in many instances in resource areas and in manufacturing, the effective choice in large-scale ventures may be between public enterprise and foreign private. A priori, the choice is not necessarily in favor of public enterprise. However, neither should our biases be strongly in favor of foreign enterprise. The policy maker should ask himself which alternative vehicle for industrialization and growth is most socially efficient. In new products in which domestic producers have no production experience, it will be the foreign firm which will respond to government support and protection. But the dependence on foreign investment may have powerful externalities, both economic and noneconomic. Short-run production increases may be more than offset by future economic liabil-

---

1. S. A. Morley and G. W. Smith, "Import Substitution and Foreign Investment in Brazil" (Discussion paper 5, Program of Development Studies, Rice University, Spring 1970).

TABLE 3

PRODUCTION SHARES AMONG STATE, FOREIGN, AND DOMESTIC PRIVATE FIRMS

	Firms	Share of Production(%)		
Iron ore mining	State	27–28		
	Foreign	57–60		
	Private	12–16		
Crude steel production:	State	48–60		
integrated mills	Foreign	8–13		
	Private	27–44		
Lead: mining	Foreign	41–47		
and smelting	Local	56–52		
	State	1–3		
Zinc	Foreign	60–78		
	Local	40–22		
	State	0		
			% Private	
		Production	Refining	Market
Petroleum	Venezuela	99.8	99.8	100
	Peru	95.0	97.7	98
	Mexico—Pemex	—	—	—
	Colombia	79.0	52.0	95
	Chile	—	—	100
	Brazil	—	14.0	100
	Bolivia	4.0	—	—
	Argentina	33.0	43.0	40
Copper	Mostly private (except in Chile)			

SOURCE: Taken from J. Grunwald and P. Musgrove, *Natural Resources in Latin American Development* (Baltimore: Johns Hopkins Press, 1970), pp. 179, 211, 229, 289.

itics, an increase in political instability, capital flight, sensitivity of the economy to international forces, and some of the undesirable effects of the multinational firm.

In other instances, efforts to get the domestic firm going may involve so many undesirable and inefficient incentive devices that public enterprise might be better from the outset. My colleague Charles McLure found this to be so in a tax incentive study of Colombia.[2] And I found even the direct static welfare costs of subsidies and incentives for industrialization in Brazil to be quite high, even in the 1950s.[3]

In conclusion, it may well be true that the growth of public enterprise has been overly constricted in Latin America. At least this hypothesis seems well worth additional study.

2. Charles McLure, "Colombia Tax Incentives," mimeographed (September 1969), p. 16.
3. Donald Huddle, "Measurement of Static Welfare Losses: Horizontal and Vertical Distribution Inequities and Revenues in a Multiple Exchange Rate System" (Discussion paper 6, Program of Development Studies, Rice University, Spring 1970).

Comment—William G. Tyler

IN the economic literature related to public enterprise one can discern two separate approaches. The first is a theoretical approach focusing on the allocational question of efficiency. With the choice and specification of different social-welfare functions economists have concerned themselves with the efficiency aspects of public enterprises, analyzing such issues as externalities, pricing, and investment criteria. Inherently, welfare economists accept the postulate that the government is a social body whose rules and objectives are dependent upon the evaluations of its individual citizens. That a government could be independent of such evaluations or make separate judgments is not generally admitted by welfare economists. Yet sociologists, political scientists, and problem-oriented economists have no misgivings in making this distinction. In addition, the discussion of public enterprises does not relate directly to the allocation of society's output between public and private goods. It relates to the production of those goods—be they public, private, or some mixture of the two. In short, the matter of public enterprise is not primarily an economic issue but an institutional one. What institutional arrangements with respect to commercial enterprises are more beneficial for fulfilling certain objectives?

The second approach to the question of public enterprise has been through the instrument of the case study. By examining the experience of different countries, industries, and specific firms, insight is gained into the performance of government-owned firms. Baer's paper is one of the first attempts to undertake a comparative analysis, based upon the different case studies done regarding Latin America. As more case studies become available, we should be able to expect more contributions along comparative lines.

As Baer's study clearly points out, it is yet difficult to generalize about the experience and performance of public enterprise in Latin America. Baer notes the divergence of goals which hinders attempts at comparative analysis. The use of the economist's allocative efficiency yardstick is questionable when goals of public firms differ. It may be that a firm is effective in obtaining its objective, but that objective may itself be irrational from the viewpoint of allocative efficiency.[1] A degree of interdependency between the decisions of the public firm and the organization of the government renders it impossible to separate completely economic and political analysis. Thus it would seem that market concepts are insufficient to fully analyze governmental behavior. In the future economists may increasingly find organization theory useful in

1. A treatment of this question is undertaken in William G. Tyler, "Some Indicators of Governmental Sector Efficiency in a Less Developed Country: The Brazilian Case," *Revista de Administração Pública* (November 1970).

such analysis. While most economic studies abstract from political and administrative factors, Baer has appeared conscious of this problem and has avoided doing so. At the same time, however, one finds it impossible to agree with some aspects of Baer's political interpretation. For example, he states that ideological considerations have *not* been important in the growth of public enterprises in Latin America. Yet he goes on to assert that nationalism has been a major reason for the growth of such enterprises. This second claim is acceptable, if not patently obvious. But is he to have us believe that nationalism has no ideological content? I personally find it impossible to accept the notion that nationalism and the establishment of public enterprises in Latin America are not somehow ideologically motivated.

TABLE 1

Firm	Type of Goods	Government Organization	Reasons for Formation	Market Organization
Firm A	Public	Centralized (political constraints)	Political	Monopolistic supplier
	Mixed (externalities)			
	Private	Decentralized (absence of significant political and administrative constraints)	Economic	Other suppliers

Another difficulty in generalizing about the behavior of government firms can be seen in their disparate nature and differential circumstances. In addition to a definitional problem as to what exactly constitutes a public enterprise, public firms engage in a wide variety of activities ranging from the provision of purely public goods to the production of purely private goods. To generalize from the experiences of firms engaged in such different activities can be both perilous and misleading. Before meaningful hypotheses can be formulated and tested, it would seem that some sort of typology of public enterprise is needed. This typology should consider such characteristics as the type of goods, the nature of the governmental organization including political and administrative constraints, the reason for the existence of the firm, and the characteristics of the market. A rudimentary such typology might appear with classifications as depicted in Table 1. With the use of a typology such as this, hypotheses could be formulated and tested with cross-sectional data according to firms.[2] I would think that a more concrete methodology would provide greater insights into the behavior and performance of public firms than off-the-cuff generalizing.

In his examination of reasons for subsidization of a public enterprise, i.e., the arguments of marginal cost pricing and externalities, Baer briefly treats the allocative issue. In my view this is a matter of some importance in the discussion of the public firm in less-developed countries, bringing to mind a number of relevant and unanswered questions. In light of the numerous recent developments in the theory of public pricing policy,[3] how do the public firms in Latin America price their output? What are the welfare costs of their pricing behavior? Are there significant differences between public and private firms in pricing? How do public and private enterprises differ in the economizing and use of scarce entrepreneurial talent? How do production functions differ? How does investment behavior differ? To what extent can the operating deficits of many public firms in Latin America be justified by the existence of real and unimagined externalities? Should public enterprises follow social marginal criteria even if this means significant deficits or the lack of competitiveness with private firms in the industry? There is much work still to be done by economists in developing operational rules for pricing and investment behavior and in undertaking empirical study to evaluate the performance of public firms in less-developed countries.

When referring to private enterprise performance criteria, it is important to remember that efficiency in the use of the factors of production and profitability is not the same. Even using the market valuations of factors, this similarity does not necessarily follow. Either public or private firms may have access to certain advantages denied to others that may affect their profitability, even though efficiency in factor use is unaffected. For example, in a recent study Roberts evaluates the performance of public and private development banks in less-developed countries and discovers significant differences in profitability and factor use efficiency.[4] He finds that, while private development banks tend to be more profitable than public development banks, the latter exhibit a tendency

2. For example, profitability or factor-use efficiency in public firms could be correlated with the characteristics in the typology of Table 1. Using dummy variables with increasing numerical value for traits in each of the four categories of characteristics, a positive coefficient would be hypothesized for all four when correlated with either profitability or efficiency. For example, in category 1 dealing with the type of goods, it would be hypothesized that profitability for firms would increase as the goods and services produced become increasingly private in character.

3. See, for example, M. H. Peston, "Aspects of the Pricing Policy of the Nationalised Industries," in Julius Margolis and Henri Guitton, eds., *Public Economics: An Analysis of Public Production and Consumption and Their Relations to the Private Sectors* (New York: St. Martin's Press, 1969).

4. Paul E. Roberts, Jr., "Development Banking: The Issue of Public and Private Development Banking," *Economic Development and Cultural Change* (April 1971).

towards greater factor use efficiency. The reason for the difference in profitability is attributed to the ability of the private development banks to avail themselves to a far greater degree of relatively cheap financing in foreign exchange afforded by such lending agencies as the World Bank Group and AID.

Although Baer provides a contribution in his treatment of the distributional aspects of public enterprise operations, a number of important questions regarding the growth aspects related with such firms remain unanswered. What is the relationship between the formation and growth of government enterprises and the growth of the economy? Under what circumstances does the formation of such firms facilitate or hinder growth? What insights into this relationship are offered by the Latin American experience?[5] Baer cannot properly be criticized for not having resolved these questions, because in great part the answers to these and related questions necessitate greater information about individual experiences than is currently available. While it appears that the public firms in Latin America have been unsuccessful in contributing to savings, they can exert a positive influence on growth in other ways, such as providing for growth sequences, bringing about attitudinal change (à la Hirschman's hiding hand), and facilitating the growth of the entrepreneurship.

Another dimension of the growth aspect of the government firm's role is primarily a political one. In the absence of a dynamic and economically oriented entrepreneurial elite, a government intent on bringing about development may be confronted with the choice of forming public firms or allowing the establishment of dominant foreign firms. Intuitively, the preference would seem to be with the former. In addition, the estab-

5. In a rudimentary attempt to shed some light on such questions, I regressed average annual GDP growth rates on the government percentage of ownership among the largest enterprises. A cross-section of six major Latin American countries was selected, based upon data availability. With average growth rates as the dependent variable, the following regression equations were estimated for the percentage of public ownership among the largest twenty and thirty enterprises, respectively.

(1) $Y = .0494 + .0666X$
$\quad\quad\quad\quad (.0646)$
$R = .46$
$R^2 = .20$
(2) $Y = .2996 + .0686X$
$\quad\quad\quad\quad (.0681)$
$R = .45$
$R^2 = .21$

In both equations X is only significant at about the 35 percent level. Nevertheless, the positive correlation coefficient suggests a moderate degree of positive association between a country's growth performance and the importance of its public enterprise. If growth of public firms were substituted for the importance of such firms, I imagine that the level of association would be greater still.

Data were obtained from various UN publications and Frank Brandenburg, *The Development of Latin American Enterprise* (Washington, D.C.: National Planning Association, 1964), pp. 54-66. Growth rates covered the 1950-63 period and public ownership data were for 1963.

lishment and growth of public firms may facilitate the development of a national industrial elite. Historically, in the presently developed countries a transfer of political power has always been made from an agriculture-oriented, traditional elite to an emergent industrial elite. In Latin America this process has been stymied (with attendant political chaos, military dictatorships, and the like), in part because the emerging industrial elite is foreign and politically nonparticipatory (at least in the traditional sense). This situation has resulted in a political vacuum. On the other hand, the formation of public firms could prompt the development of a national industrial elite—an occurrence which seems to be taking place in Latin America.

Discussion

A. CHURCHILL: I would like to take issue with a point raised concerning the amount of knowledge available on public enterprises. The World Bank at the moment spends, or is committing, something over $2 billion a year, mostly for public enterprises. At the moment the bank is producing many reports every year concerning public enterprises. Most of these unfortunately are not available to the public. We have tried summarizing some of the data, however, to determine how important these institutions are and how they affect rates of growth. For example, if one takes a worldwide sample of all underdeveloped countries and correlates both cross-section and time-series data—say, on the size of the public sector relative to the rate of growth—one gets significant correlations. Unfortunately, they are negative. Similarly, if one uses rates of growth over time in individual countries, in only one country in Latin America—Colombia—has there been a positive correlation between the rate of overall growth and the rate of growth of public enterprises. Others are all significant but negative. These results are discouraging, and I am not quite sure how one should interpret them.

R. THORN: Regarding the question of the efficiency of state firms, I think we could say that as a generalization for the major portion of public enterprises, inefficiency is due to their being operated for other than purely economic ends; they are operated to achieve many social ends. In all the countries without exception, there is a social pressure that must be relieved, and it often turns out that the state enterprises provide the path of least resistance. I do not think one will find the answers to questions about the efficiency of state enterprises within the state enterprises themselves. It is part and parcel of the problem of overall growth in the country. When one can discharge workers and know that they will be absorbed in some other sector, it is quite a different decision than when one knows that they are going to remain unemployed and on the streets to agitate or worse. I do not, however, want to underemphasize efficiency; it is obvious that state enterprise inefficiencies create problems for economic growth.

Concerning the question of information about state enterprises, I find that having access to some of the reports which are in restricted files is not always illuminating. In my own experience, I have had the privilege of looking at not only official restricted reports, but even operating reports within the government trying to show what is going on; often it is simply not possible to understand what is going on. There are two things to be mentioned in this connection. The first is that the governmental organization, whether a state enterprise or autonomous, often issues poor information. The average level of accounting of the state enterprises often is not in accord with or up to the general accounting standards of the governments within which they operate, at least in their published accounts. The second point is although the operating people may have better information, I am not at all sure that this information is made available to the political decision makers. If the political decision makers possessed better information about the state enterprises, in many instances their decisions might be altered by the evidence.

There are many relationships between the state enterprises and the government that require a tremendous amount of analysis, in addition to the pricing problem. In talking about efficiency I would distinguish between accounting efficiency—what the enterprises publish as their net loss or gain—and allocative efficiency—what their drain on the resources of the country really is. The latter is what Baer and the rest of us are interested in, but we are very far from really knowing these answers even for those state enterprises with the best published accounting information.

H. HINRICHS: I want to support Thorn's observation by pointing out that it is a gross error to assume for public enterprises the profit maximization motive of private enterprises. If one took a systems analysis approach to the public sector and the whole country, one would doubtlessly find that the objective function includes employment, social stability, and certain externalities through infrastructure development which do not exist in a pure neoclassical model. In Argentina, for example, over a fifteen-year period in which employment on the railways increased by 50 percent, traffic fell by 25 percent—the point being that there are two different phenomena here, and one must look at more sophisticated objective functions in analyzing public enterprises in Latin America.

D. MAHAR: Another question that enters here, with which I have had problems in my research, is how to define the public sector. In Baer's paper, for example, I see evidence of this problem in Tables 3b and 3c. In 3b, he has "public sector" and then "publicly owned firms," and in the next table "investment of wholly or partially owned government firms."

Where do we put this type of firm? In the Brazilian national accounts, for example, government enterprises are included in the private sector; and in calculating our usual government expenditure to GDP ratios, using these figures, we probably underestimate the role of government in Brazil. But if we add the "mixed corporations," as they are called in Brazil, and derive these ratios, we overstate the relative role of the public sector. One should decide what is meant by the public sector, instead of arbitrarily counting government corporations as either part of the public sector or not, which is particularly confusing when trying to do comparative work and using data from different sources.

N. KALDOR: Concerning public enterprises, the absence of native private enterprises in Latin America seems to me the most interesting problem to investigate, whether it is for economic or sociological reasons. No country has succeeded in developing and industrializing, with the possible exception of Canada, when its development was largely based on foreign-owned or foreign-controlled enterprise. If one looks at some of the most successful late industrializers, like Japan, foreign enterprise played no role whatever for the simple reason that it was never allowed to establish itself, nor was it in the case of Sweden. One ought to learn, by looking at those countries that have succeeded in the development process, why other countries fail. I am convinced Latin America will never develop so long as it is largely based on foreign-owned firms as it is today, a condition which is by the way almost peculiar to Latin America. In other countries that have been successful lately, like the smaller countries in Asia, foreign enterprise plays a much less important role in industrialization than it does in Latin America.

The distinction between public and private enterprises may be considerably overdone. At the critical stages of Japanese industrialization, enterprises were formally private but they were organized, controlled, and directed by the government in their investment policy; they were run by managers who were ex–civil servants, which is even true today of the six largest corporations in Japan. The trouble in Latin America is the lack of native managerial and entrepreneurial talent, which is bound to make for inefficiency whether it is in native private enterprise or native public enterprise.

9

Industrial Structure, Industrial Exporting, and Economic Policy

An Analysis of Recent Argentine Experience

David Felix

TAX rebates, export credit arrangements, and regional tariff preferences to promote industrial exports are very much in vogue in Latin America. The appearance of these stimuli during the 1960s has been paralleled by a noteworthy expansion, albeit from a small initial base, of the range and volume of industrial exports, mainly from Argentina, Brazil, and Mexico, the largest and most industrialized of the Latin American countries. For the "Big Three," industrial exporting has become a modest alleviant for industrial excess capacity and foreign exchange shortage, but whether it will also develop in time into an important curative for many of the industrial problems that overaddiction to import substitution has engendered is still problematical. Such a development depends not merely on the effectiveness of the promotional stimuli, but also on the ability of the respective countries to supplement them effectively with measures to rationalize their overprotected and high-cost industries, and that is as much a question of flexibility of political power relationships as of technical efficacy of the measures.

Faith that where there's a way there's a will does permeate much of the postwar development literature, although the basis for the optimism is not always clear. Thus "two-gap" theorists expect a "rising propensity to export," induced somehow by rising per capita income, to eliminate in time the dominance of the foreign exchange gap over the saving-investment gap.[1] Their key assumption is that rising per capita income will tend to be accompanied not only by improvements in the supply of productive inputs, but also by policies appropriate for utilizing effectively the greater productive potential. In the same vein but with somewhat greater specifics, Linder sees industrial exporting as the second half of a two-stage process. Via import substitution and rising per capita income the less-developed country must first approximate the "representative

1. Ronald McKinnon, "Foreign Exchange Constraints in Economic Development and Efficient Aid Allocation," *Economic Journal* 74 (June 1964).

demand" and industrial structure of advanced economies, generating thereby the requisite productive skills, marketing experience, and other externalities for moving into industrial exporting.[2] The unstated assumption is that the market structure, price behavior, and political relations generated by import substitution will not be enduring obstacles to the sustained growth of industrial exports.

This study examines this assumption for one of the Big Three, Argentina. A decent respect for the complexities of each country's socio-economic structure and politics precludes, therefore, extending the findings herein to other Latin American countries, particularly since development taxonomists cannot even agree whether Argentina is a genuine Latin American less-developed country or merely a backsliding developed country. Still, Argentina's industrial growth since the early thirties has, *estilo latinoamericano*, occurred almost entirely under the aegis of import-substitution industrialization policies. Its industrial value-added to GNP ratio, around one-third, is currently the highest in Latin America. Since World War II Argentina has been troubled, more severely than other industrializing Latin American countries, by two- to four-year business cycles reflecting recurring balance-of-payments deficits that, in turn, have been accentuated by the inability of import substitution to reduce the postwar import/GNP ratio. And like the others, it turned in the 1960s to industrial-export promotion as one means of easing the foreign exchange bind, vying in the course of the decade with Brazil for the lead in Latin American industrial exporting to LAFTA (Latin American Free Trade Association) and the rest of the world.[3] Thus, perhaps some of the findings herein have broader Latin American significance.

The first part of this study assesses the relative contribution of tax subsidies, LAFTA concessions, and excess capacity to the recent expansion of Argentine industrial exports. Because the period of observation is short the regression model used is unavoidably crude, but the finding— that tax subsidies apparently contributed relatively little to the expansion of industrial exports as compared to LAFTA and excess capacity—may be of interest since the second part of the paper buttresses the plausibility of the finding by indicating various perverse factor-intensity biases in the industrial export mix. The third part then links these biases to characteristics of Argentina's industrial market structure and price behavior, while the fourth part suggests that stalemated sectoral conflicts over policy continue to block the rationalization of the industrial sector

2. Staffan B. Linder, *Trade and Trade Policy for Development* (New York: Frederick A. Praeger, 1967).

3. See the industrial trade statistics through 1967 compiled by the Instituto para la Integración de America Latina, in *Argentina: Exportación de Manufacturas a America Latina* (Buenos Aires: Banco Interamericano de Desarrollo, 1969), and an equivalently titled study for Brazil, same source and date.

needed to establish a more effective stance for sustained industrial exporting.

NONTRADITIONAL INDUSTRIAL EXPORTING IN ARGENTINA

Industrial exporting is not a new experience for Argentina. Indeed, as Table 1 shows, its highest importance in the Argentine export mix was reached in World War II when manufactures averaged 13.6 percent of all exports.[4] The proportion fell off rapidly with the postwar return of U.S. and European competition, despite bilateral trade agreements with neighboring Latin American countries and preferential export exchange rates in the Perón era. After the fall of Perón, bilateral trade agreements were progressively liquidated and in 1959 preferential export rates were

TABLE 1

ARGENTINE EXPORTS, 1938-69

Years	Total Annual Average Exports (Millions of Dollars)	Percentages of Total					
		Livestock Products	Crop Products	Forestry Products	Minerals	Fish and Game	Diverse Manufactures
1938-40	436.8	46.1	46.1	2.8	1.3	0.4	3.3
1941-45	577.3	56.6	25.0	2.4	1.6	0.8	13.6
1946-50	1,324.3	43.1	49.4	2.5	0.2	0.3	4.5
1951-55	987.5	50.5	40.6	5.2	0.4	0.1	3.2
1956-60	1,000.1	50.6	44.0	1.7	0.6	0.3	2.8
1961-65	1,277.2	45.6	46.2	1.1	1.2	0.4	5.5
1966-69	1,509.3	43.8	44.1	1.1	1.2	0.5	9.3

SOURCE: Dirección Nacional de Estadística y Censos (DNEC), *Anuario de Comercio Exterior,* various issues.

terminated. Concurrently, industrial exporting reached its nadir—less than 3 percent of all exports—in 1956-60.

By 1961, however, stagnating primary exports and a rapidly mounting foreign debt service revived governmental interest in industrial export promotion. Duty drawbacks on industrial exports went into effect in 1961. Negotiations to reestablish Latin American trade preferences burgeoned into the formation of the Latin American Free Trade Association, which inaugurated operations in 1962. In 1963 export tax subsidies were further augmented by rebates (*reintegros*) for domestic taxes

---

4. Diverse manufactures in Table 1 include some processed primary products, e.g., sugar, but excluded flour, vegetable oils, corned beef, and similar mildly processed crop and livestock products.

on inputs incorporated in "nontraditional" industrial exports. Still other government promotional measures of the 1960s were intended to reduce risk and enlarge market information. These include export insurance, medium-term financing for durable goods exports, permanent exhibit centers abroad, credits to Argentine firms for displays at international fairs, the creation of a consular market information service, etc.

The measures were accompanied, as Table 1 shows, by a fairly substantial rise of industrial exports. Complicating the causal linkage, however, is the effect of rather severe industrial excess capacity in the 1960s, reflecting overoptimistic expansion of some industries during the 1960-61 investment boom and a greater frequency of depressed home demand during the 1960s for most of the industrial sector. Some of the industrial exports, according to trade gossip, were sold below full cost, and excess capacity was widely believed to have been an important motive for the increased industrial exporting. For example, a late 1963 survey of leading trade associations (to identify industrial products with the best chances for exporting to LAFTA) came up with a list selected mainly from the technologically sophisticated end of the Argentine industrial spectrum where excess capacity was particularly pronounced.[5] The four main reasons given by the respondents for their choices were, moreover, in order of frequency: current excess capacity, minimum production in other LAFTA countries, future excess capacity, and progressive management. Despite prodding by the interviewers, few mentioned cost competitiveness—an astute omission, since most of the product classes selected had above average Argentine/U.S. price ratios.[6]

To sort out the influence of LAFTA, tax subsidies, and excess capacity, groupings of nontraditional industrial exports were regressed on the "real" exchange rate including export tax subsidies, capacity utilization in the exporting industry, and the number of LAFTA tariff concessions applicable each year to the export class. The time series, except of course for LAFTA concessions, cover 1955 to 1968.[7]

Nontraditional industrial exports are those receiving both duty drawbacks and *reintegros*. For some of the regressions, these exports are subdivided into Type I and Type II—the former receiving, in addition to drawbacks, *reintegros* equal to 12 percent, and the latter to 18 percent of their respective FOB values. The 18 percent products, according to

5. For example, tractors, motor vehicles, electric and nonelectric machinery, organic chemicals, railroad equipment, rubber products. See José M. Dagnino Pastore, *Productos Exportables: Resultados de Encuestas* (Buenos Aires: Instituto Torcuato Di Tella, 1964).

6. For Argentine/U.S. price ratios by industry, see David Felix, "The Dilemma of Import Substitution—Argentina," in Gustav F. Papanek, ed., *Development Policy: Theory and Practice* (Cambridge, Mass.: Harvard University Press, 1968), p. 85, Tables 3.6 and 3.7.

7. Space constraints prevent the inclusion here of a detailed description of the

official pronouncements, incorporate more value-added per unit in the manufacturing stages than do the 12 percent products. Apart from some deviations made for political or other reasons (described in Appendix A) the Type I-II separation seems, on inspection, to conform to the value-added difference. Regressions were also performed on data subdivided by destination—to LAFTA, and to the rest of the world. In addition, Appendix A lists exports to bordering countries, a subdivision of LAFTA separately delineated to indicate the "neighborhood store" nature of much of Argentine industrial exports prior to establishment of LAFTA. All the export series are deflated to 1960 dollar prices.

Analytically, the distinction between "nontraditional" and "traditional" industrial products is less arbitrary for Argentina than for advanced industrial economies. The Argentine industrial sector divides readily into a small group of long-established industries processing agricultural and forestry products for domestic and foreign markets, and a wide array of industries whose sales have been almost exclusively domestic. In 1963 the first group, while supplying only 11 percent of all industrial value-added and about 7 percent of industrial employment, produced over half the nation's exports.[8] The remaining industries, by contrast, supplied less than 5 percent of all exports, although the percentage doubled by the end of the sixties. Moreover, the value-added to gross output ratio of the small exporting group of industries averaged 32 percent as compared to 54 percent for the larger, domestically oriented group. Finally, the two groups diverge as regards the sources of excess capacity. Because of superior export competitiveness, excess capacity in the first group has been mainly governed by fluctuations in the supply of raw material inputs, whereas for the second group excess capacity has been mainly determined by fluctuations in domestic demand. The official designation of most exports of the first group as agricultural, livestock, or forest products rather than industrial products thus has a plausible basis.[9]

Turning to the explanatory variables, the tax rebates (drawbacks and *reintegros*) are treated as upward adjustments of the "real" exchange rate. The adjusted "real" exchange rate is thus the peso/dollar rate multi-

---

data sources and data massaging techniques (Appendix A) and the various data series (Appendix B). These are available directly from the author. Included here is a brief general explanation of the data inputs.

8. The group consists of the following five-digit ISIC industries:

Meat packing	(20101, 20104)	Wool washing	(23102)
Dairy products	(20201)	Preparation of vegetable fibers other than	
Flour milling	(20502)	cotton	(23103)
Sugar refining	(20701)	Salting and depilating hides	(29101)
Oilseed refining	(20911)	Quebracho extracting	(31106)
Cotton ginning	(23101)	Fat rendering and bone milling	(31201)

Value-added and employment data are from the 1963 Census of Manufactures.

plied by the ratio of the relevant components of the U.S./Argentine wholesale price indices, multiplied again by one plus the percentage value of the tax rebates. Excess capacity is measured by capacity utilization indices derived from annual estimates for the 1960s by the Argentine National Development Council and extended back to 1955 by the author's use of deviations from 1954-61 output trends. The LAFTA variable is simply the annual number of LAFTA concessions outstanding for the relevant Argentine industrial product class.

Finally, lags must be considered. A lagged relationship between exports recorded at shipment time and the explanatory variables is likely, since exporters can have reasonably good knowledge only of current and past values of these variables at the time export contracts are being sought. One-year lagging of the independent variables, in fact, gave much better fits and fewer "wrong" signs than did unlagged regressions. One-year lagging probably conceals some misspecification, since the true lags must surely differ with respect to each of the various parameters. But with four variables and only fourteen observations per variable, extensive experimenting with alternative lag structures was not possible.

Table 2 presents the results of lagged regressions performed on log transforms of more aggregated groupings of the data, so that the coefficients of the independent variables are elasticities.[10] The high statistical significance of the LAFTA elasticities is to be expected. Also unsurprising is the low value of these elasticities, since the concessions are not weighted by relative size and since many concessions have had little effect on trade flows—LAFTA negotiators having a penchant for granting concessions on imports that do not compete directly with domestic products.

More interesting is the unimportance of the "real" exchange rate embodying tax subsidies for nontraditional exports. With two exceptions the elasticities have the "right" sign, but their values are low and statistically insignificant at even the 10 percent level. Capacity utilization fares better. Eight of the nine elasticities are negative, six of these are also statistically significant at the 10 percent level or better, and most of the negative elasticities have values well above unity.

The industry regressions of Table 3 show a similar pattern.[11] LAFTA elasticities are low but significant except for paper products exports to

9. As, for example, in Table 1.

10. The log regressions usually gave slightly better fits than did those run on the original data, possibly because the influence of extreme deviations was dampened. Log transforms, of course, yield constant elasticities, but in all cases the values are fairly close to the elasticities calculated at the mean of the corresponding regressions on the untransformed data. The log regressions are really hybrids, since the LAFTA variable, which has zero value before 1962, could not be transformed into logs. LAFTA elasticities in Table 2 were calculated, therefore, by multiplying the LAFTA coefficients by the arithmetic mean of the LAFTA series.

LAFTA. The exchange rate including tax subsidies again appears relatively unimportant in most cases; nineteen of the twenty-eight elasticities have positive signs, but only nine of the nineteen are significant at the 10 percent level or better along with three of the negative elasticities. Capacity utilization again shows up as somewhat more important; twenty of its elasticities are negative and fourteen of them are significant at the 10 percent level or better, but six others with the "wrong" sign also meet the significance test.

The importance of the exchange rate falls further and that of excess capacity rises, however, if the seven regressions with annual export flows in 1959-68 of under $500,000 are excluded (see last column of Table 3). In the twenty-one regressions that remain, only fourteen of the exchange rate elasticities are positive, of which only five are also statistically significant, whereas seventeen of the capacity utilization elasticities have the "right" sign (−), thirteen being statistically significant.[12]

The regressions thus suggest the following generalizations about Argentina's nontraditional industrial exporting: (a) exports to non-LAFTA countries during the 1960s have been more responsive to excess capacity pressures than to price/cost changes resulting from exchange rate fluctuations and tax subsidies, and (b) exports to LAFTA during the same period have been largely unresponsive to either stimulus, but have been motivated mainly by LAFTA tariff concessions. To be sure, LAFTA tariff concessions affect price/cost ratios, but they also operate to reduce risk, since they give access to a regional market protected by high third-country tariffs against full competition from advanced country suppliers, and since intra-LAFTA competition has been restrained by the tendency of member countries to concentrate their concessions on noncompetitive imports.

Generalizing from the regressions is, to be sure, risky, since their short time span precluded efforts to purge them of possible misspecifications and multicollinearities. The generalizations, however, merit a modest bet, for they tend to be supported by factor-intensity analysis, also crude, of the exporting industries.

11. Table 3 records only the twenty-eight that were significant at the 5 percent level or better out of a total of thirty-six industry regressions. The latter total excludes wood products, for which data were available only for 1958-68. Exports of wood products for the available years are included, however, in the data used for the Table 2 regressions.

12. Of the three statistically significant excess capacity elasticities with (+) signs remaining in the twenty-one, two are for Food and Beverages, for which a (+) may not be analytically perverse, since the capacity utilization of at least some of the Food and Beverages activities fluctuates positively with the supply of raw material inputs rather than with home demand. This has been true, for example, for cheese products, a Type I nontraditional export. See Fundación de Investigaciones Económicas Latinoamericanas, *La Industria del Queso en la Argentina* (Buenos Aires, 1966).

TABLE 2

Log Regressions of Nontraditional Industrial Exports, 1956-68, on "Real" Exchange Rates, Capacity Utilization Rates, and Number of LAFTA Concessions[a]

Category and Destination	Constant	Real Exchange Rate (Lagged 1 Year)	Capacity Utilization Index (Lagged 1 Year)	LAFTA Concessions (Lagged 1 Year)	R^2	F-Ratio
All nontraditional industrial exports						
To all areas	6.084	0.271 (0.686)	−1.865[d] (−1.665)	0.481[b] (5.281)	0.910	30.48[b]
To LAFTA countries	5.152	0.312 (0.667)	−1.912[d] (−1.445)	0.613[b] (5.687)	0.916	32.62[b]
To rest of world	12.630	0.079 (0.124)	−5.184[b] (−4.075)	—	0.639	8.85[b]
Type I						
To all areas	2.936	0.065 (0.213)	−0.225 (−0.223)	0.426[b] (7.779)	0.906	28.83[b]
To LAFTA countries	1.222	−0.193 (−0.399)	0.283 (0.176)	0.664[b] (7.599)	0.901	27.28[b]

TABLE 2—Continued

Category and Destination	Constant	Real Exchange Rate (Lagged 1 Year)	Capacity Utilization Index (Lagged 1 Year)	LAFTA Concessions (Lagged 1 Year)	R^2	F-Ratio
To rest of world	8.339	0.072 (0.129)	-3.212[c] (-1.941)	—	0.318	3.32
Type II To all areas	4.561	0.821 (1.120)	-2.275[c] (-1.734)	0.675[b] (3.864)	0.880	21.96[b]
To LATFA countries	3.252	0.721 (1.007)	-1.675 (-1.232)	0.657[b] (3.853)	0.864	19.05[b]
To rest of world	16.856	-0.131 (-0.098)	-7.883[b] (-4.557)	—	0.828	10.384[b]

[a]Numbers in parentheses are t-values.
[b]Indicates is significant at the 1% confidence level (one-tail t-test).
[c]Indicates is significant at the 5% confidence level (one-tail t-test).
[d]Indicates is significant at the 10% confidence level (one-tail t-test).

TABLE 3

Log Regressions by Industry of Nontraditional Industrial Exports, 1956-68, on "Real" Exchange Rates, Capacity Utilization Rates, and Number of LAFTA Concessions[a]

Industry and Destination	Constant	Real Exchange Rate (Lagged 1 Year)	Capacity Utilization Index (Lagged 1 Year)	LAFTA Concession (Lagged 1 Year)	R^2	F-Ratio	Average Annual Value of Exports 1959-68 ($1,000 at 1960 Prices)
Food and beverages							
To all areas	0.360	−0.319 (0.781)	1.589[d] (1.733)	0.141[b] (3.397)	0.628	5.07[c]	12,885
To LAFTA	−4.028	−1.526[c] (1.965)	4.686[c] (2.690)	0.388[b] (3.925)	0.746	8.79[b]	3,130
Textile products							
To all areas	4.117	0.080 (0.059)	−2.242 (−0.702)	0.655[d] (1.746)	0.611	4.72[c]	2,328
To rest of world		−1.706 (−0.939)	−9.920[b] (−3.087)	—	0.501	5.01[c]	1,049
Chemical products							
To all areas	2.595	0.401[d] (1.677)	−1.064[d] (−1.560)	0.495[b] (7.437)	0.947	53.14[b]	7,818
To LAFTA	2.495	0.451 (0.987)	−1.468 (−1.126)	0.543[b] (4.267)	0.863	18.84[b]	3,999
To rest of world	8.806	0.351 (0.666)	−4.189[b] (−4.690)	—	0.624	8.29[b]	3,819

TABLE 3—Continued

Industry and Destination	Constant	Real Exchange Rate (Lagged 1 Year)	Capacity Utilization Index (Lagged 1 Year)	LAFTA Concession (Lagged 1 Year)	R^2	F-Ratio	Average Annual Value of Exports 1959-68 ($1,000 at 1960 Prices)
Rubber products							
To all areas	−20.283	3.977[c] (2.785)	4.180[d] (1.633)	1.318[b] (5.142)	0.748	8.92[b]	630
To LAFTA	−6.864	−0.526 (−0.324)	2.233 (0.937)	1.127[b] (4.475)	0.757	9.35[b]	229
Stone, glass, ceramics							
To all areas	−12.491	1.040[c] (2.098)	4.348[b] (3.261)	0.461[b] (5.413)	0.800	12.03[b]	370
To LAFTA	−14.434	0.887[d] (1.633)	5.478[b] (3.752)	0.447[b] (4.758)	0.780	10.651[b]	342
Printing and publishing							
To all areas	5.165	0.825 (1.051)	−4.006[d] (−1.776)	1.127[b] (7.768)	0.933	41.68[b]	4,675
To LAFTA	3.174	1.016[d] (1.486)	−3.298[d] (−1.679)	1.212[b] (8.529)	0.942	48.30[b]	3,118
To rest of world	39.053	−1.542 (0.567)	−19.286[b] (−3.038)	—	0.486	4.73[c]	1,557

TABLE 3—*Continued*

Industry and Destination	Constant	Real Exchange Rate (Lagged 1 Year)	Capacity Utilization Index (Lagged 1 Year)	LAFTA Concession (Lagged 1 Year)	R^2	F-Ratio	Average Annual Value of Exports 1959-68 ($1,000 at 1960 Prices)
Leather products							
To all areas	−0.498	0.602 (1.089)	−0.747 (−0.432)	0.339[c] (1.857)	0.631	5.126[c]	758
To LAFTA	−39.192	1.386 (1.065)	14.741[b] (3.625)	1.414[b] (3.294)	0.627	5.04[c]	89
To rest of world	7.800	0.223 (0.372)	−4.250[b] (−3.883)	—	0.602	7.55[b]	669
Paper products							
To all areas	−9.770	5.121[b] (4.140)	−1.909 (−1.101)	0.843[b] (4.111)	0.798	11.88[b]	303
To LAFTA	−10.775	5.237[b] (4.058)	−1.541 (−0.252)	0.815 (0.786)	0.777	10.48[b]	258
Metal products							
To all areas	7.069	−0.080 (−0.084)	−3.608[c] (−2.263)	0.545[b] (3.447)	0.761	9.538[b]	8,233
To LAFTA	4.980	−0.244 (0.291)	−2.330[c] (−1.845)	0.645[b] (3.243)	0.707	7.226[b]	4,558
To rest of world	35.500	−8.742[c] (−2.417)	−9.634[c] (−2.756)	—	0.676	9.41[b]	3,675

TABLE 3—Continued

Industry and Destination	Constant	Real Exchange Rate (Lagged 1 Year)	Capacity Utilization Index (Lagged 1 Year)	LAFTA Concession (Lagged 1 Year)	R^2	F-Ratio	Average Annual Value of Exports 1959-68 ($1,000 at 1960 Prices)
Vehicles and nonelectric machinery							
To all areas	4.213	0.529 (0.820)	−2.510[d] (−1.707)	0.765[b] (3.005)	0.900	27.13[b]	8,406
To LAFTA	3.584	0.513 (0.860)	−2.249[d] (−1.655)	0.695[b] (2.956)	0.897	26.06[b]	5,855
To rest of world	15.899	0.472 (0.378)	−9.040[b] (−5.927)	—	0.792	19.04[b]	2,552
Electrical machinery apparatus							
To all areas	−5.223	2.021[b] (5.767)	0.661 (0.862)	0.458[b] (3.897)	0.876	21.28[b]	2,141
To LAFTA	−1.275	1.165[c] (2.628)	−0.723 (−0.746)	0.447[b] (3.013)	0.802	12.159[b]	1,711
Clothing							
To rest of world	19.781	−3.149[d] (−1.621)	−8.356[b] (−4.005)	—	0.681	8.028[b]	31

[a] Numbers in parentheses are t-values.
[b] Indicates significant at the 1% confidence level (one-tail t-test).
[c] Indicates significant at the 5% confidence level (one-tail t-test).
[d] Indicates significant at the 10% confidence level (one-tail t-test).

FACTOR-INTENSITY CHARACTERISTICS OF ARGENTINE NONTRADITIONAL
EXPORTS

Excess capacity is a dubious basis for sustained export growth, while the
ability of exchange rate manipulations to force long-run changes of relative prices is limited at best. Hence, despite its inadequacies, one tends
to lean on relative-factor proportions theorizing for at least partial guidance as to long-term exporting prospects—particularly since, for technologically dependent economies, other long-run deterrents to industrial
exporting (such as marketing costs and the risk of product obsolescence)
probably correlate at least roughly with the physical or human capital-
intensity of the products.

To get around formidable data gaps, factor-intensities were estimated in two alternative ways, both shaky but each reinforcing the other's
findings. The first ranked two-digit Argentine industries along a skill
index using Argentine manpower data, and along a physical capital/labor
index derived from U.S. industry data (no comparable Argentine data
being available). Using U.S. capital/labor ratios may not be all that
extraordinary, however, since it is likely that the strong factor-intensity
axiom is alive and well in Argentina, sustained by the almost total dependence of modern Argentine industries on imported technology. The
second approach uses H. B. Lary's value-added per person technique[13]
which also assumes strong factor-intensity ordering, plus some other
analytic question marks.

Table 4 presents various features of Argentine industries that shed
flickering light on factor-intensities and technological characteristics.
Column 1 shows that in the mid-1960s nontraditional exporting was a
very minor sales outlet for the industrial sector. More recent information
indicates that this has continued to be so, the ratio to total industrial output rising only to around 1 percent in 1969.[14] This implies that industrial
investment and other long-run enterprise decisions in the 1960s were
still guided almost exclusively by domestic market expectations, which
strengthens the likelihood that excess capacity has been an important
motive for industrial exporting. Individual industry ratios diverge, but
except for Printing and Publishing, the export market remains of very
minor importance. The apparent unimportance in some cases is, however,
a consequence of the high level of industrial aggregation in Table 4, and
amends are made for this in data presented further on.

The remaining columns of Table 4 compare structural features of the
thirteen industries, while rank correlations between these indices and the

13. Hal B. Lary, *Imports of Manufactures from Less Developed Countries*
(New York: National Bureau of Economic Research, 1968).
14. The estimate was given in a speech by José M. Dagnino Pastore, Minister
of the Economy from June 1969 to June 1970.

export ratios are presented in Table 5. What do these correlations indicate about relative factor-intensities?[15]

One message is that the industry export ratios show no apparent bias as regards physical capital-intensity, the correlation being only 0.082. A second is that the exports may be relatively skill-intensive by Argentine standards, the correlation of 0.407 mildly supporting the view that Argentina with its literate labor force, sizable cadre of university-trained professionals, and modest real wages and salaries may have a potential advantage in various skill-intensive industrial exports to Latin America and perhaps to advanced markets as well.

A third message, however, countermands the second by suggesting that Argentine industries have been violating Heckscher-Ohlin dicta in their nontraditional exporting. This is implied by the −0.729 correlation between Argentine skill ratios and Argentine/U.S. skill ratios, and by the −0.412 correlation between the latter and the industry export ratios. That U.S. industries have higher proportions of skilled personnel than their Argentine counterparts, as column 5 of Table 4 indicates, should not be disturbing to Heckscher-Ohlin aficionados; but that the industries with the greater comparative skill disadvantage vis-à-vis their U.S. counterparts should have higher export ratios of nontraditional products surely is.

Deviation from proper factor proportions behavior is also implied by the import coefficients. Since technologically complex products usually require a wide range of specialized material as well as skilled labor inputs, one would expect the more technologically complex j^{th} industries in an input-output matrix to have the wider ranges of positive but low-valued a_{ij}'s. For technological borrowers like Argentina, however, some of the manifestation of technological complexity should be diverted to the direct and indirect import coefficient vector, the more technologically complex product classes having the higher import coefficients. Similarly, the more technologically complex the product class, the higher the associated skill ratio is likely to be. Skill ratios should thus correlate positively with import-intensity for technology-borrowing countries.

Turning to Table 5, we indeed find a positive correlation of 0.522 between the import coefficients and the Argentine skill index and an even

15. Going beyond rank correlations is unwarranted in view of the crude nature of the skill ratios. The construction of these ratios, described in the footnotes to Table 4, has two main weaknesses: (a) It was not possible satisfactorily to separate skilled workers from the semi- and unskilled. Weighted proportions of technical and administrative employees were used, therefore, to devise the comparative skill index. (b) While weighting was necessary, the weights used were arbitrary. Technical and professional employees were assigned a higher weight than administrative staff because their relative importance is probably a better proxy for the degree of technological sophistication of the industry than is the proportion of administrative employees. Proprietors were excluded from administrative staff to reduce the distorting effect of differences in the size of enterprises between industries on the skill ranking.

TABLE 4

COMPARATIVE STRUCTURAL RELATIONSHIPS OF ARGENTINE INDUSTRIES

Industry	Average Annual Nontraditional Exports, 1963-66 (as % of 1963 Total Output)	1960 Argentine Skill Ratios as % of Industry Average	1958 Capital-Labor Ratios (U.S.) (as % of Industry Average)	1960 Direct and Indirect Current Import Requirements (per Unit of Output)	1960 Argentine/ U.S. Ratio of Skills	1963 Value-Added (per Employee as % of Industry Average)
	(1)	(2)	(3)	(4)	(5)	(6)
Printing and publishing	5.24	107.2	62.6	0.1284	0.937	66.4
Metals and metal products	1.77	97.8	138.4	0.1786	0.900	114.8
Chemical products	1.72	110.6	186.2	0.1017	0.874	157.5
Electrical machinery and apparatus	1.12	100.6	72.2	0.1622	0.814	147.9
Nonelectric machinery and vehicles	0.99	104.3	107.5	0.1492	0.894	101.0
Food and beverages	0.65	98.5	125.3	0.0346	0.968	91.7
Textiles	0.28	97.0	76.6	0.0427	0.962	91.8
Clothing	0.13	94.5	32.8	0.0638	0.977	69.6
Leather products (including shoes)	0.08	96.8	52.6	0.0327	1.004	73.7
Furniture and wood products	0.06	95.1	59.1	0.0739	0.971	38.9
Paper and paperboard	0.02	98.9	117.6	0.1054	0.939	149.1
Rubber products	0.02	100.0	99.3	0.1937	0.934	137.0
Stone, glass, and ceramics	0.01	98.6	170.0	0.0629	0.935	72.4
All industry	0.09	100.0	100.0	—	—	100.0

SOURCES: 1963 output and value-added per person were computed from the 1963 *Censo Nacional Económica: Industria Manufacturera* (Buenos Aires: Instituto Nacional de Estadística, 1968).

1963-66 average annual nontraditional industrial exports were computed from Appendix Table B-4.

The Argentine 1960 skill ratio index was computed by: (a) giving the number of professional and technical employees (per 1,000 employed) a weight of 3.0, the number of administrative employees (excluding proprietors, per 1,000 employed) a weight of 2.0, and the remaining employees (per 1,000) a weight of 1.0; and (b) dividing each industry ratio by the weighted average for all industries, using value-added weights from Consejo Nacional de Desarrollo (CONADE), *Distribución del Ingreso en la República Argentina*, and *Indice Provisional de la Producción de Industria Manufacturera, Anexo Estadística* (Buenos Aires, May 1964).

The Argentine/U.S. ratios of skills were obtained by computing U.S. 1960 industry skill ratios with the same source and method as in preceding paragraph, and dividing higher negative correlation, -0.725, between the import coefficients and the Argentine/U.S. skill ratios. Apparently, the industries with the greater comparative skill disadvantage have been the more import-intensive Argentine industries, as well as the more intense exporters of nontraditional exports. The beauty of these findings is marred, however, by the direct correlation of only 0.281 between export ratios and import coefficients; the sign is right, but the value is depressingly small. Nevertheless, the messages do lend some support for the view that the nontraditional industrial export mix of the 1960s may have been inappropriate for either sustained long-term expansion of industrial exporting or for maximizing the net foreign exchange earnings from such exporting.

Could these results reflect an industry aggregation bias or merely that nontraditional industrial exports to LAFTA have been more skill-intensive than those to non-LAFTA countries? These possibilities were tested by the second alternative method, using value-added per employee as an index of capital-intensity for lack of more direct disaggregated data.

The rationale for the index was developed by Hal B. Lary in his study of LDC industrial exporting.[16] Lary found that wages per employee correlates fairly well with relative skill ratios for a broad array of three- and four-digit U.S. SIC industries, and that physical capital per employee correlates respectably with nonwage value-added by industry. From this he deduced that for manufacturing activities total value-added per employee is a good proxy for combined human and physical capital per worker. He then also found that the three categories of value-added for U.S. industries correlate moderately well with those for arrays of comparable industries of the United Kingdom, Japan, and India, and deduced, therefore, that strong factor-intensity ordering is a worldwide characteristic of modern manufacturing production functions, so that value-added per employee can be used to indicate the combined physical plus human capital-intensity ranking of LDC industries. Interindustry and inter-

---

them into the skill ratio for the corresponding Argentine industry. The skill data were obtained from M. A. Horowitz, M. Zymelman, and I. L. Hernstadt, *Manpower Requirements for Planning, an International Comparison Approach*, vol. 2 (Boston: Northeastern University, 1966).

Capital/labor ratios were constructed from 1957 U.S. physical capital per worker data at the 4-digit SIC industry level in Hal B. Lary, *Imports of Manufactures from Less Developed Countries* (New York: National Bureau of Economic Research, 1968), Appendix Table A-2. The 4-digit data were aggregated to the 13-industry level using Argentine 1960 value-added weights. They were then expressed as a percentage of the weighted average for all 13 industries. Source of the weights: CONADE, *Distribución del Ingreso*, 1964.

Direct and indirect import coefficients were computed by the author from the inverted table of 1960 input-output coefficients and vector of current input requirements for Argentina, constructed by CONADE. See David Felix, *Did Import Substituting Industrialization in Argentina Save Foreign Exchange in 1953-1960? A Report on Some Findings* (Buenos Aires: Instituto Torcuato Di Tella, 1965), Table 2.

16. See Lary, *Imports of Manufactures*, chaps. 2, 3.

country deviations from competitive behavior and dynamic disequilibria were distributed, in his judgment, with sufficient randomness as not to block the relative factor-intensity relationships from shining through statistically.

Table 6 adds U.S./Argentine correlations to Lary's intercountry value-added correlations. The total value-added correlation is consistently the highest of each country set, although it still leaves unexplained variance of from 22 percent for the U.S./U.K. correlation to 38 percent for

TABLE 5

RANK CORRELATION MATRIX OF STRUCTURAL RELATIONSHIPS
BETWEEN ARGENTINE INDUSTRIES

	Non-traditional Export Ratios	Argentine Skill Index	Capital/ Labor Index	Direct and Indirect Import Require- ments	Argentine/ U.S. Ratio of Skills	Value- Added per Employee
Nontraditional export ratios	1.000	0.407	0.082	0.281	−0.412	0.143
Argentine skill index		1.00	0.516	0.522	−0.729	0.533
Capital/labor index			1.000	0.171	−0.555	0.561
Direct and indirect import requirements				1.000	−0.725	0.451
Argentine/U.S. ratio of skills					1.000	−0.665
Value-added per employee						1.000

SOURCE: Table 4.

the best of the U.S./India alternatives, the U.S./Argentine residual falling encouragingly below the midpoint of the range. The wage and non-wage correlations are usually much poorer, the worst by far being U.S./Argentina nonwage value-added, an anomaly left for later discussion. In general, neither the presence of occasional factor reversals nor of varying degrees of monopoly embodied in factor and product prices can be rejected on the basis of the regressions. But invoking the BTN theorem for moral support,[17] we have nevertheless used total value-added per employee to rank Argentine nontraditional industrial exporting activities.

Charts 1 and 2 indicate that the factor-intensity deductions based on Tables 4 and 5 are probably not due to industry aggregation bias or a higher skill content in the exports to LAFTA.[18] On the contrary, at the

17. The BTN (Better Than Nothing) theorem was first developed by B. T. Nemesio, an eighteenth-century Neapolitan logic chopper, during his honeymoon.

five-digit ISIC industry level of Chart 1, 59 percent of the exports embodied value-added ratios above the average for all Argentine industry, by 20 percent or more, whereas in Table 5 the correlation of value-added per employee with export ratios is significant. Similarly, Chart 2 indicates that 61 percent of the exports to non-LAFTA countries emanated from the higher end of the value-added per employee range, implying that exports to non-LAFTA countries were somewhat more skill- and/or

TABLE 6

CORRELATIONS OF VALUE-ADDED, WAGE VALUE-ADDED, AND NONWAGE VALUE-ADDED PER EMPLOYEE OF THE U.S. WITH ARGENTINA AND OTHER SELECTED COUNTRIES

Countries Compared and Year of Census	Number of Industries	Value-Added per Employee		
		Total	Wage	Nonwage
U.S. (1965) and Argentina (1963)	64	0.839	0.699	0.171[a]
U.S. (1958) and U.K. (1958)	103	0.882	0.849	0.855
U.S. (1962) and Japan (1962)	178	0.753	0.778	0.690
Excluding 9 extreme observations	169	0.806	0.782	0.743
U.S. (1963) India (1961)	117	0.600	0.494	0.599
Excluding industries under 2,000 employment	83	0.634	0.553	0.658
Excluding also 7 extreme observations	76	0.786	0.518	0.785

[a]Not statistically significant.

NOTE: U.S. correlations with U.K., Japan, and India are between the logs of dollar value-added per employee for the various countries. The U.S./Argentine correlations are between unlogged ratios of industry value-added to the national industrial average of each of the two countries.

SOURCES: U.S. correlations with U.K., Japan, and India taken from Lary, *Imports of Manufactures,* p. 75, Table 6; U.S./Argentine correlation computed from U.S. data, ibid., pp. 24-29, Table 2, and Dirección Nacional de Estadística y Censos, *Censo Nacional Económico: Industria Manufacturera, 1963* (Buenos Aires, 1968).

capital-intensive than were those to LAFTA. Disaggregation and value-added per employee ranking thus strengthens the inference that Argentina has been violating at least static comparative advantage in its nontraditional industrial exporting.

18. In these charts, value-added per person data were obtained from the 1963 Argentine Census of Manufactures. Nontraditional exports by the five-digit ISIC industries include only those four-digit NABALALC "items" whose export value averaged over $100,000 per annum during 1963-66, and also exceeded $100,000 for at least three of those years. The purpose of the procedure was to eliminate mini-items, of which there were a great many, and one- and two-shot large items, of which there were also a fair number. Forty-four items met both criteria, but the forty-four accounted for 82 percent of the total value of nontraditional industrial exports during 1963-66. Similar processing was done on exports to non-LAFTA countries. Only nineteen items, collating with sixteen five-digit ISIC industries, met both criteria. The nineteen made up approximately 93 percent of all non-LAFTA exports in 1963-66.

CHART 1

FACTOR-INTENSITY OF LEADING ARGENTINE NONTRADITIONAL INDUSTRIAL EXPORTS
BY ISIC 5-DIGIT INDUSTRY, 1963-66

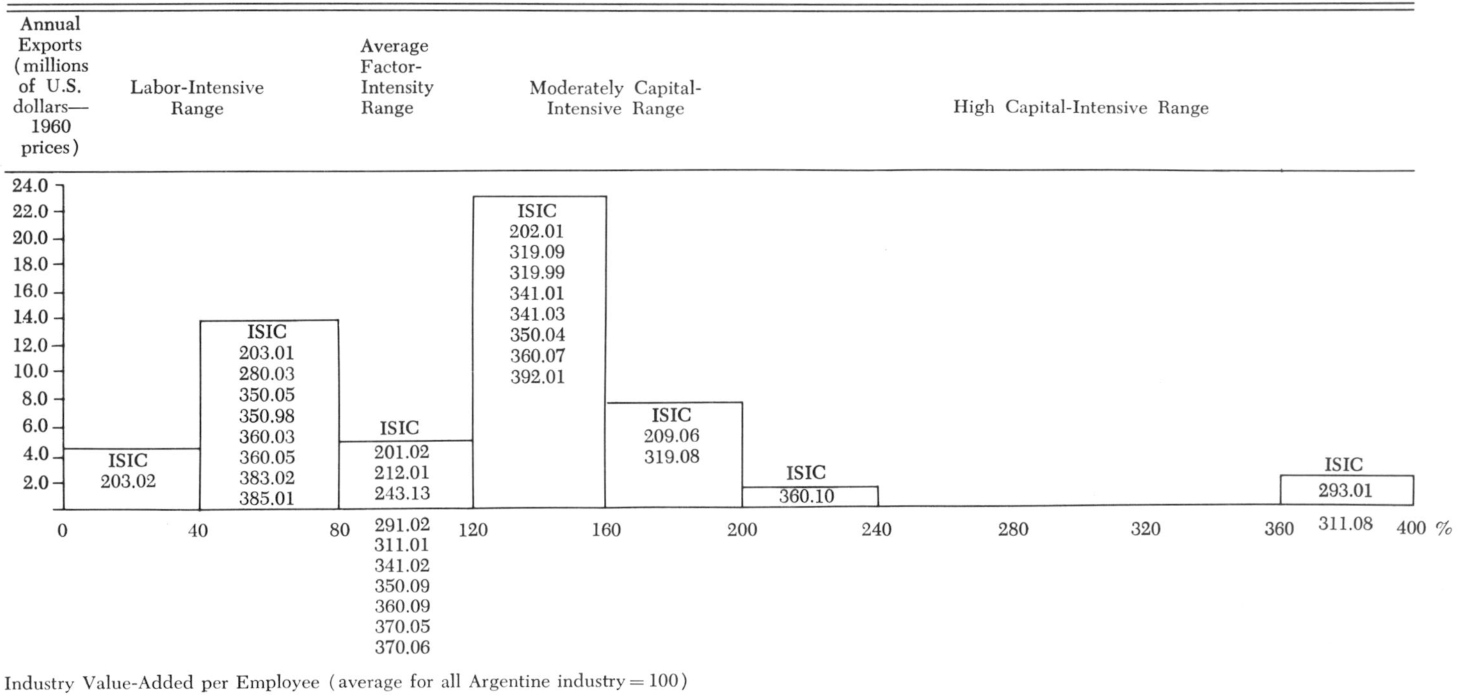

Annual
Exports
(millions
of U.S.
dollars—
1960
prices)

| Labor-Intensive Range | Average Factor-Intensity Range | Moderately Capital-Intensive Range | High Capital-Intensive Range |

24.0 –

22.0 –

20.0 –

18.0 –   ISIC
                                          202.01
16.0 –   319.09
                                          319.99
14.0 –   341.01
                                          341.03
12.0 –   ISIC   350.04
              203.01   360.07
10.0 –   280.03   392.01
              350.05
8.0 –   350.98
              360.03   ISIC
6.0 –   360.05   201.02
              383.02   212.01   ISIC
4.0 –   385.01   243.13   209.06
        ISIC   291.02   319.08
2.0 –   203.02   311.01   ISIC
                             341.02   360.10   ISIC
                             350.09   293.01
                             360.09
                             370.05
                             370.06

0   40   80   120   160   200   240   280   320   360   400 %
                                                                                      311.08

Industry Value-Added per Employee (average for all Argentine industry = 100)

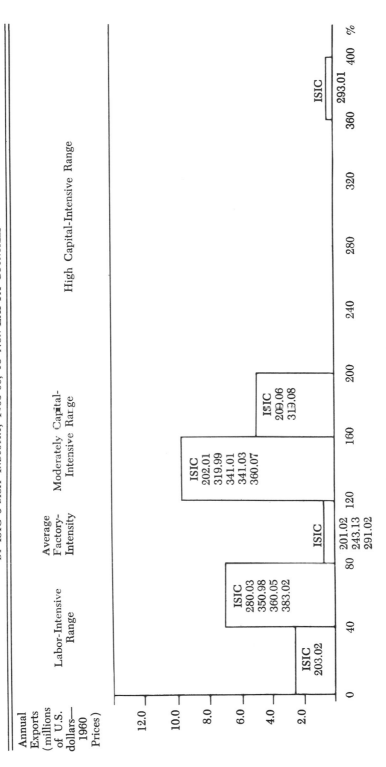

CHART 2

FACTOR-INTENSITY OF LEADING ARGENTINE NONTRADITIONAL INDUSTRIAL EXPORTS
BY ISIC 5-DIGIT INDUSTRY, 1963-66, TO NON-LAFTA COUNTRIES

Annual Exports (millions of U.S. dollars—1960 Prices)

Labor-Intensive Range

Average Factory-Intensity

Moderately Capital-Intensive Range

High Capital-Intensive Range

ISIC
203.02

ISIC
280.03
350.98
360.05
383.02

ISIC
201.02
243.13
291.02

ISIC
202.01
319.99
341.01
341.03
360.07

ISIC
209.06
319.08

ISIC
293.01

Industry Value-Added per Employee (average for all Argentine industry = 100)

MARKET STRUCTURE AND PRICE BEHAVIOR OF ARGENTINE INDUSTRY

These findings would be difficult to explain if Argentine industries were operating in open, highly competitive markets; they fit rather well with other evidence indicating the dominance of oligopoly and cartelized price behavior. The two are mentioned conjointly because the most common Argentine intraindustry size distributions are either simple oligopolistic or dualistic, i.e., a few relatively large firms at one end and a large cluster of small firms at the other. This observation is impressionistic, since only sketchy data on size distribution are available. However, according to a recent overall estimate, less than 2 percent of all industrial firms had over 100 employees, but these produced over half of Argentina's industrial value-added.[19]

Many small firms are linked symbiotically with large ones as parts suppliers or as specialized final processors, but even where small and large compete in the same markets, "live and let live" industry pricing behavior tends to prevail. In part, this is because the large and the small tend to be organized in industry trade associations that frequently speak for the industry on policy matters affecting costs and prices. But also contributing to "umbrella" pricing is the high percentage of large firms that are foreign subsidiaries or are government owned.[20] Foreign firms in a heatedly nationalistic climate tend to keep their market power sheathed as regards pricing. Similarly, government firms prefer to minimize political rancor by not engaging in *competencia desleal*, the general Argentine term for underpricing one's competitor.

The industry structure and price behavior, not atypical for Latin America, were nurtured by the import-substitution industrialization strategy that has dominated industrial promotion in Argentina since the mid-1930s. But the prevalence of undersized plants and their survival under "live and let live" pricing behavior was accentuated by two Argentine features of the strategy. The first was the tendency to make promotional inducements, such as import protection, credit, tax and import subsidies, available generically for classes of products rather than more selectively

19. Cited in a speech by General M. Chescotta, secretary of industry and domestic commerce, as reported in Servicia de Prensa del Ministerio de Economía y Trabajo, *Información Económica de la Argentina* (September 1970).
20. "Large" mainly by Argentine standards. Only eight industrial firms, all foreign subsidiaries or government owned, had gross sales in 1967 in the $100-$400 million range. Three of these were petroleum firms, four were in transport and heavy engineering equipment, and one was in basic steel. If output were valued at international prices, the sales of the transport firms and of the steel firm would each drop below $100 million. In 1969-70, two industrial firms quoted on the Buenos Aires exchange had sales of $100 million, including one of the above-mentioned transport manufacturers, and only five others had sales of between $50 and $100 million, two of these being foreign-controlled subsidiaries with minority local ownership. See *Primera Plana* (30 January 1968), p. 21, and *The Review of the River Plate* (30 September 1970), p. 518.

to applicants who also met efficiency criteria such as a reasonably adequate scale of operations and cost competitiveness. This tendency was augmented after the overthrow of Perón by the ideology of the victorious anti-Perónist business elite, which accepted the compatibility of protection and subsidies with "free enterprise," but insisted on nominally equal access to the unequal privileges, opposing as government interference proposals involving bureaucratic selectivity such as had intermittently marked Perónist practice. The second was the tendency for the postwar level of protection to be set high enough to eliminate the danger of competitive imports disrupting domestic pricing arrangements.

The price behavior of the industrial sector has shown, therefore, the following manifestations. The first is that paralleling the apparent price inelasticity of nontraditional industrial exports, import demand in the postwar era has also been unresponsive to changes in external/domestic price ratios.[21] Imports have varied chiefly with the level of industrial activity, devaluations resulting in declining imports mainly when accompanied by fiscal and monetary constraints sufficient to depress aggregate industrial demand. Secondly, wide intraindustry differences in firm size and cost structures have probably ruled out marginal cost–marginal revenue pricing by the large firms, implying rather that, through informal price leadership or by more formal arrangements, prices have tended to be set at some "satisficing" markup over full cost.[22] Thirdly, interindustry price changes have tended to correlate negatively with relative output growth between industries,[23] the slow-growing industries being able at least partially to ease their problems through above-average increases in prices.

The maintenance of a sort of capitalist egalitarianism through compensatory price increases is illustrated by Tables 8 and 9. As further background for interpreting the tables, however, three dynamic features of post-1950 economic policy should be noted. One was the effort to stimulate agricultural output by raising relative agricultural prices through devaluation and an easing of price controls. After Perón's overthrow, this was complemented by efforts to weaken the Perónist-controlled unions, partly to subvert the base for the return of El Tirano, but also to hold

21. Richard D. Mallon writes, "No investigator has yet to my knowledge been able to discover a regression equation for import demand which turns up a coefficient of relative import prices that is statistically significant." *Balance of Payments Adjustment in a Semi-Industrialized Export Economy: The Argentine Case* (Paper delivered at Harvard Development Advisory Service Conference, Sorrento, Italy, 5-12 September 1968).

22. Partial evidence that price leadership may be the more common of the two is provided by the incomes policy that was maintained fairly successfully from the March 1967 devaluation until the May 1969 labor riots. Wages were frozen by edict, but the industrial price freeze was accomplished through "voluntary" agreements with about 150 large firms.

23. For some statistical support for the period, 1946-60, see Felix, "The Dilemma of Import Substitution," p. 73, Table 3.2.

down wages so as to free a larger share of agricultural staples for export and to raise the profit share as a stimulant to private investment. The third was to promote the establishment of capital-intensive and technologically sophisticated import-substituting industries, relying heavily on liberal inducements to foreign private investors.[24]

The wage-price objectives were attained during the first post-Perónist decade, as shown by Table 7. By the early 1960s, agricultural prices had

TABLE 7

TRENDS IN RELATIVE PRICES, WAGES, VALUE-ADDED, AND RELATIVE SHARES, 1951-69.

	1951-54	1955-58	1959-62	1963-66	1967-69
Relative prices					
$\dfrac{\text{Agricultural prices}^a}{\text{Manufacturing prices}^a}$	100.0	102.3	118.1	118.8	113.3
$\dfrac{\text{Manufacturing prices}^a}{\text{Industrial wages}^b}$	100.0	112.2	122.0	104.1	116.2
Real industrial wages^c	100.0	110.3	97.4	114.1	110.9
Wage share of national income^d	48.9%	46.1%	40.9%	43.7%	

Industrial value-added from 1953 and 1963 industrial censuses	1,000 Pesos (1953 Prices)	
	1953	1963
Annual value-added per employee	34.6	45.5
Annual wages and salaries per employee	11.9	11.0
Wage-salary share of industrial value-added	35.5%	25.0%

^{a}Wholesale price index subseries, 1951-54, from central bank wholesale price index; for 1955-66 from DNEC index.
^{b}Weighted DNEC index of wages according to trade union agreements (*convenios*); skilled-labor index weight = 0.3, unskilled = 0.7.
^{c}DNEC weighted wage index deflated by DNEC cost-of-living index.
^{d}1950-63, from CONADE National Accounts; 1964-66, from central bank national accounts; wage share includes employer social security taxes.

risen almost 20 percent more than industrial prices and the latter had risen over 20 percent more than industrial wages. Average industrial real wages fell around 2-3 percent, and the wage share of national income by a whopping 16 percent. Industrial value-added per employee rose around 30 percent, while labor's share of industrial value-added fell by the same percentage. The fall concealed, however, a widening dispersal of wages, for the attempt to weaken unions succeeded mainly in subverting the

24. Many of these policies, it should be noted, did not emerge *de novo* with the overthrow of Perón, but were an extension of tendencies initiated under Perón during his second term.

rather egalitarian wage structure of the Perónist era. Individual unions remained strong, and in the faster-growing capital- and skill-intensive industries, were able to make real wage gains.

The price paid for these changes in accelerated inflation, depreciating exchanges, and rapidly rising foreign indebtedness was quite high. Following the abandonment of the incomes policy that Perón imposed fairly

TABLE 8

CHANGES IN ANNUAL OUTPUT AND VALUE-ADDED OF ARGENTINE INDUSTRIES, 1953-63

		Percentage Change, 1953-63[b]			
Industries	%Output Growth 1953-54/ 1963-64	Value- Added per Employee	Wages- Salaries per Employee	Nonwage Value- Added per Employee	Ratio of Wages- Salaries to Value- Added
Above-average growth					
Vehicles and nonelectric machinery	143.0	75.7	11.3	137.9	−35.6
Electric machinery and equipment	115.2	51.1	36.3	58.6	−10.0
Metals and metal products	104.2	68.9	28.1	96.8	−24.2
Petroleum refining	90.9	52.4	10.2	133.1	−25.6
Paper and paperboard	75.5	78.3	32.9	102.4	−25.0
Rubber products	66.0	65.4	−0.2	92.6	−39.5
Chemicals and chemical products	64.2	33.3	8.8	40.2	−40.6
Group average[a]	108.9	57.9	17.8	80.1	−25.3
Below-average growth					
Printing and publishing	38.6	3.6	1.0	−3.0	−2.8
Food and beverages	31.2	13.9	−27.4	29.9	−36.1
Stone, glass, and ceramics	15.5	11.1	−1.8	17.4	−11.8
Misc. manufactures	14.7	10.6	−19.9	26.7	−27.7
Tobacco products	6.1	34.1	−7.4	38.6	30.6
Textiles	−0.1	23.9	−16.0	38.7	−32.2
Clothing	−9.6	−11.3	−64.0	−7.1	−48.8
Wood products	−11.8	−6.6	−21.8	3.8	−17.7
Leather products	−15.4	−23.4	−41.4	−12.4	−25.0
Group average[a]	28.6	5.5	−32.4	27.3	−35.8
All industry	46.9	31.3	−7.5	51.6	−29.7

[a]Weighted average.
[b]1963 wage and value-added for each industry were deflated to 1953 prices using respective industry price series.
SOURCES: Industry output rates and price series, from National Development Council (CONADE), *Distribución del Ingreso en la República Argentina* (Buenos Aires, 1965), Anexo No. 4 and Anexo No. 12. Wages and value-added data, 1953 and 1963, from Argentine Censuses of Manufactures, deflated to 1953 prices by respective industry price indices.

effectively in 1953-54, the implicit merchandise exchange rate rose over 1,900 percent between 1954 and 1963, leading the GNP deflator which rose by 950 percent in the same interval—much of the difference being accounted for by lagging prices of public services, frozen house rents, lagging indirect tax receipts,[25] and inadequate depreciation allowances. Public and private foreign indebtedness rose from a negligible figure in 1954 to over $3 billion in 1963, about two and a half times the value of that year's exports, while net foreign services on current account fell from +$12 million in 1954 to −$151 million in 1963. Nor were these

TABLE 9

CORRELATION OF VALUE-ADDED, WAGE VALUE-ADDED, AND NONWAGE VALUE-ADDED
PER EMPLOYEE FOR ARGENTINE INDUSTRY, 1963 AND 1953[a]

	r[b]	r without 5 Extreme Observations[b]
1953 with 1963		
Total value-added	.801	.870
Wage value-added	.309	.558
Nonwage value-added	.838	.864
Intra-1953		
Total value-added with wage	.432	.460
Total value-added with nonwage	.972	.994
Wage with nonwage	.214	.363
Intra-1963		
Total value-added with wage	.677	.692
Total value-added with nonwage	.977	.997
Wage with nonwage	.622	.642

[a]90 industries in the sample.
[b]All correlations except .214, column 1, are significant at the 1% confidence level.
SOURCE: Dirección Nacional de Estadística y Censos, Censo National Económico: Industria Manufacturera, 1963 (Buenos Aires, 1968), and Censo Industrial, 1954 (Buenos Aires, 1958).

disruptive developments compensated by accelerating economic growth; the real GNP growth rate in 1955-63 was no higher than in 1950-55.

These trends are also reflected in the intercensal industry comparisons of Table 8. Output of the first group of industries—the focal point of ISI strategy in the intercensal period—grew, of course, much faster than the average for the industrial sector. They also had by far the higher increases in value-added per worker, unequally distributed between wages and nonwage value-added.[26] But note that the slow-growing second

25. Between 1953-54 and 1962-63, the ratio of indirect taxes to GNP fell from 10.7 percent to 9.1 percent and that of all taxes to GNP from 15.9 percent to 11.4 percent.
26. Most of the increase probably reflects increased capital-intensity rather than either sustained bonanza profits or a relative rise in indirect taxes. The enduring col-

group of industries, with little apparent improvement in labor productivity, not only had a positive growth of nonwage value-added per employee, but succeeded in lowering the wage to value-added ratio by more than the fast-growing group.

Other indications that egalitarianism was more operative in industry pricing than in wage determination during this period are provided by Table 9. Note the weak correlations for 1953 of wage value-added with the other two value-added categories and the low correlation between 1953 and 1963 wage value-added, whereas in 1963 wage value-added correlated fairly strongly with the other two categories. Turning to Table 6, note that Argentina's wage value-added distribution in 1963 also correlates fairly well with the wage value-added distribution of that paragon of market efficiency, the United States, whereas the negligible correlation between U.S./Argentine nonwage value-added in that table contrasts sharply with the high 1953-63 nonwage correlation in Table 9. These data, plus the low incidence of bankruptcy and take-overs during the post-Perónist years, suggest that disproportionate price increases and product/wage cuts were major mechanisms by which firms in the slow-growing industries survived. In effect, only the wages half of the restructuring of relative industrial wages and prices for competitive exporting had been realized by 1963.

Finally, was the anti-Heckscher-Ohlin bias of the nontraditional industrial export mix in the 1900s due also to the dominance of multinational corporate subsidiaries in many of the high-technology industries? These have an advantage over national firms by being able to reduce exchange rate uncertainties and excess capacity through intracorporate international trade at in-house prices. LAFTA complementary agreements furthered this advantage by allowing a few Argentine subsidiaries to expand regional specialization and interchange with intracorporate LAFTA subsidiaries. Whether this contributed on balance to the anti-Heckscher-Ohlin export bias could not be determined—information on foreign subsidiary participation in Argentine nontraditional exporting and on the special contribution of LAFTA complementarity agreements being only sketchy and anecdotal. The following are merely two opposing examples.

First, under a 1963 complementarity agreement covering business machines, IBM and Olivetti reshuffled production among their respective LAFTA plants, IBM-Argentina concentrating on a line of accounting machines and Olivetti-Argentina on a line of simple desk calculators. In both cases, specialization, cheap skilled Argentine labor, and duty-free intra-LAFTA trade of parts and accessories evidently made exporting to advanced countries as well as to LAFTA profitable. By 1967 the value of

---

lapse of share prices on the Buenos Aires Bolsa after 1961 is incompatible with the first possibility; the decline in the ratio of indirect taxes to GNP (see note 25) undermines the second.

business machine exports reached $12.8 million, or 39 percent of Argentine exports of engineering goods on a gross value basis,[27] substantially less when import content is netted out. These exports merit, therefore, the blessings of Heckscher-Ohlin. But they also merit the more ambiguous benediction of Raymond Vernon,[28] the products being apparently old models near the end of their international product cycle whose production was shifted from subsidiaries in more technologically advanced centers to Argentina. Given the rapid obsolescence characterizing such products, sustained expansion of exports would appear to depend not merely on comparative wage rates and production skills, but also on technological developments, production, and marketing decisions over which the Argentine subsidiaries probably have negligible influence.

The second example involves Argentine motorcar firms, which in 1965 were given tariff exemptions for balanced bilateral trade with Chilean counterparts. In the following year, Ford-Argentina, whose deluxe Argentine passenger model was then a 1963 U.S.-styled six-cylinder Falcon, shipped some 3,000 engines to Ford-Chile at an FOB price, according to Argentine export statistics, of $673 per engine. In this case, the Chilean government and Ford-Detroit willing, Ford-Chile could have done better ordering its engines from Sears-Roebuck U.S.A.

INDUSTRIAL EXPORT PROMOTION AND
TRENDS IN ARGENTINE INDUSTRIAL POLICY

Although sustained growth of nontraditional industrial exports seems to require, as complements to the export promotion program, policies to modify the industrial market structure and price behavior, little movement has been initiated. Most of the economic and sociopolitical crosscurrents that have buffeted policy making since the early 1950s still prevail, generating irresolute marches and countermarches over a policy terrain that remains circumscribed by unresolved sectoral conflicts reinforced by ideological disagreements on the desired shape of Argentine society. Industrial exporting is a desideratum for all the major competing policy camps, but a minor one to which they are not ready to subordinate more basic objectives on which they fervently disagree.

Nontraditional exporting now receives prominent play in the Argentine press, minor shipments of technologically sexy new items getting well-publicized send-offs. This reflects government efforts to imbue the inner-directed Argentine industrial sector with export-consciousness, and attempts of Argentine firms to gain goodwill and local market prestige by

27. General Agreement on Tariffs and Trade, *International Trade, 1968* (Geneva, 1969), p. 70, Table 18.

28. Raymond Vernon, "International Investment and International Trade in the Product Cycle," *Quarterly Journal of Economics* 80 (May 1966): 190-207.

publicizing that their products are good enough to be sold outside of Argentina. The public relations barrage contrasts, however, with the hard fact that the cumulated increase of nontraditional industrial exports in the 1960s totaled only 3-4 percent of the increase of industrial output. Industrial investment and output decisions, therefore, have continued to be governed almost entirely by domestic market appraisals, and major fissures have not yet appeared in the solid opposition of the industrial sector to attempts to dismantle the high tariff wall that protects its price behavior.

Even the LAFTA market continues to be viewed ambivalently— indeed, with less enthusiasm now than in its initial years. This may reflect disillusionment with the retreat of LAFTA from its original goal of regional free trade by 1973 to its current half-life as a mere preferential tariff arrangement. Since 1964, new concessions for Argentine industry have become much harder to extract. But Argentina, the largest inside industrial exporter to LAFTA, also shares the blame for the succession of bargaining stalemates that have brought LAFTA to its present stagnancy. Yet this has not split Argentine industry into fervid pro- and anti LAFTA trade liberationists battling for public support. The LAFTA market, present or prospective, is evidently not all that important to any substantial segment of Argentine industry.

At the governmental level, the attitude has also been ambivalent. Measures to promote industrial exports are acceptable to both of the vague economic ideologies—economic liberalism, Argentine style, and "developmentalism" (*desarrollismo*)—that have alternately influenced Argentine industrial policy since Perón. Some in each camp seem now to accept the need to restructure relative industrial prices and costs if exporting is to become a major industrial activity. But disagreement is rampant on how to accomplish this, and in the alternating periods when one or the other ideological camp has had the larger say on economic policy, neither has done more than nibble intermittently at the task.

The chief liberal instrument has been tariff reductions, two attempts having been made to date (both post-1966). To neutralize opposition, the cuts were in each case made coincidently with exchange rate devaluation and were justified primarily as antiinflationary measures rather than as moves toward industrial rationalization. Neither tariff cut resulted in a sustained invasion of competitive imports, partly because for many products the cuts merely reduced the extra margin of safety incorporated in the precut tariff rates to insure exclusion of competitive imports, but also because incipient invasions were quickly cut off at the pass by other defenses. Thus, half a year after the March 1967 tariff cuts, industrial trade associations were invited by the Ministry of the Economy to assist in constructing a comprehensive system of "antidumping" index prices for customs valuations. Similarly, the June 1970 tariff cuts were rescinded in November 1970 for a wide range of goods that were beginning to feel import competition. Tariff cutting has been hit-and-run rather than orderly and progressive.

Desarrollistas generally oppose tariff liberalization as premature, but some have been attracted to French or Nipponese-type measures to prepare the industrial sector for exporting: the promotion of mergers, rationalization of selected industries with good export potential, export cartels, subsidization of indigenous R and D (research and development), etc. This is a change of emphasis from the *desarrollismo* of the Frondizi period, which was indiscriminately ISI-oriented. Thus far, however, the change has been more verbal than substantive and the *desarrollista* schemes that get embodied in government action remain ISI-oriented. There is greater insistence now than heretofore that government-subsidized industrial plants be built to reasonably adequate scale, so that some of the most recent projects approved—e.g., in aluminum, steel, and petrochemicals—will initially have planned capacities in excess of projected domestic demand, the surplus to be exported until home demand catches up with capacity. But, in general, *desarrollistas* give top priority to filling out the Argentine industrial structure with more intermediate capital goods and high-technology activities, which, they believe, would save foreign exchange and reduce the structural weaknesses that inhibit industrial exporting.

The failure to reach a workable consensus on economic policy also reflects, however, basic disagreement over the questions *cui bono?* and *quis regit?*—that is, over the social welfare function and the distribution of power. Cutting back the public sector, import liberalization, higher relative prices for agriculture, a good climate for foreign investors, and overall policy direction safely in the hands of a coalition of *estancieros*, Buenos Aires financiers and export-import houses, agricultural processors, and foreign investors—this is the lost but not forgotten world that inspires the economic liberals. And it is hostility toward that world and the socioeconomic groupings that seek to restore its essentials which unites otherwise disparate elements in opposition and draws them to vague nationalistic and populist counter-ideologies, to Perónism, or to various versions of *desarrollismo* that seek to replace legally proscribed Perónism as ideological rallying points. This unresolved sociopolitical disagreement, easily visible during the intervals of parliamentary rule, surfaces again as military factionalism when the Argentine military, as it has frequently done since 1930, seizes formal control. For, as the self-appointed counter-parliament of Argentina, the military (despite its rhetoric of professional unity) soon becomes riven and immobilized by the same unresolved disagreements that divide the society it attempts to rule.

Two consequences of this sociopolitical impasse for economic policy making are worth noting. The first is that even narrowly technical economic policy decisions tend to be viewed, suspiciously or hopefully, as promoting a broader ideological objective. The second result is to shorten the politically acceptable pay-out period for economic policies. The first makes cautious, incremental economic policy making politically difficult to sustain. There has been a strong temptation, therefore, to which those in high office or seizing it frequently succumb, to concoct dramatic, comprehensive policy packages in hopes that the results will be so widespread and irreversible as to sap permanently the basis of the sociopolitical impasse. But even where the concoctions have made plausible economic sense—some, e.g., Frondizi's, clearly did not—their benefit streams usually could not reach flood within the constrained pay-out period. Either the effort would recede into immobilism under the weight of politically necessary ad hoc compromises, or the unsuccessful initiator would be replaced by another pretender. Thus, another facet of the Argentine impasse.

This is frustrating also to U.S. economist-observers, nurtured in an orderly political environment where consensus politics and the age of the technical advisor replaced ideology some two decades ago, according to the dating of some U.S. political sociologists. For example, buttressing the export promotion measures with some combination of progressive tariff-cutting rationalization measures selectively concentrated on key industries with export potential, plus transitional compensation for the industrially disabled, ought to be an economically feasible and politically possible compromise. Perhaps it would be, if economists could also predict with reasonable accuracy the extent and duration of the structural adjustments that would be imposed on the industrial sector and their interim consequences for the level of industrial investment and employment. But economists are not very good at answering such reasonable questions. As a weak alternative they could fall back on the standard ploy that gives economists their reputation for being status-quo-minded, and advise an incremental approach that minimizes the risk of large errors. But that would only minimize the risk of large errors of commission—not of omission, which would result from not seizing economic and political opportunities or having the small results inundated by other economic trends which a bolder approach might have diverted. Simple, all-purpose policy formulas get easily swallowed up by the Argentine impasse.

If this political appraisal is correct, Argentina's industrial structure will be pushed slowly and haltingly at best toward a more viable exporting stance, and the statistical patterns in the earlier sections of this paper will remain relevant for some years at least. This presages, in turn, a diminution of the growth of nontraditional industrial exports from the 1960s rate.

One reason for projecting a slowing is that many of the items instigated by excess capacity in the 1960s industrial export mix are probably not profitable long-term bets. Some of these may revive intermittently during depressed phases of the recurring Argentine stop-go cycles, and they will be supplemented, no doubt, by similarly motivated exports as new import-substituting activities in the high-technology and scale-intensive segments of the industrial gamut continue to be encouraged by import constraints, by the consumerist influences of technically advanced cultures, and by the persistent bias of Argentine industrial promotion policy in favor of backward linkage development. Since these are not the Argentine industrial activities that can compete confidently and profitably in open international markets, the new items are also likely to be exported, for the most part, evanescently or intermittently.

A second reason for expecting a slowdown is the stagnant status of LAFTA, the most important single stimulus to Argentine nontraditional industrial exporting in the 1960s, as a regional trade-promoting institution. Indeed, Big Three industrial exports may be faced soon with subregional trade diversion from the Andean Common Market, should that scheme be implemented. But, apart from this threat, the institutional obstacles and disagreements over the sharing of costs and benefits of regional integration seem too deep-rooted and complex for a quick revival of LAFTA's dynamism to be likely.[29]

Increasing the "real" exchange rate for industrial exports through more generous subsidies, or through a dual exchange rate scheme, could counter these depressing factors. In contrast to global devaluation, devaluing the industrial export exchange rate will not, in the present Argentine setting, generate major offsetting increases in the prices of wage goods and industrial materials. Also, there are probably "real" industrial exchange rates falling outside the range of rates assessed in the regressions (presented earlier) that could significantly stimulate industrial exports. Assuming the fiscal and financial burden of such rates is politically manageable, their economic desirability is, however, still open to question. For excess-capacity-motivated industrial exporting in the Argentine setting is double-edged. It has a desirable countercyclical effect, particularly for industrial activities with high fixed costs. But insofar as it makes new ISI in capital- and scale-intensive activities more feasible, it also helps divert investment toward the portion of the industrial gamut with the poorer prospects for sustained exporting. The second effect could be minimized by appropriately selective subsidy measures, but this would require reversing the bias of current industrial export subsidies toward high value-added products. In sum, Argentine industrial export promotion thus far has been not so much a major departure from the extreme ISI orientation of postwar Argentine industrial policy as an attempt to

29. See David Felix, "The Political Economy of Regional Integration in Latin America," *Studies in Comparative International Development* 5, no. 5 (1969-70) for my attempt to analyze the problem.

preserve its problematic viability, and this subordination is unlikely to change soon.

Acknowledgment.—An initial version of this study was issued in mimeograph as Economic Development Report No. 107 of the Development Advisory Service. I have benefited from critical comments on that version by Daniel M. Schydlowsky of Harvard University and Nathaniel Leff of Columbia University.

I am also deeply grateful to the Harvard Development Advisory Service for its hospitality and generous research support for the initial study, to Washington University for computer time, and to Robert Woodward of Washington University for processing and programming the additional data incorporated in the current version.

Comment—Joseph Grunwald

ARGENTINA has long been considered a puzzle by economists. Why has this economy, which reached a high level of development more than half a century ago, been characterized by a lack of dynamism for so long? Even today its per capita income is too high, the degree of inequality of its income distribution too low for Argentina to be classified as a "less-developed country." The composition of its national income and labor force also makes it look like a developed industrial nation. Yet, its economic growth has been below that of most developed and developing countries, certainly well below the Latin American average. Periodic economic progress has been short-lived and nearly offset by periodic backsliding. With all the preconditions seemingly existing, it is difficult to understand why the economy has not "taken off."

Despite the fascination, not many economists have dared to delve into Argentine studies and fewer still have emerged with sensible explanations. Felix, who has studied the Argentine economy extensively, makes a contribution in his paper to our understanding of the sluggishness of that country's industrial exporting.

Unquestionably, much work has gone into the preparation of Felix's paper, more than two-thirds of it being devoted to quantitative analysis. Many time series were collected, most of them shown in an appendix not published here, and many regressions were run. The conclusions arising from this effort are that within a framework of import-substituting industrialization, Argentine nontraditional exports have not responded to export promotion and relative prices, have not conformed to Heckscher-Ohlin behavior, have reacted primarily to intra-Latin American concessions and excess capacity. I do not have any strong quarrels with the general thrust of the findings, but I do not think that they are firmly based on the empirical analysis.

Those of us who have been doing empirical work for a long time are well aware that it is relatively easy for a critic to shoot holes into the nature and reliability of data, the methodology used, and the interpretation of tests. Also, we find quite often that after much effort the data manipulations do not support many worthwhile results. The Felix paper is subject to both types of critiques.

Felix analyzes Argentine exports primarily from the supply side. Leaving aside wild assumptions about international free trade and demand elasticities, the demand of importing countries clearly plays an important role in the determination of Argentine exports. Most nontraditional exports of the country go to other LAFTA nations and the United States. Using LAFTA concessions as the only external variable is inadequate. Felix uses cumulative LAFTA concessions, which almost by definition gives an increasing time series. It is not surprising that he got a significant and high correlation coefficient—as a matter of fact, the best correlation in his experiment to explain nontraditional export behavior. One would suspect that one could show good correlation with nearly any upward-moving time variable. More significance could have been attached to this correlation if it derived from a weighting of concessions classified by preconcession traded and nontraded goods. Other changes in trade policies of the importing countries, including tariffs, exchange rates, and quotas, probably have been more important for Argentine exports than LAFTA concessions. They should be taken into consideration, especially for the neighboring countries with which Argentina maintains special trade relationships.

Though the "real rate of exchange"[1] variable used by Felix neglects demand and concentrates on supply factors, important supply items were omitted. Thus, subsidized credit is at least as important as drawbacks and rebates for export promotion, but was not included in the "real rate of exchange." It is obvious that some factors are difficult to take into consideration because of the problems of data availability and quantification. But one has reason to suspect that if the "real rate of exchange" could have been adjusted to take into account at least the credit element, its correlation with nontraditional exports might have been significant.

In the second section of his paper, Felix turns to an examination of

1. Felix's adjusted "real rate of exchange" contains heterogeneous factors: for example, tax rebates are certificates, not cash, and can be sold only at a discount; drawbacks are cash, but not a flat rate and therefore difficult to calculate; and not all nontraditional exports receive drawbacks. There are, of course, many shortcomings in the basic "real rate of exchange" concept used by Felix (the official rate adjusted by the ratio of the respective wholesale price indices), the most serious one being that it depends so heavily on the base period selected. For a discussion of this subject and an attempt to calculate an "implicit rate," see Joseph Grunwald and Jorge Salazar, "Economic Integration, Rate of Exchange and Value Comparisons in Latin America," in Don Daly, ed., *International Comparisons of Prices and Output* (National Bureau of Economic Research).

factor proportions to shed some light on Argentine industrial export performance. Again this is a difficult area for data manipulation and Felix has used some ingenious devices for his analysis. But, apparently necessary shortcuts bring with them also unavoidable shortcomings. Thus the use of U.S. industry data as a proxy for unavailable Argentine data may be justified for specific (at least five-digit) industries; in two-digit aggregations, however, the United States and Argentina have very different output mixes. Moreover, Argentine industry is still strongly dual: there is a technologically sophisticated sector for which the U.S. proxy would be more reasonable, and there is also a substantial artisan sector for which it would be nonsense. The use of nonwage value-added as a proxy for capital in a country like Argentina is subject to question as well. Value-added can also be an indicator of inefficiency, excess profits, or high protection, possibly reflecting the opposite of technical advancement.

Felix concludes from his examination that Argentine nontraditional export behavior contravenes the Heckscher-Ohlin thesis. This is not much of a conclusion. In a world of tariff protection, rate of exchange controls, direct restraints on competition, excess capacity, unemployment and underemployment, different social legislations, not to speak of different production functions in the various countries, can one expect anything else but distorted factor prices? But Felix insists on pursuing this theme and devotes almost the entire next section on market structure and price behavior to a sometimes elaborate chase of what he calls the anti-Heckscher-Ohlin bias of Argentine exports. One is tempted to respond: so what? Not that the discussion does not contain some interesting bits of information and insights, but why beat a dead horse and spend so much effort in an attempt to get to the roots of something which is generally recognized, fairly well understood, and certainly not unique to the Argentine economy?

Inevitably, any real-world examination of the Argentine economy must eventually turn to a sociopolitical discussion. How else can one deal with the phenomenon of Argentine policy making and the resulting impasse? The last section of the paper contains such an analysis and Felix is very good at it. There are incisive comments and a convincing appraisal of the prospects for nontraditional exports.

On balance, the paper constitutes a valuable contribution to the literature on the Argentine economy despite its weaknesses, which occur especially in the quantitative analysis. One can go further and say that much of what Felix has to say about Argentina has implications for those other developing countries, particularly in Latin America, which are caught up in a continuing process of import-substituting industrialization.

Comment—John F. Morrall

AS is true of most good research, Felix's paper raises more questions than it answers. A major theme running through his paper which may be classified as one of his "answers" is that twenty-five years of import-substitution industrialization has left Argentina's export sector totally unprepared to act as the engine of growth now that import-substitution possibilities are becoming exhausted. Felix's regression results, showing that Argentine exports are not responsive to world price changes but are mainly explained by excess capacity and LAFTA concessions, support this conclusion.

Felix is not very optimistic that the increase in Argentina's non-traditional exports in the sixties can be maintained in the seventies for at least two reasons, the first being that excess capacity is not a viable long-run basis for comparative advantage, and the second that the LAFTA stimulus is becoming stagnant. Felix sees little hope that economic advisors can have much effect in resolving Argentina's problems due to a "basic sociopolitical impasse" which holds back the rationalization of Argentine industry and the development of a vigorous and effective export promotion program. The point should have been made here that this "sociopolitical impasse" is not unique to the Argentine experience but rather is characteristic of most countries engaging in import-substitution industrialization.[1]

Although Felix's major conclusions appear to be reasonable and consistent with existing studies, some of his preliminary statistical evidence and conclusions appear to be a bit premature. We are left with some questions still unanswered and some ends still loose. Although it may well be that the questions are unanswerable given our present state of empirical knowledge, there is more to it than that.

To begin with, when attempting to test the Heckscher-Ohlin theory in either its traditional or its human capital modified form, one should not repeat the mistake of Leontief by failing to establish empirically beforehand whether the country in question is abundant or scarce in the relevant factors of production vis-à-vis that country's main trading partners. Felix is hazy on this point, but he appears to hold "the view that Argentina with its literate labor force, sizable cadre of university-trained professionals, and modest real wages and salaries may have a potential advantage in various skill-intensive industrial exports to Latin America and perhaps to advanced markets as well."

The .407 Spearman correlation coefficient between an Argentine skill index and exports as a percentage of output reinforces his belief and, according to Felix, is consistent with neo-Heckscher-Ohlin reasoning.

---

1. For this point, see Albert Hirschman, "The Political Economy of Import Substituting in Latin America," *The Quarterly Journal of Economics* (February 1968).

But what Felix has done at this point is to set up a straw man. A much simpler and more basic explanation of this positive correlation coefficient (which, by the way, Felix fails to mention is not statistically significant at the .05 level) is that skill- or technology-intensive products usually have a high value to transportation costs ratio, and are therefore likely to be exported *and imported* in greater amounts than non-skill-intensive products. Better indices of comparative advantage (which, in fact, have already been developed and used by many economists[2]) would be exports minus competitive imports divided by production, or exports as percentage of the total exports of the country's main trading partners. This index would probably show that Argentina's net exports are non-skill-intensive. This would agree with what Lowinger found to be true for Brazil.[3]

When Felix next finds a −.412 correlation coefficient between Argentine gross exports and an index showing Argentine skill-intensity relative to U.S. skill-intensity (which, again, he fails to point out is not statistically significant), he then claims that this must be disturbing to Heckscher-Ohlin *aficionados.* In defense of Heckscher-Ohlin, it should be pointed out that their theory does not predict that a skill-abundant country will have a comparative advantage in industries that are skill-intensive relative to corresponding industries in other countries. It does assert that a country will have a comparative advantage in industries that are skill-intensive relative to *other* industries. Felix's Argentine-to-U.S. skill index tells us nothing about comparative advantage. All it tells us is that the elasticity of substitution of skills for nonskills with respect to factor price changes appears to be higher in the more skill-intensive industries. The correlation coefficient of −.729 between the Argentine-U.S. skill index and the Argentine skill index, which is the only correlation coefficient that is statistically significant at the .01 level in Felix's Table 5, actually supports the Heckscher-Ohlin theory by indicating a positive correlation between U.S. and Argentine skill requirements. In fact, the direct correlation (calculated by this writer) between U.S. and Argentine skill indices produced a Spearman coefficient of +.868. This, of course, is evidence in support of the absence of factor-intensity reversals in skills between the United States and Argentina, a requirement that is crucial to the Heckscher-Ohlin theorem.

Even if Felix's criticism of the Heckscher-Ohlin theory were not based on a theoretical misspecification of the theorem, the empirical evidence on skill endowments still indicates, contrary to Felix's view, that

2. See, for example, Donald Keesing, "The Impact of Research and Development on U.S. Trade," *Journal of Political Economy* 75 (February 1967): 38-48, and Thomas Lowinger, "The Neo-Factor Proportions Theory of International Trade: An Empirical Investigation," *American Economic Review* 61 (September 1971): 675-81.

3. See Lowinger, "Neo-Factor Proportions Theory."

Argentina is not skill-abundant relative to her main trading partners. In another study, calculations from OECD data show that "skilled workers" make up from 9 percent to 5 percent of the labor force in manufacturing in Sweden, the United States, France, the United Kingdom, Canada, and Germany, and only about 3 percent in Argentina, Panama, and Mexico.[4] Felix's own data, showing the Argentina-to-U.S. skill ratio, indicate that only one industry in Argentina is more skill-intensive than its counterpart in the United States. The industry is leather products, which is just barely relatively skill-intensive with an index of 1.004.[5] On both theoretical and empirical grounds, Felix's point that Argentina is violating Heckscher-Ohlin postulates must be placed in serious doubt.

Felix attempts to explain this "apparent" violation of Heckscher-Ohlin principles by disaggregating trade into a non-LAFTA component in order to determine if this subset of trade is less skill-intensive than Argentina's trade with the rest of the world. Because of lack of data availability, Felix has to invoke the "BTN theorem" to justify use of total value-added per worker as a proxy for skill-intensity. Previous work, including that of Leontief, has demonstrated that the use of physical capital statistics in explaining trade flows can lead one down a one-way street in the wrong direction. From Leontief, Vanek, and Kenen's work, one now should expect that the exports of less-developed countries to industrialized countries are capital-intensive due to the complementarity between natural resources and physical capital. Thus, this effect may have hidden the expected finding that Argentine exports to LAFTA countries are more human capital-intensive than her exports to non-LAFTA countries. The use of total value-added data probably leads Felix to an unsubstantiated, if not faulty, conclusion. He states that this evidence strengthens the inference that Argentina has been violating at least static comparative advantage in its nontraditional industrial exporting.

Perhaps the paper's major empirical contribution is the extensive number of log regressions that were run in an attempt to explain the growth of Argentina's nontraditional industrial exports over the period 1956-68. LAFTA concessions seemed to explain exports to LAFTA countries, while excess capacity explained exports to non-LAFTA countries. The real exchange rate was not statistically significant in most cases. Although high R^2's were attained in the majority of cases, unfortunately there appear to be some problems in the specification of the model. To be specific, Felix has left out the demand side. What Felix should be trying to explain is not the increase of Argentina's industrial exports over a thirteen-year period, but the change in Argentina's share of world exports of manufactures over this period. Almost all the major countries

4. See J. F. Morrall, "The Human Capital and Product Cycle Explanations of Trade" (Ph.D. diss., University of North Carolina at Chapel Hill, 1971), p. 114.
5. See Felix's Table 4.

of the world had an increase in their exports of manufactures over this time period. Thus, a proxy for world demand, such as world exports of manufactures, should have been included in the regression analysis as an independent variable. Also, it is usually the case when economists use time series annual data, and especially when some key variables have been left out, that serial correlation becomes a problem. However, Felix evidently did not test for this since the Durbin-Watson statistic does not appear anywhere in the paper. If serial correlation is significant, his conclusions may have to be modified.

To check for this possibility, Felix's equations A-1, A-2, and A-3 were rerun and it was found that serial correlation does indeed present a problem. The Durbin-Watson statistic indicates significant positive correlation for A-3 and indeterminate results for A-1. Only in equation A-2, all nontraditional exports to LAFTA countries, does there appear to be no serial correlation.

Second, to test for the importance of world demand, these same three equations were rerun, this time including a time variable as a proxy for increasing world demand. These results appear in Table 1. The inclusion of a proxy for world demand does raise adjusted R^2 when exports are disaggregated to LAFTA and non-LAFTA countries, but it does not in the case of exports to the whole world.[6] The time variable is almost significant at .10 in the LAFTA case, reducing the significance of the concessions variable and capacity variables about equally, and it is significant at .05 in the non-LAFTA case, reducing the significance of the capacity index from .01 to .10. The results from this additional empirical work are that the Felix conclusions should not be accepted wholeheartedly (because of the auto-correlation problem) and that external influences are probably as important in determining non-LAFTA trade as are internal influences.

One way out of the problem posed by serial correlation is, of course, to use cross-sectional analysis. In fact, Felix provides as many cross-sectional observations, i.e., industries, as he does time series observations, i.e., years, there being thirteen of each. As a quick check, Spearman rank correlation coefficients were calculated for the year 1964 between exports as a percentage of output for the thirteen industries, which is the same measure of export competitiveness that Felix uses later in the paper, and the three independent variables used by Felix plus one proxy for the LAFTA effect. The Spearman coefficients between the export index and the real exchange rate, the capacity utilization index, and LAFTA concessions are −.29, −.33, and .59, all insignificant at the .05 level except the last and the coefficient for the exchange rate having a sign opposite

6. Note that the adjusted R^2's in Table 1 cannot be directly compared with the R^2's in Felix's Table 2 because Felix does not adjust his R^2 for loss of degrees of freedom.

the one expected. Although the LAFTA coefficient is significant, it may be misleading because of reverse causality. One would expect export-oriented industries to lobby for a greater number of concessions than import-competing industries.

To check out the LAFTA effect more fully, exports to LAFTA as a percentage of total exports were calculated and correlated with the export index. The result was a coefficient of − .13, which has the wrong sign and is insignificant. Thus, the LAFTA influence does not appear to be

TABLE 1

Log Regressions of Nontraditional Industrial Exports, 1956-68, on "Real" Exchange Rates, Capacity Utilization Rates, and Number of LAFTA Concessions (All Lagged 1 Year)

	Constant	Real Exchange Rate	Capacity Index	LAFTA Concessions	Time Variable	R^2	Durbin-Watson F Ratio
A-1 to all areas	4.672	.223 (.539)	−1.577 (−1.283)	.0207[b] (2.700)	3.358 (.689)	.873	1.72 21.6
A-2 to LAFTA	3.674	.208 (.459)	−1.279 (−0.951)		7.321 (1.374)	.898	2.08 27.4
A-3 to rest of world	3.628	.073 (.136)	−2.548[a] (−1.584)		9.007[b] (2.211)	.689	1.01 9.84

[a]Indicates significance at the .10 level.
[b]Indicates significance at the .05 level.

important in explaining Argentina's export competitiveness, and the cross-sectional results appear to be in conflict with Felix's time series approach.

Certainly further work, especially of this cross-sectional nature, remains to be done. The results above may reflect more the inadequacies of the available data than the validity of the hypothesized models.

The most surprising result to me of both Felix's regression analysis and the rank correlation analysis above is that the exchange rate does not turn out to be statistically significant. This is especially surprising since a similar study of Brazil done by William Tyler using quarterly data did find the adjusted real exchange rate to be statistically significant.[7] But perhaps Felix's result is due to the formulation of the exchange rate variable that he used. One of the most important recent develop-

7. See the discussion of Felix's paper by Tyler in this volume.

ments of tariff and exchange rate theory is the concept of the effective rate of protection. This development has been associated with Bela Balassa and Daniel Schydlowsky.[8]

The idea is that it is not just the exchange rate on the finished product that determines the full effect of a country's exchange rate structure on an industry's competitiveness; the exchange rates applicable to the inputs of that industry are also important. An industry that has to pay an above-average price for its inputs will certainly have difficulty in exporting its output to other countries. Given Argentina's multiple exchange rate system, which ranged in 1966 from 200 pesos per dollar for agricultural exports to 700 pesos per dollar for finished-product imports, and taking the full structure of the exchange rate into account, Felix's conclusions are likely to be significantly altered. One might find that, indeed, the exchange rate has played a significant part in determining Argentine export competitiveness. Again, there are some unanswered questions and a need for more work in refining and testing these concepts.

Finally, let me emphasize that I do agree with Felix's main general conclusion, i.e., that the many years of import-substituting industrialization which Argentina has gone through have now made it extremely difficult for Argentina to undertake a vigorous export expansion phase. Felix seems overly pessimistic, however, about Argentina's potential for success. First of all, it does not appear that Argentina has been exporting products in which it has a comparative disadvantage. Second, the time variable regressions indicate that world demand has played an important part in increasing at least the absolute volume of nontraditional exports. Third, the evidence for Brazil and most other countries indicates that exchange rates do matter and can be manipulated to promote export growth, and finally, it may well be that economic determinism usually prevails over "basic sociopolitical impasses."

Discussion

N. KALDOR: Felix's regression equations do not prove much about the lack of importance of competitiveness in exports. On the contrary, I would say that the excess capacity variable tends to prove the opposite. I presume you calculate a real exchange rate by taking wholesale prices

8. B. Balassa, "Tariff Protection in Industrial Countries: An Evaluation," *Journal of Political Economy* 73 (December 1965): 573-94. See also B. Balassa and D. M. Schydlowsky, "Effective Tariffs, the Domestic Cost of Foreign Exchange and the Equilibrium Exchange Rate," *Journal of Political Economy* (June 1968), and Schydlowsky's paper in this volume.

and adjusting them for various things. But this is quite irrelevant from the point of view of export competitiveness of industrial goods, because the difference between Argentine and world prices is not in price *levels* but in price *structures*. Therefore, a real exchange rate based on price *levels* reveals nothing about the real exchange rate applicable to a particular class of goods, such as manufactured products. The higher and more extreme the protection, the greater the difference between the internal price relationship of agricultural and industrial prices and the world price relationship, the less appropriate that indicator is. On the other hand, the fact that exports are sensitive to excess capacity does mean, in my view, that prices *are* important. In economic terms, the significance of excess capacity is that exports are marginal and the greater excess capacity is, the more manufacturers are willing to dump exports at prices below the prices at which they sell at home. The lower the excess capacity, the less is this difference between the two prices. Therefore, the very fact that excess capacity is important means also that competitiveness is important.

I think the Heckscher-Ohlin theory is complete nonsense. Its main presumption is that there exists a production function which, in some sense, applies equally to the United States, Argentina, and any other country at any one time. This is obviously untrue. One of the reasons why it is untrue is that the function is assumed to be linear—this is critical to the theory. That is, the theory assumes constant returns to scale, whereas the most important thing about industry is the existence of increasing returns to scale, both of the static and the dynamic type, due to learning-by-doing and economies of differentiation, specialization, etc. Therefore, theorizing about "factor endowments" determining what a country should or should not export is irrelevant. Argentina cannot export because Argentine industry is inefficient, which means it has a very *low* production function in neoclassical, or Heckscher-Ohlin, terms. It has a *different* production function and a very low one.

Finally, the value-added measure is arbitrary, because one can always increase the "value-added" merely by increasing the measure of protection. If one had a 500 percent duty on motorcar imports, it follows that the "value-added" in the motorcar industry would be very much higher in terms of local prices than if one had only 100 percent protection. To make any sense of "value-added" it must be measured at international prices, not domestic prices.

I. NAVARRETE: I have great intellectual admiration for the Heckscher-Ohlin theory, but I also think there are several important factors that it does not take into account. More important than factor endowment is the size of the market. The existence of potentially large markets makes it possible to gain certain advantages by negotiation of power groups, which the Heckscher-Ohlin theory does not take into account. Nor does it consider the increasing importance of international corporations, common markets, and the economics of big and competing economic units. Another neglected aspect is the possibility of manipulation of relative prices, like the exchange rate.

H. HINRICHS: Felix might have said something more about not only the weird production functions within Argentina, but also the weird consumption functions. That is, in a sense the pricing policies within Argentina not only for capital goods but also for consumption goods affect the capacity to export, especially in the beef industry. I think that looking more at pricing within Argentina is really the only way to explain what is happening to both traditional and nontraditional exports.

W. TYLER: Although there are many facets of Felix's study, some of my own recent work done with Brazil coincides well with his analysis and findings. As is the case with Argentina, the composition of Brazil's industrial exports is capital- and skill-intensive. Although this situation raises questions in terms of the Heckscher-Ohlin theorem, the apparent paradox in the case of Brazil's industrial exports can be resolved within the general framework of Heckscher-Ohlin.[1] When adjustments are made for natural resource content, market destination, and other factors, the paradox disappears. In the Argentine case, contrary to Felix's interpretation, it may well be that the findings are also consistent with Heckscher-Ohlin. Given the intermediate range of Argentina's per capita income and supposed skill and capital endowment, we would expect that her exports to less developed economies would be more capital-intensive than those going to more-developed (and more capital- and skill-rich) countries. The data that Felix presents suggest support for this hypothesis. Felix does not discuss the natural resource content of Argentine industrial exports, but one suspects that such an examination might also provide some clues for better understanding the nature of Argentine comparative advantages.

An attempt, similar to Felix's, was made to utilize regression analysis to explain variance in Brazil's manufactured exports. The basic regression equation included independent variables representing the real exchange rate, tax incentives, capacity utilization, industrial production, the LAFTA effect, and the growth of total world demand.[2] In contrast to the Felix study, all data were broken down on a quarterly basis, thereby expanding the degrees of freedom. In order to complement the regression analysis, in-depth interviews were conducted with thirty-one varied industrial producers.

The results of this statistical analysis parallel Felix's. In the Brazilian

1. See William G. Tyler, "The Labor Skill Content of Brazilian Trade in Manufactures," mimeographed paper for AID (October 1970).

2. See William G. Tyler, "Manufactured Export Promotion in a Semi-Industrialized Economy: The Brazilian Case," *The Journal of Development Studies*, October 1973.

case, the recession-boom effect, as manifested through decreasing and increasing capacity utilization, exercises a significant influence on the performance of industrial exports. In periods of industrial recession exports of manufactures grow rapidly, whereas in times of rapid industrial expansion such exports grow at a rate below the trend. This suggests that in Brazil, as perhaps in Argentina, industrial producers view the export market as only a complement to the domestic market.

While in the Argentine case the exchange rate variable does not appear as statistically significant, this is not the case in Brazil. The regression analysis produced a statistically significant, "correct" positive sign for the real exchange rate coefficient. This finding was further supported by the interviewing survey, in which producers not only noted the importance of the real exchange rate but also emphasized the manner of its adjustment. In mid-1968 the Brazilian government announced a policy of more frequent devaluations, occurring every three or four weeks, in order to allow for a more orderly depreciation of the currency accompanying the inflation. Producers stressed the fact that such a policy better enabled them to predict export profitability when domestic production costs were continuously increasing.

Tax incentives have occupied an important position in the Brazilian government's attempts to promote the export of manufactures. As is the case with Argentina and most other less-developed countries, Brazil's indirect taxes on industrial products are considerable. To provide for greater competitiveness of its manufactures in international markets, Brazil has exempted exports from the payment of certain indirect taxes and has established a subsidy element as well. It is estimated that by mid-1969 the tax incentives had risen to a magnitude of some 42 percent of the domestic market price. This would correspond to devaluation of the same amount.

Contrary to the impression gathered in the interviewing survey, the regression analysis did not indicate much effectiveness for the tax incentives in promoting exports. This was due to the recent nature of tax incentive implementation (important incentives only after mid-1965) and to what I interpreted as a natural lag in their effect. Almost without exception, the firms interviewed attached great importance to the tax incentives both because of their magnitude and because of the confidence inspired by the government through its indication of an interest in export promotional problems.

Regression analysis approaches to this type of problem, while conceptually correct, are fraught with practical limitations. Problems with serial correlation of residuals, multicollinearity, and identification provide constraints on the use of regression analysis for explicating export performance. In addition, there are very serious problems in quantifying certain intangibles, such as confidence, uncertainty, etc., which play important roles in determining export behavior. All this suggests that such analysis alone is not adequate for making policy decisions.

D. FELIX: My paper does not test the Heckscher-Ohlin theory, but rather uses part of it provisionally to analyze a subset of relatively highly processed industrial products—the so-called nontraditional exports—that Argentina has been attempting to promote. The techniques used in producing these products—at least as concerns equipment and product specification—have been largely imported. There are no visible mechanisms in Argentina for doing much in the way of local adaptation of these imported technologies. Many of the plants are foreign subsidiaries, local R and D outlays are minimal, machinery is either imported or produced locally under foreign licensing, and many consumer manufactures are also constrained to imported specifications by licensing arrangements. Undoubtedly, scale differences have impelled some modifications of the imported technologies, and lower wages as well as organizational inefficiencies have probably also somewhat altered factor proportions from the norms of the countries exporting the technologies. I do not believe, however, that Argentine industries share the same efficiency envelope with, say, the United States and Japan, but that they are largely scattered in the interior space.

Under these conditions and with the price of comparable equipment and industrial materials generally higher in Argentina than in the technology-exporting countries, the more physical capital-intensive Argentine industry is, the less likely it is to be able to export profitably in open markets.

The effect of skill-intensity is somewhat more complex. Argentine skilled labor is generally judged to be good and cheap by American and West European standards. But there is also probably a positive correlation between the relative skill-intensity of an industry and the level of technological sophistication of the industry product mix, to blend Heckscher-Ohlin with Raymond Vernon. The businessman's ceaseless quest for temporary and quasi-permanent monopoly devices—the driving force that makes the capitalist world go round—is thus pursued with particularly powerful weapons in the technologically sophisticated industries: heavy marketing and R and D outlays, rapid product obsolescence, etc., with large-scale operations an essential means of reducing unit costs of these outlays and spreading risk. If high skill-intensity is a rough proxy for these competitive attributes in the industrially advanced economies, then counterpart Argentine industries are probably at a serious long-run disadvantage in competing with them in open markets, despite the relative cheapness of Argentine skilled labor.

Concerning the regressions, there is probably a time trend built into the LAFTA concessions; exports in period t are likely to be influenced by concessions made in t–2 . . . , t–k as well as by those made in t–1. If each of the concessions were fairly generic one might even expect the weights of the distributed lag relationship to rise with age of concession, although I suspect this is not so for the highly specific and circumscribed LAFTA concessions. In any event, one would need another ten years or more of data before it becomes feasible to experiment with various lag structures. A poor excuse, but unavoidable.

As for bringing world demand into the regressions, this would be silly in my view. Given the minute Argentine share of world industrial exports, demand is probably infinitely elastic and virtually impervious to shifts in the level of world income. For LAFTA, demand elements might be a bit more relevant, although probably not by much in view of the small portion of industrial output that LAFTA countries exchange with each other. In any case, three lagged variables for fourteen years of observations is already pushing the limit of creaibility, although this again is no justification for not taking my results with a grain of salt.

On the use of value-added as a proxy for capital-intensity, I use the Lary approach merely to test whether the anti-Heckscher-Ohlin relationships suggested by two-digit industry analysis fade away when more disaggregated industry data are used. The fact that the two alternative approaches to ranking industries by factor-intensity generate similar results somewhat strengthens the validity of each approach as well as of the industry ranking. Industry differences in value-added per person may, of course, also incorporate differences in indirect taxes, wage rates, and profit margins, and it is unlikely that these interindustry differences will be the same in each country. The fairly high correlations in Table 6 suggest that the intercountry differences may be moderate, but not that they do not exist. Similarly, Table 8 indicates that in Argentina the more capital- and skill-intensive Group I industries had on the average a smaller decline in the wage share and a higher increase in nonwage value-added per worker than did the Group II industries. Nevertheless, Group II was able to increase its nonwage value-added share despite a negligible rise in its value-added per worker, implying an intertemporal improvement in relative prices and labor market bargaining power for that slow-growing group of industries. Thus, while I believe that the factor-intensity rankings in the paper are plausible, they should not be digested unsalinated.

I did not do a survey as Tyler did in Brazil, but referred to one made by Dagnino Pastore in late 1963, which indicated that the industrialist respondents assigned little importance to comparative cost when asked to select likely exporting industries. The industries chosen were mainly those producing technically sophisticated products, and the four chief reasons given for the choices were: other LAFTA countries did not produce the products, i.e., reduced risk; current excess capacity; future excess capacity; and progressive management. Favorable production cost was far down the list of reasons, even though the survey instructions urged respondents to consider comparative costs as a prime criterion.

The sensitivity of exports or imports to exchange rates is likely to vary considerably with the conjuncture of circumstances. I would suggest than an essential element in the relative effectiveness of current Brazilian exchange policy is that its hard-line military regime has been able to hold down wages. This has not been possible for long in Argentina during the postwar era even during the frequent periods of military rule. The feedback of devaluations on domestic wage demands, and of these two on domestic prices, has been so powerful that Argentine governments, regardless of their original intent, have usually wound up using exchange rate overvaluation as an antiinflationary device. Sustained relative price shifts between internal and external prices have thus been hard to effect in Argentina, and this awareness permeates both government and business decision making. The price of a more effective price mechanism in Latin America today may well be weak labor organization, muzzled intellectuals, and military diktat in place of parliamentary politics. I offer this as a *wert-frei* analytic proposition qua economist; as a human being, the price is excessive to me.

10

Fiscal Policy for Full-Capacity
Industrial Growth in Latin America

DANIEL M. SCHYDLOWSKY

A LATIN AMERICAN ENIGMA: KEYNESIAN UNEMPLOYMENT?

THE Latin American economies are generally thought to be amply endowed with labor and rather scarcely endowed with capital. It is usually concluded that this structure in the relative availability of factors of production leads to the existence of unemployment and of low-productivity employment of labor. Unemployment is indeed high in Latin America at the present time and appears to be growing. The Latin American Institute of Economic and Social Planning has estimated the level of unemployment in Latin America to be about 11 percent. If the underemployed are included, this figure rises to 25 percent. If output grows at historical rates, overt unemployment is estimated at 18 percent for 1980.[1]

While the existence of unemployment is indisputable, evidence is also gradually accumulating on the presence of underutilization of capital. Not only do many of the Latin American economies periodically use their installed productive capacity at levels below their own customary norm, the norm itself is based on utilization of capital at less than 24 hours a day for 365 days a year less maintenance. Whereas in the developed countries, the relative factor endowment makes it undesirable to use the capital stock around the clock day in and day out, in economies with a surplus of labor of the magnitude that the Latin American countries apparently have, it is to be expected that the optimal use of factors would require much more intensive utilization of the capital stock than is observed in developed countries or than is in fact observed in the Latin American economies themselves. While systematic information of the extent of multiple shifting is not available at the present time, it is common knowledge in Latin America that on the average a plant and equip-

1. "The Unemployment Problem in Latin America," Organization of American States, Third Inter-American Conference of Ministers of Labor of the Alliance for Progress, Document 10 (18 September 1969).

ment are used on a one-shift basis, the exceptions being process-centered industries in which around-the-clock operation is required for technical reasons. Deviations from the usual norm have been tabulated in Argentina for the periods 1961-65 and show capacity utilization to have fluctuated between 55 percent and 67 percent of this norm on the average. The sectoral details of these data are shown in Table 1.

The existence concurrently of unutilized labor and unutilized capital throws considerable doubt on the prevailing hypothesis that unemployment in Latin America is of the structural kind. Rather, it suggests the

TABLE 1

ARGENTINA: UTILIZATION OF INSTALLED CAPACITY

Sector	Percentage of Actual Output with Respect to Maximum Output			
	1961	1963	1964	1965
Food and beverages	48.8	53.2	48.9	51.5
Tobacco	82.7	81.9	88.6	91.2
Textiles	83.2	59.2	68.9	77.1
Clothing	88.3	64.2	72.5	78.4
Wood	72.7	48.6	55.2	70.4
Paper and cardboard	55.1	48.3	52.7	62.4
Printing and publishing	73.3	58.3	62.4	70.8
Chemicals	73.4	59.9	68.1	73.8
Petroleum derivatives	87.9	78.?	84.7	83.6
Rubber	80.5	54.0	66.2	77.6
Leather	84.2	66.8	77.8	79.9
Stone, glass, and ceramics	70.2	59.0	68.7	71.8
Metals (excluding machinery)	59.4	40.8	50.3	66.6
Vehicles and machinery (excluding electrical equipment)	78.6	44.6	56.5	65.6
Electrical machines and equipment	59.2	43.5	47.6	61.0
Weighted average	67.2	54.6	59.5	66.1

SOURCE: CONADE, results of the Survey on Production and Investment Expectations of Industrial Enterprises (Buenos Aires: CONADE, March 1965), Table 3.

possibility that Latin America is faced with a typical Keynesian unemployment problem. Such a conclusion is tempting; however, it must be borne in mind that production cannot simply go forward on the basis of capital and unskilled labor as the only factors of production. In the Latin American context, skilled labor, management, and foreign exchange are equally crucial factors of production. Yet none of these factors can be thought of as existing in absolutely fixed supply. Surely skilled labor can be trained if there is a demand for it; entrepreneurs will appear if there are profit opportunities or if they themselves have "excess capacity"; and finally, foreign exchange is a produced input and, with suitable macroeconomic policies, is available as any other intermediate product rather than as a primary factor of production. Thus it does seem appropriate to conclude that Latin America is at present beset by an unemployment problem more akin to a Keynesian situation than to a structural development one.

If this conclusion is correct, Latin America has a very considerable potential for increasing its level of income, its growth rate, and its employment simply by using its existing factors more fully. The growth problem in Latin America then becomes very closely entangled with the problem of utilization of resources rather than being in the first instance a problem of allocation.

Such a change in emphasis also makes considerable difference to the framework of analysis in which Latin American policy is conducted. For example, in such a context import substitution *à outrance*, which has been repeatedly criticized on allocation grounds, appears more reasonable. If *all* domestic factors are in excess supply, any and all foreign exchange saving activity is desirable. It is only when at least one of the domestic factors has nonzero costs that a comparison of different ways of saving (or earning) foreign exchange becomes relevant. Although Latin American import-substitution policies offer some grounds for believing that policy makers were aware of the nature of their economies' unemployment, such a recognition, if extant, clearly did not carry over to other areas of policy.

BARRIERS TO CAPACITY UTILIZATION

A number of factors inhibit the fuller utilization of installed capacity on the part of industrial firms. The main ones are the following.

Unavailability of Market for the Product

The domestic markets of the various Latin American countries are of such limited size that the productive capacity, operating at one shift or less, is able to satisfy the total demand forthcoming at prices that allow the accustomed profit to be made. It is of course true that any one of the firms in an industry could reduce its price and attempt to drive its competitors out of business in order to then satisfy the whole market at a fuller level of utilization of its installed capacity. From the point of view of the economy as a whole, such a development primarily reallocates excess capacity, capacity usage only expanding to the extent that a lower price increases the total industry sales.

Price cutting of this kind happens only rarely, if at all, because of the oligopolistic structure of the market, each participant knowing that the others will retaliate and uncertain of his own final success. At the same time, the government is aware that an artificial expansion of the domestic market through the extension of consumer or producer credit is not feasible in the long run due to the balance-of-payments effects of expanding output. Since Latin American industry by and large requires some imported material inputs in order to be able to operate, an expansion of demand in the domestic market and the consequent increase in domestic production to supply it implies immediately a rise in imports which is not sustainable over the long term, given the balance-of-payments situations of these countries. Finally, the export market is not a relevant one for most Latin American producers due to the level of their costs, which at the current exchange rates is considerably above the prices they can obtain in the export markets. Market conditions are such, then, that there is nowhere to place the increased output arising from fuller utilization of capacity.

Unavailability of Working Capital

Since production is not instantaneous, a certain amount of working capital is needed for maintenance of stocks of raw material, goods in process, and finished products. Latin American industry typically finances this working capital with bank credit. This implies that unless credit for working capital were expanded, fuller utilization of capital would be made impossible through a constraint on the possibility of maintaining the required inventories of various types of materials and goods in process.[2] In addition it must be borne in mind that some of these inventories consist of imported products and thus their increase has balance-of-payments effects.

Unavailability of Skilled Personnel

Skilled and supervisory labor are inputs complementary to capital, unskilled labor, and foreign exchange. The total unavailability of such labor could therefore prevent any production from taking place. The extreme case of such unavailability arises in the family firm wherein the management is fully concentrated in the owner himself, who, of course, cannot work twenty-four hours a day. In larger firms, with hired management, this problem becomes less acute. Nevertheless, the procurement of supervisory labor of adequate quality to work the second and third shifts is no negligible problem. At the same time, the process-centered industries in which the nature of the technical process requires working around the clock, have found it possible to obtain the requisite type of labor; thus

2. For a general argument in favor of considering credit a factor of production, cf. G. Maynard and W. van Rijkeghem, "Stabilization Policy in an Inflationary Economy," in G. F. Papanek, ed., *Development Policy: Theory and Practice* (Cambridge, Mass.: Harvard University Press, 1968).

it is difficult to believe that other industries would not be equally success-ful. It appears useful, therefore, to think of this element more as gener-ating an extra cost rather than as raising a question of absolute avail-ability.

Labor Cost Structure

The movement to a second and/or third shift implies a discrete enlarge-ment in the labor force in industry. In the context of labor regimes in which hiring is considerably easier than firing due to laws protecting the stability of employment, regulations governing severance pay, vacations, etc.,[3] such a commitment on the part of industry has aspects similar to those of investment in a fixed asset.[4] In addition, labor laws or collective bargaining contracts often specify higher pay for second- and third-shift work, thus making the hiring of additional labor for fuller-capacity utiliza-tion through multiple shifting more expensive than the acquisition of a similar amount of labor to work a first shift on additional capital goods.

Tax Legislation

Depreciation rules for corporate income tax purposes are typically related to a number of calendar years according to the type of equipment. No allowance is made for the level of intensity with which the equipment is used. As a result, the total allowable depreciation can be used as a de-duction from taxable profits arising out of first shift operation. If a second or third shift of production is added, no further deduction for deprecia-tion can be taken from taxable profits. In consequence, the same tax rate has a higher incidence on each peso of profit earned from a second or third shift than it does on a peso of profit earned from the first shift. However, such a differential impact is equivalent to a higher corporate tax rate on second- and third-shift profits and constitutes a disincentive to the operation of such shifts.

THE AVAILABILITY OF A MARKET AND OF FOREIGN EXCHANGE INPUTS

We have noted before that the internal market, at current levels of ag-gregate demand, is not sufficient to absorb the additional output arising from fuller utilization of the industrial capacity. At the same time, it is

3. The current *cost* of fringe benefits to the hiring enterprises was estimated in 1957 by R. A. Ferrero for Peru at 41.4 percent of wages for blue-collar workers and 45.9 percent for white-collar workers. The impact of a substantial dismissal on com-pany liquidity requires a different analysis, however. Cf. R. A. Ferrero and A. J. Alt-meyer, "Estudio Económico de la Legislación Social Peruana y Superencias para su Mejoramiento" (Lima, 1957).

4. For a more general discussion of labor force hiring as a fixed investment, cf. Raymond Vernon, "Organization as a Scale Factor in the Growth of Firms," in J. Markham and G. F. Papanek, eds., *Industrial Organization and Economic Develop-ment* (Boston: Houghton Mifflin, 1970).

not possible to expand the aggregate demand without placing an intolerable strain on the balance of payments. The obvious solution is to look to the export market, which has sufficient capacity to absorb the additional output of any one Latin American country and indeed of all of them together. In addition, the placing of output on the foreign market would provide the necessary foreign exchange to acquire the imported inputs necessary for production to go forward. The problems of market availability and foreign exchange availability are therefore interdependent and can be solved simultaneously. Moreover, it is worth bearing in mind that as industrial exports increase and the availability of foreign exchange is thereby augmented, it becomes possible to adopt a more expansive aggregate demand policy, thus absorbing some of the increased industrial output in the domestic market. In consequence, the balanced policy will be one in which only a part of the additional industrial product gets exported, the remainder being absorbed by the domestic market through an expansion in the aggregate demand therein. The precise point of balance is one in which the new industrial exports cover precisely the new import requirement generated by the output itself as well as by the additional domestic aggregate demand.

A necessary condition for such a policy to be feasible is the price competitiveness of industrial output.[5] This condition is generally thought to be so difficult to fulfill that the Latin American policy makers have typically not looked at the export market as a likely place for absorbing any industrial output. The prevalent view is that Latin American industrial production is "very high-cost" and "inefficient." Such a conclusion is derived from a rather simple cost analysis which consists of taking the costs of production in local currency, dividing these costs through by the exchange rate, and comparing the resultant foreign exchange amount with the current price in the international markets. Such an analysis is fortunately highly misleading.

The Latin American economies all operate with an implicit multiple exchange rate system which consists of a unified financial exchange rate and a highly differentiated set of import and export taxes and other restrictions. The financial exchange rate, i.e., the amount of units of local currency for which a unit of foreign exchange sells in the local financial market, is the figure that receives most attention; but from the point of view of the impact on the economy's performance, the influence of the trade taxation and other trade restrictions is at least as important. Indeed, the whole "exchange rate system" is composed of the financial exchange rate and a large number of commodity exchange rates which are the multiple exchange rate equivalents of the existing taxes and other re-

5. This condition is not by itself likely to be a sufficient one. Quality of product and marketing channels with appropriate information feedback are two other conditions which are necessary in most situations.

strictions on commodity trade. Each commodity exchange rate is defined as the number of units of local currency for which a dollar's worth of imports at CIF prices (or exports at FOB prices) sells for (is bought at) on the domestic market. Each commodity exchange rate is equal to the financial exchange rate plus all the trade taxation and restrictions assessed on the import or export of that particular commodity. A single commodity may naturally have more than one commodity exchange rate depending on whether it is imported, exported, or traded under a variety of regimes.

A typical Latin American exchange rate system is structured like that of Argentina in 1966, which consisted of the following rates:[6]

Rate	Composition	Pesos/Dollar
Agricultural export	= Financial less 10% tax	= 200
Financial	= Financial	= 220 = official
Nontraditional export	= Financial + 18% tax rebate	= 260 rate
Raw material import	= Financial + 50% duty	= 330
Semimanufactures import	= Financial + 120% duty	= 460
Components import	= Financial + 175% duty	= 600
Finished products import	= Financial + 220% duty	= 700

Examining now the cost structure of the typical Argentinian industrial producer, we find that his imported material inputs would be acquired at an exchange rate ranging from 330 to 600 pesos per dollar. His domestic material inputs would be supplied by local producers at prices somewhat below the import point, i.e., at prices reflecting an exchange rate range of, say, 310 to 580 pesos per dollar. Finally, the typical producer's wage rate would reflect an exchange rate approximating the average exchange rate applying to industrial output in general, or about 600 pesos per dollar.[7] Thus our producer's cost exchange rate would approximate 450 to 500.

Two conclusions can be drawn from this calculation of the cost exchange rate. The first of these is that at a nontraditional export exchange rate of 260, the typical Argentinian producer could not have been expected to export. Indeed, he was implicitly subject to a substantial export tax through the relative exchange rates for costs and sales with which he was confronted. This situation, of course, generalizes to Latin America as a whole: the import commodity rates are very disparate and invariably higher than the financial and the nontraditional export rates. Table 2 shows the ratio of commodity import rates to the financial rates for two-digit industries in Brazil, Chile, and Mexico.

6. "Proyecto de Modificación de la Estructura Arancelario-Cambiaria," Camara Argentina de Radio, Televisión, Telecomunicaciones y Afines (Cartta), September 1966.
7. w = marginal physical product (MPP) × price of output. If the unit of output is set at an amount costing one dollar CIF, then we have w = marginal physical product × average commodity exchange rate for output.

The second conclusion is that it is inappropriate to take local currency costs and compare them to world prices by means of the financial exchange rate. Since costs are based on an exchange rate substantially above the financial exchange rate, the comparison of these costs with world prices by means of the financial rate implies an overstatement in the dollar costs. The standard cost calculations, therefore, generate an

TABLE 2

IMPORT COMMODITY RATES IN SELECTED LATIN AMERICAN COUNTRIES
(FINANCIAL RATE = 1.00)

Sector	Brazil (1967)	Chile (1961)	Mexico (1960)
Nonmetallic mineral products	1.40	2.39	.96
Metallurgy	1.34	1.66	1.30
Machinery	1.34	1.84	1.30
Electrical equipment	1.57	2.05	1.25
Transport equipment	1.57	1.84	1.26–1.52
Wood products	1.23	1.35	1.14
Furniture	1.68	2.29	—
Paper and paper products	1.48	1.55	1.35
Rubber products	1.78	2.02	1.33
Leather products	1.66	2.61	1.20
Chemicals	1.34	1.94	1.24
Pharmaceuticals	1.37	—	1.12
Perfumes and soaps	1.94	—	1.10–1.22
Plastics	1.48	1.50	—
Textiles	1.81	2.82	1.30
Clothing	2.03	3.55	1.10
Food products	1.27	1.82	1.18
Beverages	1.83	2.22	1.28
Tobacco	1.78	2.06	1.31
Printing and publishing	1.59	1.72	1.13
Metal products	—	1.59	1.31
Fertilizers and insecticides	—	—	1.09

SOURCE: Joel Bergsman, and Pedro S. Malan, "The Structure of Protection in Brazil," Table 6.6, col. 5; T. Jeanneret, "The Structure of Protection in Chile," Table 7.8, col. 1; and G. Bueno, "The Structure of Protection in Mexico," Table 8.7, col. 3, in B. Balassa et al., *The Structure of Protection in Developing Countries* (Baltimore: Johns Hopkins University Press, 1971).

"inefficiency illusion" which "substantiates" the conviction that Latin American industrial production is high-cost and inefficient. An impression of the importance of the inefficiency illusion can be derived from Table 3, which presents estimates of the excess of local costs over the world price for Brazil on the basis of the financial exchange rate and an average industrial cost exchange rate.

Several additional factors need to be mentioned at this point. The antiexport bias introduced by the inequality of the industrial cost exchange rate and the nontraditional export exchange rate is made worse by the impact of transportation costs which reduce FOB prices below the CIF prices for equivalent commodities. Import duties in the developed countries serve to widen this FOB/CIF gap further and to reinforce the antiexport bias of the exchange rate system. On the other hand, if exports would be additional to rather than substitutive of domestic sales and if excess capacity is available, they might well have a marginal cost below the average cost of output for the domestic market. If such were the case,

TABLE 3

THE "INDUSTRIAL INEFFICIENCY ILLUSION" IN BRAZIL: EXCESS OF DOMESTIC
PRICE (COST) OVER INTERNATIONAL PRICE

Sector	At Financial Exchange Rate(%)	At Industrial Cost Exchange Rate(%)[a,b]
Nonmetallic minerals	40	− 5
Metallurgy	34	−10
Machinery	34	−10
Electrical equipment	57	6
Transport equipment	57	6
Wood products	23	−17
Furniture	68	13
Paper and paper products	48	0
Rubber products	78	20
Leather products	66	12
Chemicals	34	−10
Pharmaceuticals	37	− 7
Perfumes and soaps	94	31
Plastics	48	0
Textiles	81	22
Clothing	103	37
Food products	27	−14
Beverages	83	24
Tobacco	78	20
Printing and publishing	59	7

[a]Derived as follows: rate for intermediate products, 1.49; rate for wages, 1.48; average, 1.48.
[b]A negative sign indicates domestic price is below international price.

SOURCE: Joel Bergsman and Pedro Malan, "The Structure of Protection in Brazil," Tables 6.6, 6.8.

the antiexport bias in the exchange rate structure and in the world price structure would be somewhat offset. Further offsets could come from monopolistic market structures in the domestic commodity markets of potential export products of Latin America. Such structure essentially implies a marginal cost below the domestic price. Finally, monopolistic pricing in developed countries by producers of potential Latin American export products would also generate an offset by providing a higher price floor which must be undercut.

THE PRIVATE AND SOCIAL BENEFITS AND COSTS OF CAPACITY UTILIZATION

We have already established that utilization of capacity requires industrial exporting. We have also suggested that the generation of such exports is hampered by an exchange rate system that has a sufficiently large antiexport bias to make exporting unprofitable, i.e., at private prices benefits from export sales (revenue) fall short of costs (expenditure).

An estimate of the excess of costs of production in Brazil, Chile, and Mexico over prices in developed countries (on the assumption of fully competitive markets all around and no excess capacity) is shown in Table 4. Due to the various considerations discussed at the end of the last section, these figures overstate the true cost/price gap; however, the precise extent of this overstatement awaits a quantification of the impact on marginal costs and prices of levels of capacity use and market structure in both the exporting and importing countries.

The effect of the antiexport bias in the exchange rate system can be expressed as the percentage of per unit current value-added that could be paid to factors on the basis of revenue from export sales under the existing exchange rate structure. Table 5 shows such data for Brazil, Chile, and Mexico. It will be noticed that in some cases the antiexport bias is such that revenue from export sales would be insufficient to cover the costs of the material inputs required by such sales.

The social cost, i.e., the cost at shadow prices, of additional industrial production is substantially below private costs for a number of reasons. Labor costs would be much lower on several counts: unskilled labor is generally recognized to be in surplus supply and thus would have no opportunity cost from the point of view of the economy as a whole. Semiskilled and skilled labor is not so extensively available, but could be generated through the training of some of the existing surplus of unskilled labor. This training cost, however, when viewed in relation to the useful lifetime of the trainees, becomes a negligible magnitude. Nor is it appropriate to include in the shadow price of labor an item for reduction in society's investment,[8] except in the unlikely case that consumption out of the new wage bill caused a reduction in the absolute level of investment that would be forthcoming in the absence of the capacity-utilizing production. The social cost of labor in production is therefore negligible.

The social cost of capital is also substantially below the private cost. Since the use of installed capacity is at issue, the capital outlay has already been made. The only relevant cost for utilization is a possible user cost. This in turn depends on whether scrapping of installed capital is the result of actual physical deterioration or of technological obsolescence. If scrapping arises from wear, the social cost is equal to the present value of the output foregone due to earlier scrapping. Assuming

8. The "Little-Mirlees" adjustment. Cf. OECD, "Manual on Project Analysis."

TABLE 4

THE EXCESS OF COST OVER EXPORT PRICE FOR SELECTED LATIN AMERICAN COUNTRIES

Sector	Brazil				Chile				Mexico			
	Own Tariff (%)	Industrial Country Tariff (%)	Freight (%)	Total (%)[a]	Own Tariff (%)	Industrial Country Tariff (%)	Freight (%)	Total (%)	Own Tariff (%)	Industrial Country Tariff (%)	Freight (%)	Total (%)
Nonmetallic minerals	40	5	5	62	139	5	5	177	-4	5	5	11
Metallurgy	34	5	15	86	66	5	15	131	29	5	15	78
Machinery	34	22	8	90	84	22	8	103	30	22	8	84
Electrical equipment	57	22	8	122	105	22	8	191	25	22	8	77
Transportation equipment	57	22	8	122	84	22	8	161	26[b]	22	8	78
Wood products	23	5	30	119	35	5	30	140	14	5	30	103
Furniture	68	16	8	117	129	16	8	210	—	16	8	—
Paper and paper products	48	5	8	81	55	5	8	89	35	5	8	65
Rubber products	78	8	8	124	102	8	8	154	33	8	8	67
Leather products	66	16	8	114	161	16	8	252	20	16	8	62
Chemicals	34	8	8	69	94	8	8	54	24	8	8	56
Pharmaceuticals	37	8	8	73	—	8	8	—	12	8	8	41
Perfumes and soaps	94	16	8	162	—	16	8	—	10[c]	16	8	48
Plastics	48	8	8	87	30	8	8	64	—	8	8	—
Textiles	81	8	8	128	82	8	8	255	12[d]	8	8	41
Clothing	103	16	8	174	255	16	8	380	10	16	8	48
Metal products	—	8	8	—	60	8	8	100	31	8	8	65
Fertilizers and insecticides	—	8	8	—	—	8	8	—	9	8	8	38

[a] $\text{Total} = \left(1 + \frac{\text{own tariff}}{100}\right)\left(1 + \frac{\text{industrial tariff}}{100}\right)\left(1 + \frac{\text{freight}}{100}\right)^2 - 1$

[b] Railway equipment only.

[c] Soap only.

[d] Cotton textiles only.

SOURCES: Own Tariffs—Bergsman, Malan, Jeanneret, and Bueno, in Balassa, *Structure of Protection in Developing Countries*. Industrial Country Tariffs—Balassa, "The Structure of Protection in Industrial Countries and Its Effect on the Exports of Processed Goods from Developing Countries" (Paper submitted to UNCTAD II), Table 1. Freight—Balassa, footnote in above source taken from "Trade Prospects in Developing Nations."

the production from years twenty to forty is at issue, this will be substantially reduced by any reasonable discount rate. If scrapping is due to obsolescence, be it at private or social costs, then the marginal cost of using installed capacity is zero, except for additional maintenance cost.

The social benefit of capacity-utilizing industrial production can take two forms, depending on whether the output is (a) exported or (b) used to increase domestic absorption of the goods produced over the level obtaining in the absence of such production. In the first case the social benefit is equal to the net foreign exchange made available, i.e., to the difference between the foreign exchange value of the output and the foreign exchange value of the material inputs. For the output, FOB prices are relevant and for inputs, FOB or CIF prices should be used, depending for each material input on whether it is exported or imported (or is substituting for imports).

TABLE 5

THE ANTIEXPORT BIAS OF THE EXCHANGE RATE SYSTEM IN SELECTED LATIN AMERICAN COUNTRIES (PERCENTAGE OF ACTUAL FACTOR REMUNERATION PAYABLE ON THE BASIS OF EXPORT SALES)

Industry	Brazil	Chile	Mexico
Nonmetallic mineral products	.64	NVA[a]	—
Metallurgy	.68	NVA	.49
Machinery	.71	.03	.57
Electrical equipment	.36	.11	.71
Transport equipment	.46	.15	.57[b]
Wood products	.78	.30	.75
Furniture	.32	NVA	—
Paper and paper products	.54	.21	.38
Rubber products	.41	NVA	.53
Leather products	.43	NVA	.61
Chemicals	.66	NVA	.5
Pharmaceuticals	.06	—	.65
Perfumes and soaps	NVA	—	.50–.77
Plastics	.49	.34	—
Textiles	.68	NVA	.79[c]
Clothing	.34	NVA	.83
Food products	.66	NVA	.59
Beverages	.14	NVA	.55
Tobacco	.40	.04	.53
Printing and publishing	.52	.31	.77
Metal products	—	.28	.48
Fertilizers and insecticides	—	—	.77

[a]NVA = negative value-added, i.e., no payments to factors feasible.
[b]Railroad equipment only; motor vehicles have NVA.
[c]Cotton textiles.
SOURCES: Bergsman and Malan, "Structure of Protection in Brazil," Table 6.6; Jeanneret, "Structure of Protection in Chile," Table 7.8; and Bueno, "Structure of Protection in Mexico," Table 8.7.

If the output is used to increase domestic absorption, the social benefit is equal to the excess of the marginal social utility of the good whose absorption is increased over the marginal social cost of the material inputs required for production. This cost will equal the foreign exchange value of the material inputs converted to local currency at the marginal social utility of foreign exchange, if the material inputs are traded on the margin. It is worth noting that an activity may have negative social benefits under (a) and still yield positive benefits under (b) if the commodity concerned has a demand price (i.e., marginal utility) greater than the demand price for foreign exchange in general (i.e., marginal utility of foreign exchange), as is likely to be the case with commodities at the higher end of the protection spectrum.[9]

From an empirical point of view, most productive activities in Latin America yield positive social benefits under (a) and of the remainder only a few would fail to do so under (b). Thus, it can be concluded in general that the social benefit of using installed capacity is positive. Whether the social benefit will also exceed the social cost depends on the size of the benefit as well as on the importance of the user cost of capital as a social cost. It is to be expected, however, that utilization of installed capacity in a broad spectrum of activities would have a high excess of social benefits over social cost.

Fiscal Policy for Capacity Utilization

So far we have argued the following:

(a) The utilization of capacity requires that some of the new output generated with that utilization be exported.

(b) At social (shadow) prices, the export of part of the production arising from capacity utilization will leave a positive net benefit for a wide spectrum of activities.

(c) At private prices, exports are unprofitable.

It follows, therefore, that fiscal policy for capacity utilization must consist of making the export of industrial production profitable in those sectors in which it leaves a net benefit at social (shadow) prices. A version of such a policy is one which subsidizes exports.

Export subsidies have traditionally been opposed by the policy makers of Latin America on the grounds that they foster inefficient indus-

---

9. Given some level of availability of foreign exchange, the marginal utility of foreign exchange is equal to $1 + \sum m_i t_i$ where the m_i are the marginal propensities to import and the t_i are the tariffs or tariff equivalents of import restrictions. The marginal utility of a tradable commodity is given by $1 + t_i$. Defining a_{ji} as the input of material j into one unit of i, all taken at free trade prices, it can easily be seen that negative net benefits under (a), $1 - \sum a_{ji} < 0$, do not in general imply negative benefits under (b), $(1 + t_i) - (1 + \sum m_i t_i) \sum a_{ji} < 0$. For the derivation of the marginal utility of foreign exchange, cf. D. M. Schydlowsky, "On the Choice of a Shadow Price for Foreign Exchange," Economic Development Report 108, Harvard University Center for International Affairs.

tries and that in addition they draw on very scarce fiscal resources which are better employed elsewhere. The first of these reasons is based on the comparison of domestic industrial costs and international prices by use of the financial exchange rate. This procedure has already been shown to be an inappropriate way of undertaking these comparisons. It is biased against the conclusion that industrial cost will allow exporting and instead gives rise to the phenomenon of "industrial inefficiency illusion." The second objection is not conclusive either. An export subsidy, once enacted, will only generate fiscal expenditure if exports in fact take place under it. Such exports would at the same time, however, imply additional economic activity which in itself and through the foreign trade multiplier would generate a substantial increase in the tax base. This increase in the base would in turn generate additional revenue for the exchequer. This new revenue would serve to cover in part or in whole the subsidy necessary to generate the exports in the first place. Thus, through a combined foreign trade and fiscal multiplier, the export subsidy generates its own (partial or total) financing. Under the Latin American conditions in which the marginal import propensities are rather low, foreign trade tax multipliers tend to be high, and as a result fairly large export subsidies can be supported by the revenue generated in this form, particularly if they are paid only to new exports.

In essence, what is at issue is the use of a full-capacity utilization budget to estimate the fiscal impact of export subsidies. This full-capacity budget is analogous to the full-employment budget introduced recently in the United States. However, whereas in the U.S. version the issue is a spending (reduction) of government revenue to generate domestic activity and additional domestic employment which in turn will then finance the government expenditure, in Latin America we are faced with a situation in which it is the expenditure of public funds for the creation of exports which generates a higher level of economic activity and in consequence an increase in revenue.

A simple model of the following kind allows the calculation of a full-utilization budget and specifically of the maximal subsidy payable without net fiscal cost to the exchequer. Define: P as total expenditure of the private sector; p as marginal propensity to spend of the private sector; M as imports at CIF prices; m as marginal ($=$average) propensity to import; Y as income at market prices; E as exports at FOB prices; G as government expenditure; T as fiscal revenue; a as rate of ad valorem import duties; td as rate of direct taxes on income; and ti as rate of taxation on domestic transactions expressed as a percentage of national income. Then:

$$P = p_o + p(1 - td - ti - a\frac{M}{Y}) \; Y \qquad (1)$$

$$M(1+a) = m(1-td-ti-a\frac{M}{Y}) \ Y \tag{2}$$

$$E = E_o \tag{3}$$
$$G = G_o \tag{4}$$
$$Y = P + G + (E-M) \tag{5}$$
$$T = aM + (td+ti)Y. \tag{6}$$

This system of equations tells us that gross private disposable income[10] determines the level of final demand for domestic goods and for imports measured in domestic prices (equations 1 and 2), that exports and government expenditure are exogenously determined (equations 3 and 4), that income must equal expenditure (equation 5), and that fiscal revenue comes from several kinds of taxes.

The total differential of fiscal revenue with regard to income from exports will show the net increase in fiscal resources per peso of additional income of exporters.

$$dT = \frac{am(1-tx) + (1+a)(td+ti)}{(1+a)\{1-(1-tx)[p-(m/1+a)]\}} dE \tag{7}$$

where
$$tx = td + ti + a\frac{Y}{M}.$$

Incorporating export subsidies explicitly requires substituting E by $E^* = (1+s)E$, where s = rate of subsidy on FOB value of exports. The net fiscal change after export subsidy payments can now be written as:

$$dTn = \frac{am(1-tx) + (1+a)(td+ti)}{(1+a)\{1-(1-tx)[p-(m/1+a)]\}} dE^* - \frac{s}{1+s}dE^*. \tag{8}$$

Applying these formulae to Argentina with $tx = .43$, $td = .0467$, $ti = .07$, $a = .024$, $m = .159$, $p = 1$, one obtains:

$$dTn = .566 \ dE^* - \frac{s}{1+s}dE^*. \tag{9}$$

To obtain the maximal subsidy rate, s, which causes no net deficit, equation 9 is set equal to zero and s is 1.3, which means that in Argentina a subsidy rate of up to 130 percent of the FOB value of the export will not disimprove the fiscal balance.[11] Other countries will surely have

10. Note that this is defined at factor cost—hence, the terms for indirect taxation and import duties.

11. For more detail on this model including period analysis, sectoral disaggregation, and sensitivity analysis of the parameters, cf. D. M. Schydlowsky, "Short-Run Policy in Semi-Industrialized Economies," *Economic Development and Cultural Change* (April 1971).

different and probably lower cutoff points, but economies as closed as those in Latin America cannot fail to have high foreign trade multipliers and hence room for substantial export subsidization without a negative net fiscal impact.

THE EFFECTS OF MULTIPLE SHIFTING

Fuller utilization of capacity will naturally generate a once-and-for-all increase in the level of income. Since second and third shifts are typically somewhat less productive than the first shift, one can expect the addition of a second shift to somewhat less than double the contribution of industry to GNP, and the addition of a third shift to add again somewhat less than the second shift. Assuming that the complementary factors of production can all be made available and fiscal policies adopted to

TABLE 6

ESTIMATED REAL PER CAPITA INCOME OF SELECTED LATIN AMERICAN COUNTRIES AT DIFFERENT NUMBER OF SHIFTS WORKED IN INDUSTRY, 1967 (U.S., 1960 = 100)

	1 Shift	2 Shifts	3 Shifts
Argentina	26.0	30.4	34.0
Brazil	13.0	15.0	16.5
Chile	21.0	23.6	25.9
Colombia	12.0	13.1	14.0
Peru	10.0	10.8	11.4

achieve the macro balance necessary, ball-park levels per capita income at one, two, and three shifts of operation of industry can readily be calculated. Table 6 presents such estimates for Argentina, Brazil, Chile, Colombia, and Peru for the year 1967 in terms of index numbers of real per capita income based on Beckerman's study[12] in which U.S. per capita income in 1960 is taken at 100. In this calculation it is assumed that industry operates on the average at one shift of capacity.

In addition to producing a once-and-for-all increase in the level of income, full utilization of capacity reduces the capital output ratio. Furthermore, if the marginal savings rate is above the average, there will be an increase in the average savings rate. These two factors together will generate a higher rate of growth. Unless the level of demographic increase is strongly and positively affected by the level of per capita income, the higher level of aggregate growth will also signify higher per capita income growth. The combination of a larger base and a higher rate of growth arising from multiple shifting generates much quicker increases in the level of income in multiple-shifting countries.

The implications of applying full industrial capacity growth can

12. W. Beckerman, "International Comparisons of Real Income," OECD.

be seen by comparing income on the assumptions of one, two, and three shifts of operation of the industrial sectors of Argentina, Brazil, Chile, Colombia, and Peru in the year 2000. This comparison is presented in Table 7, which shows that triple shifting can almost double the per capita income attainable in the year 2000.

Conclusions

In this paper we have argued that unemployment in Latin America co-exists with underutilization of capital. This quasi-Keynesian situation cannot be eliminated with a simple expansion of domestic aggregate demand in view of the balance-of-payments situation facing these countries. As a result, a part of the new output generated by putting the excess capacity to work must be exported in order to pay for the imports necessary for higher levels of utilization to be sustainable.

TABLE 7

Estimated Real Per Capita Income of Selected Latin American Countries at Different Number of Shifts Worked in Industry for Year 2000
(U.S., 1960 = 100)

	1 Shift	2 Shifts	3 Shifts
Argentina	42	80	87
Brazil	25	41	47
Chile	35	70	97
Colombia	20	35	38
Peru	23	29	31

The structure of the exchange rate system has a substantial anti-export bias, thus hindering the generation of industrial exports. In addition, the "industrial inefficiency illusion" operates to reinforce the conviction that industrial exporting is impossible. For this and other reasons arising from the labor and tax legislation, putting capacity to work is not profitable at private prices.

At social (shadow) prices, however, the benefits can be expected to be substantial. A fiscal policy is therefore needed to bring private profitability in line with the net social benefits. Such a policy would be one of export subsidization.

Contrary to common belief, such subsidies need not represent a net outflow from the treasury. The higher level of activity concurrent with an increase in capacity utilization generates a greater tax base and more revenue. The total effect of the foreign trade and tax multiplier may well pay the whole cost of the subsidy or more.

Finally, the implications of full-capacity growth for several Latin American countries were estimated for the year 2000. The ball-park figures indicate that per capita income at three shifts of operation would be almost double the level achievable in 2000 at one shift of operation and historical growth rates. It seems, therefore, that a vigorous fiscal policy of capacity utilization and industrial export promotion holds the promise of an impressive pay-out for the Latin American economies.

Acknowledgment.—The underlying research for this paper has been supported in part by the Development Advisory Service, Harvard University, from AID grant CFD-1543; however, the views expressed do not necessarily reflect those of AID. The compilation of some of the tables by David Dapice is gratefully acknowledged.

Comment—Juan Pablo Pérez-Castillo

SCHYDLOWSKY'S paper is essentially an attempt to implement the useful conclusions of his research on Latin American exchange rates. Schydlowsky intends to show that under certain conditions which call for exports, Latin American governments will have to subsidize producers. He stresses further that those conditions do in fact exist, arguing that the solution to the unemployment and unused industrial capacity problems is to be found in the exportation of a sufficiently large portion of an expanded industrial output. He feels that the proper fiscal policy measure is export subsidization, because the Latin American exchange rate systems are so significantly anti-export-biased that only at "social" prices are exports profitable.

His reasoning views Latin America as suffering from unemployment "more akin to a Keynesian situation than to a structural development one," and from underutilization of (industrial) capital. Theoretically, these gaps could be reduced substantially by expanding aggregate demand. In fact, however, due to the high import content of industrial production, imports would rise significantly with the expansion of output. Most of these countries already have balance-of-payments problems and are thus unable to finance such additional import requirements. Moreover, the internal markets of these countries are insufficient to absorb the additional output in its entirety. Hence, part of the output would have to be exported, reaching an equilibrium when the new industrial exports just compensate for the new import requirements generated by the expanded production. This means that output would have to be price-competitive in order to make exports profitable; however, in point of fact the financial exchange rates are poor measures of competitiveness because they provide an "inefficiency illusion." As a result, "socially corrected prices" must be used, via subsidization, in order to provide the necessary profitability that will make such a venture economically feasible (to private enterprise).

From a strictly technical point of view his argument is sound, provided that the assumptions upon which it is based and the objectives of the proposed corrective measures are either logically acceptable or empirically verifiable. This comment will concentrate on two aspects only, without going into great detail due to limitation of space: Schydlowsky's explanations and interpretations of the phenomena of unemployment, unused capacity, and export possibilities; and the implications of the policy measures in terms of economic development.

The concurrent presence of unutilized labor and capital suggests to Schydlowsky that the arguments of the "structuralists" are incorrect, because in the long run the major obstacles are solvable by providing only the necessary incentives (such as export subsidies) for the economy to adjust automatically to eliminate these two unemployment problems. Unfortunately, his position is not entirely convincing due to the fact that it implicitly rests on (among other things) a specific conception of underdevelopment (and, thus, of development) that takes for granted the sociopolitical framework and the historical process of its formation. This is a value judgment *not* based on scientific observation and is precisely one that is under study in Latin America by many of its social scientists. Moreover, there is strong evidence suggesting that the price mechanism is quite inefficient in the performance of its functions. Profit opportunities have been abundant, yet entrepreneurs are still scarce; and the demand for skilled labor has been increasing rapidly with the supply continuously lagging significantly, unable to reduce the gap.

Individual country markets are indeed small and the import content of industrial production is truly high; but these are not the underlying causes of unemployment, excess capacity, or balance-of-payments problems. Proposals of fiscal policies to eradicate these problems must rest upon a full understanding of the process by which they arose in the first place; otherwise, the proposals will be mere temporary remedies at most, and they may even aggravate the situation. The problem of small markets is at once quantitative and qualitative, involving population size as well as income distribution and consumption habits. Similarly, the problem of high import propensities is quantitative and qualitative, for it concerns the degree and nature of economic and social development achieved, consumption patterns, and technology uses. Indeed, the whole issue of economic development is fundamentally qualitative, involving national objectives, cultural values, and type of social system desired. A high level or rate of growth of per capita income is not necessarily indicative of a high level or rate of growth of economic development unless accompanied by massive participation of the population, a guarantee of the basic social requirements (such as food, housing, education, and health), and nationalization of the basic dynamic forces of the economic process (that is, the endogenization of the key variables making for a long-lasting, self-sustaining process). In other words, the mere expansion of production and income is not necessarily development; one must inquire as to the nature and type of that expansion of economic activity.

It is unlikely that the simple exportation of excess production will solve the unemployment problem, since it does not get to the root of the problem. Industrial production is not employment-elastic because the technology used is of foreign origin, created by foreign productive forces; thus, the technology is not the result of the degree of development of the national productive forces which employ it. As a result, industrial enterprise is absorptive of foreign capital equipment, including foreign methods of production, administration, and organization. Under these circumstances and given the nature of the domestic market, which has already been molded by consumption patterns formed via imports and under conditions of extremely unequal income distribution, the real issue cannot be centered on the trade-off between new imports and exports, but rather on the trade-off between foreign and national decision making. We will return to this point later.

In explaining the barriers to capacity utilization, Schydlowsky correctly cites five causes, all of which are significant: small market size, scarce working capital, insufficient skilled personnel, high labor costs, and the tax legislation. He then goes on to explain the reasons for the "inefficiency illusion," announces the corrective measures that should be taken, and estimates the gains from capacity utilization. But, in his argument Schydlowsky does not take into account explicitly those barriers to capacity utilization that also limit the export possibilities of Latin America *as a whole*. In a recent study by the Latin American Economic and Social Planning Institute (ILPES),[1] the various causes of capacity underutilization were analyzed (including technological backwardness and ignorance and oligopolistic agreements, among others), reaching the conclusion that it is an illusion to expect Latin America to increase substantially its industrial exports outright and without radical structural changes and intensive technological research for the following reasons: the exportables are import competitive and widely produced; plants are of minimal-size scale by international standards and therefore are marginal relative to foreign companies and/or parent firms; there is neither technological originality nor commercial organization on an international scale; and, enterprises too often are prevented from exporting by their parent firms and/or suppliers of technology and patents.

The argument of the Schydlowsky paper rests on the assumption that Latin American countries have deviated from the comparative advantage principle in selecting the industrial areas in which to operate, attributing

1. *Elementos para la Elaboración de una Política de Desarrollo con Integración para America Latina* (Mexico: Seminario sobre Desarrollo Nacional con Integración, August 1970).

their lack of specialization to the exchange rate systems. It would then follow that the recommended fiscal policy measure would lead to specialization along the lines of the comparative advantage principle. It is not only difficult to see how this would happen or how long it would take, but—more significantly—it would apparently mean that the Latin American countries must accept and exploit their existing relative conditions, not attempting any changes before implementing the subsidy program. Yet these conditions were historically formed more as a function of the social, political, and international relations dominating the Latin American scene since colonization than as a result of the natural and inherent economic conditions of each country. Moreover, foreign enterprises are placed on an equal footing in the paper with national firms, tending to overestimate the effects of the policies on the development of the *national* enterprises.[2] Finally, the presumption that demand for Latin American exports is highly price-elastic and large enough to absorb the whole of supply does not seem reasonable, particularly after consideration is given to the types of goods subject to exportation and their quality. Furthermore, among the countries that comprise the region there is a great deal of competitiveness and very little complementarity. And where favorable export conditions are found, according to the Brazil study cited in note 2, foreign enterprises are the most likely to benefit from an unrestrictive subsidy program, in which case the result will be a deepening of dependence (foreignization of industrial production), especially within the leading (and most critical) sectors.

This returns us to the question raised earlier regarding decision making and to the meaning of a long-lasting, self-sustaining development process. A discussion of the instruments of fiscal (and other) policy should take into account the premises and assumptions underlying the design of the strategy recommended, which in turn involves specific characteristics of the economic (and sociopolitical) system desired. Yet the available literature, which is primarily a product of those economists greatly influenced by the performance of the industrial countries, fails to consider these issues explicitly. In fact, it presupposes that underdeveloped countries must follow the path of industrial countries, particularly the capitalist ones, since a major premise is that economic development is a process that occurs in stages that are nothing more than stages leading toward the same type of social system which those countries possess.[3]

As such, then, this literature takes for granted that the objective is to produce a large and increasing quantity of goods and services, and fur-

2. A recent study on Brazil concludes that such an export program would have the foreign firms as the great beneficiaries: F. Faynzylber, *Sistema Industrial y Exportación de Manufacturas en Brazil* (CEPAL, November 1970).

3. For an interesting opinion on this topic, see the interview with Father Benjamín Núñez referred to by Wilkie in his paper in this volume.

ther admits the need for an appreciable change in the structure and level of domestic demand, which calls for the structural transformation of production (a process known as industrialization). However, both the literature and its approach to development (implicitly, or even explicitly at times) postulate that the future structure of that demand and production must be similar to that of the presently industrialized countries (with minor differences, if any).

This result is understandable because the structure of demand and supply and their time paths are quite similar among the leading countries. In fact, this pattern is the only visible and existing example available. Nevertheless, this fact does not make it immutable and historically deterministic, and we may be committing a grave error by accepting a priori a specifically determined development pattern without exploring other possibilities. This is extremely important since we are actually dealing with the cultural systems of underdeveloped countries. Thus, for example, we should study, thoroughly and concretely, the structure, historical formation, and present dynamics of the domestic demand (consumption patterns) to which we will accommodate production. Policy recommendations to accelerate output should take into account the socially desired future structure of final demand for that output. To the extent that the present structure of output is demand-specific, and thus income-distribution-specific, increments in production based on nonselective criteria may well mean that the historical consumption patterns of the high-income groups are being regarded as socially desirable. This in turn may mean that production will be foreign-dominated (via the technology used, the goods produced, and the decision-making process used), as the consumption patterns are foreign-determined and foreign-oriented.

Underdevelopment, as many economists argue, is an historical process, dynamic and capable of self-sustainment, resulting from the international relations which in part gave rise to those countries as nation-states and which have since dominated their economic, political, and cultural conditions. Such countries are foreign-dependent, with their social systems and power structures conditioned accordingly. They have passed from a situation of mono-production for export and importation of almost everything else (from ideas, technology, and legal systems to final consumer goods) to a situation of quasi-import-substitute production, a process which has produced new forms of dependence and foreign orientation.

Industrial production requires more complex technology, organization, and capital goods, all of which must be imported because they are not internally produced. Hence, the driving force of the process remains foreign, in part due to technological and financial reasons but in part also due to political and ideological considerations. As the industrialization process continues its greater complexity results in even greater foreign participation and control, which further aggravates the structural deformation of the system, for it is a foreign crust unrelated to the national reality. Having been nurtured on imports, the domestic market to which industrial production caters is geared to the foreign consumption patterns of the wealthy. As a result, industry operates at low levels of output capacity and absorbs relatively small quantities of domestic resources (particularly labor).

Since dependence (foreign influence) transcends the economic sphere into the political and cultural areas, the economic system accommodates and becomes conditioned by the development style of the foreign country (or countries). In fact, the whole system will adjust accordingly to satisfy the needs and requirements of this exogenous industrialization process. In a very real sense, supply creates its own demand, and a "foreign" supply creates a "foreign" demand. Production provides those goods that satisfy existing needs, but it also creates the needs for those goods. There is a dynamic interdependence, which reinforces dependence in all its ramifications and expressions. Under these circumstances, when a country does not control the reins of its own economy because the basic decisions are made elsewhere and respond to other interests, it makes little sense to talk about self-sustained growth.

Furthermore, attempts to accelerate the rate of growth will actually increase dependence. The reason is that such an acceleration will depend precisely upon those changes consistent with the dynamic functioning of the economic system, accommodating and molding resources and institutions to its needs. It will depend upon the right type of labor resource, demand structure, laws and regulations, human relations, etc. The output of these factors will have to be linked to the foreign-dominated productive process. Increments in productivity, and thus the personal income of labor, will be linked to foreign technological advances. Research, education, even the arts, will be linked to the process with the communications media playing their role. The propagation of the process, through the economic system to the social classes, to cultural values, and to the political machinery will lead to an increasing loss of autonomy and independence. As the national physical, economic, and social infrastructure becomes consistent with the productive process, it will also become subject to evaluation by foreign standards, so that, in terms of the potentiality of. the *national* productive forces, underdevelopment *increases*.[4]

4. For several years, the research group under my direction at CENDES was concerned with this problem, both as advisors to the Planning Office and in our own personal research. To this end, we had in operation a very large and complex computer decision model, which we were using to test and evaluate alternative long-run (thirty years) development patterns for Venezuela. The study clearly showed that there is a logical and economically feasible alternative to the historical development pattern. It also questioned the feasibility of the capitalistic economic system for overcoming its underdevelopedness. For more information on this work, see our article

Notwithstanding these criticisms, Schydlowsky's paper is noteworthy and merits careful analysis. It correctly questions the overall industrialization policy of Latin American governments and calls attention to problem areas that should be swiftly tackled. The myopia of these governments regarding their foreign trade policies (including their exchange rate policies) is exposed and measured. The method of calculating export possibilities can be properly used to implement a selective subsidy program consistent with a development plan aimed at achieving greater technological and administrative autonomy and, therefore, at achieving development. The way is open for serious thought and work toward economic development with integration on a continental scale that combines the internal potential of each country with the overall potential of the integrated whole. Of course, this calls for radical structural change on the part of each national economy, as well as a different conception of development and a different structural relationship with the industrialized nations. Complete overhauls are called for especially in the educational system, the system of mass communications and diffusion of information, the power structure, and above all the property system.

Comment—Anthony Churchill

I do not worry much about definitions of economic growth. I think Arthur Lewis put it nicely when he said it was a matter of choice. The rich can choose to be poor, but the poor do not have any choice. In my own country, Canada, we worry a great deal about foreign investment and foreign control of the economy. But we seem to keep getting richer and the enthusiasm for doing something effective about it seems to diminish. Whether that is a good thing or not is up to one's own judgment.

An important point made in Schydlowsky's paper is the use of tax or fiscal policy to stimulate the fuller utilization of capacity. Usually, measures taken by governments are in the form of incentives—tax credits, depreciation allowances, custom duties exemptions, and so on. Not enough attention is paid to the impact of public policy on the relative price structure of the factors of production. In too many countries, the effect of government measures is to insure the underutilization of both labor and capital. This applies in both industry and agriculture. Latin America is full of modern plants operating at a fraction of their capacity and most policy measures are aimed at adding to this capacity. In India and Paki-

---

"Estilos de Desarrollo," *El Trimestre Económico*, no. 144 (Mexico, 1969) and our book *Estilos de Desarrollo*, published by CENDES in a limited edition, and a shortened revised edition in one volume, prepared for publication by the United Nations.

stan, where there are large surpluses of labor, government policy encourages the use of tractors.

In many cases, particularly in agriculture, the production function is more or less neutral between capital-intensive and labor-intensive methods. One can produce rice by using airplanes, as in the United States, or by using much labor, as in Indonesia. It is a question of relative prices.

The problems of distorted relative prices are equally applicable to industry in Latin America. The fiscal system as it has developed through time by use of various tax, expenditure, and social policies has so distorted the factor mix that we wind up with underutilization of both labor and capital.

In Colombia, for example, there exist restrictive labor practices which require much higher pay for shift work or for overtime work, other legislation which makes it impossible to fire people, and taxes on payrolls. At the same time there are lower tariffs on investment goods, tax credits, overvalued exchange rates, and the usual package of incentives for industry. In general, the use of capital-intensive methods is made so attractive that there is more and more unemployed labor sitting around and more and more expensive capital being imported.

How can fiscal policy change this? I think that when one sits down and works out what the production functions look like, sometimes the conclusions are surprising. No one should talk about general taxes on capital and general subsidies to labor, or vice versa, depending on the economy. These do not seem to work. There are particular forms of taxes, and these again turn out to be so particular that one must be very careful about whether one is talking about capital-intensive industries or labor-intensive industries. Taxing capital-intensive industries does not necessarily mean using more labor; sometimes it may mean using more capital and less labor, depending on the production functions. Those of us who have tried to take a look at this statistically have found that it is necessary to look at more than just one section of the world. If one looks at most Latin American countries, the industrial structure is not too dissimilar; however, for the world, there is a very wide range of experience and very different industrial structures. Take, for example, the textile industry, which happens to be common to most underdeveloped countries and has a large export market and therefore a world price. It is an industry where, surprisingly enough, there is a tremendous variation in production techniques. One can go from a country like Korea, which has an extremely high labor-intensive textile industry, to a country like Colombia, which has an extremely high capital-intensive textile industry. The degree of capital-intensity of the industry is explained by the wage scale; in other words, it is directly dependent upon the wage rate. By this I do not mean just money wages; one has to take into account the whole package of labor costs and the whole package of capital costs. We find a huge difference in these two countries, both of whom produce textiles for the export market, using different production techniques. This suggests that, at least in textiles—and it could also be the case in many other industries— if we got busy and found the evidence we would see a wide variety of production functions.

Fiscal policy can influence the choice of techniques through shifting relative prices, and I would suggest that perhaps some of the work of economists interested in this area should lie in trying to find out what kind of tax policies we should use, or perhaps misuse, in order to encourage the kind of production mix which is more suitable to the factor endowment of the economy. Of course, this means an increase in efficiency and, hopefully, an increase in output and economic growth. Some countries have done this through export subsidies with some degree of success. Looking at the experience of Colombia, one finds that industry is very sensitive to the international market; change the exchange rate in Colombia and there is a big shift in exports. What we have failed to do, though, is to go back a little further and see if we could get an even greater increase in exports not by just subsidizing exports, but by changing factor prices so that we in fact get more efficient output and larger amounts of output. The only country I can think of that has gone this route quite consciously is a very small, labor-intensive one, Singapore. It has had a very rapid rate of growth and is consciously following a policy of making sure that wages—a good socialist government, too, by the way—do not rise too fast and that capital does not have too great an incentive. In other words, it has tried to combine its factors and get the kinds of industries or production functions most suitable to its particular factor endowment.

Discussion

W. TYLER: Based on limited observation, it appears that in many Latin American countries the greatest extent of capacity underutilization occurs exactly in those industries that have been most stimulated by import-substitution policies and are, by their nature, the most capital-intensive. This apparent association between capacity underutilization and capital-intensity suggests two things if subsidies are to be provided to stimulate output in these industries. First, the employment effect may well be exaggerated by the proponents of such subsidies. Second, there is the question of international comparative advantage of the products produced by the subsidized industries. Are these the types of products in which Latin American or other less-developed countries can successfully compete in the international market? Do these countries (generally considered capital-poor) possess a comparative advantage, or a potential comparative advantage, in the types of goods produced by the underutilized industries? Probably not.

In addition, one might also question the likelihood of the developed countries cheerfully accepting the exports resultant from subsidies of the type Schydlowsky suggests. The recent revival of protectionism, notably in the United States, lends slight promise.

F. ANDIC: Schydlowsky begins with the view commonly taken by economists that unemployment is high in Latin America (10 percent or more). In my opinion, this is not the best premise with which to start the discussion of the problem of full capacity. The issue at stake is not the existence of unemployment as such, but of *unemployables*, i.e., masses or groups of workers who for various reasons are unemployable in the industrial sense but who cannot be forced to return to the agricultural sector. To take the example of Puerto Rico, with which I am most familiar and where the problem is very apparent—despite the enormous size of the market for industrial production (the United States), the non-existence of excess capacity in plants, and a three-shift working day in many establishments—unemployment of 10 percent or more continues to be a persistent phenomenon. This is unemployment in a statistical sense; in reality, at least 70 percent of the registered unemployed are unemployable. They have no industrial skill, having moved from the rural areas to the urban solely with training in cutting sugar cane and harvesting coffee. There are also many high-school dropouts in this group who are not willing to take blue-collar jobs. Unemployment remains high because of the unemployables rather than the scarcity of jobs. I suspect that this situation also holds in many Latin American countries. Although Schydlowsky touches upon the problem of scarcity of skilled labor in Latin America when discussing aspects of capacity utilization, we should place greater emphasis on separating the unemployed from the unemployables not only in Latin America but in all the developing economies.

My second point refers to the question of export subsidies. I am worried about this concept because of its distributional effects. Given the tax mix as it is in Latin America (and in fact in many of the underdeveloped countries) with its heavy bias on indirect taxation, to allocate a certain portion of the revenues to export promotion may create more problems of a social nature than the economic ones it tries to solve. If some sort of value-added tax existed rather than such a heavy emphasis on other types of indirect taxes, then exporters could be exempted from it. Consequently, changes in the tax mix or the composition of revenues could be made into a more effective instrument to improve the distribution of income, and the burden on the indirect taxpayers need not be increased in order to subsidize a small exporting sector.

H. HINRICHS: I have four brief comments on Schydlowsky's paper, which I found somewhat reminiscent of Lauchlin Currie's *Accelerating Development*. There are four problems which are not insurmountable, but which are nevertheless problems. When one subsidizes exports, one may have certain GATT problems in terms of dumping. Secondly, to the degree that one pushes exports faster than imports, perhaps with a lag, one could have an inflation problem structurally built in. I also question Schydlowsky's tax multipliers; I do not know how rapidly the taxes, with a lag, will come in after one passes out all these export subsidies. Fourth, and the real issue, is that a country may have a greater supply of industrial goods to sell, but I doubt if it will have the world demand or the buyers.

J. GRUNWALD: I agree with Schydlowsky's implied emphasis on export promotion, yet one cannot ignore the justified fears of Latin American countries that a massive promotion of exports might provoke negative responses by the developed countries. It surely would be frustrating to see full-capacity utilization thwarted and government subsidies wasted because surplus production cannot be exported due to more quotas, higher tariffs, and other protective measures by the developed countries.

As for the comment on Schydlowsky's paper by Pérez-Castillo, I think all of us are in agreement that development implies many more things than simple economic growth. Yet, I have rarely heard Latin American policy makers spell out their social goals. What is confusing to economists is that policy makers' pronouncements concentrate on economic growth as the principal development objective. Other goals should be spelled out specifically. Thus, two major noneconomic objectives implied in a broad concept of development are a better distribution of income and greater control over one's own affairs (control of foreign capital and foreign investment). But the cold fact remains that in addition to these objectives there is still the problem of feeding the poor and increasing the standard of living of the masses—in other words, economic growth in the traditional sense. It then becomes an operational matter of how to implement a development strategy that combines a better distribution of income and a greater control over one's own affairs with the need to accelerate economic growth.

W. BAER: In pointing to the necessity for export diversification many economists have commented on the foolish behavior of Latin American countries undergoing import-substitution industrialization over the past twenty to thirty years in neglecting exports. Although these economists are right in showing how this neglect has placed many countries in a prejudicial position, the righteous tone of the critiques is often out of place. Most economists forget that these countries relied in many key sectors on foreign capital. In order to attract the latter, Latin American countries used the large and protected internal markets as their principal bait. It would have been very difficult to attract firms if from the start they had been required to export a large proportion of their output. Although I do not want to justify what happened, our critique should be more balanced in the light of historical knowledge.

Turning specifically to Schydlowsky's paper, I wonder how valid is the underlying assumption concerning international price competition. Even if measures are taken to reduce costs, subsidize exports, and adopt more realistic exchange rates, would this help exports of manufactured goods if no additional measures are taken? Credit conditions, marketing outlets, terms of delivery, brand names, etc., might be just as, if not more, important in promoting industrial exports. To the extent that this is true, Schydlowsky's remedies are only partial in nature.

R. MUSGRAVE: First of all, there is the problem of how full-capacity use should be defined, whether it should be defined with regard to eight hours or with regard to twenty-four hours. This brings in the questions of how scarce is capital relative to labor and how expensive is nighttime labor as against daytime labor and what are the preferences of the labor force in this respect. Full capacity would probably call for a lower number of hours, the less capital-scarce the country is. The question is how to define the problem so that it can be applied to different countries.

Moreover, the remedies for undercapacity utilization will depend on why this underutilization exists. The fiscal techniques that are to be used will differ with the situation. If underutilization reflects excessively restrictive firm policies, then the question is what kind of tax devices or tax subsidy schemes, such as the antimonopoly tax suggested by Joan Robinson long ago, might be used to induce the firm to produce at a more nearly competitive output. But this makes sense only if there is a market for the product. If instead the problem is one of lack of markets, these tax gimmicks will not do, and the solution lies with macro-policy.

The argument of the paper is largely that the lack of market should be remedied by devices to increase exports. But why has this expansionist policy to go via export markets? Why not just give people at home more money so that they can purchase the output of this excess capacity? One basic reason is that the nature of the capital stock might be unsuitable to increased production for domestic consumption, especially if demand were to be distributed more equally; it may be geared to produce for export markets. If so, the basic policy problem—at least the longer-run problem—is one of changing the capital structure so that it can meet a policy of domestic demand expansion. And will not the export encouragement serve to worsen the misfit of the capital stock? In answering these questions it remains to be seen, of course, whether export-oriented capital equipment is superior, from the point of view of comparative advantage, to domestic-consumption-oriented capital equipment. In this respect, the choice of capital equipment becomes part of the broader problem of export orientation versus import substitution.

Given higher-capacity use, more labor would be used with the given capital. But there is a further problem, which may be more important. The amount of labor which is combined with capital, assuming capacity use, depends on the nature of the technology. This raises the whole question of capital-intensive versus labor-intensive technology and of employment in relation to growth. I think that a good case can be made for using tax devices to induce people to substitute more labor-intensive technologies and, indeed, to create such technologies.

D. SCHYDLOWSKY: Expansion should be via the foreign market basically because a country needs imported raw materials. If the economy did not have that problem, it could just pump in money to increase domestic demand of whatever kind, giving selective credit, say, for consumer durables, and in principle place any amount of product. But this cannot be done, because all Latin American countries have some import component in their industrial output. If the economy does not increase exports, it cannot sustain the higher level of industrial output.

R. MUSGRAVE: Increased use could be made of export proceeds to import the kind of appropriate capital equipment which a country needs to produce output for domestic use with a lower import content.

D. SCHYDLOWSKY: An economy has only a certain amount of export revenue, which can be divided between maintenance imports and capital imports. The only way to obtain more output is to shift from capital imports to maintenance imports, in which case the rate of growth is reduced in order to obtain higher output. This is why I am suggesting that in order to maintain the growth rate, possibly raise it, and at the same time increase the level of utilization, more foreign exchange is needed. The plausible way to obtain it is to sell abroad some part of the new output—not all of it, but at least enough to pay for the import component of the new output.

A fundamental issue running through various comments is factor mix versus factor utilization. We have almost come to a situation of a Keynesian contra-position to a neoclassical full-employment world. Churchill notes that countries ought to be looking for more labor-intensive technology, and Musgrave notes that the most important problem is to use more labor-intensive technology. I disagree with these positions. Factor substitution is important, and countries ought to have better labor-intensive technologies. But economists have been looking at that kind of issue for a long time, while in the meantime underutilization of installed capital and a Keynesian-type unemployment situation exist. Whatever we think about the current capital-labor ratio, if the factors of production exist and if they can produce outputs that add to the wealth of the country, they should be used. This does not deny the importance of the relative factor price issue.

Andic is concerned about the distributional effects. I suggest that the economy generate more output and more taxes and use those new taxes in a particular way. Thus, the country does not have a fixed pie which it is redistributing. It would require a very marked redistribution for the poor, on balance, to be worse off. If the economy can produce more of everything, some of the "more" is going to accrue to the bottom-income groups.

On the issue of independence, raised by Pérez-Castillo, some of the crucial elements in the dependence of Latin America on the rest of the world are the facts that its exports are specialized, that it has a constrained balance-of-payments situation, and that it is forced to accept foreign capital because that has been the only way it has been able to grow. If Latin America managed to diversify its industrial exports it would escape this bind, and then it would be possible to become much more selective in accepting foreign investment. So I suggest that putting existing capital and labor to use, even if that capital is foreign-owned, in the medium term will give Latin America more independence, defined in the conventional sense of less dependence on the foreigner. If the economy can achieve more exports and more diversification, it will not need as much foreign capital inflow.

This point applies to technology as well. If a country has a small market and a highly diversified economic structure, it is very difficult to develop indigenous technology. The Argentines have tried, and it was very difficult. They found that both overhead costs, such as operations research departments, and line production costs rose. They now find themselves having to plan for flexibility, which is very costly. But if the economy could break into the export market effectively and achieve longer production lines, then it could support an indigenous technology. Unless a country succeeds in this, it is hard to visualize how it can reduce its dependence on foreign technology.

The policy package of producing more with what a country already has and breaking into the export market is a necessary but not sufficient condition. The same applies to the restrictive practices problem. Undoubtedly monopolies exist in Latin America, to a large extent because protected markets exist and so something precise exists to divide up. In the export market, monopolistic price-fixing is much more difficult. It is impossible to get out of a boxed-in monopolistic market unless the country breaks into the export market. Thus, to have a sufficient policy it may be necessary to break up the monopolies. But to attack the monopolies without entering the export market is self-defeating.